OTHER BOOKS BY HENRY W. CLUNE

Seen and Heard 1933
Seen and Heard 1935
The Good Die Poor
Monkey On A Stick
Main Street Beat
By His Own Hand
The Big Fella
Six O'Clock Casual
The Genesee
The Best of Henry Clune
O'Shaughnessy's Café
The Rochester I Know

I ALWAYS LIKED IT HERE

Henry W. Clune at ninety-two

HENRY W. CLUNE

I Always Liked It Here

REMINISCENCES OF A ROCHESTERIAN

Rochester, New York 1983
FRIENDS OF THE UNIVERSITY OF ROCHESTER LIBRARIES

Author's note:
I am beholden to Joan S. Hart for her professional editing and meticulous proofreading, to Daniel G. Kennedy for his counsel and help with my manuscript, and to Marion B. Kaiser for the skillful typing she has displayed in typing manuscripts for me for forty years. Acknowledgment is also made for the assistance of Gail Ferris.

This book has been designed by
Horace Hart
and manufactured by the
Vail-Ballou Press

ISBN 0-9610824-0-2

For Peter Dzwonkoski

INTRODUCTION

What literate citizen of Rochester, young or old, native or recent resident, has not heard of Henry W. Clune? Many have read one or more of his six novels, many more are familiar with his books of non-fiction, *The Genesee* (1963) and *The Rochester I Know* (1972) in particular. Many Rochesterians have the pleasure of recalling Henry's "Seen and Heard" columns in the *Democrat and Chronicle,* which he produced regularly until 1968. Since then he has gone into active retirement at his home in Scottsville, where he lives—has long lived!—with his charming wife Charlotte. Here, at ninety-three, he reads voraciously—Dickens and Montaigne are favorites—walks a mile a day, maintains a vigorous social life of entertaining and visiting that would weigh heavily upon a hardy soul half his age, and has recently finished the book you have before you. In the phrase with which Henry concludes this volume, he is "*locally,* internationally famous," and it is more than probable that at this moment in Paris, London, and Canada a reader or two or three remembers with pleasure a Henry Clune novel or column. But Henry belongs to Rochester, to its history and culture, and many who know him would say that he reflects, in his own animated personality, much of the charm and sparkle of that multifaceted city.

Why should the Friends of the University of Rochester Libraries publish a book by Henry W. Clune? Reasons leap quickly to mind. Henry is Rochester's author. From the vantage point of a long and happy life he offers a perspective on the city—its history, activities, citizens, visitors—which illuminates, informs, and entertains. Though it visits other places such as Alaska and New York City, the book is full of Rochester. In publishing it we honor its author, who has honored us by donating the manuscript. At the same time, we record his recollections and impressions forever and convey them to interested people in and outside of the Rochester community.

The Friends Publications Committee has an unwritten bias toward publishing materials from the Library's collections, and there is a strong sense in which we are doing just that when we publish *I Always Liked It Here.* In 1980, inspired partly by the observance of Henry's ninetieth birthday, we were fortunate in acquiring the Clune archive from Syracuse University Library, where it had been since the mid-1960s. Realizing that Rochester is the proper home for the Clune papers, the Syracuse Library kindly turned them over to us. The manuscript of this book is as much a part of the Clune archive, now housed in Rare Books and Special Collections, as any other item therein. Thus, we are publishing from the Library collections in publishing this book.

And what a fine book it is, full of wit and insight, history and humor, characters famous and fleeting, all done up in the gentlemanly, warmly ironical, faintly Victorian style of Henry W. Clune, a Rochester original.

Peter Dzwonkoski, *Head*
Department of Rare Books
and Special Collections
The University of Rochester Library

I have seen the birth of many miracles in my time.
Montaigne

PROLOGUE

John Steinbeck's remark that the profession of book writing makes playing the races seem like a stable and conservative occupation, I often recall when I ruminate on the rich promises and the modest rewards I received from my own practice of the art.

But there are compensations, I suppose. When I read of the millions paid Judith Krantz for *Princess Daisy* by the same paperback publisher who paid me peanuts, I realize that if my novel had brought me a million or two, my wife would have had a diamond as big as the Ritz, I a race horse and probably an early demise as the result of profligacy and dissolute practices instead of carrying on to the golden age of ninety-odd.

Early one August afternoon while I was resting in a room in the Adelphi Hotel in Saratoga Springs before going out to the race track, the telephone rang and a male voice with a cultured English accent inquired if I were Henry W. Clune.

"That's me," I answered ungrammatically.

The speaker identified himself as Cecil Scott, senior editor of the Macmillan Company. He had learned from a telephone conversation with my wife in Scottsville that I was somewhere in Saratoga Springs, and he had called half a dozen hotels before locating me at the Adelphi.

"Mr. Clune," he continued, "we have given careful consideration to your manuscript. We think it a very impressive performance. We would like you to come to New York to talk about it."

I asked Mr. Scott when he wanted me in New York.

"Friday of this week," he said. "At twelve noon in our office. We'll have lunch."

This was Tuesday. When I put the receiver back on the hook I looked at myself in the wall mirror, studied my countenance closely, and told myself confidently that I was going to be a great man. Adjusting my necktie, I left the room and went out to the race track.

My stay at the track was brief. Handicapping horses seemed a trivial pursuit in light of the momentous news I had just received. I was being solicited by a great publishing house, who must believe they had a hit on their hands with all the trouble they had taken to ferret me out. I left the race track after the third race and sped home, knowing I would have to cram on my newspaper work if I were to take time off later in the week.

I arrived in New York Friday morning, and in the taxi ride to the Macmillan Company at 60 Fifth Avenue, I reviewed the fortuitous circumstances that were responsible for this eagerly anticipated meeting.

In late spring, at a cocktail party at the home of Mrs. Whitney Allen, I had met an engaging young man from the Macmillan Company who was to join the company's sales force in London the next week. As the party was breaking up I invited the young man to dine with me at a downtown restaurant; I told him during dinner that I had been struggling for a long time with a novel that I should like very much to show to a publisher.

"You know of Max Perkins?" the young man asked.

"The great Scribner editor?"

He nodded. "Perhaps we haven't a Max Perkins, but our senior editor has somewhat similar talents. Cecil Scott. Why don't you mail your manuscript to him?"

"May I use your name?"

"Surely. I'll drop Scott a note and tell him to expect it."

I mailed what I had written—a bulky package of several hundred typescript pages—and heard no more about it until

Cecil Scott telephoned me at Saratoga Springs more than two months later.

This Friday noon as I left the taxi that carried me into lower Fifth Avenue and looked up at the large and very solid building of the Macmillan Company, I wondered how such an imposing edifice could have been erected merely on the practice of persons like myself stringing words together on paper. I was fidgety. I had lost the confidence I had had when I studied my countenance in the wall mirror in the Adelphi Hotel, thinking then it reflected a prescience of greatness. I did not enter the building immediately but crossed the Avenue to a café for a very dry martini, a bracer for a meeting that now seemed as formidable as a summit conference.

The receptionist at Macmillan's put me at my ease. She smilingly informed me that I was expected and directed me to the office of the senior editor, a brisk, chubby, genial man, a native Scotsman, who had come to the United States and joined the publishing firm not long after he had been graduated from Cambridge University.

"I'm sorry," Cecil Scott apologized, "but we've got to go across the street for lunch. We have excellent dining facilities here, but unfortunately they are being renovated. You won't mind?"

I assured him I wouldn't.

"Well, come along," he said, and we entered an elaborate office where I was introduced to George P. Brett, Jr., president of the firm, and Harold Latham, who was soon to retire as editor-in-chief.

I had heard of Harold Latham. He had become almost a figure in folklore.

There were legends about Margaret Mitchell's *Gone With the Wind,* and Latham was central in several of them. He had learned while on a southern scouting trip for Macmillan that Miss Mitchell had written a novel, and he asked her to allow him to read it. It was a manuscript of interminable dog-eared, scrawled-over, and tattered pages; the physical burden of it, one story went, made it necessary for the editor to purchase two suitcases to carry it out of Atlanta. He was engrossed by the manuscript, reading it all night on the train that took him to New Orleans; his absorption continued when he reached that city and he knew, as he later reported, that he had something of "tremendous importance. . . . Any publisher would have recognized that fact. I was fortunate to come along at the right moment."

Latham was still in New Orleans, not yet finished with the story, when Miss Mitchell wired, "Please send my manuscript back. I have changed my mind."

He persuaded her to allow him to keep it, and he took the mountainous mass of paper to New York, where his associates at Macmillan were as excited as he was about the story. It was Harold Latham who directed the publication of the novel that became a publishing phenomenon.

This noon, sitting across from me in the office of the Macmillan president, Mr. Latham said, "Mr. Clune, your manuscript has been read by a number of outside readers. If we didn't know they are honest people, we'd believe there was collusion, they are so unanimously enthusiastic."

Mr. Brett nodded as if to affirm Mr. Latham's remarks. He had not previously mentioned my manuscript but had questioned me about my family, my home, my newspaper career, and he wondered if I had any hobbies. Now he referred for the first time to the subject that was the purpose of this meeting. "We all feel," he said, "that you have a fine story. It needs some work done. But what you've written has the elements a fine novel should have. We would like very much to publish it. We have had our share of best sellers and books that have won prizes—Pulitzer, and other awards. You of course know of the tremendous success we made of Margaret Mitchell's novel."

He paused a moment, and looked at me intently. "Mr. Clune," he went on, "I can tell you this. It is our considered judgment if we publish your novel, that it will be the greatest popular success we have had since *Gone With the Wind.*"

It was a heady pronouncement and I managed to take it holding to my chair, not leaping wildly into the air. Perhaps I had never been more excited than I was at that moment, but my response was controlled and modest. "I'm glad," I told the president of the publishing firm, "that you find it interesting."

Mr. Brett picked up a legal looking document from his desk and began to read it. It was a contract, with stipulations about royalties, foreign sales, movie rights, and whatnot, to which I listened superficially. The great thing was they were eager to publish a story I had worked on for a long time, that ran out to hundreds of typed pages, and that I was sure would be an "important" novel, if, indeed—and in the light of Brett's prediction, the speculation was rife with me—it was not proclaimed The Great American Novel.

When he finished reading, he moved the paper across the desk with one hand, the other holding a pen. I hunched forward in my chair and signed on the dotted line. We then went across Fifth Avenue for a gay and sumptuous lunch at the Grosvenor Hotel, during which Brett echoed the remark of the young man I had met at Mrs. Allen's that Cecil Scott was considered a sort of Maxwell Perkins and would work with me as Perkins had with Scott Fitzgerald, Thomas Wolfe, Marjorie Rawlings, and other Scribner authors. Before lunch was over, it was agreed that Scott would come to Rochester to discuss revision of the opening chapters of the novel, not to change the plot but to "light up the vestibule," to give drama to the opening scenes.

I left for home that night in a trance, wondering if the critics would compare me with Tolstoi, or Thackeray, or Arnold Bennett, or half a dozen other famous novelists into whose empyreal realm I believed I was about to enter.

CHAPTER ONE

About the worst thing that happened to me in my youth was when my father lost his temper and flailed me with a razor strop because I balked at taking swimming lessons at Dockstader's Baths on North Water Street in Rochester, New York.

My father was this sort of a man:

One day, when I was in my fiftieth year, he called me to his small office on an upper floor of a Rochester bank building and handed me a rectangular slip of paper he drew from a pigeonhole of his roll-top desk. It was a demand note for $25,000 lent by my father to John—, a former president of a Sioux City, Iowa, bank. Across the right hand corner of the note were two words in my father's cursive script, "No interest."

"If anything happens to me," my father said, "I never want you or anyone else to attempt to collect a penny of this money. If John is able to pay, he'll pay without anyone asking him to do so. He got hurt in the crash. I tried to help him. I'm not sure my help did much good. But he is never to be badgered for the money. You understand?"

I told him I did.

"You see," my father went on after a moment's reflection, "John did a very kind thing for me once."

"What kind thing?"

"He revived my faith in Christmas."

"When you were a kid?"

"Yes." He moved slightly in his swivel chair, his eyes averted from mine, and told of an episode of his youth.

It was a year or two after the surrender at Appomattox, and my father was five or six years old. He was a frail, sensitive child, the only surviving issue of parents whose marital life had been grossly interrupted by four years of war.

A few weeks before Christmas my father's mother gave her small son to the charge of an elderly, childless couple in the Iowa village in which she was then living and bid him a tearful goodbye.

"I'll be back before Christmas," she promised.

She was leaving on a sad mission. Her husband, Colonel William H. Clune, a young lawyer and four-year veteran of the Civil War, commissioned by the government to attempt to resolve a legal-military problem relating to the operations of the army on the Mexican border, had died in a yellow fever epidemic in Galveston, Texas.

Left with scant means and possessed of meager information concerning the circumstances of Colonel Clune's death, my grandmother essayed the long journey south in the hope of locating her husband's burial place and of reclaiming any assets he might have had on his person at the time of his death. Neither of these purposes was achieved. Abandoning her investigations, the widow started back to her Iowa home. Her intention was to arrive in time to devise some form of Christmas celebration for her son, but a few days before the holiday she was halted by a prairie blizzard that held stage coaches tightly in their relay stations and made any travel impossible.

On Christmas Eve, my father, a lonely little boy with no hope that his mother would return that night, tacked a stocking to the chimney piece and rose next morning to see what it held.

It was empty—as dejectedly and prosaically limp as a washed stocking hung on a line to dry.

The elderly couple who had taken the lad into their house for a small fee that would help eke out their narrow resources, probably had no understanding of the ardent expectations of youth and had not thought to add Christmas cheer to the routine hospitality they provided their small guest.

Their unwitting neglect caused cruel disappointment and all but extinguished the last spark of faith the boy had in the miracle of Christmas. The spark was kept alive only by the knowledge that that night Santa Claus was scheduled to appear at a celebration in a community church, which the boy's guardians, when he petitioned their consent, said that he might attend.

Sitting alone in a back pew of the small church, he heard the names of youthful contemporaries called out and saw each designated child dart forward to receive one or two and sometimes three presents from Santa's bag, toys which had been provided by the parents of the assembled children.

There was great bustle and stir and exultant "oh's" and "ah's" as Kitty was handed a doll, Tommy a sled, and Frank a tiny replica of a Mississippi steamboat; and so it went all down the line until Santa's bulging bag was empty and the bewhiskered distributor of these good things descended from his throne.

Only one child was empty handed. His name had not been called. For the second time this Christmas day he suffered a bitter disappointment and as he left the pew sobs choked his throat and tears bubbled in his eyes. Half blinded by tears, he was pressing through the happy throng toward the door when a small miracle, on this day of miracles, occurred.

A friendly arm fell over the slim shoulders of the empty-handed child, and a boy of his own age spoke with friendly concern. "Why, George, you don't have a present. Here, you have this, I've got three." And he thrust an iron horse, a curvetting little horse, gaily caparisoned like a trick horse in a circus, into the other's hand.

The boy pressed the gift close to him, his heart overflowing with happiness. For all its lack of value, the iron horse seemed a wonderfully ingenious thing; he cherished it for months, and he never forgot the kind youth who had given it to him.

The two boys grew to manhood. The good Samaritan remained in the west and became a figure of prominence in the second city of his native state; the other moved, shortly after he exceeded his nonage, to Rochester, New York, where he lived for the remainder of his long life. In a period of more than fifty years the two friends of youth saw one another less than half a dozen times.

Four or five years before his death and a couple of years after my father told me of the Christmas Miracle, he called me to his office and again drew from a pigeonhole of his desk the note signed by the Sioux City banker.

"John—died suddenly this morning." My father's eyes were sad. "Heart. I told you before what a kind thing he did for me many years ago. He was a very kind man." He waved the demand note for $25,000 slowly in his hand. "No use keeping this any longer," he said; and he tore the slip of paper into a dozen pieces and dropped them into a trash basket atthe side of his desk.

* * * * * * * * * *

My father moved to Rochester, New York, in 1882, at the age of twenty-two. His youth had been almost no youth at all, and its single highlight may have been the gift of a toy horse which he valued in later years at $25,000. His formal schooling ended when he was nine. From then on he worked at a variety of scratch jobs to help support his widowed mother. The boy's mother applied for a Federal pension. She mentioned in the application that during four years of conspicuous war service her husband had been wounded and cited for valor. The application apparently was lost in the bureaucratic labyrinths of the Johnson and Grant administrations, and years passed before she was granted a stipend of thirty dollars a month. In the meantime she moved from Iowa to stake a Homestead claim in the southern part of Dakota Territory. The venture failed. The widow and her preteen-age son were incapable of operating a 160 acre farm and cattle ranch on the unfenced steppes of what was then the western frontier. They moved again, this time into Yankton, not far from the Homestead site. My father could read at the age of fifteen, but he could not write. He learned in the next year or so and also learned (for one of his jobs was working around the Yankton station of the recently established Sioux City and Dakota Railroad) the Morse Code. At seventeen he was an accredited telegraph operator for the railroad, assigned first to the station at Yankton, then to the one at Vermillion, also in Dakota territory, and finally, to the eastern terminus of the road at Sioux City, Iowa.

When the superintendent of the Sioux City and Dakota accepted a similar position with the Buffalo, Rochester and Pittsburgh Railroad, whose headquarters were in Rochester, New York, he persuaded my father to come east, where he was first employed by the railroad and later by a Rochester company that operated bituminous mines in western Pennsylvania and used the railroad as a carrier for large shipments of its coal.

In Rochester my father's life brightened. He had come a long way from the drudging tasks of odd-job boy in an opening western land. On the Homestead acres his mother tried to settle, he had sat long lonely hours on a cow pony with nothing in visual prospect beyond the grazing critters except the waving grass of the interminable prairie. He worked as a hired hand for other settlers, walking mile-long furrows barefoot, behind a mule-drawn plow. He found no romance in the "wild and woolly west." Once in the east, he was a committed urban dweller; country life had no appeal for him.

Denied during his formative years the diversions and activities of youth, my father attempted to compensate for this denial by engaging in recreational pursuits that his liberated life in Rochester permitted. He learned to dance and play whist. He skated on the frozen surface of the Genesee River. He enjoyed the theater. He joined an athletic club, became a competent gymnast and, when the bicycle craze was at its zenith, was an amateur record holder at the distance of one mile.

His social life expanded. Among the friendships he formed was a brief one with the city's most eminent woman. For a time he sat once a day at a boarding house table with Miss Susan B. Anthony. Young and impressionable, my father, at first, was diffident in the presence of a woman whose fame had spread across her native land and even to Europe. Susan B. ("Saint Susan," as her ardent disciples canonized her) was then in her sixties, old enough to be my father's grandmother. As their acquaintance improved he found that she was not the abrasive and pugnacious harridan newspaper artists delighted to caricature, but a woman of wit and charm. He was won to the causes she espoused. He particularly admired her unremitting effort to obtain political suffrage for the members of her sex. My father followed her career until it ended with her death more than twenty years after he first met her. And though he himself was hardly a reformer—and perhaps something of a reactionary in his later, more affluent days—his respect for the famed feminist was profound.

In 1885, George H. Clune married Hattie Bruman, a lovely blonde young woman, in the home in which the bride was born in Rochester. The next year the oldest of the couple's three daughters was born. I came along four years later. I suspect that on the day of my birth my father was the most exultant man in Rochester and my mother the most bewildered and perplexed woman. My mother was totally feminine. I am sure she never wanted a son, and I doubt if she was conscious of her capacity to conceive one.

My father had looming hopes for the only male issue he would have. He would instruct him in his own athletic pursuits, carefully educate him, endow him with all of the advantages his own youth had lacked. The two, father and son, would be boon companions. He would send his son to Yale, since the man by whom he was ultimately employed went to Yale's Sheffield Scientific School, and my father knew almost nothing about any other college or university.

His hopes, as I advanced from childhood to adolescence, were shattered by an almost pathological resistance I displayed toward education and by a sort of paranoiac contrariness that caused me to oppose every design my father had for me. I was deliberately over-indulged by my mother and unwittingly by my father. I was weak, stupid, soft. In the end, my educational failures broke my father's heart.

My father was an unusual man. He was a man of certitude and rectitude. He had a bag full of theories, some of which seemed to me hardly rational. During all the years that I knew him I never heard him use profanity or a vulgar four-letter word. He never attended church, except possibly once every fourth or fifth Easter Sunday at the earnest behest of my mother. He neither smoked nor drank. He never gambled. He eschewed tea and coffee. He dressed with extreme conservatism, and his tailoring, in time, was the best to be had in town. But he never wore an undershirt, a waistcoat, or an overcoat, and he walked a mile and a half to and from his office on the bitterest winter days in this scant attire.

He took a cold shower every morning of his life. He believed that most physical disorders were caused by over-eating and lack of exercise. On those rare occasions when he was ill he refused all medication and took no food until he recovered. Very late in life he had all of his remaining teeth drawn without the use of novacaine. In his late sixties he could still do the giant swing and a running front somersault off a mat. In his mid-seventies he was doing, with little grace but with considerable courage, a one-and-a half somersault from the high board of the swimming pool of Rochester's leading social club, the Genesee Valley.

My father read Elbert Hubbard's *A Message to Garcia,* thousands of reprints of which were handed out by business houses to their employees, and he became a Hubbard disciple. He subscribed to and avidly read Hubbard's little butcher paper monthly, the *Philistine,* issued from the author's Roycroft print shop in East Aurora, New York. Hubbard harped continually on the idea of hard work and dauntless resolution. He castigated the clock-watching employee. My father tried early to instruct me in the doctrine that loyalty to the one for whom one worked always paid off; that the man who always did a little better than his best succeeded. He was curiously naive about the inhumanity of large employers to labor, although he surely knew of the brutalities of the Pullman and steel strikes, the sweatshops in the clothing industry, and the criminal abuse of labor by many great corporations, including perhaps the bituminous mining company which employed him. He held the quixotic notion that one should never ask for a raise; if a worker merited a raise, it would come to him automatically. I learned differently from hard experience.

He had an abhorrence of debt and a theory of economics which would bring ruin to General Motors and probably the country at large if put in practice today. He was inexorably opposed to installment buying. "Buy now, and pay later," would be anathema to him. Whether it was a baby carriage, a lawn mower, a bicycle, a piano, or a house, he would buy only what he could pay for at once, cash on the barrelhead. My mother liked to adorn her handsomeness. She had natural style. She liked fancy dresses, small luxuries, whist parties, and dancing clubs. She had a mild desire to keep up with the Joneses. My father wanted nothing to do with that sort of competition if the costs were more than he could afford.

I am sure he was skeptical of Revelation, but he had very strong beliefs in other areas. One concerned the sacredness of private property.

"Never—never," he impressed upon me, "touch another person's property unless you have the owner's permission to do so. The jails are filled with people who break that rule."

I heard, but failed to heed the injunction.

Before I reached my teens (perhaps when I was ten or eleven years old) I occasionally walked to and from school with a tough little hombre whose mother took in washing. His name was Frankie, and he lived at some remove from the bourgeoise exclusiveness of our own home on Linden Street, in a neighborhood commonly spoken of as Swillburg. We would meet on South Avenue and walk to No. 13 School, passing on the way Mr. Schultz's grocery store at the corner of South Avenue and Cypress Street.

In clement weather, the grocer displayed an assortment of perishable produce in crates and barrels on the sidewalk in front of his store. One morning on our way to school, Frankie suggested, "Let's grab a couple of ol' Schultz's apples."

"How can we do that?" I asked.

"You do what I tell you, and I'll show you."

Frankie was never too clean. He was ragged-assed and tatterdemalion. But he had a certain imperiousness, a command presence. Boys of my age were not inclined to cross him or defy his orders.

As we reached the front of the Schultz store, he told me to snatch his cap from his head and throw it into the apple barrel, which I did.

"Hey, what t'hell you mean doing that?" Frankie cried

angrily. He reached into the barrel, reclaimed his cap, and we passed on. "Look," he said, grinning, and he showed me three apples he had concealed in his cap when he picked it out of the barrel.

It seemed to me that there was something here of genius. Frankie was a smart one, all right.

For a few days after that when we passed the Schultz store, either I threw Frankie's cap into the barrel or he threw mine. And whoever reached into the barrel came up with two or three apples.

The next Sunday my oldest sister had a girl friend for Sunday night supper. She was a stranger to me and it struck me that she was putting on airs. I wanted to make an impression.

So I told boastfully, and with graphic detail, how Frankie and I had mastered the trick of snatching apples from the barrel as we passed the Schultz store. I finished, expecting my cleverness to be applauded. Instead, there was an ominous silence.

From his place at the head of the supper table, my father fixed me with the eye of a hanging judge.

"Do you know what you've done, young man?" he asked in a tone of utter condemnation. "You've stolen. You've done what thieves do."

"B—but just a couple of apples," I protested. "What's a couple of apples?"

"You've stolen," my father repeated. "You've taken another man's property. Those apples belong to Mr. Schultz. He sells them to make a living. And you—you sneaked your hand into his barrel like a thief and took what didn't belong to you."

"Wh—why," but I was whimpering now, my puff gone, my boast deflated.

My father reached into his pocket and rang a quarter down on the table top. "You take that," he commanded, "and tomorrow you stop and tell Mr. Schultz what you did and pay him for the apples you stole."

I saw my sister's girl friend, whom I had been trying to impress, looking at me as if I were a roach or some other odious insect, to be crushed by the sole of her slipper.

I leaped up from my chair, and ran upstairs to my room,

hot tears scalding my cheeks, a hate formed against my father that I was sure would never abate.

Half the night long my mind seethed with schemes of revolt. I would never suffer the ignominious act of restitution my father had ordered. I'd run away. And perhaps in my wayfaring career I'd be killed riding the brake beam of a freight train and then a wicked old man would realize what he had done to his son. Murdered him!

My father was gone when I came down in the morning. My mother was at the breakfast table. Never having wanted a son, and never quite understanding the one who had come to her by an untoward accident, I knew she loved me. I could see sympathy and sorrow in her eyes. But she knew no way to ease the ordeal to which I was committed. On the way to school I crossed South Avenue and passed the Schultz store on the opposite side of the street. I followed a similar procedure going home for lunch and returning to school for the afternoon session.

But I knew, as older persons were sensible of the inevitability of death and taxes, that I could not appear at the supper table that night unless I was able to report that I had executed the obscene order my father had given me.

I approached the Schultz store on my final return from school with lagging steps and anarchy in my soul. I told myself a dozen times I'd walk boldly past the store without entering it to confess my theft and hand Mr. Schultz the quarter that had become as evil as a hoodoo in my pants pocket. In the end, my dread of the scene at the supper table if I failed to report the expiation of my crime overcame every instinct of revolt. I stumbled into the store, trying to pull my head down between my shoulders as a turtle draws its head into its shell at a moment of menace. I drew the quarter from my pocket and fumbled it onto the counter.

"I—I gotta pay," I stammered to Mr. Schultz.

He was a kindly little man with a little pudding of a belly rounded over by a soiled white apron. He peered at me over his spectacles.

"Pay? Pay for what?"

"Apples. I took a couple of apples from your barrel.

M—my father says I gotta pay for 'em." I was blubbering. I knew I was making a holy show of myself. I turned from the counter and bolted for the door.

"Wait! Wait!" Mr. Schultz called, and when I paused and turned, he beckoned me back to the counter. He dropped my quarter into a cash drawer (there was no register) and returned twenty-three cents. "A couple of apples. A couple of pennies ought to do it."

There was a cage on the counter, almost like a birdcage, except that it was tightly screened against flies. He took from this a creampuff and handed it to me. "Don't be worrying about a couple of apples," Mr. Schultz said. "Pshaw! I was a boy myself once."

"Oh, thanks—thanks, Mr. Schultz."

I left the store thinking Mr. Schultz the kindest man in the world and ran all the way home, eating the pastry as I ran, my panting lips foamed with its creamy contents.

The experience perhaps was not as painful a one as the time my father flailed me with a razor strop, but it impressed upon me a lesson that I never forgot.

Many years later I related the incident in a newspaper column that dealt primarily with the tragic fate of two supposedly well brought up youths who were found guilty of a series of thefts and sent to prison. A few days later I had a note from the then head of the Federal Bureau of Investigation:

> Dear Mr. Clune:
>
> The Honorable John A. Doyle, Commissioner of Police of Brighton, has just forwarded me a copy of your article appearing in the April 26, 1938 issue of the Democrat and Chronicle entitled "Bad Start—Tragic End."
>
> Your keen analysis of the tragic youth problem in crime was most interesting to me. I thoroughly agree with you that the stealing of apples from the corner grocery store, if unchallenged, is the beginning of a career of tragedy. There is much to be done for the youth of America and you may be sure that the law enforcement profession deeply appreciates the assistance which articles such as yours render in bringing

before American parents the crying need for proper early training of youth.

With best wishes and kind regards.

Sincerely yours,
J. Edgar Hoover

* * * * * * * * * * *

My father tried hard, as the YMCA slogan has it, to "Make a Pal" of his son. It didn't work. Our relations were taut when I was a small kid and they did not relax when I advanced into adolescence. He took me to a football game one Thanksgiving afternoon. The University of Rochester had taken up football within the last ten years. This was the "big game," the annual match with Hobart. It was a time when players wore shin guards and nose guards and heavily padded combination uniforms but thought it mollycoddlish to wear helmets. They let their hair grow thick, but not as long as the hippies wear it today. The game was played on a campus field not far from downtown Rochester. There may have been a small grandstand, but I do not recall it. We stood on the sidelines to watch the play. The spectators were in continual movement as they followed the ball from one part of the field to another. I was tall for my age but not rugged. I was buffeted and jostled. I cried. I told my father I wanted to go home and presently, in disgust, he took me.

The following summer I learned to swim, partly under the propulsion of a razor strop.

I had learned to ride a bicycle. Odd as it may seem today when athletic aptitude is common to youth of both sexes, there were schools for instruction in cycling in the last decade of the last century. One of these was conducted by a downtown bicycle dealer named Robert Thompson. Class was held in a large hall similar to a roller rink. The instructor would support the beginning cyclist by holding one hand on the saddle post and the other on the handle bars and run with him around the hall until the student learned to balance and pedal off by himself. My father bought me a bicycle and I learned to ride in the Thompson school. It was a small red bike with wooden handle bars.

My father owned two racing bicycles and a tandem. The front of the tandem was V-shaped, like a woman's bike. There was no crossbar from saddle to handle bars. Occasionally on pleasant Sunday afternoons, my father, with my mother on the front seat, made short runs into the country. My mother went without protest but with very little spirit. She wore a long divided skirt (the chain on her part of the tandem had a guard to protect a woman's skirt from being caught in the chain or sprocket) and bicycle shoes that laced up to the calf of her leg, although of course the tops of her shoes were never exposed.

I never became an enthusiastic cyclist but learning to ride hadn't been difficult, and sometimes I rode behind my parents on their Sunday excursions. Learning to swim was another matter.

Kids I knew less favored than myself learned to swim in a shallow piece of water known as The Pebbles on the west side of the Genesee River, a few hundred yards south of Clarissa Street bridge. They were self taught. They would pee on their left leg for luck and wade out to where the water was breast high and try and try until they managed to raise both feet from the floor of the stream and execute a dog paddle. After that they might master the breast stroke or the single overarm.

For the most part they swam in the altogether, and occasionally a Mrs. Grundy, crossing Exchange Street bridge, found offense in this distant display of youthful nakedness and complained to the police, and the bathers would be chased from The Pebbles. These were not, however, serious interdictions. A couple of days after a "raid," if the weather continued warm, the swimmers and learners would be again disporting in the cool waters of the river.

Downtown there was a plunge, or swimming pool, at a place on Water Street known as Dockstader's Baths, and it was there that my father sent me to learn to swim. The pool was a tiny wooden basin of muddy water pumped up from the Genesee River. Its four walls were of equal length and ten or twelve strokes would take a swimmer from one wall to another. The place seemed to me as grim and forbidding as a catacomb. Its few narrow, high-placed, dust-covered windows admitted little light. There was a row of rickety lockers with broken locks. There was no springboard, but one could swing out from a ledge of the pool on a pair of Roman rings and drop into the water. There was a vile odor from a sulphur spring that bubbled up somewhere in another part of the establishment, where Dockstader treated adults suffering from rheumatism, arthritis, and allied diseases. The swimming pool was a sideline. It derived its greatest patronage from newsboys who hawked the five daily newspapers then in circulation in Rochester. Each paid five cents for the privilege of stripping naked and plunging into the opaque but cooling waters.

The pool, of course, was used only during warm weather. One summer Mrs. Henry J. Moore arranged with Dockstader to lease it for a couple of hours two mornings a week in order that the younger of the ten Moore children and their youthful friends might learn to swim.

Mr. and Mrs. Moore and their numerous issue occupied a large three-story brick house set on an acre of ground on the west side of Mt. Hope Avenue. The house faced the western terminus of Linden Street, the modest but extremely pleasant residential street on which our family lived, which extended half a mile between South Avenue and Mt. Hope. It was staffed by six or seven servants and composed a domestic establishment unique in Rochester and one it is difficult to conceive being duplicated in this age. The entertainment provided for the Moore children and the neighborhood kids fortunate enough to enjoy their friendship was bounteous and varied. There might be twenty at a Sunday night supper, which would be prepared by a male cook who wore a hat like a hotel chef's and served by a butler and a couple of maids. The Moores had riding horses, a menagerie in the barn, and a stage for amateur theatricals. They had the finest private tennis court and the largest bobsled in town. They gave box parties in the grand old Lyceum Theater and coasting parties at the newly founded Oak Hill Country Club. They had a canoe and a skiff for use on the river, the right bank of which was a short distance from the rear of the Moore property. They had skis before any of the rest of us knew of these slender wooden boards used by the Scandinavians, a motorcycle, and a sailing yacht that defended Canada's Cup on Lake Ontario. My first ride in an automobile was in the Moore's Rambler.

My father knew and admired Mr. Moore, who was head of John C. Moore Corporation, a large printing plant, and I was friendly with the younger members of the family and often played in the Moore yard. Mr. Moore was a kindly, even-tempered man who encouraged his children to confine their recreational pursuits to their own home. He took delight in witnessing these activities. He provided a prodigal way of life for his family; but it was his wife, who administered the Moore menage, set rules of conduct for her numerous brood, and acted as disciplinarian. With ten children, Mrs. Moore was hardly a doting or over-sentimental mother. She was a tiny woman of enormous energy, considerable competence, and an air of command. When she organized the swimming class, I was invited to join.

I went to the first session not knowing what to expect. Dockstader, the instructor, was a large, slow-moving, taciturn man, usually with a cold cigar in a corner of his mouth. His teaching technique consisted of fitting the learner into a canvas harness which was attached by a rope to a stout pole Dockstader held in his hands as he moved slowly along the edge of the pool. "Kick, kick,—stroke, stroke," he'd call down to the youth in the water. He was always fully dressed; there was a legend that he himself was unable to swim. "Kick, kick,—stroke, stroke." That was the extent of his teaching text.

The others in the small class took readily to the water. Indeed, Jean, the youngest of the Moore daughters, a slim, pretty, spiritied girl, who seemed to rush headlong at anything that excited her enthusiasm, was able to do without the harness after two lessons. I descended into the pool shuddering and frightened, but ashamed to protest in front of my peers. Once out of the water and free of the instructor's harness, I was determined never to return. I hated the place. The vile smell from the sulphur spring seemed to symbolize everything that was evil about Dockstader's. And the next lesson day I rebelled so vigorously that my father blistered me with a razor strop. He had not been present at the swimming lesson, which was ably directed by Mrs. Moore. Now he ordered me to mount my small red bike, and he set off on his racing Columbia. As we proceeded through Linden Street on the way to Dockstader's, my howls of anguish were so loud that neighbors rushed out to the curb expecting catastrophe.

Once I mastered the trick of keeping afloat and propelling myself through the water with a frog kick and a breast stroke, I enjoyed swimming. And in time my father permitted me to use the summer clubhouse of the Rochester Athletic Club. This was a green-shingled, two-story building that stood at the edge of the Genesee Valley Park athletic field. The field had a third of a mile bicycle track, a quarter-mile cinder track, and jumping pits. The clubhouse faced the Genesee River. Its lower floor was used for the storage of canoes and three or four racing shells. Upstairs was a locker room and two shower baths that expelled only unheated river water.

I swam off the clubhouse dock, used the skiff that was assigned to the kindly boatman in charge of the clubhouse, and presently was given the privilege of my father's canoe.

In the last years of the old and in the early years of the present century, canoeing on the upper Genesee was a favorite pastime. Recreational pursuits were more leisurely in those days. For many of us they were quite simple, requiring no great expenditure of money or a need to go far from home. The internal combustion engine was being developed, but the automobile was a curiosity rather than a vehicle of practicability; and motorboats had not yet disturbed the placid waters of our river or befouled the air above it with their oily stench.

Leaving the clubhouse dock with a duffle bag under the deck of their canoe, two young men paddling south would soon be on a waterway almost as primitive in aspect as it had been a century before, when the Genesee was a main artery of travel for the Seneca Indians. There would be thick wooded areas along the shore and winding tributaries to explore. There would be fish in the stream to catch for a campfire breakfast. The canoeists might proceed twenty miles south and see little more of man's handwork than the span of a railroad bridge. They might be away overnight, or for several nights, living like the *courreur de bois* of long ago.

Young men were proud of their canoes. They scraped

and varnished them in the spring in preparation for a summer on the water. They were careful after a day's paddling to swab the hull clean of any adhesive shoreline mud. They swept the carpeting that lay along the flooring, particularly if their craft were used at times to entertain young women. There were canvas canoes; Oldtowns, broad-beamed and suitable for water much rougher than that encountered on the gentle Genesee; and narrower, crankier wooden ones. But the canoe that gave cachet to its owner and set him apart as an aristocrat on the river was a Threehouse.

Mort Threehouse was a crotchety little man, a gunsmith by trade, a crack shot, and an expert fisherman, who, during the winter months, might condescend to build a canoe in a shed behind his home in a modest west side neighborhood.

He built, in all, not more than fifteen or eighteen, and each was a superb example of the woodworker's craft. His canoes were constructed with the exquisite care Duncan Phyfe might have exerted in the creation of a lyre table or a mahogany sofa. I think it was during the last winter of the last century that my father persuaded Threehouse to build a canoe for him.

My father strove for excellence in anything he attempted. He greatly admired the perfected skills of others. He told me that Threehouse was a mechanical genius. Occasionally on a Saturday afternoon he took me over to the gunsmith's shed to see how the work was progressing.

Threehouse struck me as an over-fussy man. I have seen him fling away strips of wood that seemed perfectly good with an angry expletive that he had been sold rotten lumber. He was meticulous in every detail. The hull of our canoe was made of basswood, and seven other different woods were incorporated into its construction. It was sixteen feet in length, narrow of beam, with a sharp prow and stern. It had a brass keel and only brass screws were used in the wood. The mahogany planking of its deck was divided by a strip of white cherry. The building of the boat was exasperatingly slow. Threehouse would not permit urgency to detract from care of workmanship. But once the *Owana* (as my father named the craft) arrived at the clubhouse and was launched, the lovely blending of its woods, its grace, its maneuverability, and speed made it a standout. Proudly my father flew the club's burgee from a staff in the bow. Other canoeists passing on the river all but genuflected, for this was a Threehouse—the smartest thing on the upper Genesee.

When canoeing was in great vogue on the Genesee, an upriver excursion was an exciting adventure for a canoeist's best girl. The girls of some of the canoeists worked half the winter making sofa pillows, sometimes with the name of the boy friend's boat embroidered on them. Not many girls paddled. In summer finery, perhaps wearing a flower bedecked hat with a broad limber brim, a girl would ensconce herself among a clutch of sofa pillows in the bow and sense the elegance of Cleopatra on her Nile-floating barge. Suntan oil was unknown. Pretty girls were as protective of their complexions as a Jane Austen heroine. Exposure to the sun brought out freckles; to become as sunburned as a field hand would be gauche. Girls held parasols over their heads when the canoe left the shade of the riverbank's overhanging cottonwoods for the open stream. They faced the paddler in their pillowed luxury. There would be a shoebox under the bow deck with a carefully prepared lunch: deviled eggs, ham and cheese and jelly sandwiches; potato salad; possibly a cold chicken or half a chocolate cake.

I was only an occasional canoeist, never an expert. Our Threehouse was narrow and tippy. Its occupants needed to be carefully balanced; deftness was needed in its management or over you'd go. My father had a second canoe, a broad-beamed canvas craft. It was as stable as a scow. He had hoped to use this to entertain my mother on the river, but her interests were almost entirely sedentary.

Two or three experiences on the Genesee, when she sat in a nervous twit with her back to a cork-filled pillow that served as a life preserver, her hands clutching the gunwales so tightly that the knuckles whitened, were all that she wanted. She couldn't swim. "George, if we capsize you couldn't save me," she protested ominously.

"I *could* save you," he boasted grimly. "But we're not

going to capsize. Besides, that pillow back of you would float you all day."

She had little confidence in my father, none in the cork-filled pillow or canoe. She found no charm in the river scenery. She went once without a parasol. The brim of her hat was not broad enough to protect her face from the sun. Her nose reddened and peeled. That was the final excursion. She never went out in the canvas canoe again, and my father relegated it to the racks in the clubhouse until he had an opportunity to sell it.

My few companions on the river were boys of my own age. I was timid and withdrawn with girls. I was invited to a birthday party for a pretty little girl who lived on the east side, the fashionable section of town. I had been asked because my parents were friends of her parents. It was a large party. After supper a game called Post Office was played. I was called in from one room to another, ostensibly to receive a letter. Instead, I was virtually grappled by a girl who tried to kiss me. I escaped, ran up the front stairs of the large house and locked myself in the bathroom until I found an opportunity to sneak down the back stairs and run home bare-headed, my best cap sacrificed to my shameful lack of gallantry.

Later I had an apocalyptic experience with the fair sex which increased my timidity and excited my curiosity about them. Our sixth grade at No. 13 School must have been of ideal size. There were seven girls and five boys. The teacher was a handsome young woman. She wore her hair parted precisely in the middle, and an attractive shirtwaist, ornamented by a billowing jabot, covered her bosom and reached to her belted waist. I have a large photograph of the teacher and the members of the grade standing around a table-size relief map of the western Rockies. The boys, of course, were all in short pants. I wore a sailor blouse with white piping at the collar. The boy next to me, the son of a physician and the brightest boy in the class, wore a jacket, a shirt with a stiff linen collar, and a bow tie. We all wore high shoes. The shoes of some of the girls laced up to the calves of their legs. A girl named Cora had the desk directly in front of me and girl named Theresa sat directly behind me. Cora was large for her age, tall and slim. In the relief map photograph she is wearing a dress with white flounces at the shoulders and a gaudy ornament at her throat. Theresa was small and demure. One day, during study period, Cora surreptitiously handed me a sheet of paper and whispered, "Give it to Theresa."

In this relayed passage I glanced at the unfolded paper. On it was a crude drawing which, when I looked a second time, made me gasp. It was obviously intended to represent a penis. Under the drawing Cora had scrawled, "How'd you like to have this in you?"

Sex education was not part of sixth grade curriculum at No. 13 but apparently Cora, and perhaps Theresa, were precocious in these matters.

I was disturbed and unsettled by the incident. It was as if I myself had lost my innocence. After that I was always put out of countenance when face to face with Cora. She would look at me with bold eyes and laugh, or rather smirk. The smirk seemed to say, "Why don't you wise up, kid?"

When the school term ended, workmen began the demolition of old No. 13, which was to be replaced by a larger building. In the fall I was transferred to a school across the river. Cora and Theresa went somewhere else. The thought of the passed paper lingered in my mind for a long time. It aroused speculation. I wondered if "nice" girls were as interested in male genitalia as were Cora and Theresa and found in the end that many were.

CHAPTER TWO

I signed the Macmillan contract in late August 1951. The week after Labor Day Cecil Scott came to Rochester and took a suite in the Hotel Seneca, where, for several hours each day of his three-day stay, we discussed the alterations I was to make in the early chapters of the story.

I had put a title on the manuscript which the editor thought awkward and unconvincing; and I had intended for the frontispiece a quote from one of Sir Francis Bacon's essays . . . "the mold of man's fortune is in his own hands," which I felt would represent the manner in which my hero achieved, by his own exertions, tremendous material success. The line was never used, but from it Scott devised what became the novel's registered title, *By His Own Hand,* thought by many readers to indicate the hero's death by a self-inflicted bullet.

Scott was jealous of my script. *By His Own Hand* was not my first novel but my third, and there had been also three books of nonfiction. He wanted nothing said of these. *By His Own Hand* was to be a smashing novel by a new author he had uncovered as Harold Latham had introduced Margaret Mitchell and *Gone With the Wind.* I consented to the slight. The other novels had had promise, and one flourished for a time; but this was to be my *chef d'oeuvre,* and I was agreeable to anything that would advance it to the predicted success.

Eighteen years before, I had compiled, at the request of the *Democrat and Chronicle,* a book of my newspaper columns, which sold several thousand copies at Christmas time at one dollar a copy. There was also a two dollar deluxe binding, and later, with the war, a paperback edition which the newspaper distributed to members of the armed forces from the Rochester area. Ed Sullivan, the New York *Daily News* columnist, reported that *Seen and Heard* was the best selling book in Western New York.

The first *Seen and Heard* was my first book. Two years after it was issued, *Seen and Heard* Volume II, with new material and a foreword by my friend, George S. Brooks, was put out by the newspaper. I was busy at the time writing a novel and not particularly interested in a second locally printed book, so I made the selections hurriedly. Volume II sold well but did not match the success of its predecessor.

My first novel, *The Good Die Poor,* was a raffish tale of a picaresque newspaperman told in lively vernacular prose, and it caught on at once. It went into a substantial second printing before it even hit the stands, and when it did, the *New York Times* gave it a booming review. The book briefly made the best seller list; it was a Book of the Month Club option; and Methuen published it in England, where it received good notices.

Miss Bernice Baumgarten, my agent, sold the picture rights to Warner Brothers, and the *Hollywood Reporter* front-paged the news that Bette Davis and Edward G. Robinson would co-star in a film version to be produced by Edmund Grainger from a script by Michael Fessler.

This was heady stuff for a small city newspaperman living in the rural community of Scottsville, and my hope for fame and riches zoomed into the stratosphere.

Presently, Miss Davis and Robinson were withdrawn, and Humphrey Bogart replaced Robinson in the leading male role. Warners sent me an elaborate press book telling of the change. Time went on. I waited to be summoned to Hollywood as an expert adviser, and I had visions of a grand premiere of *The Good Die Poor* in Rochester, perhaps in the Eastman Theater.

I had received not an astronomical sum, but several thousand dollars for the movie rights, and I would be paid no more, for the sale was outright. But a picture starring Miss

Davis and Robinson, or Bogart, would surely be an "A" film, and that would mean prestige for the author. Nothing happened and the picture was never made.

The Good Die Poor was published in early autumn, 1937. William Morrow published my next novel, *Monkey on a Stick,* in May 1940. It was a fatal month for fiction.

History was being made, and the tremendous happenings in Europe were announced in staccato sequences over the air and in screaming headlines in the newspaper. Nazi hordes were pushing into the Netherlands, Belgium, and Luxemburg. Chamberlain quit as Prime Minister of Britain and Winston Churchill took over. In a blitzkrieg move, the Germans crossed the French border and were soon to enter Paris. Then the quintessential disaster, the evacuation of British forces from Dunkirk and the exposure of the Motherland to what the world believed would be imminent invasion.

Monkey on a Stick was light fiction. It told about a mousey little man whose hypnotic radio voice beguiled millions into believing that he should be president of the United States and brought him within an ace of being nominated. But it had no chance of attracting the attention of the reading public whose eyes were fixed on the catastrophic war dispatches in the newspapers.

Nonetheless, the book had fine notices. The *New York Herald-Tribune* reviewed it in both daily and Sunday editions. In the first, the prestigious Lewis Gannett, said that except for a lack of sure-footedness in the closing chapter (a chapter that an equally distinguished critic pronounced "artistically right") it would have been "first rate American satire." "As it is," Mr. Gannett added, "it provides a chuckle-full evening." The *Times* spoke glowingly of the novel; it was well received by the *New Yorker,* the *New Republic,* called by the *Daily News* "the best novel ever written about radio," and the *Daily Worker,* radical, and prejudiced on the side of Communism, found it "significant." "On the surface, *Monkey on a Stick* is light comedy . . . But beneath the absurdities, flippancies and wise-cracks, the novel contains an intelligent warning about wolves in clowns' clothing, and brings to mind Adolf Hitler being derided and scorned as a comic figure in the very years when international capital, unaware that the stooge would turn, was priming him as a hatchetman against the Soviet Union . . ."

The book was approvingly discussed at the celebrated Round Table in the Algonquin Hotel, where a group of such smarties as Heywood Broun, George S. Kaufman, Dorothy Parker, Franklin Pierce Adams (F.P.A.), Alexander Woollcott, et al., gathered each noon to exchange *bon mots* and be gawked at adoringly by tourists from Biloxi, Mississippi, and Punxsutawney, Pennsylvania, dress buyers from Wichita, Kansas, and other hinterland areas; but Woollcott, who could put a seed catalogue or a telephone directory on the best seller list with a word of commendation, never gave public mention to *Monkey on a Stick.*

A playwright wanted to dramatize the novel for the stage, but Miss Baumgarten touted me off the proposal.

"He'll want to tie it up for six months if we give it to him," she said. "We'll make a quick sale to Hollywood, and later sell it for a price for the theater."

And in time, she did sell it to Warner Brothers. My wife got a mink wrap but no diamonds. The price was far from spectacular, and they put this novel on the shelf as they had *The Good Die Poor.*

CHAPTER THREE

The business of growing up in the last decade of the last century and in the early years of this one may have been as perplexing as it is today, but in my recollection it doesn't seem so. I knew no great anguish in the transition from childhood to puberty. I was awkward and shy and chary of girls; but any teenage love sickness I knew was much less virulent than a bellyache I got from eating green apples.

I had prurient stirrings, of course. I knew high school girls who were spoken of as "fast", who were supposed to countenance an extensive laying-on of hands. They excited my curiosity, but they were not my intimates. And if they went, as the saying was, "the limit," I heard of no pregnancies among them. If there were youthful junkies, they were out of my ken. I was goodie-goodie to the extent that on the night of our high school fraternity's grand ball I was untempted by the sneaked-in hard liquor that rendered some of the brothers *hors de combat.* I was fortunate in the choice of parents and in their selection of a place in which to live and raise a family. I thought of my father with his steady job as an infallible provider, a stout bastion against impoverishment and want. And if in a rare wakeful hour of the night I heard my mother's muted sobs and knew that my parents were quarreling in their darkened room, I was distressed but never fearful that my father would run away and leave us.

I suppose our neighborhood was typically bourgeois. We were "squares." We lived quite orderly lives under quite favorable auspices. In the full length of the street on which I passed the first three decades of my life I knew of no home that was broken by divorce, no quarrels over the custody of children, no court disputes over the division of property.

People moved into our street and "stayed put." There were residents who remained forty, fifty, even sixty years. I knew two women, each of whom died in the house in which she was born. My mother may have typified the neighborhood. In her nearly eighty-five years of life she moved four times, but never farther than a twelve-minute walk from her place of birth.

Our immediate neighbors were at variance in numerous ways. There was among them a disparity in tastes, practices, occupations, politics and religious beliefs; but always there was great good will and fellowship. There were no quarrels except minor ones among the small fry, which were quickly over. If there was illness in a family, right away the next door neighbor or the neighbor across the street called to offer assistance: to come with hot broth, or jellies, or some delicacy to tempt the patient's appetite. Housewives traded gossip and recipes when they came out in the morning to shake small rugs over porch railings. Elaborate preparations were made for a neighborhood picnic. It was the main topic among us for days. We envisioned it as a shining adventure. It was hardly that; the sumptuous picnic supper was spread on outdoor tables in Highland Park, less than a mile from home.

On rare occasions when the newspapers found need to mention our street, they gently lampooned it as "sleepy Linden Street." We were not annoyed. We knew no turmoil or undue commotion; the nights were as quiet as they might have been on a road in the boondocks. Until the automobile came into common use there was almost no traffic after nightfall. I was a boy in knee pants when the dirt road was replaced by a macadam pavement. I remember lying over-long abed on a drowsy vacation summer morning and hearing what sounded like a horse at mad gallop. The illusion was very real. Actually, what I heard was the cadenced fall of hoofs of one of the teams of draft horses that at intervals slowly hauled carts loaded with sand over the new macadam. The grocer's wagon came through in the morning, later, a delivery rig from a downtown store. It was quiet on our street, even in the daytime.

A few years after I was born in a house on the north side of Linden Street, we moved into the second house to stand on the south side of the street. Both properties indented into the beautiful display nursery of the Ellwanger & Barry Nursery Company, in which Mr. Maloy, our next door neighbor, served as secretary. He had been hired at the age of thirteen years as an errand boy in the firm's small, picturesque, stone office building (the two bookkeepers sat on high stools at breast-high desks, and cannel coal burned in open hearths in each room) on Mt. Hope Avenue, a short distance from the upper corner of Linden Street; he was still there fifty-six years later when the firm disbanded. He lived virtually all of his life on Linden Street, first in the home of his parents, and then in the house next to the one in which we moved. In the second dwelling all seven of the Maloy children were born and there, after the house had known a great deal of living, Mr. and Mrs. Maloy died.

Mr. Maloy was something of an institution in the neighborhood. A kindly, gentle-mannered, pipe-smoking man, he walked four times daily over a half mile course that separated his home from the Ellwanger & Barry office. His pedestrian habits had a chronometric regularity. He left his home precisely at nine o'clock each morning and returned for lunch at exactly 12:15 P.M., and housewives, observing his departure or his arrival ran to set their clocks aright.

Directly across the street from the Maloys were the Tiefels. Mrs. Tiefel was a large, witty, sharp-tongued Irish woman. She was deeply loyal to her forebears and pugnacious in its defense. Under a crustacean exterior she secreted her softer sentiments and hid a heart as large as the face of a grandfather's clock. "You come back," she angrily admonished her older son, who complained that a boy at school was "picking on him," "and tell me that kid whipped you, and I'll whip you till you blister." One day I saw her in tears. It was the day the news came through that the lank, red-headed Englishman, Fitzsimmons, had won the world's heavyweight boxing championship from James J. Corbett with a blow to the solar plexus. It was the worst possible day for the defeat of the handsome Corbett, whose lineage, like Mrs. Tiefel's, was Irish. St. Patrick's Day, 1897!

"Oho! Oh-o-o," she moaned. "That—that scum! That filthy English son—son . . ." She was never a profane woman. Now she strove to find a word that would properly denigrate the new champion that she would not need to repeat in the confessional box. None came. "That—that . . ." she said again, and gave up, dropped into a chair, and sobbed.

Mrs. Tiefel was a notable cook. The concoctions she contrived in her small kitchen on a coal-burning range, the surface of which was half the size of a folding card table, made her a culinary conjurer in the eyes of her neighbors. Every Saturday morning she forked out of a kettle of boiling grease on her tiny stove the finest friedcakes I have ever tasted. I would be drawn to her kitchen on these mornings, ostensibly to wait until her older son finished his Saturday chores, but actually to receive the first friedcake to come from the grease kettle. I would mumble my compliments with a mouth full of deliciously crisp hot dough and usually be rewarded with a second sample.

Mrs. Tiefel's husband was a quiet, bandy-legged little man employed by a large plumbing establishment. My father said that he was the most skillful man with tools he had ever known. His reputation was wide. Residents of the great houses on the city's fashionable east side gave their plumbing contracts to his employers with the stipulation that Mr. Tiefel make the installations or attend to the repairs. He could fix anything it was said, even repair a watch. After his working day, he often lent his mechanical skills to his neighbors. He would hang a door, install a gutter pipe, open a clogged drain, or replace the glass in a broken window. He would perform these services quietly, with great expertness, and be affronted if a neighbor attempted to pay him.

* * * * * * * * * * *

I have spoken of the neighborliness of residents of Linden Street when perhaps I should have been more specific.

The street was approximately half a mile in length, and though I had a speaking acquaintance with most of its residents, my neighborly relations (and those of my parents and sisters) were confined to five or six families who lived a little east of the middle of the block. We were a coterie. We were friendly with the other householders, but they were outside of our parochialism which, if the truth be told, was tinged faintly with snobbery. We had a sneaking and unwarranted feeling of superiority. This may have derived from our fecundity. Large families were advocated in the early days of the century, and there were few children on Linden Street outside of our small social unit, where every family had two, three, four or, as in the case of the Maloys, seven kids. Every family except one. Across the street from us and two doors west of the Tiefels were the childless Herbert Joneses.

The Joneses were small, delicately made people who had an elegance that might have been stamped upon them with a die. It was difficult to conceive of either of them in the slightest disarray. The perfection of their exteriors aroused speculation as to whether they ever sweat, defecated or engaged in the sexual act; one wondered, indeed, if they ever got fully out of their impeccable investitures.

We liked the Joneses. They were an integral part of our small society. But their tastes were different from the tastes of most of us, and although they tried to adapt to our practices and amusements, the buckram stiffness of their stylishness never allowed them to unbend fully.

Mrs. Jones had a wasp waist and tiny hands and feet. My mother, whose fine figure, if not Reubenesque, was full and blooming, envied her petiteness. She thought Mrs. Jones the height of fashion, which she was on Linden Street. She sighed longingly when she spoke of Mrs. Jones' wardrobe, of the delicate appointments of her home, of the food served and the exquisiteness of the service when she entertained her whist club. I once heard my mother, in a moment of extravagance, compare Mrs. Jones with the celebrated stage beauty, Maxine Elliott, whose figure was considerably more ample than our neighbor's, to say nothing of other pulchritudinous differences.

Mr. Jones' tailoring complemented his wife's fashionable attire. On the warmest days of summer he was never without waistcoat or jacket. His clothes fitted over his minuscule stature as if they were a natural integument. The creases in his trousers were as sharp as a snickersnee. The derby he wore in winter and the boater in summer sat on his head as if each was as inherently a part of him as the fabrics that enfolded him.

The Joneses inspired attempts at caricature by the youngsters of the neighborhood. The preciousness of Mrs. Jones' attitudes and the precise manner in which Mr. Jones spoke, as if each word was deliberated over and tested before it was uttered, encouraged exaggerated imitation. I never indulged in this mimicry. I had heard from my parents the story of Mr. Jones' thwarted ambition and I sympathized with his frustration. I saw nothing comic in the little man.

In his youth his engulfing purpose had been to play *Hamlet,* to move in tragic majesty about the stage giving off such soliloquies as,

> . . . O God! O God!
> How weary, stale, flat, and unprofitable
> Seem to me all the uses of this world.

He had gone off in early manhood with a Shakespearian repertory company but never rose much above the bottom line of the program's *Dramatic Personae.* He carried a halberd in the chronicle plays; was cast as a watchman, masker, or attendant in *Romeo and Juliet.* Principal roles evaded him. He was too small. He tried block or platform shoes. The contrivance failed to elevate him to the princely presence of *Hamlet.* Sadly he abandoned his Grail-like quest. He quit the "road" and settled into a clerkship with a canning company. He rose, in time, to become treasurer of the company. If he felt his confined routine "weary, stale, flat," it was not unprofitable. I thought Mr. Jones the most interesting person on our street, not the stuffy little dandy he seemed to my contemporaries. I had become an enthusiastic playgoer, clattering up the long iron stairs to the Lyceum gallery on Saturday nights where one might relish for a twenty-five cent ticket the great mimes of the American stage. I was fascinated by the theater and its players. I found in the story of Mr. Jones' aborted career, both romance and tragedy.

* * * * * * * * * * *

Besides the Joneses, the Tiefels, the Maloys, and ourselves, our small social unit included the families of a railroad carpenter, a compositor in a print shop, a noted horticulturist employed by the city's park department, and a salesman for a firm that manufactured office supplies.

Our communal relations were instinctive rather than deliberate. By tacit agreement all in our group patronized the same grocery and the same meat market; we bought our butter and eggs from Mr. Kiefer, who drove his carriage into Linden Street every Saturday morning; our milk man was Mr. McNall.

I have often wondered how Mr. McNall put it all together every day of the year without the aid of General Electric or the automobile. His dairy farm was eight or nine miles from Linden Street on the far side of a formidable eminence known as Methodist Hill in the rural township of Henrietta. He must have been up shortly after midnight to milk his cows, strain the milk into galvanized cans, and set out over a dirt road in his two-horse rig for Rochester. He never failed, not even during a February blizzard, when his sleigh would rock crazily in drifts that reached the bellies of his horses. We would hear him before we were up, ladling milk from one of his large cans to the small can we had left in the milkbox near the back door. It was raw milk, of course. It was some time before a stubborn health officer compelled the politicians to pass a city ordinance prohibiting the sale of unpasteurized milk. I knew no one on our street who contracted undulant fever. Our neighborhood seemed a singularly healthy place to live. Rochester suffered two smallpox epidemics during the first three or four years of the century, but no one from Linden Street was removed to a disgraceful lazaret on a back road near the Erie Canal feeder (the site is now part of the University of Rochester campus) known as the "pesthouse." We went through a series of infantile diseases without a fatality. None of our houses was quarantined with scarlet fever or diptheria signs.

The physician who attended us may have been to a considerable degree responsible for our excellent health record. He was Dr. William A. Keegan, a bachelor, whose sole agency in life seemed to be the practice of medicine, which engaged him twelve or fifteen hours a day. He was the pet of the city's tight little social hierarchy, the east side "fashionables," and beloved in our modest neighborhood and in other districts.

I remember his coming into the sick room, blowing a little from the exertion of his ascent to the second floor, his ample figure draped in a finely tailored suit of wide checks, gaudy as a riverboat gambler's, a hothouse flower in his lapel.

"Hul-lo, hul-lo," he would say. "What in the world's happened to you?"

"Good morning, doctor." Even if the pain was sharp, or the ache acute, you would try to smile. You knew he would expect that. He would be smiling.

He would move a chair near the bed, and wiping the outdoor moisture from his glasses, he might chuckle over an incident of the road. "A fellow was coming down the street in a light cutter driving a dapple gray mare. Wanted to give us a brush. I told Otto to stir up our pair, and off we went." He chuckled again. "Devil take the hindmost. But we pulled up and let him go. It's fine sleighing. Fancy, though, a man of my age, racing horses."

You found yourself chuckling, too. It wasn't much of an incident, but the way he told it made it sound amusing. You felt the least bit cheery already.

His well worn and capacious medicine case rested on the floor at his side. There was more talk, but it was general, not clinical. Various members of the household dropped what they were doing to come and see the doctor. He would tweak the nose of the little boy and put his arm around the little girl and say, "Hul-lo, puddin'." He had a dozen calls to make and perhaps a dozen behind him but now he seemed merely to have stopped by for a social visit. There was nothing hurried about him. So far he hadn't asked or been told a thing about the invalid's symptoms.

The talk would become general. Occasionally the patient would be included in it. His opinion would be asked on some subject.

Presently, the doctor would take from a vest pocket his thick gold hunting case watch and click back the cover. "Hm-mm, quarter to twelve. It's a cold morning. I hate to go out again."

He would take your wrist in the most casual manner and count the pulse. He would place his thermometer under your tongue, cautioning you not to bite it—"it's not peppermint, y'know." He would go over you with a stethoscope, remove the ear pieces, continue his conversation and occasionally, in the most offhand manner, question his patient about his complaint.

"Hm-mm, that's it, eh? Funny thing for you to have. Well, let's see. I guess we can fix that."

He would raise the medicine case to his knee, open it and remove a couple of thin cylindrical vials. Someone had hurried to fetch two water tumblers with butter plates to cover their tops. He would pour a small potion of evil looking liquid into each of the glasses and lumberingly get to his feet.

"Just lay up for a few days, now. No ice skating tonight. No jumping around."

He would pat the patient on the shoulder and start for the door. When he was at the threshold, someone might question him about the dosage; how should it be given?

"Oh, yes. Two teaspoons every two hours today and one teaspoon every two hours tomorrow. I'll look in tomorrow if I'm around this way. He's going to be all right."

Then he would go down the stairs, bundle into his great beaver coat, and go out to his Victoria cutter, the numerous brass fittings of which glowed like the fittings of a fire cart. And Otto, the little German coachman, with a trim military moustache and very correct livery, would raise the reins, cluck to the stylish matched pair of bays, and off Dr. Keegan would go to his next visitation.

And the patient upstairs would draw a deep breath, sigh, and know that no reservation would be needed in Charon's skiff this trip. Hadn't the doctor said, "He's going to be all right?" What further assurance was needed that the return to complete health was just around the corner?

Dr. Keegan's knowledge of medicine was rudimentary compared with today's scientific advances, but he had a Hippocratic devotion and the balm of his presence at a sickbed which, if not as sovereign a remedy as today's wonder drugs, often had a very curative effect. He was a memorable character. His image is still vivid in my mind.

* * * * * * * * * * *

In its early years, Rochester, New York, was known as the Flour City, a term derived from the flour produced by the numerous mills that stood along the banks of the Genesee River, which flowed north through the heart of the city's business district. At the beginning of the twentieth century, the city acquired a new distinction, which resulted in the alteration of the spelling if not the pronunciation of its sobriquet. It became, because of the celebrity of its municipal parks and their notable flora displays, the Flower City. It was an embowered community. Matching rows of fine trees graced its residential streets. Looking down upon it from the eminence of Cobb's Hill, which marked the city's eastern boundary, one saw what appeared to be a settlement designed in a woods. It was a quiet place; it was rare that anything spectacular occurred within its corporate compass. It was a neat, cozy, complacent little city—very sure of itself.

In winter the cheaper saloons posted Free Hot Soup signs in their windows. The trolley cars were heated with coal burning stoves. The famous aqueduct that carried the waters of the Erie Canal across the Genesee River made a popular ice rink, and occasionally Hebing's Band quickened the tempo of the skaters with hard-blown martial airs or synchronized their rhythm to the softer strains of a Strauss waltz. The big downtown stores kept open Christmas Eve and weary, foot-sore clerks straggled home toward midnight for a single day of rest after weeks of frantic holiday selling. At the fall of evening, all-night lunch cars were hauled by horses to stations in downtown streets and returned to their places of replenishment when the sun came up in the morning. Ambulances, fire engines and the police patrol were horse-drawn. There was a malodorous rig driven by a man known as the "honey-dumper" who cleaned the privies that still remained in our neighborhood. Bock beer signs were the harbingers of spring. Then came a fellow with a bell and a loud voice, crying, "Knives ground! Scissors sharpened!" Still later the hurdy-gurdy man appeared with a monkey on a leash. In the summer a white waffle wagon moved creepingly through the streets behind a sad-eyed horse which needed no command to stop when a parcel of kids clamored at the wagon's counter-like opening for the waffle man's brown, sugar-coated confections.

Rochester had five or six theaters playing flesh shows. There were twice-weekly band concerts in the city parks which attracted large, attentive, and orderly crowds. The town loved parades, and downtown streets were given over to them on the slightest provocation. An elaborate water carnival with a long procession of decorated floats brought thousands to the banks of the upper Genesee. The one-day stand of the circus was a notable summer occasion. It made an all-day spectacle for scores of circus buffs who showed up at daybreak to watch roustabouts sledge tent poles into the ground with the rhythm and exquisite timing of a Rockettes dance routine. They would see the elephants herded into their tethering area, the construction of the zoo, the quick setup of the side show, and, finally, the climactic event of the morning—the raising of the vast spread of canvas, the Big Top, under which the matinee and evening performances would be given. There would be a morning parade through downtown Rochester. And late at night, after the show was over, and the wooden stands had been knocked down, and the Big Top had collapsed like a stricken dirigible, there was still the procession of elephants, caged animals, and horses through flare-lighted streets to the train that would move the nomadic enterprise to a new stand.

The city's downtown section first became known to me when my father occasionally took me on a winter Saturday afternoon to the gymnasium of the Rochester Athletic Club. It was part of his program to make a pal of his son. He would drag me on a sled over snow-covered walks, and after each gym session we would stop at a drug store in the famous Powers Hotel for a chocolate ice cream soda. They were five cents in those days, except at the fashionable Whittle's Candy Store on East Main Street, which made the best chocolate ice cream sodas I have ever tasted. Those were a dime.

The Athletic Club had no junior members. An applicant for membership needed to be eighteen years old. I was a privileged guest. My father was president of the club and chairman of a committee that was raising money for a fine modern clubhouse on the east side of the city, which would open early in the new century. The club, when I first knew it, occupied two floors of a West Main Street loft building. The lower floor had locker and shower rooms, a reading and a billiard room, and a tiny cubicle that served as an office for the Professor, Louis D. Eldredge, a remarkable little man who was the club's physical director. The upper floor was a large, draughty room, permeated with the smells indigenous to gymnasiums. It was heated by two or three potbellied stoves similar to those used in the shanties of railroad switchmen. The room was equipped with the usual paraphernalia of such places. A narrow strip of padded fabric lay in an oval pattern around the perimeter of the gym and over this middle-aged men with swaying bellies, wearing the most god-awful costumes, jogged twenty-four laps to the mile.

The oval running track was the only thing that interested me. I liked to tag behind the puffing, sweating, fat men in their grotesque costumes for a few turns and then dart past them. The fat men never deigned to give me an eye, and my flashy exhibition inspired no quickening of their sluggish pace.

I was prohibited by my father from frequenting the reading and billiard rooms downstairs, but Professor Eldredge was a friendly little man and I would stop in his office to examine the pictures of champion athletes that hung on the narrow walls and read the legends below them. The professor was an expert wrestling and boxing coach, and two of his protégés had won national championships in these sports at a tournament in far away San Francisco. He also knew a good deal about track and field. He told me about some of these champions: The Englishman, W. G. George, who had run a mile in time that had never been equalled; Mike Sweeney, the great high-jumper; Bernie Wefer of the New York Athletic Club, who had run one hundred yards in nine and four-fifths seconds, a world record.

I recounted the exploits of these celebrated performers to my youthful contemporaries on Linden Street and we decided to organize an athletic club of our own. My father had a steel tape. With this we measured a course of 100 yards. I delighted in running, not in the smelly gymnasium, but outdoors, over country roads and meadowlands and on the sidewalks of Linden Street, and after a few weeks of fairly arduous practice I essayed a trial against a second-hand silver pocket watch my father had given me. It seemed a memorable effort. When my father came home for supper that night I met him with the thrilling announcement, "I ran a hundred yards in nine seconds this afternoon."

"Silly! Nonsense!" my father said testily. "You never did anything of the kind. Have you swept the cellar floor, as I told you to do this morning?"

I answered surlily that I had. I completely discounted my father's grouty skepticism, attributing it to ignorance. John Tiefel had timed me with the second hand of the watch in nine seconds, which was a lot faster than Wefers had run.

My maternal grandmother lived with us. She was a churchly woman of very upright principles. She was in bed a good deal of the time, and complained of a stomach disorder. She kept a couple of bottles on a shelf in the clothespress of her room, the contents of which appeared to give her relief. I knew her strict principles would not permit her to lie. She was in bed after supper, and I went into her room.

"Grandma, I did, didn't I, run a hundred yards in nine seconds?"

"You did what?" she asked.

"Run a hundred yards in nine seconds."

"Dearie," she said, "would you hand me one of those bottles on the clothespress shelf and then get me a glass with a tiny bit of water from the bathroom?" I did as she requested. I watched her pour a shot of what I later learned was gin into the glass with the "tiny bit of water."

She drank off the potion, which she always said settled her stomach, smacked her lips, and put a hand on her abdomen.

"I did though, didn't I Grandma, run a hundred yards in nine seconds?"

"Why, of course you did, dearie," she said, taking another quick swallow of the "medicine." "Would you please put the bottle back where it belongs?"

I replaced it on the shelf and left the room exultantly. Grandma was a very staunch Christian and she didn't lie. She had corroborated the figures on the watch John Tiefel had held. I *was* the fastest runner in the world.

Many years later, I was talking with Piper Donovan, an old professional sprint runner, whose brother, Pooch Donovan, was the Harvard track coach. We were discussing what seemed an incredible performance by a sprinter on the West Coast where timing, in that particular era, unlike Caesar's wife, was not above suspicion.

"I care not," said Piper Donovan, "who runs one hundred yards in nine seconds until I know who held the watch."

Long since I had become convinced that my own performance of nine seconds with John Tiefel holding a battered pocket watch was somewhat in error.

CHAPTER FOUR

Miss Bernice Baumgarten was a tiny, spirited lady, the right hand "man" of Carl Brandt, head of Brandt & Brandt, the literary agency of Park Avenue, New York City. She represented a number of well-known authors, including J. P. Marquand and her husband, James Gould Cozzens, both Pulitzer prize winning novelists.

Although she did not sell my fifth book, *Main Street Beat,* a series of newspaper reminiscences which W. W. Norton published a couple of years after the close of World War II, she arranged the contract and refused to accept a fee for her service. Later, she worked intermittently with me for several months on what I hoped would be my "big book" (which eventually became *By His Own Hand*), but somewhere along the way lost what she called her perspective, and I lost an agent who, I am sure, would have been of incalculable benefit to me. She was aggressive in the interest of her clients and enormously knowledgeable in the matter of writing and in the business of marketing literary wares.

I had formed a friendship, before I lost Miss Baumgarten, with Samuel Hopkins Adams, a man I came to revere more than any other man I knew except my father. He had read *Monkey on a Stick* twice and wrote me, after the second reading, to tell me in flattering language how much he liked it. A close friendship evolved out of the correspondence which continued until Mr. Adams' death in his late eighties. He was a wise and kindly counselor. He had written probably two dozen books, fiction, biography, history; he was a literary figure and also a client of Miss Baumgarten's. A short story of his, adapted for the screen, became a great Hollywood hit, *It Happened One Night,* co-starring Claudette Colbert and Clark Gable. Mr. Adams read the draft of the novel Miss Baumgarten had given up on, suggested some reconstruction, and his suggestions were incorporated in the manuscript that Macmillan accepted.

The alterations Cecil Scott wanted in the forepart part of the novel were made in a high pressure job of rewriting early mornings, nights, on my days off from the newspaper, from shortly after Labor Day until Christmas. Preparations were then made for publication in the autumn. There were delays. A famous Wall Street law firm read the manuscript for libel and after several weeks of scrutiny pronounced it free of hazard. It was then given to the most conservative law firm in Rochester (the elderly members all seemed to wear hearing aids and stiff stand-up linen collars), who raised a question about one of the very minor characters, and Cecil Scott came bounding into town to see what needed to be done to make the script dead safe. The adjustment was small. In two paragraphs I changed the sex of the minor character, and we were then, the elderly gentlemen of the law firm said, "home free."

Between his second visit to Rochester and Pub day—the day a book is issued—I conferred with Scott a couple of times at his home in Chappaqua, New York. I was there one day when a woman guest came for lunch in a great shining motor car that looked to me as long as a Coast Guard cutter. I myself, that year, was driving a small, three-year-old Plymouth with manual shift. Perhaps I was envious as I glanced through a window at the expensive vehicle. "Here's your guest," I remarked, half-sneeringly, to Scott, "in another one of those damn Cadillacs."

"Poof, Poof," Scott scoffed. "In three months (it was three months to Pub day), you can have twelve of those and a Rolls Royce to boot."

I more than half believed him.

By His Own Hand was boomingly promoted at first. There were full page, three-quarter page, and half-page advertisements in the newspapers and periodicals. If my ego was not like a raging tooth, it was stimulated and inflated. "Powerful in its theme and characters, this is a novel as big as life itself. . . . Alan Wesley (the hero of the novel) is a name destined to be on the lips of thousands of excited readers."

And the jacket copy made me wonder who was the greater, Charles Dickens or me.

"From its opening pages this extraordinary novel will hold you in its spell . . . the author has created a character, titanic, disturbing, and yet sympathetic. But he has done more than this—he has created a world peopled with living men and women and filled his background with a sense of time as only the great novelists can, so that when you have finished the book you will say, 'This has been one of the rare experiences in my reading life.' "

Cecil Scott came up for Pub day. It was like a coronation. Sibley's, the leading department store, in a huge newspaper ad, affirmed that *By His Own Hand* was "already an American saga," and urged the public to meet "the famous author" at an autograph party. Scrantom's, the leading book store, sold more than 1,000 copies the first day, a record sale for a novel that has not been beaten. It was fantastic, and I believed everything that was said about the novel and myself.

Then the roof fell in.

Orville Prescott, the day-to-day book review man for the *New York Times,* fell upon the book—mangled it tooth and claw. He called what I had written a *roman à clef* and asserted that "seldom have well known individuals had their lives retold in fiction with the combination of accuracy and license that the late George Eastman, founder and guiding genius of the Eastman Kodak Company, suffers in Henry W. Clune's tiresome novel, *By His Own Hand.*"

The man then really vented his spleen. What I had written was "vulgar petty gossip. . . . soggy and repetitious, old-fashioned in its technique (he tells about his characters instead of letting them speak for themselves) . . . One just doesn't believe in these people."

There was much more of the same.

It smashed me, of course. I couldn't understand why

the book and I had become the victims of a hatchet job. It seemed to me that the reviewer's vitriolic attack had been made, not because the book was as bad as he professed it to be, but because he felt he detected a resemblance between its main character and the great Rochester industrialist. I wondered bitterly why he had been so sensitive on this point, and in time I discovered what I am sure was the reason. Mr. Prescott was the scion of a great industrial fortune, the grandson of the founder and president (until his death) of the Sherwin-Williams Paint Company, which does a billion a year. He was true to his class, and in defense of it he employed all the weaponry he could command. What he wrote wasn't a critique; it was an act of blind savagery and as stupid as acts of blind savagery usually are.

At one point in the latter part of *By His Own Hand,* it is told of one of the younger characters, "Judy had come from a lunch party a girl named Alice Rogers had given and was loosely committed to a dull young man from Williams College. She was tired of his talk of Psi U house parties . . ."

Mr. Prescott was Psi Upsilon at Williams.

The novel was reviewed extensively from coast to coast. It had its detractors, but nothing said against it remotely compared to the splenetic onset in the *Times.* Clark Kinnard, a syndicated book critic whose readership exceeded that of Mr. Prescott's, suggested that "an unusual treat will be missed by any whom the flood of fall fiction causes to overlook Mr. Clune's opus. It is a long time since we have had as conscientious, dispassionate, and realistic a study of a genius in the exalted American arts, manufacturing and business."

Lewis Gannett, in the daily *New York Herald Tribune,* spoke well of the book and called its protagonist a "memorable character," and Mary Ross, in the Sunday edition, said that I wrote "straight forwardly but without special distinction, but with mastery of the setting, situation and characters of the novel." She remarked that *By His Own Hand* was a "substantial achievement as a recreation both of a period and segment of American life." Miss Ross, countering the *Times'* review, said that while the career of the novel's main character might seem to parallel the career of Rochester's leading citizen, "For the purposes of fiction such conceivable identifications are unimportant, for most readers will find that Alan Wesley and Minerva live in the novel even if they have not existed in real life."

By His Own Hand excited a great guessing game in Rochester. Readers, convinced that I had been writing about Mr. Eastman, his confreres and his social acquaintances, strove feverishly to give the identity of living or dead Rochesterians to the fictional characters in the novel.

Some of the city's most solid citizens, to whom George Eastman had become almost a diety, were outraged that the character in my story, whom they accepted as the great industrialist, had a mistress. I recall meeting Alexander M. Beebee, chairman of the Rochester Gas & Electric Company, as the light changed at a downtown intersection. Beebee was an honorable member of the community, an outstanding business and civic leader, but not a fellow to tolerate nonsense or indulge in light fancies. There was very little give to him. He was a friend of mine, but on two or three occasions, as we passed not too close to one another on the sidewalk, he had strangely failed not only to respond to my called greeting but to favor me with so much as a nod. I now confronted him in the middle of the crosswalk.

"What in the world's the matter with you," I asked, "that you don't speak to me?"

He moved his hands in a gesture of revulsion.

"You've put yourself beyond the pale," he answered angrily. "That vile and vicious book. Scandalizing that great man."

"What great man?"

"You know you were writing about Mr. Eastman." A hand went up to his eyes, and I was astonished to see tears trickling down his cheek. "Putting a woman in his life—having him *keep* a woman."

"Alex," I said, "the man in my story is Alan Wesley, not George Eastman. But I'll tell you this, if George Eastman didn't have at least one cutie in his life, they better not boast about it."

Not all Rochesterians disapproved of the novel. It had a wildfire sale in every bookstore in the area, and I had scores of letters from local readers who enjoyed it greatly. The managing editor of the *Democrat and Chronicle* devoted a full page to a glowing review which he himself wrote, and Rabbi Philip S. Bernstein of Temple B'rith Kodesh, one of the most brilliant theologians in the community, found *By His Own Hand* "a powerful novel, strong, deep and gripping."

Subsequently, I had several notes from Rabbi Bernstein commending the book, in one of which, received more than a dozen years after its publication, he wrote, "I still consider *By His Own Hand* one of the finest novels I have ever read."

I'll let the statement stand, conceding that the Rabbi's enthusiasm may have tricked him into hyperbole, but suggest that in the matter of writing he is a man to reckon with.

In its 11 September 1950 issue, *Life* devoted most of its editorial space to an article by Rabbi Bernstein, *What the Jews Believe,* which Henry R. Luce, co-founder and then head of the Luce publishing empire, told the rabbi produced a greater reaction than any article previously published in the magazine. In time, *What the Jews Believe* was reprinted in an anthology, *Great Readings from Life,* and the Rochester rabbi shared space in the volume with such world figures as Sir Winston Churchill, Dwight D. Eisenhower, Field Marshal Montgomery, Harry Truman, and Ernest Hemingway, whose short novel, *The Old Man and the Sea,* first appeared in *Life.*

Rabbi Bernstein was urged to expand the *Life* article to book length, which he presently agreed to do, and when *What the Jews Believe* was issued by Farrar Straus, queues of purchasers formed near the publishing firm's Fifth Avenue office as, a hundred years before, eager readers lined up at the New York wharves to receive the latest installment of a Charles Dickens novel.

The book was translated into numerous foreign languages, it went through twenty-seven editions, and its sale greatly exceeded the sale of any other book by a Rochester author with the possible exception of *Christianity and the Social Crisis,* the major work of the distinguished Protestant theologian, Walter Rauschenbush.

Orville Prescott, forsaking the function of critic to savage *By His Own Hand,* was applauded by a group of Eastman worshippers, some of whom may never have seen so much as the back of the industrialist's neck. His assertion that Mr. Eastman was the prototype of the novel's main character touched a sensitive nerve in the Macmillan office. A few years before, the firm had published a better than eleven-hundred page work, *The Theory of the Photographic Process,* by Dr. Kenneth C. E. Mees, the Eastman Company's leading scientist and head of its research department; moreover, Mr. Brett, the Macmillan president, had close relations with some of Kodak's top executives. I myself heard howls of protest, and probably Mr. Brett did, too. The advertising for *By His Own Hand* shrank, and the promotion effort lost its early vigor. The wonderful Miss Baumgarten would never have taken this lying down; I missed her grievously.

I had been, briefly, the fair-haired boy at Macmillan's. Prescott's diatribe put me somewhat out of favor. The novel performed nothing like its pre-publication promises, and rather than becoming affluent enough to afford a dozen Cadillacs and a Rolls Royce as Cecil Scott had predicted, I ended up with my three-year-old Plymouth with manual shift. The book did, however, have a respectable sale, something between 45,000 and 50,000 copies in this country. Macmillan (I had had no agent since Miss Baumgarten) sold the novel to a newspaper syndicate, which issued it in abridged form, and the foreign rights went to William Collins Sons & Company, Ltd., of London. The English edition came out in July 1953, and the following month I had an optimistic letter from Mr. Collins, which opened:

> "Dear Mr. Clune:
>
> "I thought you would like to know how we are going with *By His Own Hand.*
>
> "We printed a first edition of 10,000 copies and were able very quickly to put on a reprint of 6,000, and we shall be putting on another reprint shortly . . . There is no doubt that the public is enjoying this fine story and we are getting repeat orders from the leading libraries and bookshops in London. . . . We hope to keep the book selling right on to Christ-

> mas. Our Australian branch is particularly interested, and I am sure they will do very well with it."

In a postscript Mr. Collins wrote, "I did enjoy the book *so much*. It is a fine novel."

There was never a hint in the English reviews that *By His Own Hand* might have had biographical implications. The readers liked the story for itself. I fancied a line from the *Dublin Evening World,* which Collins prominently displayed in their advertisements, "Never a dull page."

In Rochester, where the book sold more than 6,000 copies, the guessing game continued for years and may still be played; but the anger the novel excited among a small group of Rochester readers subsided long ago. Twenty years after its publication, *By His Own Hand* was staunchly defended by Mrs. Marion Gleason in an issue of the University of Rochester Library Bulletin, which was devoted exclusively to articles about the famed Rochester industrialist and the university's greatest benefactor.

Mrs. Gleason came to Rochester shortly after World War I with her husband, Harold, who was to become Mr. Eastman's private organist and establish an organ department for the Eastman School of Music. A handsome, spirited, and extremely intelligent young woman, she fell quickly into favor with the Kodak head, and the friendship continued until the latter's death.

Once settled in Rochester, Mrs. Gleason and her husband were astonished to discover that many of Rochester's so-called best citizens had a feeling close to hatred for Eastman, which she attributed to a change in public thinking.

"In the 1800's," Mrs. Gleason wrote in the Library Bulletin, "the rich man was regarded as a good man no matter how his wealth was acquired. Then, during the first half of the 1900's public opinion swung away from the hero worship of the wealthy to the muckraking scramble to reveal the ruthless business methods of the leading industrial giants, the Rockefellers, the Morgans, the Mellons. In the case of George Eastman, one of the last of the generation of self-made tycoons, this shift in attitude reached its culmination in the book,

By His Own Hand, written by Henry Clune, a Rochester newspaper man."

Further along in her essay, Mrs. Gleason reported that two friends of hers, J. P. Marquand, author of the Pulitzer Prize novel, *The Late George Apley,* and André Maurois, distinguished French writer, both had entertained the notion of doing a fictional story on Eastman. They came to Rochester at different times, and Mrs. Gleason provided each with some material for the proposed project, but neither writer went on with it. "Perhaps there was not enough romance in G.E.'s (George Eastman) history to relieve the bleakness of his personal life. . . .

"On the other hand, Henry Clune perhaps had a more facile imagination and fewer inhibitions. It's possible, also that he had a deeper insight into G.E.'s character. I have just reread *By His Own Hand,* and my reaction is about the same as it was when the controversial book first appeared. I don't believe that G.E. would have rejected the romantic escapades that Clune attributed to Eastman's fictional counterpart as violently as did many of Rochester's outraged citizens—offspring of the same people who rejected G.E. in 1919. In fact, I have a notion that G.E. would have been somewhat pleased to think that such episodes could have been imagined as happening in his romance-starved life."

CHAPTER FIVE

As a high school kid I had a dreamy notion of marrying a celebrated actress, and I was in love with Elsie Janis, the adored mimic of musical comedy who married late in life. Her protective and determined mother, who started to make a star of her daughter before she attained her tenth birthday (and succeeded by the time the girl was fifteen) wouldn't permit her to get far away. I saw Miss Janis for the first time in *The Vanderbilt Cup.* Before she returned in another show I had accompanied Edward Payson Weston, the famous pedestrian, on twenty miles of his walk (at the age of sixty years) from Portland, Maine, to Chicago, and boasted that I could walk sixty miles in a day. Gaius Moore, fourth oldest son of the multitudinous Moore family on Mt. Hope Avenue pooh-poohed my boast. He bet me five dollars I couldn't perform the feat. I lacked money to cover the bet. Gaius (we called him Cap for some unexplained reason) then said he'd pay me five dollars if I made the walk.

I set off one morning for the village of Geneseo, which was thirty miles from Linden Street. I left early, at four o'clock. I was home that night at seven, tired but gloating in my triumph. When I went next day to collect the prize money, Cap refused to pay. He protested that a day was twelve hours, and I had taken fifteen to do the sixty miles.

We didn't quarrel over the issue. Cap had done me numerous favors in the past and he was soon to do me another.

Miss Janis was coming back in a new musical, *The Hoyden,* and Cap, aware of my infatuation, agreed to purchase two front row seats in the Lyceum and a dozen American Beauty roses if I would fling the flowers over the footlights at the dark-haired beauty.

It seemed like a sure way to win the lady's love. We went on opening night of the show's three-day stand. It was a gala. Miss Janis had an enormous following in Rochester. The fanciest people in town came in smart horse-drawn vehicles and in limousines and glass-enclosed electric automobiles, many in formal attire. It was a resplendent audience. This was an era when a woman might publicly display a rope of pearls or a lavalier of rubies and sapphires and a man might secure his stiff shirt with diamond studs without fear of being mugged or robbed at gunpoint. I carried my long-stemmed bouquet under my overcoat. It was tied with a silk ribbon and an attached card bore my name and address.

As the first act ended and a salvo of applause boomed down from the galleries and rose from the lower floor of the house, I stood up and flung the roses. It was a hurried pitch and too vigorous. The flowers struck the lady in the stomach and fell to the floor. She stooped and picked them up and bent a fleeting smile upon me. It was like the touch of an accolade. The curtain fell, the house lights sprang up, and Will Corris, the meticulous little showman who managed the Lyceum, came bounding down the aisle.

"Who did that? Who threw those flowers?" he demanded angrily.

Corris took great pride in his theater and in the stylish audiences who turned out for his opening nights. Rochester was a tightly-knit little city in those days, and the manager knew most of the occupants of his orchestra chairs. Wearing a handsomely tailored dinner jacket, he would greet the arriving main-floor ticket holders very much in the manner of the gracious host receiving guests in his own home. He wanted the proprieties to prevail in his theater and throwing flowers over the footlights seemed to him a disorderly act. He glowered at Gaius Moore and me, but he was uncertain as to which was the culprit. Gaius was a large, lumbering young man, enormously good-natured but not unformidable in aspect. He grinned down at the bristling little showman.

"Why it's a tribute," he said. "A tribute to your star. What's wrong with a tribute?"

People were moving into the aisle for the first act break, and after a moment Corris turned away with a muttered threat about calling the police.

Miss Janis's over-the-footlights smile was not the only reward derived from my act of bravura. On the last night of the show's stand I hung around the stage door of the Lyceum until the star and her mother, who was never more than an arm's length from her precious and richly-rewarded daughter, left the theater in the company of two handsome, beautifully dressed young beaus, passed through the stage alley and entered the Hotel Seneca which stood next door to the theater. The maitre d' in the Pompeian Room greeted the party with a bow that dipped his head almost to his knees and escorted its members to a prize table. "Here! Here!" he called sharply, and clapped his hands to summon waiters to attend them.

I waited at the threshold of the Pompeian Room until the party was well settled. The conversation seemed lively and amusing. I observed that the young men looked upon Miss Janis with eyes as adoring as my own. I took a deep breath, screwed my "courage to the sticking place," and crossed the room. I bowed. "Good evening, Miss Janis."

"O-oh," she said, and I could see that she was striving to identify me. Then the vagueness vanished. She smiled; I thought her smile celestial. "Oh, mother," she said, "this is the boy who threw the roses."

"Oh," Miss Janis' mother said, and nothing more.

I mostly wore my father's cast-off but never badly worn trousers. They were tight for me; they sheathed my long legs like a drainpipe. I was never sartorially magnificient. I saw the young men glance at me not with condescension, but with something like revulsion. I fumbled a few words, shook hands with Miss Janis, and left, moving as airily as a phantom, head-over-heels in love. I had had not only a smile from my goddess, she had spoken to me. I had touched her!

A week or two later I received in the mail a small photograph inscribed to me and signed, "Sincerely, Elsie Janis." I framed it and placed it atop the small desk in my bedroom, where it was accessible to my eyes at all times. I cherished it as a sacred icon until, eight or ten months later, I saw Julia Sanderson and faithlessly abandoned my dark-haired love for the blonde star of *The Girl from Utah.*

At the time, Miss Sanderson must still have been married to the great race rider, Tod Sloan, whom I met years later in a shabby hole-in-the-wall gambling hall in Montmartre. He was then through as a jockey and long since divorced from Miss Sanderson. He was a tiny, pinch-faced, sunken-eyed man in flashy clothes, a huge cigar caught in the corner of his mouth. He had been ruled off the American turf for illegal practices and the English disbarred him from their courses after he whacked a waiter over the head with a champagne bottle at Ascot and was ill-mannered in the presence of the King.

My acquaintance with Miss Sanderson was more extensive than my brief meeting with Miss Janis. I was with her on several occasions and saw her in most of her starring roles. As a young man, I thought her the most beguiling lady of the musical stage, and the passing of many years has not debased this impression. Meeting Sloan in the sleazy Montmartre resort, I wondered how the lovely Julia had taken this raffish little man to wed.

Then I remembered that Tod Sloan had once been the idol of the racing public of two nations, a familiar of royalty and of men of mighty millions; at the summit of his fame he would have had a good deal to commend him to a youthful chorus girl, which was Miss Sanderson's status at the time she and Sloan were married.

I knew something of the Sloan legend. If his winnings were not actually in the millions, he lived in the manner of a millionaire in what was probably the most profligate epoch in American history. He had come from Kokomo, Indiana, and in an attempt to convince the civic leaders that he was the native son most deserving of a statue in the public square, he returned to Kokomo in a private railroad car with a party of high-flying friends, quantities of champagne, and a retinue that included a butler and a valet.

In Paris he was living in the past, basking in retrospective triumphs. He was a monologist and I was fascinated by his ceaseless talk. A stable boy at the old Sheepshead Bay race course in New York, he had been picked up by trainer named Huggins and put on a horse as an apprentice jockey. He had little success; he was considered a mediocre rider until, so he said, he invented the crouch seat.

Rather, he said, it was taught him by George E. Smith, better known as Pittsburgh Phil, who emerged from a Pittsburgh cork factory to become one of the turf's greatest plungers and to die not broke, in opposition to the axiom that all horse players do, but with an estate of $2,000,000.

Smith, who had never put a leg over a horse's back, was an astute student of racing form. Straddling a kitchen chair, he demonstrated to Sloan how a rider hunched forward on the withers of a horse would become part and parcel of the galloping animal and relieve it of part of the burden imposed upon it by riders who rode straight up or in a semi-upright position.

He further explained his theory by the analogy of a man running across a field with a small child in his arms. If he ran with the child held at arm's length from his body two objects would be in motion. If the child were held close to the man's breast the burden of its weight would be lessened, the man and child would become a single object, and the man would be able to move with greater facility and speed.

Sloan went to England with his tricky new seat and almost got laughed off the race course. "They guyed me," he said, "the newspapers, the toffs around the ring, the experts. Shit! Experts! Once I begin to win, they're laughing out of the other side of their puss. I win like crazy. Pretty soon every boy in England is trying to ride my way. They called it 'monkey-on-a-stick.' I met kings and duchesses and earls, God knows what all. I was big. Bigger' n all—" he waved a hand in a wide inclusive arc and stopped abruptly. A man whispered in his ear and the two moved quickly across the room to join a third man in low-voiced conversation. I soon quit the resort. Later I was told that the roulette wheel was being manipulated; that the croupier was a "mechanic." I heard also that Sloan had been asked to leave Paris under threat of arrest. It all may have been rumor. But the little man had had little luck after his riding days ended. When he died in Hollywood in 1933 of cirrhosis of the liver, he was said to be penniless but buoyant, still boastful, game. "Sit down," he is said to have invited two visitors to his deathbed, "Sit down and take the weight off your feet. And have a drink."

* * * * * * * * * *

Although my father must have deplored my teen-age indolence, he knew no way to inculcate me with the stern purposes he himself had formed in his early years and that had made possible his rise from youthful indigence to a rewarding and responsible position in industry. In the benign bourgeoise ambience of our home and neighborhood I enjoyed a soft and pleasurable existence. I did little studying and not much work. I never had a paper route. Unlike many of my male contemporaries in high school, I never strove very hard for a job during the weeks of summer vacation. One summer, however, my father committed me to a team of surveyors who worked in the western Pennsylvania coal fields owned by the mining company which he then served as auditor and treasurer. My job was chain boy. Most of our work was above ground, but occasionally we were required to take linear and angular measurements in either a slope or a shaft mine, wearing illuminated miners' caps. I hated it. It seemed to me that every time we entered a chamber to set up a transit the ceiling began to chip and fall away. We boarded in shabby houses or even shabbier small town hotels. One was a temperance hotel. I have been leary of temperance hotels ever since. I, and I presume my companions, was besieged for two nights by a resolute army of bedbugs which mottled my body with red and itching welts.

I had been in the mining country before. When my father left the railroad that carried shipments of bituminous coal to Buffalo, Rochester and Pittsburgh to work for the mining company, his first job was as pay master. The corporate offices of the company were in Rochester, and the money paid the miners was sent in cash from there to the mining district in Indiana County, Pennsylvania.

Twice my father took me on these payday excursions. He put me in a berth on a sleeper that ran from Rochester to Pittsburgh, and he himself sat all night in the baggage car among metal boxes that contained the miners' wages, a loaded pistol in his pocket. I was proud of his authority. I thought him a very important man, when, next day, he stood behind a wicket in a shack-like mine office handing out pay envelopes to a long line of grimy-faced miners, each of whom had a view of the pistol that lay on the counter ready to my father's hand. The men were foreigners for the most part, and many were unable to write. They would put down a metal identification disk and mark X on a piece of paper and receive their pay, meager enough in an era before the union was strong enough to enforce a decent wage for digging in a black pit below the earth's surface.

When I returned to the mining country to work with the surveyors I hated the experience and pleaded with my father to be allowed to come home. He was adamant for a time. He detested what he called a "quitter", and it seemed to him that I was always looking for an easy out. He himself had invincible resolution. Once committed to a project, he was unremitting in its pursuit; he gave it his fullest effort and devotion. I was awed sometimes by my belief that he could surmount all obstacles by the mere exertion of his will. As a small boy, I had the fanciful notion that he could leap over the top of our house if he actually put his mind to it. Now he told me to stop my "crybabying" and "stay on the job."

The mining company by which he was employed and the Buffalo, Rochester & Pittsburgh Railroad for which he had formerly worked, were closely allied. Both were largely controlled by the wealthy Swiss-American Iselin family of New York. The operating head of the mining companies was an extremely able executive, Lucius W. Robinson. Robinson was a Yale graduate. He was a handsome, beautifully tailored man, with graceful manners. He had numerous financial and social connections in New York and Palm Beach, Florida, but he sought no prominence in Rochester. He had three homes, one in Rochester, another in DuBois, Pennsylvania, and a third in Hobe Sound, Florida. The Rochester house was one of the finest residences in the city. It stood next door to the larger but architecturally less distinctive house of George Eastman, the Kodak tycoon, who once made a statement that surprised many people in Rochester who had never before heard of Robinson. On an occasion when funds were being raised for some philanthropic agency, Mr. Eastman said that his neighbor, Robinson, had more money than he had.

Robinson lived quietly, but elegantly. The story was that as his two daughters and one son came of age each was endowed with $1,000,000. He was a man who always traveled, as the saying is, "first-cabin." His frequent visits to DuBois and the mining region farther south in Pennsylvania were made in his private railroad car, on which I was once a luncheon guest.

The miners were on strike during part of the time I worked with the surveyors and their bitterness toward the operating company and their militant attitude toward the Pennsylvania State Constabulary had brought about an ugly situation. The mining company was talking of bringing in scab labor and the constabulary was prepared to defend these interlopers if they were put to work. The countryside was at hair trigger tension.

During this period of crisis, Robinson arrived one Sunday morning in the mining town in which I was staying. He had come to learn what efforts were being made to settle the strike, and that morning he sent for me. With him on his private car, which stood on a railroad siding, were two or three adult guests, one of whom was an Iselin from New York. The car was staffed with a butler and male cook. Accustomed as I was to the poor fare of third-class boarding houses and small town hotels, I thought the lunch Lucullan.

Before the meal was finished the butler handed a written message to Robinson. He read it and passed it around the table. Below a crude drawing of a dagger dripping blood these words were scrawled on a smudgy piece of paper:

Be prepared to meet your God today.

Robinson seemed unmoved by the threat which excited alarm among his guests. He was to confer that afternoon with representatives of the strikers in a mine office a short walk from the railroad siding. His friends urged him not to leave the car without a constabulary escort. He laughed and shook his head.

"I'll manage," he said.

When he finished lunch, Robinson put on a boater, adjusted his necktie in front of a mirror in the paneling of the wall, and ignoring the pleas of his friends that he not depart without an armed guard, picked up a gold-headed cane and left the car. His friends did not volunteer to accompany him and I deliberately delayed the consumption of a second dessert my host had ordered for me. The railroad yards were in the scrubbiest part of the mean little mining town. A group of men in working clothes lounged outside a jerry-built saloon a short distance from the siding on which stood Robinson's car. They were rough looking characters. Beyond was a dirt road, a rickety wooden sidewalk and on each side of the narrow street stood the miners' cabins.

Unhurried, erect, stylish, lightly touching the tip of his cane to the broken sidewalk, Robinson moved past the men in front of the saloon, who fixed him with glowering eyes but made no menacing move. From the car window we followed his progress until he turned a corner of the street and disappeared from our view. We waited apprehensively, half expecting the report of an assassin's gun or the louder sound of an exploding bomb. After a minute or two, one of the guests spoke, and his words reflected the sentiment of all on the car. "That Robinson," he said. "That Lucius Robinson, certainly has moxie."

* * * * * * * * * * *

My father acceded in time to my pleas that I be permitted to return home, and after a month in the mining country I was back on Linden Street pursuing the vacuous life that had marked most of my summer vacations. I ran and walked and sometimes went canoeing on the river. Soft as I was, I indulged a fantasy that I was destined for immortality, and I resumed my preparations for the moment when fame would flower upon me and the world would be stirred by my momentous performance.

I had known for a long time that my maternal grandmother had inadvertently committed an untruth when she conceded that I had run 100 yards in nine seconds, and I had no belief that such a performance was possible. But at least a year before I entered my teens, I had conceived the notion that it was possible to run a mile faster than 4:12 ¾ seconds, a feat that seemed to me then, and continued to appeal to me for years, as the limit of any normal man's desires.

You walk, you walk a little faster, and still faster, both feet, as your step hurries on, suddenly leave the ground—neither heel nor toe touching—and you are running. It was that way with me since early youth. The tough kids from what we knew as Swillburg, who would see me running through the nursery property of the Ellwanger & Barry Company on my way to Highland Park and the open country beyond, fixed me with the epithet, Legs Almighty. Fellows with slow moving horses, drivers of farm wagons or carts loaded with sand would shout, "Hey, you training for a race, or racing for a train?" There were times when I caused commotion running through a procession of funeral hacks turning into the entrance of Mt. Hope Cemetery. The drivers would yank viciously at their startled horses and shower me with invective. Ropes were stretched across a back road during a severe smallpox epidemic to prevent people from passing a noisome lazaret in which victims of the disease were dying or suffering treatment, but the road was one of my favorite routes and I leapt over the ropes and kept on running.

The world record for the mile was 4:12 ¾ seconds. It was made by W. G. George in London in 1886 and continued on the books for twenty-nine years, when it was lowered by a tiny fraction of a second. In August 1915, Norman Taber, a Rhodes Scholar from Brown University, ran a paced mile on the then fast Harvard Stadium track in 4:12 ⅗ seconds. This was the prodigious performance I had dreamed of and prayed

I might accomplish. It was hailed in newspaper headlines, and the solidly good newspaper, the *New York Tribune,* put this line over Taber's picture:

ATHLETE WHO HAS STIRRED THE WORLD

Stirred the world indeed! And this, mind you, in the second year of the greatest war the world had ever known, and the world shaking in its boots, fearful that this was Armageddon.

But I agreed with the *Tribune's* caption writer.

What human achievement could match Taber's?

There was a theory in those days that by doing too much running a growing boy would burn himself out, become, as the trainers said, "stale as boarding house cake," and I was often torn between the need to run many miles a week and the fear that I was over-doing and should substitute walking as a conditioner. It was during one of these interludes of non-running that I plodded along with Edward Payson Weston when, after a brief rest in a Rochester hotel, he resumed a pedestrian journey to Chicago that had started in Portland, Maine.

Weston was the first person of sporting fame I had ever met, and I was proud to be his unsolicited escort. He was a wiry little man, then in his sixties, who had come through Rochester forty years before on a hike from Portland, Maine to Chicago. There was nothing of the freak about him. He had been a well-known pedestrian since early manhood and had competed in those drudging, dreary contests that once attracted the sporting public called "Six-day-go-as-you-please" races. In these tests a man ran or walked six days and nights around a ten or twelve lap track, choosing what time he would eat and sleep, and the winning purse went to the athlete who totaled the greatest number of miles. Weston was known for his ability to continue in movement unconscionably long hours, but he did not run—only walked—and the winner of these contests was usually a fellow who alternated between a walk and a jog trot. The "Six-day-go-as-you-please" was the precursor of the infinitely more exciting six-day bicycle races that every winter for years attracted all day and all night crowds to Madison Square Garden.

Weston's capacity to keep everlastingly going was evidenced when he arrived in Rochester a few hours after midnight one raw, rainy November morning. He had come from Syracuse, a distance of ninety miles, which he covered in twenty-seven hours with only brief pauses along the way. He flopped on a bed in a downtown hotel, dead beat out; but at nine o'clock, with only three or four hours sleep, he was up, breakfasted, and ready to resume his westward journey, and it was then that I joined him. The rain of the night before had not abated. At the Rochester city line, Weston was photographed by Al Stone, crack newspaper photographer, who years later was to become my friend and associate on the Rochester *Morning Herald.* There were few paved roads in the countryside, and the dirt road we followed after leaving the city was puddled, rutty, and slimy. Weston welcomed my companionship, but he did not ask and I did not tell him my name. He called me "Boy".

"Boy," he said, "there are a lot of old codgers still living along these roads who remember me coming through forty years ago. They come running out of farmhouses to greet me. You get back of me then, and stay close. If you don't, the dumb fools are like to step on my heels. My heels are like Achilles'."

I shortly discovered this was not an idle apprehension. In the early days of the century, before the proliferation of the motor car and the restlessness that today causes people to be continually on the move, people felt that if they had roots they had a good thing. Sometimes we saw names and dates on barns that indicated that the farm property had been in the same family for two or three generations. And now and then, as Weston plodded along the muddy road, a farmer would come hurrying out of a farmhouse, perhaps accompanied by his family and the hired hands, to bustle about him, impede his progress, menace his heels (except for my protection), and remind the pedestrian that the farmer had greeted him forty years before, and didn't Weston recall the incident?

"Yes, yes," he'd lie. He'd shake hands hurriedly, squirm through the small assemblage surrounding him, and press on with a flourish of the short staff he carried as a repellent to unfriendly dogs.

Rain fell unceasingly for a couple of hours after Weston left Rochester, but he was prepared for it. Bundled in yellow oilskins with a yellow seaman's hat sloped almost to his shoulders, his drooping grizzly moustache dripping rainwater, he looked for all the world like the skipper of a trawler off the Grand Banks. He was a picturesque and conspicuous figure. And while he protested at the annoyance caused by "old codgers" who greeted him, he would have felt neglected without their attentions and tributes.

He was a stickler for clean living, exercise, and orderly habits. He said he was making this hike to demonstrate his principles about health and physical care. There was also a financial motive. He was receiving an honorarium from the *New York Times* for dispatches he sent to that newspaper telling of his experiences en route, and a national baking company was rewarding him for plugging the wholesomeness of its bread. He hummed a march tune as he walked, which he occasionally interrupted to deliver a brief homily for my ears.

"Boy," he said, "when you marry, be sure to marry a good cook. And one who doesn't have a frying pan in the kitchen. Fried foods are the ruination of the stomach. And be sure she's chaste." He paused in the road, partly turned his back to me. He was a mannerly little man. He fumbled with the stubborn clasps of his oilskins. "Boy," he said again, "You'll excuse the vulgarity of the expression, but it's the devil's own job to take a piss in this coat."

He trudged on steadily but not at a taxing pace. We passed through Churchville and Bergen and stopped at a farmhouse east of Batavia where Weston, after a cup of tea and a light lunch, stretched out on a bed. I waited in the parlor. He was up in less than an hour, whistling, as cheery and bright-eyed as if he had had a night of unbroken rest. His recuperative powers were remarkable. At the outskirts of Batavia, a representative of the baking company, whose car had been mired for hours in a sticky road between Syracuse and Rochester, caught up with us. I told Weston I was leaving. He pleaded that I continue with him to Olean, near the southern border of the state, but I was illegally absent from school and one day of truancy was enough. I shook hands with the old man and left, feeling I had had a sort of bid at fame.

CHAPTER SIX

A miserable failure in Rochester high school, I left to enter Phillips Academy at Andover, Massachusetts. I professed, and my father believed my professions, that in this new environment I would succeed. I didn't. I blew a golden opportunity to acquire an education and at the same time pursue under excellent auspices the grail of my dreams and what I secretly defined as the prime aspiration of my life. I wanted to quit one of the greatest schools in the country and come home. But I hung on at my father's insistence, and suffered the ignominy of being relegated to the freshman class after having been exposed to nearly three years of secondary education.

In those days Andover sent many of its graduates to Yale and Harvard and its athletic teams regularly scheduled contests with the freshman teams of these institutions. The school's football, baseball, and track teams were often interscholastic standouts, matched only by teams from Phillips Academy at Exeter, New Hampshire. The track coach, who served also as trainer for the football team, was Sid Peet, who would be unacceptable in today's Andover with its multisplendored millions, its elaborate buildings, its exclusive admission requirements, and its co-eds. He chewed tobacco. He wore a celluloid collar. His formal education had ended at the sixth or seventh grade.

Nonetheless, Sid Peet was venerated by some of the glittering athletic heroes at Yale, Harvard, and Princeton who had learned a lot from his coaching at Andover. I absurdly marked him as the great man in a school that was directed by a celebrated headmaster, Alfred E. Stearns, and included among its faculty several exceptional educators. Peet had no faculty status, but he had been a long time at the Academy. He knew a great deal about athletics, and his pronouncements on the subject of foot racing struck me as oracular.

He had been a professional sprinter and had competed with success in the famous handicap races in Sheffield, England, where thousands of pounds were wagered and where the winning runner himself had a chance to win a pot of money. He had had a variety of experiences, and he recounted them with gusto. Peet had associated with prizefighters, carnival pitchmen, pool hustlers, and other grifters. He had traveled with the Barnum & Bailey Circus, running twice daily around the Big Top oval against a horse. In the locker room after track practice, I sat before him like a disciple at the knees of Socrates as he meticulously cleaned the short-nosed pistol he had used while coaching the sprinters. He had, I was sure, the knowledge I needed to achieve my dedicated purpose.

In time our rapport ended. My academic grades fell off so badly that I was ineligible to represent the school in track and during a full year at Andover I ran only two races, both against intramural competitors, which I won in scrubby times. Peet angrily accused me of being a malingerer and the captain of the track team excoriated me for lack of school spirit and ceased speaking to me.

With numerous strikes against me, I was also penalized by being confined to the school yard while students of standing were granted passes to visit Boston at the close of Saturday morning classes. I had become, if not infatuated, as I had been with Elsie Janis and Julia Sanderson, sensually excited by photographs of Annette Kellerman, who was diving into a pool of water as a vaudeville headliner wearing black silk tights that adhered as tightly to her form as the skin of a seal.

In every city in which she appeared meddlesome dogooders and professional spoilsports inveighed against the daring of her costume. Their wails and protests were trumpet blasts for the managers of the theaters in which the Australian naiad was booked. They made better promotion than flamboyant press agentry. Queues formed at box offices. Standing Room Only signs were dusted off and erected in theater foyers. For a period of time, Miss Kellerman was the biggest hit on the vaudeville circuit.

I was desperately determined to see this sensational performer, who promised to reveal even more of the female form divine than the Corybants who cavorted on the stage of Boston's venerable burlesque house, the old Howard. I worked out a stratagem two weeks before Miss Kellerman opened at Keith's famed vaudeville theater. I acquired from a theatrical costumer in New York a ferocious black moustache and needed, once it was attached to my upper lip, only a broad-brimmed, soft-crowned hat to impersonate a blackhander. I was sure the moustache was a suitable disguise. And Saturday noon of the week of Miss Kellerman's engagement at Keith's I rode into Boston on a train on which three Andover masters also were passengers, impervious to the threat of being expelled if discovered. Reaching the city, I was hurrying along Washington Street when I heard the taunt of a newsboy, "Pipe the guy with the false spinach." Frightened by the disclosure I ran up an alley and examined my image in the mirror of a gum machine. To my horror I saw that two metal clasps that reached into my nostrils to give added security to the glued-on moustache had come loose and dangled over my disguised upper lip.

I snatched off the moustache, went on to the theater barefaced, obtained a front row seat, and felt divinely anointed when Miss Kellerman did what was called the Australian Honey-Pod, and water splashed out of her tank and wet my best suit. She was all that I anticipated. Once her black silk tights were slicked down by the water of the pool there was very little one did not know about her physical lineaments, and all that was revealed was enormously alluring.

I got back to school that night after a long drawn-out and circuitous journey on interurban trolley cars, my malefaction undetected. But the story of my escapade had wide circulation in the school yard and gave me the single distinction I knew in a full year at Andover. I had established a sort of benchmark in student idiocy.

At the close of the school year I devised another absurdity that further denigrated my standing as an ideal product of this fine institution and added to my notoriety as a schoolyard clown. With the annual competition in declamation coming up, I promoted a campaign to raise money to encourage a youth named Harris to participate. Harris was a senior who was to matriculate at Yale in the fall. He was in love with a girl in his native city of Denver; he had over-spent his allowance; her birthday was imminent; and he was distressed at the prospect of not being able to send her a present. I suggested that I could raise as much as ten dollars provided Harris allowed me to select the recitation he would deliver. He agreed, and I managed to increase the prize to fifteen dollars.

Harris was a short, squarish young man of considerable courage who was desperately in love. On the night of the august occasion, with the chapel filled with an audience that was largely adult he mounted the rostrum, his face as white and expressionless as a polished china plate, not to deliver Washington's *Farewell Address,* or Lincoln's immortal words at Gettysburg, or Demosthenes' defense of himself against Aeschines, but to recite these words in a monotone clear enough to reach to every corner of the chapel:

> Two lonesome skunks by the roadside stood,
> as an automobile whizzed by,
>
> The smell it left was far from good,
> and a tear was in one's eye.
>
> "Oh, why do you cry?" asked his anxious friend.
> "Why do you sob and quake?"
>
> "Because that smell," said the other skunk,
> "Is like mother used to make."

Harris stepped quietly down from the dais. There was a hush in the chapel followed by a faint tittering, but no applause. Then the orderly voice of Doctor Stearns, who presided, announced the next speaker, who, if I recall correctly, spoke lines from Keats' sonnet, *On First Looking into Chapman's Homer.* I sat in a rear pew with my collaborators in this absurd canard, a handkerchief pressed to my mouth to prevent an explosion of laughter. We quickly sneaked out of the chapel. Outside, we gave vent to our merriment, confident that our jape was an enormous success. We paid off Harris, who, probably because of his academic excellence, suffered no reprimand. The housemaster in the dormitory where I lived said sarcastically, "Well, Clune, I suppose that was your great triumph."

The school term was over a few days later, and I left Andover. I returned home limp with failures. My father was heartbroken at the sorry mess I had made of the school year and that I seemed determined to make of my life.

Both in high school and at Andover I had had some small success with English composition, and for some time I had cherished in the back of my head the notion that once I achieved my great goal I would stop running and dedicate myself to a new purpose: I would become a writer. I applied to the city editor of a Rochester newspaper for a job. He agreed to a trial, but at no pay—I was not a cub, but a *sub* reporter. The staff worked unconscionably long hours; and since I aspired to become a staff member, I gratuitously equated my working day to that of the paid hands.

My devotion to this unpaid job and the efforts I was making on the outside to master it (I was an atrocious speller and each morning my mother gave me spelling lessons) permitted me little time to train on the track. Ill-prepared, I went to New York to run in the Metropolitan Championships, and, indoctrinated with failure, failed again. Failed miserably!

Throughout my youth my father often insisted that he was the best friend I had, he urged me to trust and confide in him, and he avowed that under no circumstances would he let me down. And he didn't now. He provided me with board and lodging and spending money, but I seemed committed to a career of futility and he was distressed by my series of failures. He told me to abandon the notion of being a world beating miler, an ambition I had once thought integral to my being, and try to find something useful to do in life; he proposed a job with a man he knew who owned a large fruit farm.

The proposal had a hint of command. I was fearful that my father would compel me to leave what I considered the exciting milieu of the newspaper office and farm me out as an apple picker. I was aroused belatedly to a sense of my inutility and a realization of my wasted youth. I declared that no matter what happened, I'd make good in the newspaper business. A coldness had developed between my father and myself. He thought newspaper reporters were generally a shabby, poorly paid lot, inclined to debauchery. He asked scornfully what talent I thought I had for the craft when, after an extended apprenticeship, I hadn't mastered it enough to command a wage?

The question had a stinging pertinency. The truth was that my reportorial efforts appeared hopeless. I was given only the most trivial tasks in the city room or sent out to write three or four paragraphs about a lodge, church, or factory picnic; or to fetch from the home of someone recently deceased a photograph to accompany the obituary notice. My father, with whom I now had very little contact, continued to tolerate this seemingly endless unpaid apprenticeship. Weeks passed into months. Presently Morris Adams, the city editor, firmly but not unkindly, told me that I was unfitted for what I was trying to do and suggested I try something else. I couldn't fail again. I pleaded that my trial run be extended, and with some reluctance he acceded to my pleas.

I had abandoned the quest of my prime objective and now I would become first a newspaper reporter, and then an author of books. I looked at the set of Charles Dickens on our library shelf and told myself that the trick of writing was merely persistence in putting down one word after another. I seemed, however, unable to achieve in this practice a rhythmic or meaningful sequence, and it was not until I had continued in my profitless experiment more than six months that, one triumphant day, Mr. Adams called me aside and told me I had arrived. He had put me on the payroll—at eight dollars a week!

Once I became an accredited member of the newspaper staff, the confidence this new status gave me helped improve my competence. I was proud of my professionalism and I was completely dedicated. My ten and eleven hour work days (with a once-a-week trick known as the "dog watch," when I reported in the city room at 2:00 P.M. and finished at four o'clock the following morning) seemed not unreasonable. The young unmarried members of the staff, unlike veteran reporters who were supporting families on a meager wage, were romantic about their calling. We felt that we were important personages. There was no radio or television; no news media. We were the news *medium,* members of a noble fraternity who gathered and composed the tidings of the world; who sent zinging over telegraph wires or through underseas cables accounts of news events in such disparate places as the Czar's palace or the pampas of the Argentine; who reported what was happening at the Court of St. James, in Washington, or on the Shanghai bund; and we told also in graphic prose of the havoc wrought by a runaway horse in Main Street, Rochester, New York.

As time went on and my newspaper skills were sharpened by experience and practice, I ran the gamut of reportorial duties. I was listed in Mr. Adams' day book under the heading of General Assignments, but I was also a sort of utility man. I was sometimes put on Police when the police reporter was off; on Courts when the court man was absent. I substituted on Federal, City Hall, on all of the routine beats that were covered every day. On Monday afternoon I often reviewed the opening of the vaudeville bill at the Temple Theater. I began to meet people of prominence: President Taft, who had come to town for a dinner in his honor; Barney Oldfield, the famous auto racer, who was passing through; Scott Nearing, the eminent sociologist who was lecturing at the City Club; Kid McCoy, the great middleweight boxer who was in Rochester, not to demonstrate the corkscrew punch, which he professedly invented, but to expound the mysteries of theosophy. I began to think I was a newspaper man of parts. But it was the sinking of the great White Star liner *Titanic* in the North Atlantic on the morning of 15 April 1912, that gave me, more than any other experience I had had in nearly two years in the newspaper business, the feeling that I had arrived; that I was destined for great things in the field of journalism.

CHAPTER SEVEN

Sunday was usually my one day off each week, but Sunday, 14 April, I substituted for Will Richards, one of the younger men on the reporting staff of the *Democrat and Chronicle,* which meant—since Sunday was also Richards' day to hold the long watch—that I would come in early Sunday afternoon and work until four o'clock Monday morning.

Richards was a friend of mine. He was older than I by two or three years. He was experienced, talented, and amusing; the "gay caballero" of the newspaper's city room. Unmarried, he lived with his widowed mother, a charming woman who worshipped her only issue.

I envied Richards' air of worldliness, which I often attempted to imitate. He was fond of the ladies, particularly those in the theater. He had become enamored of a girl in a musical comedy that closed Saturday night at the Lyceum Theater. The troupe was to move westward Sunday for a week's stand in Buffalo. Will had been invited to accompany the girl on the troupe car and he appealed to me to take his place on the newspaper. I agreed; I knew he would go off, twizzling like a Catherine wheel, in his best suit, a flower in his buttonhole, and a walking stick hooked over an arm.

Except on rare occasions, Sunday was a dull day for news, and our Monday morning newspaper was often thin—thin as consommé as someone said. Rochester in the early years of the second decade of the century was a pleasant, orderly city, where crime was never rampant, and where one murder in a period of six months excited city-wide interest and made headlines for a week or ten days. Today, so different has our city become in the matter of law and order, that homicide is a common crime, like burglary and armed robbery, and the newspapers often pass it off with two or three backpage paragraphs.

There was no notable crime in Rochester Sunday, 14 April, and the police had little more to do than arrest a couple of wobbly-legged, loose-swinging drunks who started a fight in the Rescue Mission. The theaters were closed. It was too early for any interesting activities at the lakeside resorts, and Lilac Sunday, which would mark the opening of a week-long display of the city's celebrated collection of these flowers, was more than a month hence. No horse ran away in downtown Rochester; no newsworthy crash of motor vehicles occurred. A male quartet was performing in the YMCA auditorium and a radical speaker was booked into the Labor Lyceum, known in our city room as Dynamite Hall, but neither of these was my assignment.

In the afternoon I interviewed a couple who were celebrating their fiftieth wedding anniversary, wrote the obituary of a fairly prominent citizen, and that evening covered a small time touring evangelist who was holding forth in an outlying church, the walls of which rang continually with cries of "Hallelujah! Praise the Lord!" as sinners pressed forward to the penitential bench.

When, after returning to the office, I finished my piece on the evangelist, Mr. Adams gave me a few inside chores, and sometime after 12:30 A.M. I put on my hat and went across Main Street to Hall's lunch room, which was busy twenty-four hours of the day. The brothers who operated the place boasted that they threw the key away on opening day, and they predicted the lunch room would go on forever. The food, which was eaten off the spatulate arms of chairs, was cheap, solid, and good. Among other favored dishes was chicken pie for twenty cents. It was a meal in itself. Concealed in a thick viscous gravy were carrots, onions and liberal slices of chicken, the concoction topped by a crust somewhat the texture of battleship plating, but tasty if one had solid teeth.

Hall's and the Manhattan Restaurant were the two most popular all-night eating places in downtown Rochester. The Manhattan had tables and waitresses and stiffer prices.

At midnight and in the early hours of the morning, Hall's was a catch-all. Policemen, motormen and conductors from the trolley cars, wassailers sobering up, compositors, pressmen, and reporters from the two morning newspapers, bartenders, gamblers, stage hands, newsboys waiting for the early editions, taximen and hack drivers, bums who had panhandled the price of a cup of Java, and numerous other night persons, gave Hall's a sort of cosmopolitan atmosphere. Its powerful lights and its white walls lent it the glitter of a nova. It was a snug haven on a blustery winter night; it was cooled by whirling fans on nights of summer's dog days. I always knew people in Hall's. There was lively talk and fellowship. I left reluctantly shortly after one o'clock to take up my lonely vigil in a soon to be deserted city room.

The newsroom of the *Democrat and Chronicle* was on the fifth, the top floor of the newspaper's building on Main Street. It was a narrow, alley-like room, shabby, as most alleys are. It was divided longitudinally by two rows of opposing desks, each desk with a well for a typewriter. Green shaded lamps hung over the desks and the reporters sat on straight-backed kitchen chairs. There were spittoons on the floor. A thin wooden partition at the far end of this cul-de-sac separated the city room from a shorter and narrower alley known as the telegraph room. At one end of this the telegraph editor had his desk. He faced the backs of three or four operators who typed out dispatches received on their "bugs," or telegraph instruments, from the Associated Press and other news services.

When I reached the fifth floor of the newspaper building on an elevator that surely must have been one of the first invented, only Mr. Adams, the city editor, and a reporter who was working on a very late story, were still in the city room. Both left within half an hour. It was now my responsibility to write and arrange the placing of any local story worthy of an extra that broke between then and 4:00 A.M. Extras were not common. I had been instructed that only a very important piece of news, a great fire, a murder, a flood, or some similar event, warranted the expense and delay of making over the front page. Mostly on the long watch, the man holding it dozed or read or amused himself by throwing hard projectiles at the large rats that came up from the river bank or out from a job-plant bindery that adjoined the newsroom (the legend was they got drunk eating the bindery glue), to gambol about the floor, squeal and fight, and hold a Mardi gras. This early morning I chose a chair in the back of the room, and, associating rat bite with bubonic plague, put my feet on top of a desk and drowsed over a magazine.

I could hear through the flimsy partition that separated the city room from the telegraph room the faint tapping of a telegraph instrument, for the Associated Press operator was still taking dispatches and would continue to do so for a couple of hours. He and the telegraph editor and myself were the only persons left on the fifth floor. The telegraph editor was a thin, nervous, conscientious man who felt that his domain was the world, a large map of which was tacked to the wall above his desk. He boasted of his cosmopolitanism, reminding his colleagues that it was he who was responsible for the vital news stories that came from such places as Buenos Aires, London, St. Petersburg, Cape Town, Peking, Cairo, San Francisco—from all over the globe. He considered himself the most important man on the newspaper staff. Now he was waiting to give his editorial scrutiny to a copy of the newspaper, which would be sent to him as soon as the presses in their catacomb down by the river bank began their run; but it was nearly half an hour before we heard their thump and rumble and another few minutes before a boy delivered two copies of the first edition, still damp with ink, one to Amos, the telegraph editor, and one to me. I was eagerly turning the pages to learn if my story of the evangelist, which I thought I had invested with sly humor, had made the first edition when I heard a shout from Mr. Petty, the AP operator.

"Amos! Amos! My God, the *Titanic*'s sinking!"

I laid the newspaper aside and went into the telegraph room. I had read with superficial interest that the *Titanic* had left Southampton in midweek on her maiden run to New York. She was the largest and most luxurious liner ever built and her first-class passenger list read like a combination of Who's Who and the Social Register. But I was no traveler; the farthest I had ever been from home was Chicago and I had never seen an ocean liner in my life. I was hardly aware of the significance of Mr. Petty's words.

Amos had left his desk and was leaning over Mr. Petty's shoulder, reading the words translated from the tapping of the Morse code as Petty typed them out.

"I don't believe it," he said. He spoke angrily, as if he had been promised a very big story and the promise had been revoked. "She can't sink. The White Star people made her unsinkable. There's a mistake. There are other ships on the high seas registered in that name, *Titanic.* I know."

He turned away, but Petty called him back. "But look—look," he cried excitedly. "There're wireless flashes. She's calling for help. She's off the Grand Banks. She's hit an iceberg."

Amos squinted again at the copy paper on the operator's typewriter. "Oh, Jesus, if it's true. If it's true, it's the greatest story to come over the wires since Appomattox. Clune," he ordered, turning to me, "run downstairs. Get John Diprose. Tell him all hell's broke loose."

I did as I was told. Diprose was boss of the composing room, on the floor directly below ours. He came bounding up the stairs with me.

Amos told him the front page would be made over with a banner line across it. There would be at least two, possibly three editions. He'd stop the presses as quickly as he had something more than bulletins.

There was an agonizing delay. Petty's bug suddenly seemed closed to the *Titanic* disaster and was tapping out small, unimportant new items. Amos was in a state of frenzy. He shouted at the instrument as if to command it to get back to the main theme. The story came in fragments; it lacked cohesion, much of it extravagant speculation. Now, however, there was no question that the foundering ship was the great White Star liner. As Petty typed a paragraph, Amos snatched it from the typewriter. He sent me to the newspaper's "morgue" for all the material we had on the *Titanic.* She was huge: eleven stories high and four city blocks long. Her weight was

46,328 gross tons. She had a displacement of 66,000 tons and a speed of twenty-five knots. I took from a folder a description of her interior which told of the beauty of her woodwork, of the luxury of her first-cabin apartments, of the elegance of her several restaurants. She had a gymnasium and a Turkish bath. Suites with a private promenade deck might be leased for the six-day crossing for $4,000. I compiled most of this information in a page or so of copy, excited by the fancy that I was collaborating on a news report of an historic catastrophe.

Amos was obsessed with the notion that several Rochesterians were among the *Titanic*'s passengers. He was sure that Warham Whitney, a world traveler, a man well known in Newport and other fashionable resorts and the husband of the city's social leader, was aboard. Sometime after three o'clock in the morning he had me telephone the Whitney residence to ask if Whitney had been on the ship. I awakened an irascible butler who admitted that Mr. Whitney and his daughter, Charlotte, had been abroad for several weeks.

"But do you know if they're on the *Titanic?*" I persisted. "She's sinking, I told you."

"Well, let her sink," the butler conceded angrily, "but don't ever call me at this hour again," and down went the receiver.

We learned the next day that Whitney and his daughter were safe in Cairo.

I remained in the office until after six o'clock that morning helping Amos get out a couple of "extras." The line he put across the front page read:

LINER TITANIC REPORTED SINKING

Gigantic Steamer
Collides with
Iceberg.

But the story below told nothing of the dreadful loss of more than 1,500 lives, a fact not even hinted at by some newspapers that were printed later in the day; indeed, several announced that all passengers and crew were rescued. It was only the next day, Tuesday, 16 April, that our newspaper and others blazoned forth the news that hundreds had gone down with the ship; and it was not until the arrival in New York of the rescue ship, *Carpathia,* that comprehensive details of the disaster began to appear in the press, together with the names of survivors and stories, sometimes highly fanciful, of the last minute behavior of prominent men and women who perished when the great man-made leviathan plunged headforemost below the sea.

Six Rochesterians were on the *Titanic* and three were saved. The most prominent of the six was Howard B. Case, London manager of the Vacuum Oil Company, a first-class passenger. Walter Lord, in his vivid recreation of the disaster, *A Night To Remember,* speaks three times of Case. He tells at one point how Case helped Mrs. William T. Graham, her nineteen-year-old daughter, and the girl's governess, into a life boat, then leaned against the rail and lighted a cigarette.

"Men would go on being brave, but never would they be brave in quite the same way," Lord wrote. "These men on the *Titanic* had a touch—there was something about Ben Guggenheim changing to evening dress . . . about Howard Case flicking a cigarette as he waved to Mrs. Graham . . . or even about Colonel Gracie panting along the deck, gallantly if ineffectually searching for Mrs. Candee. Today nobody would carry off these little gestures of chivalry, but they did that night."

CHAPTER EIGHT

In 1955 I was finishing a political novel, *The Big Fella,* and Cecil Scott was jubilant. *By His Own Hand,* though far from a failure (a novel that sold better than 50,000 copies could hardly be called that), had failed to achieve the sensational success he, Mr. Brett, and Harold Latham had predicted for it, but with this one we were going to have a sure hit. There was no wild talk of its being a *Gone With the Wind* sort of thing, but *The Big Fella* would come out, smack-dab, the first of the new year, the first political novel of a presidential year.

"We'll knock 'em dead this time," Scott enthused, his correct Cambridge diction lapsing into American vernacular.

Then, to damp his ebullience and water down my own soaring hopes, he suffered an eye ailment that interrupted his editorial work for weeks, and early in the year that President Eisenhower ran for re-election against Adlai E. Stevenson, a fine political novel, *The Last Hurrah,* by Edwin O'Connor, hit the stands, won high acclaim (and, ultimately, the Pulitzer Prize), and boomed into a best seller.

Scheduled for publication several weeks before the O'Connor opus, *The Big Fella* did not appear until three months after *The Last Hurrah.* It would not, in any event, have matched the popularity of the latter, which dealt sympathetically and humorously with the career of an Irish politician and appealed strongly to readers of that heritage; but it would have been advantaged by being the first rather than the second political novel of the year. As it was, it went quickly through three printings, sold to Collins in England, to a newspaper syndicate, and to a paperback publisher. *The Big Fella* had fine reviews, with an occasional derogatory comparison with *The Last Hurrah,* across the land. I was particularly pleased when the *New York Times,* telling that I had written "a compelling case history" with "so much corroborated detail . . . that it's authenticity is unquestioned," remarked that I was the author of a "previously notable novel based on the life of a recognizable American businessman and philanthropist, *By His Own Hand.*"

I did two other novels for Macmillan, interrupting the sequence to contribute *The Genesee* to the "Rivers of America" Series, published by Holt, Rinehart & Winston. The first of the two novels, *Six O'Clock Casual,* was considered daring enough in those days of innocence to constrain my grandniece, apprenticed to a hospital nursing school, to secrete the book in the mattress of her bed for fear of the supervisor's censure. The novel was snapped up by Bantam Books, who decorated the cover of the paperback edition with a picture of a girl wrapped in a bath towel only, a far better sales pitch than the staid profile of my heroine on the Macmillan dust jacket. The novel was also published in Spanish.

A month before *Six O'Clock Casual* was to appear in the book stores, I had a telephone call from New York from Miss Annie Laurie Williams, the play agent.

"Mr. Clune," she said, and her voice seemed very eager, "I have just read *Six O'Clock Casual.* I got the galleys from Macmillan. I'm terribly excited about it. I have exactly the girl to play the lead. She's coming tomorrow for cocktails. I'm going to insist that she does it if you'll let me offer it to Hollywood."

I had had that week a letter from a man in Hollywood, asking if he might offer the novel to the movie people. I had never heard of him and had not yet answered his letter. I did know quite a little about Miss Williams although I had never met her. It was she who had closed the deal for Macmillan for the sale of *Gone With the Wind* to film producer, David O. Selznick. As a young woman she had left her native Texas for New York, hoping to star on the stage. She failed as an actress, but failure put her into another department of show business, and one night, so the legend went, she stood at the

42nd Street intersection of Broadway, and gloated to see six theaters playing hit shows that she had sold to producers.

"Miss Williams," I said, "I'd be very glad to have you offer the novel to Hollywood. But why, if you want someone to read it, don't you wait until the book's out next month, instead of showing those galleys? They're awfully inconvenient to read."

"No, no, no," she protested. "I can't wait. I've got to have this girl play the role."

"Who is the girl?"

"Natalie Wood."

Miss Wood was just out of her nonage at the time. Her career was beginning; it had not yet blossomed into stardom. Perhaps she didn't like the story, or, if she did, she may not have been important enough to ask that it be made into a film for the display of her talents. No one ever played Ellen Rood, the heroine of the novel, for Miss Williams failed to sell it to Hollywood. I had become inured to this sort of disappointment, and accepted Miss Williams' failure philosophically. There was still some money to be had from royalties, and a few thousand dollars from the paperback sale. I dedicated *Six O'Clock Casual* to my wife, who, old-fashioned in her notion of propriety, winced, thinking it raunchy; and I bought her, with part of its revenue, not merely a mink wrap, but mink from throat to ankle, which seemed to clean up the story quickly, and make it quite palatable.

During the years that I was published by Macmillan, I was frequently in New York, sometimes at the invitation of the publishing firm. Macmillan had me at the Book Awards the year the then Senator John F. Kennedy's *Profiles in Courage* was cited as the best biographical work and John O'Hara's *Ten North Frederick* the best novel. At the time *The Big Fella* was published, Macmillan arranged to have me interviewed on the air by Martha Dean, whose specialty was talking about books with their authors.

Cecil Scott once gave a lunch at the Four Seasons for the distinguished historian, Barbara Tuchman, and myself. Mrs. Tuchman was an admirer of Scott. He had edited *The Proud*

Tower, and the first of her two Pulitzer-prize histories, *The Guns of August.* She told in the preface of each of the help and encouragement the editor had given her. We left our host after lunch and walked together to the St. Regis Hotel, where Mrs. Tuchman asked if I would write a piece for *Publishers' Weekly* telling of Scott's editorial skill and the help he had given us both. In time I composed such an article and offered it to the magazine. It was never used.

Scott retired before I finished the last novel I did for Macmillan, but he was still active when my work was in mid-career, and I spent one early autumn Sunday at his home in Chappaqua conferring with him about the script. Cecil and his wife were admirable hosts, and I always looked forward to these visits, which were professionally helpful and socially enjoyable. We had a fine lunch. In late afternoon, Scott drove me to the Chappaqua station, where I boarded a local train that made a stop-and-go run through Westchester County to Grand Central.

The sparsely occupied coach I entered had as passengers in adjacent seats a tall, athletic, Yalish-looking man in tweeds; a slim, straight, out-doorish Vassarish-looking woman in a tweed jacket and skirt and long woolen stockings that displayed her bare knees; a boy called Arthur, of approximately thirteen years; a girl whose name I did not hear and who was possibly ill; a second boy, Fred, who might have been eight; and last, a flower-like child with beestung lips and eyes of turquoise blue, who was not more, I am sure, than three and one-half or four. She wore a floppish little hat, which vaguely reminded me of the hat the lovely Miss Ina Claire used to wear in *The Quaker Girl.* It was secured by a red ribbon tied under her chin.

The train was close to Grand Central when the father, hitching himself to a rucksack and swinging a pair of field glasses over a shoulder (I suspect the family had been on a birdwatching expedition), stood up in the aisle and addressed his brood.

"Arthur, you're the leader," he said to the boy authoritatively. "We'll line up on the platform and proceed across the station to the Vanderbilt Avenue exit where we'll get a cab. There's to be no monkey business; no nonsense. And you'll *all* keep in line. Understand?"

The boy nodded, and when the family left the train its younger members settled at once into formation, Arthur at the head of the line, the older girl second, Fred third, and the smallest child bringing up the rear.

I was enormously impressed by the tractability of these youngsters, by their prompt and uncomplaining compliance with an order. This, it seemed to me, was what should be happening all over the land. Discipline! The sensible imposition of parental authority. Here indeed, as the father had decreed, there would be no nonsense, no monkey business. And, with a word from him, the children were in motion, walking precisely behind their parents, who led the way across the station with long strides.

It was a diagonal course to the Vanderbilt Avenue exit and the pace of the vigorous parents grew so swift that even Arthur and the older girl had now and then to interject a jog-trot to hold it, and soon the little girl in the rear, as they say at the race track, was in the ruck.

Her tiny feet, which were turned out to the position of ten minutes to two, beat a sharp rat-a-plan on the marble floor, but she was steadily losing ground. Her floppy hat, almost dislodged by her exertions, was held on her head by the flat of one hand, her elfin face was contorted.

Then, suddenly, her protest reverberated off the marble walls and down from the lofty dome of the famous building.

"Goddamnit," she cried, in a desperate vibrato, "wait for baby!"

* * * * * * * * * *

Before he left Macmillan, Cecil Scott suggested a title for the last novel I did for his firm. I thought it wrong but did not protest because of my habitual inclination to defer to his judgment. He called it *O'Shaughnessy's Café,* the one grievous editorial error he made in my long association with him. He also approved a dust jacket which added to the impression given by the title that the novel was merely a saloon tale. It wasn't. The protagonist was a woman, who I still believe is the best fictional lady I ever created. I delight in her; I love her. And of course she should have been by name or implication in the title. Annie Laurie Williams was enchanted by the book and the woman who dominated it. She wrote, "I hope we can make a movie deal this week. I will let you know promptly. I'm trying to get $50,000." And again, she drew a blank.

Cecil Scott had always wanted me to do a regional book on Rochester, and the bright young editor I inherited after he left was also strong on the idea. The higher-ups at Macmillan rejected the proposal. In time I did a non-fiction book of this type under a kind and talented editor, Lawrence P. Ashmead, which modestly rewarded Doubleday and myself. Later, I tried another novel which reflected my feeling that the Vietnam War was the most obscene enterprise the country had ever undertaken. It was rejected all along the line, partly because, as I was told, Vietnam was "old hat"—an overkill—, and partly, perhaps, for the reason expressed by one editor who, returning my manuscript, wrote, ". . . your story does have a slightly old-fashioned air (it had no violence, and very little sex). . . . twenty years ago we probably would have taken on your book as one that we were proud to add to the Dodd, Mead list."

Regretfully, I threw the bundle of typescript pages on the shelf and went off on the memoir you are now reading, in full agreement with Mr. Steinbeck's dogma about the vicissitudes of book writing and what a tougher gamble it is than playing the races.

CHAPTER NINE

The *Titanic* story continued for many days as front page news, but my connection with it ended with the assistance I had lent the telegraph editor the early morning it broke.

Will Richards returned from Buffalo disillusioned and envious. His amour had failed. He had spent half a week's pay for a fancy silk nightgown for the girl with whom he had left in the troupe car, and she refused to permit him to put it on her. He avowed that he was through with these so-called charmers of the stage; they were cheap, meretricious, and unfaithful. His envy had nothing to do with his frustrating experience in Buffalo; it was provoked by a reporter named Jim Frazer, who had worked with us for a few months on the *Democrat and Chronicle.*

Frazer was a tall, swaggering young man with a face mosaiced with postules and the nerve of a cat burglar. He wrote swiftly and well and he was extremely resourceful. He would stop at nothing to obtain a newsbeat. He felt, as did Richards himself, that his talents were too advanced for the town. One day he disappeared without giving a word of notice, and the next we heard he was doing very well on Hearst's *Evening Journal,* in New York.

Richards was a thoroughgoing newspaperman, fully as talented as Frazer. But he was responsible for the support of his mother and could not move about at will. He longed to be in New York. Now, back from Buffalo, he resumed the routine tasks of a small city reporter and learned, as we all did, that Jim Frazer, our former associate in the city room, was actively engaged on one of the greatest news stories of the past half century.

Frazer fitted readily into the ethic of Hearst journalism. He had the speed and aggressiveness to meet its high-pressure demands. In a surprisingly short time he had become one of the *Journal*'s crack reporters. He was up to his armpits in the *Titanic* story, and we were told that he had imperiously hired a tug and steamed out into New York Bay to meet the *Carpathia* when she returned with the *Titanic*'s survivors. We secretly admired the bravura of our former colleague, whom none of us had very much liked as a person. Richards was outspokenly envious.

"That Frazer has all the luck," he complained bitterly. "If you want to get anywhere in this business, you've got to be in New York. I'd be there tomorrow if it weren't for my mother. Here, with a story like the *Titanic* breaking, I'm sent out on the federal beat. I go over and ask the weatherman if it's going to rain tomorrow; get the names of a couple of kids who enlisted at the army recruiting station; talk to the postmaster; see what's doing in bankruptcy court. Cruddy! Small time! New York's the only place!"

I, too, began to think that I ought to be in New York. If Jim Frazer could make good there, why couldn't I? The notion of this crowded me, it became obsessive, and in less than three months after the *Titanic* tragedy I resigned from the *Democrat and Chronicle* and left for the metropolis. The members of the city room staff did not give me a going-away party, but before I quit the newspaper I attended a small soiree Will Richards arranged that encouraged a belief I had begun to cherish that I was a reporter of growing distinction and a young man of very worldly ways.

Richards' black moods were transitory; each quickly disappeared under the wave of some new enthusiasm. He was enormously good natured and incapable of a prolonged grudge. In a week, if he hadn't forgotten the girl who refused to permit him to adorn her with a nightgown, his pique at her refusal had passed. And his announced resolve to disassociate himself from the ladies of the theater was little more than an *obiter dictum.*

The Corinthian Theater was offering a double feature, the Dresden China Dolls and Jack McAuliffe, undefeated lightweight champion of the world. The Dolls were petite young women, one dark, the other with honey-colored hair. Will was in love with the blonde. He decided on a party in a suite in the Whitcomb House, the sportiest hotel in town. When I was asked, I asked in turn a lady whose former husband had been the possessor of the famous blue gem stone, the Hope Diamond. She was May Yohe, a raven-haired, frog-throated beauty, old enough to be my mother. I felt like a rajah. It was a heady experience, and it addicted me to a habit of name dropping that persisted through a long career in the newspaper business. May Yohe was the first woman of celebrity I had ever beaued about.

Her life was a sequence of lively episodes. The story was that when she made her debut as a singer in the anthracite region of her native Pennsylvania, the miners who attended her concert were so impressed by her contralto voice that they endowed her with a grant to study opera in Paris. It doesn't seem valid. In those days miners had to scrimp and scrape for the bare necessities of life; their debts at the mining companies' stores often kept them in a state of feudal servitude, and it is hard to believe that they would prodigally indulge a darling of song. But the fact is that Miss Yohe did go to Paris to study, and upon her return promptly ran off with a burlesque troupe.

That was a brief interlude. Soon she was a star in musical comedy, first in this country and then in England, where she married Lord Francis Hope, who, before the marriage, supposedly gave his bride a rope of pearls valued at more than a quarter of a million dollars. A member of an old English family which had possessed the Hope Diamond for generations, Lord Hope would be known today as a swinger. He went broke in time, the Hope Diamond left his hands, and May also left him. Known as "Madcap May Yohe," she had a penchant for running here, there, and yonder with any man who took her fancy. Quitting Hope, she went bucketing off with an attractive American, with whom she lived in Japan for some time without the sanction of marital commitment. Her career was like a teeterboard in its ups and downs. In Rochester she was in a momentary depression (not in spirit, but in circumstance; her spirits seemed perpetually effervescent), and she was singing in a small-time, six-a-day vaudeville house, the Colonial. I was sent to interview her, she was pleased with what I wrote, and I went back to invite her to Will Richards' party.

The party was late, beginning after the theater closed. Will had asked besides myself, Jack McAuliffe, since he co-starred with the Dresden China Dolls. He was a spunky, amusing little man who had won the lightweight championship in London from a boxer named Carney. He lived in the recalled flowering of past glories. Richards had provided a light collation and many bottles of beer in a tub of ice. The ex-Lady Hope, an ex-burlesque woman herself, fitted aptly into the proceedings. It struck me that she could get along with anyone; there was no side to her. Her husky contralto broke the after-midnight stillness with a couple of her famous numbers, "Honey, Mah Honey" and "What Can a Poor Girl Do?" from the musical, *Christopher Columbus*. Jack McAuliffe, getting drunk on bottled beer, had a habit of leaping on the bed, striking the pose of a boxer, and crying out, "The night I fought Carney in London!" Will Richards cooed in a corner with the blonde; the dark-haired Dresden China Doll nibbled at the food, drank beer, sang, now and then danced with McAuliffe. Hotel guests, trying to sleep, apparently complained of our revelry. There was a sharp authoritative rap on the door of the suite, the door was opened, and Jack Coyle, the house dick, inquired angrily, "What the hell goes on here?"

McAuliffe was again on the bed, bounding about so vigorously that the springs almost touched the floor, throwing punches at an imaginary adversary, and describing in stentorian voice how, Biff! he had caught Carney on the jaw, Bang! he had hooked him in the gut. At Coyle's entrance he leaped from the bed to the floor with a bellowed announcement, "I'm Jack McAuliffe, undefeated lightweight champion of the world!" He thrust forth a cordial hand. "Pal, pleasedtameetcha!"

The identification was an instant palliative. Coyle was pleased to be greeted by the great man.

He beamed, gently shushed down the noise with a finger on his lips, was introduced to the one-time Lady Hope and the Dresden China Dolls (he knew Richards and me), tried what was left of the food, sat down with a bottle of beer, and listened to McAuliffe give a more tempered description of "The Night I Fought Carney in London."

It was now far after the witching hour. Soon came another caller to the suite, Freddie Reynolds, a local café piano player, who was Miss Yohe's accompanist at the Colonial. Reynolds was a tall, lean, handsome, rakish young man adored by women. Apparently May Yohe had been drawn into his magnetic sphere. She leaped up, flung her arms around him. "Dah'lin! Dah'lin! Where have you been? We've missed you!"

No one else had missed him and Richards hadn't invited him to the party.

"I was playing cards," Reynolds said. "Win more'n a hundred."

"Over a hundred. Why, dah'lin, let's you and I have a party," and May Yohe picked up her wraps, took Reynolds' arm, and with an inclusive wave to the rest of us, went with him into the corridor and where after that I never knew. I lost my companion and never saw her again. But I could boast, and did for some time, that I had been the escort of the Lady Hope whose husband had owned the Hope Diamond, now a prize exhibit in the gem collection of the Smithsonian Institution.

In a few weeks I said good-bye to Richards and other friends in the city room of the *Democrat and Chronicle* and left for New York. Richards and I were to meet again and our friendship was to grow. In time Will would win the Pulitzer Prize for Journalism and write an informal biography of Henry Ford, which the famous Maxwell Perkins of Scribner's edited. It was called *The Last Billionaire* (the author died too soon to know of Howard Hughes and J. Paul Getty.) It was a good book which deservedly made the Best Seller List. But that was years later, after Richards had become the star man on the *Free Press* in Detroit, where, for a time, we lived together when I, too, worked for that newspaper.

CHAPTER TEN

I went to New York with a letter from a Rochester business man who introduced me, if he did not actually recommend me, to Louis Wiley, business manager of the *New York Times*.

Louis Wiley had come from Rochester. He had formerly been associated with the *Post Express,* one of the city's three afternoon dailies, which was owned by Francis B. Mitchell. Mr. Mitchell was a competent newspaperman, but the *Post Express* was more or less a hobby with him; he dawdled with it, perhaps managed a scant profit from it, but the large country house in which he lived, the racing stable he maintained, and his sumptuous style of life were made possible by a fortune derived from Vanity Fair Cigarettes, the prime product of the Kimball Tobacco Company of Rochester.

It was said that Wiley left the *Post Express* after a quarrel with Mitchell, which might very well have been true. Mr. Mitchell was a man who provoked dissension. He was an imperious employer. He had all sorts of finicky rules for those who worked for him. One day an awning on a downtown building caught fire and the expanding flame partly destroyed the structure. A new reporter on the *Post Express,* unaware that it was a cardinal sin to declare or imply that cigarettes could have a deleterious effect on man or on man's handwork, wrote, as a matter of fact, that the awning was ignited when a lighted cigarette was dropped upon it, and the next day the reporter was dropped from the payroll.

At the *New York Times,* where Wiley went from the *Post Express,* he soon established himself as an important figure. He was a bachelor, dedicated long hours each day to the advancement of a newspaper that Adolph Ochs was making into one of the greatest dailies in America, and engaged at night in advancing himself as a personage on the metropolitan scene.

As I remember him, Mr. Wiley was a man perhaps less than medium height, with a large head and a definite air of presence—an aspect of Napoleonic authority. As he read the letter I presented, I gazed nervously around the large office, the walls of which were decorated with photographs of men whose names I had read in headlines. The office overlooked Times Square. Mr. Wiley finished the letter, fixed me with stern scrutiny, and asked if I knew George Eastman, head of the great Eastman Company; James G. Cutler, distinguished architect and manufacturer, and probably the best mayor the city of Rochester has ever had; Warham Whitney, husband of the unchallenged leader of the city's tight little social hierarchy. The catechism left me wanting. The best I could do was to tell him that as a boy of twelve years I had shaken hands with Mr. Eastman as he stood in a reception line at the opening of a downtown building.

I attempted, during the brief interview, to impress Mr. Wiley with my talents as a newspaper reporter, and I related two or three small triumphs I had achieved on the *Democrat and Chronicle.* He listened with less than fascinated interest. His telephone would ring, and he seemed in each response to be engaged with momentous transactions. My presence was obviously an annoyance. Once, after replacing the receiver on the hook, he scribbled a note on a slip of paper, which he fluttered in my direction.

"Take this," he said. "Go see Mr. So and So in classified. There's an opening for a bill collector."

"Bu—but, I'm a newspaper reporter."

"You have to start somewhere if you want to work for the *Times.*"

I took the slip to Mr. So and So, and two days later started pounding the sidewalks of New York, presenting bills to persons who had inserted ads in the classified section of the newspaper. It was menial work; and never after I quit it did I boast that I had once worked for the great *New York Times,* though I was sometimes tempted to do so and leave the impression that I had been employed as a reporter. The work I did was not, however, unpleasant. I lived cheaply in an excellent boarding house on West 73rd Street. New York in those days was a fascinating place for a young man fresh from the hinterland. I enjoyed roaming the streets on pleasant summer days. There was much to see, to "feel," to savor. I began to cultivate the attitude of the theatrical trouper: "After you leave New York, everything else is Bridgeport." And it seemed to me that the 42nd Street intersection of Broadway was the center of the universe.

Nights were exciting. I could occasionally indulge my taste for the theater, since the price of an upper balcony seat was not beyond my modest means. On rainy days I haunted the Public Library. I found that printed menus were issued for the free lunch in the famous King Cole Room of the Knickerbocker Hotel. I attended sporting events.

The Olympic Games were on that summer, and when the triumphant American team returned from Stockholm, its members were displayed in a motorcade down New York streets. Standing at the Fifth Avenue curb I saw Ted Meredith, the schoolboy winner of the 800 meters (in world record time), waving his boater at the adoring thousands. He seemed so young for such a triumph, and as I fixed my idolatrous gaze upon him, the yearnings I had long cherished of being a world beating miler crowded up and choked me and I felt tears on my cheeks. And there was Thorpe, Jim Thorpe, the Carlisle Indian, who had won both the pentathlon and decathlon as easily, one correspondent wrote, as picking strawberries from a bowl.

At the end of the summer, on Labor Day, I saw Thorpe win the American All-Around Championship, which is similar to the Olympic decathlon, on the grounds of the Irish-American Athletic Club. It was a raw, drizzly afternoon. Athletes in those days were not as elaborately equipped as they are today. Resting on a bench between events, Thorpe pulled on a sweater and a pair of street trousers to protect him against the chill and rain. Glen Warner, the famous Carlisle football coach, was with him. Thorpe had done poorly in one event, his point score had dropped, and Warner told him that he must do better than six feet in the high jump. He rose from the bench and without bothering to remove the sweater or pants made the leap successfully.

It was not, however, the jumping, vaulting, and weight-throwing competitions on a track field program that interested me, but the running events. From early youth until very late in life, I was fascinated by footracers, and for many, many years engaged in a grail-like enterprise to discover the beau ideal among them. I dislike to travel; abstracted from home I am unhappy until I return. But this absurd quest took me half way around the world with stops at such places as Tokyo; Lincoln, Nebraska; London; Walnut, California; Mexico City; College Park, Maryland; Oslo; Berea, Ohio; Rome; San Antonio, Texas; State College, Pennsylvania; Kingston, Jamaica, BWI; Los Angeles; New York; Boston; Philadelphia; and an unreckoned number of other cities and way stations. Then, at the Montreal Olympics, I saw John Walker, who had run a mile better than three minutes and fifty seconds; Lasse Viren, the double-winning Finn; and the Cuban, Juantorena, the most impressive of all; and I left the stadium pleased with what I had seen, but no longer interested—my enthusiasm quenched by satiation.

Since then, for me, all sports have paled, and lost their allure. There is something tacky and meretricious in today's extravagant promotions of electronic "supersports," with out-of-door games being played on artificial turf under the roofs of dome-lit auditoriums, in some instances by .226 hitters who command millions. The current crop of professional athletes may have sharper skills than their predecessors in an era before the bonanza created by television exposure, but they are somehow less interesting as personalities. They lack the spontaneity and daffiness of earlier members of the guild. They are businessmen, panoplied by agents, lawyers, and unions, who are made rich by juicy contracts for the display of their professional competencies and by substantial subsidiary contracts for promoting such merchandise as deodorants, shaving lotions, athletic equipment, and cereals that are deposed to be the breakfast food of champions.

In New York in 1912 I saw Rube Marquand pitch two of the nineteen consecutive games he won for the New York Giants; Honus Wagner, of the Pittsburgh Pirates who, before he became the greatest shortstop in baseball history, worked as a coal heaver; the big, cat-graceful Napoleon LaJoie, like Wagner, a Hall of Famer, who eked out his summertime pay playing ball for Cleveland by driving hack in Pawtucket, Rhode Island in the winter. Money was important, but the game itself was the essence of sport. I always thought Babe Ruth was one of the true amateurs of his time. I am sure he would have paid to be allowed to play if Jake Rupert, in the end, hadn't paid him $80,000 to do so. Sport in those earlier days was not so overwhelmingly commercial.

* * * * * * * * * * *

Working as a bill collector for a newspaper when I had come to New York to succeed as a newspaper reporter at times tried my patience. My discontents were, however, short-lived, assuaged usually by the discovery of some new and novel diversion in a city that seemed an inexhaustible source of novel diversions. I had the resilience of youth and youth's facility to hope. And while I realized that Mr. Wiley had not actually promised me a reporter's job, he knew that was my purpose in being in New York. Each day I anticipated being summoned from my menial pedestrian rounds and raised to the empyreal blue of the *New York Times* news room.

But time was passing. I had come to New York in the spring. Now the summer was slipping by and I was still a bill collector. I began to gloom about the future, wondering if I would ever have an opportunity to prove my reportorial talents on the metropolitan scene. Then a news story broke that made me drool with envy.

Very early one morning a gambler named Herman Rosenthal was shot a block north of the *Times'* building under circumstances that made the shooting the most sensational murder story New York had known in a quarter of a century. It involved a police lieutenant named Charles Becker and a set of hoodlums with such pseudonyms as Gyp the Blood, Whitey Lewis, Lefty Louie, Dago Frank—golden gifts to newspaper headline writers; it was front page news for weeks on end. It engaged all of the crack reporters in New York, and it left me, aspiring for recognition as a big city journalist, as remote from the action as a ribbon clerk in Woolworth's.

Becker was a crooked cop who for years had been taking tribute from gamblers who needed to "put out the ice" to protect their resorts from police harassment. Rosenthal himself had paid this tribute, and had at one time been Becker's partner in a gambling operation. Lately the pair had quarrelled and the ante was raised—exorbitantly. Angered by this increased extortion, Rosenthal announced that he would expose the lieutenant's practices to Herbert Bayard Swope, famous reporter for the *New York World,* and Rosenthal was slain, the charge was, at Becker's orders by the four hoods with the picturesque by-names.

The killing of Rosenthal had vast ramifications. It was high drama of political intrigue, wanting only the element of love to make it perfect melodrama. It rocked the city administration and rent the New York Police Department like an exploding petard. It ended the political career of Mayor William Jay Gaynor. It made District Attorney Charles Whitman governor of the state and an active candidate for the presidency. And it resulted in death in the electric chair in Sing Sing for the four "hit" men and Becker. The latter was a brutal, club-swinging, arrogant, corrupt public servant, but latter-day investigators gravely question the justice of the conviction, feeling that the evidence was set aside, due process ignored, and that Becker was the victim of public clamor and the bias and venality of the press.

At his death his widow attached a plaque to his coffin with these words:

> Charles Becker
> Murdered July 10, 1915
> By Governor Charles Whitman

Alva Johnson, who helped cover the Rosenthal-Becker story for the *New York Times,* years later wrote in *The New Yorker* that the murder had taken place during the "golden days of newspaper reporting" in New York, and his feeling was that there has never been anything like it since. There were fourteen English language dailies in the great city. Each had an identity of its own, in contradistinction with today's chain newspapers, which seem often as similar one to another as jars of peanut butter on a grocer's shelf. The competition was cutthroat. The news beat—the scoop—was the great reportorial objective; the star reporter, the Big Deal. There was the glamorous Richard Harding Davis, who might leave the opening of a Broadway play to cover a murder, still in tails, white tie, and top hat; there was the greatly admired Frank Ward O'Malley, of the *Morning Sun*. And there was Swope of the *World* who, launched into national prominence by his coverage of the Rosenthal murder, was soon to become the most famous newspaperman of his generation.

Enormously gifted, flamboyant, innovative, imperious, a legend in his own time, Swope was to make the *World* the most desirable place *in the world* for an aspiring newspaperman. Each morning I read his dazzling stories of the murder, at the boarding house breakfast table, before I set forth on my drudging round of collections. Nights I haunted the narrow segment of mid-town Manhattan that was the scene of the crime. I visited the café in the Metropole Hotel, notorious as a hang-out for gamblers, and such restaurants as the Garden and Churchill's, that had been patronized by men who were being rounded up as material witnesses.

I read in Swope's stories that some of these shady characters frequented the Lafayette Baths, and I spent part of a night in the place, hoping to hear some privy whispers concerning Rosenthal or Becker, but saw through the diaphanous fumes of the steamroom only a very fat man, a dress buyer from Kalamazoo, Michigan, who was trying to boil out a stubborn hang-over.

I had not seen Louis Wiley since he had consigned me to the classified ad department, and now I had lost faith. I was sure he had forgotten me. Sick with frustration, wondering if my destiny was forever to collect bills rather than write scintillating news stories, I quit the first named occupation a few weeks after the Rosenthal murder and managed to obtain a job as reporter on the *New York Press* at Park Row and Spruce Street. The *Press* had recently been purchased by Frank A. Munsey, who had made a success of Munsey's Magazine, a monthly. He was less successful with newspapers. He successively controlled half a dozen New York dailies, including such prestigious journals as the *Herald, Sun,* and *Tribune.* All either expired under his aegis or were merged with other newspapers.

Owing probably to the recent transfer of the property, the *Press* when I started there was in considerable disarray. The operation of the newsroom was clumsy; all thumbs. There was confusion about authority. There was shouting and ranting. It was a little like a scene from one of those popular newspaper dramas, *Gentlemen of the Press* or *Front Page.* Reporters were paid a minimal wage and eked out a livelihood on space rates. There were two or three notable newspapermen on the city staff and a number of cheap hands—eager aspirants like myself.

My own assignments were routine. I strove valiantly to keep alive in the welter and confusion of the newsroom. I hustled; I leaped obediently when shouted at by the city desk. I had had actually only a year and a half's experience as a paid newspaper reporter, and while my youthful vainglory would not permit the admission, I wasn't ready for the Big Time. The *New York Press* was too fast. I was one of the low men on the totem pole. I struggled on. One night early in October the city room rang with the cry, "Jack Zelig's been shot!"

There was mad scrambling and scurrying about. This was a couple of days before Charles Becker was to go on trial for the murder of Rosenthal. Zelig was a well known hood who, the district attorney wailed, was to be called as a witness for the prosecution. He wouldn't be called now. He had been rubbed out—shot dead as he was riding on a Second Avenue trolley car—in order, it was hinted, to silence the testimony he would give against Becker.

All hell broke loose in a city room that was already confusion worse confounded. I was screamed at to fetch from the morgue all the material on the Rosenthal murder, collate it, write a few paragraphs, not to be used as part of the story of the Zelig shooting, but to be used as reference notes by the re-write men who *were* writing it. In the morning the newspaper's headlines linked the Zelig murder with the Becker trial, and when I reported for work that afternoon, confident that I had made a small but competent contribution to the leading story of the day, I found a terse note on my hook—as did three other young members of the staff—telling me that I was through. I wired a Rochester friend who wired carfare home. Soon I was back on the *Democrat and Chronicle,* comfortable and happy in a familiar milieu.

The resentment I felt for Mr. Wiley while I was working as bill collector for the *New York Times* softened after I returned to Rochester, and although I never saw the *Times'* business manager again, twenty years after I left New York he wrote a flattering preface to the small volume of my newspaper columns the *Democrat and Chronicle* published under the column's title, "Seen and Heard."

My brief stay on the *New York Press* had not been entirely unavailing. The experience had given me new insights into the newspaper business. It had broadened my perspective and sharpened my nascent skills. I was a better reporter when I returned to the *Democrat and Chronicle.* One day about a year after I had rejoined the city staff, Mr. Adams asked me if I would like to write a column. It was a unique proposal. Newspapers at that time were not cluttered, as they are today, with the outpourings of syndicated savants who make categorical pronouncements on such varied subjects as the removal of surplus hair and the dangers of nuclear fall-out, and my column would be the only one offered to the newspaper's readers. Mr. Adams suggested that my paragraphs deal with homey and local matters, that I make no attempt at advocacy or prophecy. I began to write "Seen and Heard" as a supplement to my regular reportorial duties late in 1914. I wrote the last column under that title for the *Democrat and Chronicle* fifty-four years later.

The column did not, however, appear continuously over that long span of years. There were lapses—lenghty interregnums—caused by interruptions of my career on the *Democrat and Chronicle.* The "Guns of August" boomed in 1914, and the following year, convinced that the appalling holocaust that was scourging France, Belgium, and Italy must, because of the sheer intensity of its flame, soon burn itself out, and wanting, as a rising young journalist, a first hand view of the greatest war in history, I left the newspaper and sailed for Europe. It was a grim, gray, November crossing on the S.S. *St. Louis,* a tubby, antiquated little American liner, which, I believe without proof, was loaded to the Plimsoll mark with weapons and war materiel. We were at sea several days when the purser told me that in another hour we would pass close to the watery grave of the *Lusitania,* torpedoed six months before with a loss of two thousand souls. I wondered then about President Wilson's proclaimed neutrality and if the Germans were aware that it was more rhetorical than genuine; and if they were, wouldn't our dinky little vessel be fair game for their subs? But we reached Portsmouth without incident, and I went up to London on the boat train.

My European adventure continued until late January, when I returned to the States on the *Rotterdam,* a fine Holland-American liner, in casual association with a number of long-haired men and short-haired women, poets, artists, writers, musicians, and professional do-gooders, who had gone to Europe on Henry Ford's Peace Ship and had left it to travel home independently but at Mr. Ford's expense. I think among them was a dance group, neo-classical. They were dissidents, all; disgruntled, disillusioned, and bitter about their expansive patron.

The expedition had been an odyssey of fancy. Mr. Ford apparently believed that his vast new wealth made him omnipotent. He engaged a ship, outfitted it, peopled it with an odd assortment of peaceniks, and sent it across the seas to still the thunder of the great guns, to bring cessation to hand-to-hand fighting, and get the boys out of the trenches by Christmas. What he got for his pains were sneers, the ridicule of caricature, and the abuse of the ship's company. He rolled easily with the punches. He was on his way to becoming a billionaire as the assembly lines of his plants dropped off incalculable numbers of motor vehicles and machines that would be used to prosecute a war he had quixotically expected to end.

* * * * * * * * * *

During my several weeks stay in Europe I regularly mailed back to the *Democrat and Chronicle* dispatches which attempted to describe wartime life in London and later, when I crossed to France, represented my observations of that besieged and bleeding nation.

Nothing that I wrote was vital enough for front page display but I occasionally had an interesting experience and now and then encountered a newsworthy figure. In London I formed a brief friendship with Jack Johnson, the first black man to hold the world's heavyweight boxing championship. He was a fugitive with a white slave indictment against him. He had lost the championship to Jess Willard in Havana, Cuba, the preceding April under circumstances that were faintly suspect. Supposedly knocked out after many rounds of sparring, Johnson lay on the ring floor, hardly in a comatose state, since photographs showed him shading his eyes from the Havana sun with a gloved hand.

When I first met him he was the feature attraction—the headline act—in a variety theater in Hendon. He appeared first in a rather heavy-handed comedy sketch, then boxed a three-round exhibition with a Creole compatriot named Georgie Gunther. It was the last bit that the crowds came to see. Horribly out of condition for athletic exertions, with a great belt of loose midriff blubber, he still retained the skills that had made him in the opinion of many authorities the greatest of all heavyweights, and in the ring he was quick and graceful as a panther.

He was an amiable, gold-toothed giant who wore flashy clothes and drove a flashy motor car. He loved rich foods, the fleshpots, and crowd adulation. In the street he was always surrounded by a gaping throng. He was a curiosity, a small diversion for people who lived day to day in sorrow and fear. I became fairly well acquainted with Johnson and occasionally accompanied him in midnight rides around Hendon in his gaudy automobile. When our friendship advanced sufficiently to encourage confidences he told me a story which, when I wrote it many years later in "Seen and Heard," was picked up by various newspapers around the country.

More than five years before he appeared in London,

Johnson had defeated the white champion, James J. Jeffries, in Reno, Nevada. His victory, which was thought to have put a stigma on the white race, made him a hated figure in his native land and set off, like a string of firecrackers, a series of racial fracases across the country, in some of which men were killed.

The bitterness and vindictiveness excited by Johnson's physical supremacy—his ability to knock down with his fists any white man who confronted him in a prize ring—is difficult to understand today, when Mohammed Ali has become a folk hero and when black athletes dominate not only boxing but other sports in which they engage and star on teams even in the Deep South. But Johnson had achieved the "proud diadem of fistiani," as one flowery sports writer defined the world's title, at a time when apartheid was as prevalent in many parts of the United States as it is today in the Republic of South Africa, and the feeling was that he had to be whipped and driven into his kennel like the black cur that he was.

While he was still champion he was arrested for a violation of the Mann Act, which prohibits interstate transportation of women for immoral purposes (the indictment charged that he had taken a white woman across Lake Michigan), and he fled the country to escape arrest. What he told me in London was that he had been promised immunity if he "laid down" to Willard in Havana. He had done this, he said (he referred to the photographs showing him with a gloved hand shading his eyes from the sun after the supposed knock-out), and now learned that the promise had been fabricated; that the Mann Act indictment was still in force.

I have no proof of the validity of Johnson's story. But the fact is that he was arrested when he returned to the United States, tried, convicted, and sentenced to jail. There were other ambiguities in his career. Bill Raynor, my wife's half-brother, once beguiled me with a hairy tale of a bribe he avowed Johnson temporarily accepted to lose the fight with Jeffries and allow the world title to continue as a token of Caucasian supremacy. Raynor was married to the by-blow daughter of the notorious Tammany boss, Big Tim Sullivan, and went with Sullivan and John W. Considine, Sullivan's partner in a theatrical enterprise, to Reno. An astute gambler who reputedly controlled the gambling racket in New York City, Sullivan knew that Jeffries would have no chance if the fight was on the level. The champion had retired from the ring several years before, he had aged and softened in retirement and had been lured back to his brutal craft by a large guaranteed purse, win, lose or draw, and the clamor of a public who felt that he alone could silence the vociferous claims of the despised black man.

Raynor told me that Sullivan and Considine gave Johnson a large sum to lose, then bet a great deal of money on Jeffries, and were gulled by their own gullibility. Two hours before the fight, Billy Delaney, Johnson's trainer, entered Sullivan's hotel room, threw the bribe money on the bed, and announced, "The nigger's going to fight."

What happened in the ring wasn't a fight; it was a travesty. The woefully unconditioned champion was merely a foil for the challenger, who carried him fifteen rounds, perhaps to give the spectators a show for their money; then, seeming weary of the farce, dropped him for the count.

And Bill Raynor was sent out by Sullivan and Considine to sell off one of their theaters to obtain money to cover their wager.

* * * * * * * * * * *

I crossed the Channel in December 1915, and spent a few days at Christmastime at St. Valéry-en-Caux, a Channel town some distance below Dieppe, where Dr. Ralph R. Fitch, a prominent Rochester surgeon, and Mrs. Fitch, had established a hospital for French wounded.

It was a noble enterprise. The Fitches were deeply in sympathy with the French cause and largely at their own expense they had converted a resort hotel into a hospital. Dr. Fitch and his assistants were dealing mostly with patients who had suffered wounds that fell into the sphere of his own specialty, orthopedics. The hospital was staffed by volunteer workers the Fitches had recruited in the States and for the few days of my stay I filled in as chore man, bandage wrapper, and errand boy. A Christmas celebration was arranged by the hospital staff and it was good to see the zest and cheer with which the mangled little poilus, some with an arm shot off, some with a leg gone, some paraplegic, entered into the festivities.

I left St. Valéry-en-Caux shortly after the new year and went on to Paris. I was apprehensive about entering a great unfamiliar city where I could not speak the language and in which I knew not a living soul. I did have, however, a letter from the then Miss Maud Wilson of Rochester, commending me to a friend of hers, the wife of an American sculptor. I knew Miss Wilson through her father and brother, co-founders of Haloid, an obscure little back street firm which, many, many years later, under the inspirational leadership of Miss Wilson's nephew, Joseph C. Wilson, exploded into the miracle of Xerox.

I had intended upon my arrival in Paris to present Miss Wilson's letter to the sculptor's wife, but this purpose was delayed a few days because of the attention showered upon me by a chance acquaintance.

One gloomy winter's morning as I started across the pavement in the Place de la Concorde, a male voice called, "Oh, hello there," and a hand grasped my arm. I turned, and the man who had accosted me, seemingly abashed, apoligized. "Oh," he said, "I thought I knew you. I thought you were a fellow I met on the boat coming over. So sorry."

He had an ingratiating smile and an ingratiating voice. He was a large, soft, handsome man, very modishly dressed.

"You're the first American I've met since I've been here," I said.

He shook his head woefully. "The place is deserted. No one is in town. This damn war." He thrust out a hand. "I'm Herman Patrick Tappé."

I told him my name as we shook hands.

"Well, Henri," he said (I had been called many different things, but never "Henri" before), "you and I. We're a couple of lonely Americans. What do you say? Let's dine together tonight."

I agreed readily. I was going that day to attempt to obtain a newspaper story about Canadian soldiers, a newly arrived contingent of which was encamped on the grounds of the race course at St. Cloud, but I'd be back late in the afternoon. We fixed an hour to meet that evening, "at the Ritz," my friend suggested, since he was a guest at the hotel.

Herman Patrick Tappé I discovered, when, rather diffidently, I called at the Ritz, didn't have merely a room in the hotel, but a suite overlooking the court—a choice location, I was told. I was astonished at the interior. He must have come to Paris with a couple of trunks. He had replaced the hotel's decorations with personal knick-knacks, bibelots, and pictures of his own. There was a Persian prayer rug on the floor. There were long-stemmed roses in tall vases. The suite had the aspect of an elegantly appointed private home and its ornamentation was complemented by the attire of its occupant. He wore a gold-colored mandarin dressing gown embossed with a design of large odd-looking white birds. His feet were encased in scarlet slippers with great turned-up toes. Silken scarves were coiled loosely around his neck and a platinum slave bracelet encircled his left wrist. He looked like a rajah. He greeted me effusively; then sank among a clutch of over-stuffed pillows on a divan and fluttered his hands disconsolately.

"Henri, I so wanted to have a quiet dinner by ourselves this first day of our friendship," he lamented. "Now Monsieur———an expatriate Spaniard, who lives here, rang me up. He insists we dine with him. At Maxim's. He and Francine."

"Francine?" I asked.

"A very celebrated whore."

I am inherently a provincial small towner. Until I embarked on this European adventure I had never been more than six hundred miles from home. My few months in New York had broadened my perspective and enlarged my experience; it had hardly prepared me for Tappé and his friends.

Maxim's was quiet to what I suppose it had been in peace time. There was no music and no congestion of patrons. It struck me as the most plush public resort I had ever seen. On our brief passage from the Ritz to the café in the Rue Royale, I learned that my companion was a famous New York milliner who, even in these war years, felt the need to cross the sub-infested sea to study Paris styles in women's hats. I learned considerably more about him before the evening was over.

He apparently had high status at Maxim's. The maitre d' fussed over him as though he were royalty. We had preceded Francine and Monsieur———, who were delayed fifteen or twenty minutes. Tappé was more pleased than annoyed by their tardiness. He seemed to hope that they might not appear at all. He wanted us to be "cozy" together; "just the two of us." He was solicitous about my tastes in food, he wondered if I were pleased with the location of the table; he proposed escorting me next day to the Louvre, or "up the hill to Monmartre," where, he whisperingly hinted, he knew a couple of raunchy places that were exclusive, not for the tourist trade. He told me this was his twenty-fifth crossing of the Atlantic. He described his shop at 25 West 57th Street; reported that among his customers were ladies of the Whitney, the Astor, and the Vanderbilt families; that he made hats for Billie Burke, Irene Castle, and other prominent theatrical women; that he could create (design a woman's hat) only when a beautiful young boy in a velvet suit played soft music on a violin. He was urging me to leave the Grand Hotel to which, like so many other provincials on their first visit to Paris, I had been attracted (probably by the prefix "Grand") and move into his suite at the Ritz, free of cost, when Francine and the Monsieur entered the cafe.

The expatriate Spaniard was a tall, bony man with sallow skin, a desperado's moustache waxed to stilleto points, and sunken, world-weary eyes. He and his companion obviously had expected to meet Tappé alone and I am sure my presence was an irritant. The Spaniard gave me a quick handshake and a curt greeting. The woman was thin, very dark, and very elegantly attired. She had an enameled handsomeness, thin angry lips, and eyes that were as hard and green as the huge square cut emerald on one of her fingers. At Tappé's introduction she mumbled something in French and her hard green eyes looked at me, in my twenty-two-dollar store suit, as I imagine a duchess might look at a bug. After that I was dead removed from her consciousness: she neither spoke to me nor looked at me again. I, for my part, was fascinated by the trio:

Tappé, the male milliner; Monsieur———, about whose aspect there was something both mysterious and evil; and Francine, the celebrated whore. I felt as if I were initiated; that I had become a sophisticate.

And I was fascinated by the table talk. Francine and the Spaniard spoke English with some fluency, but with phonetic distortions that at times made it difficult for me to understand what they were saying. I derived, however, from what Francine said to Tappé, that she was eager to go to the United States, where she had never been, and that she very much wanted Tappé's sponsorship in New York.

All three dropped names with which I was familiar from reading the newspapers. Francine had been a friend of Mlle. Gaby Deslys, the "Gabrielle-of-the-Lilies," as she was known in the tiny Theater des Capucines, where she had gained her first fame. The Shubert brothers, scouting for talent in Europe, sought her for Broadway. I remember her quoted remark, "I weel go only for money. Vairy beeg money."

She was booed by Yale students when she appeared in a musical show that was tried out in New Haven. She was featured successively in the Winter Garden and the New York Hippodrome. I had thought her alluring; "quite a dish," as I remarked to Frank P. Bradley, a trick cyclist, years after her death. (So proud was she of her body that she refused to allow her abdomen to be defaced by a surgical knife, and died of a diseased appendix). "Poof," Mr. Bradley disparaged. "Poof. She was a creature of press agents. I was on the bill with her at both the Winter Garden and the Hippodrome. There were performers in those shows light years beyond her in talent."

In Maxim's I held excitedly on Francine's words as she told of parties which she and Gaby professedly had been on with Manuel, the kid king of Portugal, who, she said, had lost his head over "Gabrielle-of-the-Lilies," as, later, he lost his throne in a revolt that ended monarchial rule in Portugal. There was talk also of Harry Pilcer, Mlle. Deslys' professional dancing partner; of Harry Selfridge, who left Marshal Field in Chicago to organize in London Selfridge & Company, Ltd., the greatest department store in Europe, whom Francine and the Spaniard represented as an intimate of themselves and

Gaby. Other prominent names were batted across the table like shuttlecocks; it seemed a contest in who knew whom, and Tappé, upholding his end, named lady after lady from the New York Social Register whose hats he avowed he made.

When dinner ended presently Tappé escorted me in a cab to the Grand Hotel, protesting at my extravagance in living there when I might share his suite at the Ritz. His solicitude had become fawning, his persistence annoying. I agreed, however, to dine with him alone the next night; a third evening we went "up the hill to Monmartre" where we visited, among other places, the shabby gambling resort where Tod Sloan told me something of his beginnings as a race rider.

Tappé spent money lavishly, showily, on each of these occasions. I was never noted as a check-grabber, but I did not want to become a charity-ward; he wouldn't even permit me to tip a taxi driver. I had gone abroad with only a light topcoat to protect me from the rigors of a European winter and my companion insisted that I must have an overcoat, which he proposed to purchase. This was a little too much. We argued the issue, then quarreled, and I left him. The next day he phoned messages to my hotel and later wrote a note pleading for a reconciliation. I never saw him again but my curiosity about him continued for some time after I returned to the States and on more than one occasion, while visiting in New York, I purposely went up to West 57th Street to peep through the elaborately decorated windows of his shop in the hope of having a glimpse of the proprietor. For a time I made a practice of purchasing *Harper's Bazaar,* the women's magazine, in order to read Tappé's short essays on style trends of the haute monde which were displayed in the author's large and flowery script in the magazine's centerfold.

Breaking with Tappé, I called at the Left Bank studio of the American sculptor whose wife was a friend of Miss Maud Wilson. She had been advised by Miss Wilson to expect me and she greeted me cordially. Her husband was in Washington executing a commission for the United States government. She was a kindly lady whose name, unhappily, has long escaped my memory. I told her of my dinner with Tappé, Francine, and the Spaniard. She knew of all three, particularly

Francine. She said that Francine had been successively the mistress of an English lord and a French marquis; that she had lost her most recent "protector," a very wealthy young Frenchman, when he was shot down flying over the German lines.

"With this war, there are probably few juicy plums left for Francine in France," the sculptor's wife said. "I can understand her wanting to go to the States. And she's probably lost something of her pristine freshness. She's been a notorious figure for some time."

"And Monsieur———?" I asked.

"It's said that he acts as a sort of agent for her. I suppose, in a way, he's her procurer."

The sculptor's wife entertained me in the studio. She introduced me to a couple of elderly painters and an elderly minor poet. We went together to small cafés where the food was excellent and much cheaper than the food I had eaten in restaurants on the right bank of the Seine. I had read *Trilby* and I was imagining myself a member of the Latin quarter. My hostess showed me a side of Paris I would never have discovered alone.

But the stories I sent back to the *Democrat and Chronicle* from Paris were no more sensational than those I filed from London. They were little more than sketches of urban life and attempts to describe the Parisians' attitudes toward a war that was never very far from the city's gates. However, toward the end of my stay in Europe, through the good offices of two American newspaper correspondents who were accredited to the French army, I spent a few hours one day not far from the trenches in the Boulogne sector. The front was quiet. The only action was a desultory interchange of artillery fire, and while now and then I heard the burst of a German shell I was at considerable remove from the target.

I made a good deal of the experience in a newspaper piece and found, when I returned to Rochester, that many people were impressed with what I had written. I was looked upon as an expert on the war. This piqued my vanity and I am afraid prompted me to tell things that were more in the nature of fantasy than fact.

CHAPTER ELEVEN

In going to Europe as a civilian to learn first hand about a war in which, at the beginning I had never thought this country would become involved, I was premature. I might have waited and had a more comprehensive tour at the expense of the United States government. I was back in France in 1918, a private in the American army, if one of slight distinction. In retrospect it doesn't seem to me that I imperiled the enemy much more than my old Aunt Emma, tatting an antimacassar on the front stoop back home. I had not been taught to shoot a gun, and in any event I had no gun to shoot. I arrived in France with a medical unit from which I was soon detached and commanded to report to the office of the Army newspaper, the *Stars and Stripes,* in Paris.

There were several young men around the office of the *Stars and Stripes* who were destined to gain celebrity on the New York literary scene. One of these was Harold Ross, who was to become the founding editor of *The New Yorker.* Another was Alexander Woollcott, who each week contributed a full page to the magazine and later, as the Town Crier of radio, addressed an audience that exceeded by millions *The New Yorker's* select but limited readership. There were others. I never met any of these coming Wonder Boys. My tasks were menial. I was not in editorial, but in circulation. After several weeks in the office I was given a Model T Ford with a canvas top and detailed to join an element of the 36th Division, which was encamped not far from Chaumont, headquarters of the American Expeditionary Forces.

The 36th Division was composed of the Texas and Oklahoma National Guards and its members all seemed to be of Patagonian stature, raw-boned and hard-handed. I suspect that many of them had come from farms and cattle ranches. They looked like very competent soldiers and as they ambled along a company street or rode mules in the supply trains, they reminded me of figures in the paintings of Frederic Remington. They were friendly, unworldly, ingenuous young men. Since this was a time before the mad proliferation of the motor car, many of them had never been very far from their native prairie spreads or from such hometowns as Ardmore, Oklahoma, and Wichita Falls, Texas. I was loosely attached to regimental headquarters. The young lieutenant in command was different from most of his fellows. He was under-sized, gentle in manner, sedentary in habit, a lawyer by profession. I was amused by his odd deference. He never addressed me as "Private Clune," or "Private," or "Clune."

Not long after I joined it, the regiment was ordered to move forward to the battle lines, and as commands were ringing about and men were falling into formations, the lieutenant shyly approached me. "A-ah, do you suppose, *Mister* Clune, you'd have room in your car for my bed roll?"

I gave him an elaborate salute and a crisp response, "Yes sir, Lieutenant!" We put the bed roll under the canvas top; then, a moment before we were in actual movement, the lieutenant came to me again. "A-ah, *Mister* Clune. Do you suppose you'd have room on the seat for me?"

"Yes sir, Lieutenant!" I again gave him a very formal highball, he climbed up on the seat, and we were off.

I rode the lieutenant over every mile of our tour of duty and was well rewarded for my consideration. The *Stars and Stripes* allowed me a daily sum for rations, but the lieutenant permitted me to eat free of cost at headquarters mess and I never spent a penny of the money. The ration money I saved, added to my private's pay, gave me a monthly income equal to that of a second lieutenant's.

Joining the French Fourth Army, the 36th Division went

into action in the upper Champagne country early in October, 1918. Although its personnel had never before been under fire, the natural hardihood of these large and sturdy sons of the great southwest facilitated their adjustment to the violence and exigencies of the battlefield and they acquitted themselves gallantly. In collaboration with the French they broke the resistance of the enemy and presently drove him across the Aisne River.

This achievement came late in the month. As the division paused on the south side of the Aisne to catch its breath before resuming its pursuit of the scurrying Germans, it was replaced by other contingents of American arms and ordered to proceed south to a rest area. I went along in my Model T Ford, the lieutenant in the seat beside me. In a couple of days our regiments went into camp not far from the village of Triancourt; we were still there being re-equipped and waiting (rumor had it) to be committed to the Argonne offensive when Friday, 9 November, I received a telegram from Paris directing me to report at once to the office of the *Stars and Stripes*.

I drove that afternoon into Chalons-sur-Marne, where I would leave my car and proceed to Paris by train. There I encountered three young doughboys who flaunted before me that day's edition of the *Paris Herald*.

"Finis la guerre!" they shouted, and indicated a black line across the page that told that German emissaries had crossed American lines. They twirled in grotesque dance steps and waved the papers on high, "Finis la guerre!"

They had a bottle of wine, which they were swigging in turn, and already they had swigged quite a little of its contents. They gave me a newspaper and a hospitable chance at the neck of the bottle. The story under the front page banner line told that the German emissaries were to negotiate an armistice. It was the end, unquestionably. The very end! I took a second pull at the bottle and joined the celebration.

Chalons was a shambles after four years of battering by enemy guns and bombs from the air. But now, with the Germans in retreat, natives of the place, old men and women, and even children, some with packs on their backs, were poking through the rubble-cluttered streets in an attempt to discover some visage of their homes. And there was a restaurant where my friends proposed we have a victory feast.

The proprietor had found a tiny building, the broken walls of which still supported the remnant of a roof. He had lighted a brazier outside, and inside were two tables, chairs, a range to cook on, shiny pots and pans, and a wooden block on which to chop meat—but no meat. Fish he announced, greeting us with great geniality, was the pièce de résistance: carp. We had the fish and three bottles of wine. At the moment our feast seemed Lucullan. On the train I boarded after a rollicking farewell from my compatriots, I began to sense the wine we had drunk was not of notable vintage; the fish we had eaten was older than the wine. A queasy feeling had come on me which soon developed into the soldiers' endemic complaint, dysentary.

I arrived late Friday night in Paris. The city was shrouded and silent, the lights still dimmed. I stumbled my way to a small fleabag hotel in the Rue St. Lazare, which the army had expropriated for its personnel, and where I had lodged in my earlier stay in the city. I was assigned to a room with a cot and a bed roll. The cot was the prerogative of a technical sergeant, a much more important soldier than I, who fired a locomotive that ran to the railhead at Bar-le-Duc. The sergeant was on a short leave, and I was told that I might occupy the cot until he returned. I was ill. I lay on the cot for two days except when doubled-up on a watercloset, dosing myself with home remedies which, by Sunday night, when the sergeant returned, had pretty well cured my disorder. The sergeant claimed his cot, and that night I slept on the bed roll. Early Monday morning I was awakened by his nudging me in the ribs with the toe of his field boot.

"Get up," he said. "We're going out. The town's on the move. Things will soon be happening."

Our room was on the top floor of the hotel. Its single window overlooked the Paris chimney pots, half obscured in a gray mist; but day was breaking and thin streaks of purple stained the eastern sky. Below, when I looked down, I was aware of a massed movement in the street, indistinct in the faint light—almost spectral, except that from it rose a low scuffing sound of hundreds of feet.

The technical sergeant was already dressed. I didn't keep him waiting. In ten minutes we were in the street. There we separated, each to merge into a different segment of the pressing throng. There was some talk, which I had not heard from our top-floor window, low-key and, of course, in French. There were no shouts or manifestations of exultation. It was as if these people feared that an expression of their hopes would result in their hopes being shattered. We pushed south to the Boulevard Haussman, then into the Rue des Italiens, which, to me, had always been the Broadway and 42nd Street of Paris.

For two or three hours, as the street filled up and new crowds bore down on it and overflowed into adjacent avenues, as men, women and children continued to assemble until it appeared as if not a single person remained under a roof, there was no great noise. What had been tacitly promised, what was on the minds of everyone, seemed too good to be true. And yet, as the morning advanced, the feeling was stronger and stronger that it *was* true, that at some indeterminate hour of this day France's long travail and ravishment would end. There was an electric tension in the crowd that waited . . . waited . . . its excitement repressed almost to the point of agony until, at 11 o'clock on this morning of 11 November, the momentous news was flashed to the world. Peace! And dancing in the streets began, and cries and shouts of ecstacy, of unbelievable joy, rose on high; and perhaps there was nothing anywhere else in the world quite like the celebration in the streets of Paris.

My disorder returned the next day, more virulent than at the beginning. It persisted. Weak and enervated I worked on and off at the office of the *Stars and Stripes* for a time, then was committed to a hospital. When I recovered I did not return to Paris, but joined a minstrel show that played a circuit of hospitals and army camps in western France. I wore an ornamental costume of red pants and a red coat and a ruffled shirt with lace sleeves. I was the interlocutor. The show broke up in time and in the spring of 1919 I returned to the States in what I believe was a converted cattle boat. We sailed west through a sea so gentle that it seemed benignly in harmony with the peace that had come to the world which, now that the war to end all wars had been won, would continue eternally—or at least for the next twenty years. Discharged from the army at the port of debarkation, I was in Rochester the next day. Ten minutes after my arrival home on Linden Street, I shucked my uniform and never wore it again. Although my military career had hardly been heroic, I thought I needed a rest and a period to orient myself to civilian life. After half a week of this my father, always the pragmatist, asked, "Aren't you going back to work? It seems about time."

So I left home and caught on as a reporter for the *Free Press* in Detroit.

* * * * * * * * * *

Briefly, I enjoyed Detroit. The city had grown enormously in the 19 years since the turn of the century, more than tripling its population. I had visited it once as a teen-ager and remembered it as having something of the character of my native Rochester. The similarity was no longer marked. There were, to be sure, in various nooks and corners quiet, tree-shaded streets with dwellings not unlike the pleasant modest homes of the Linden Street where I had lived all my life. For the most part, however, the place was a bustling, hustling community with megalopolitan aspirations, the booming automotive center of the world.

I lived with Will Richards, my friend from the *Democrat and Chronicle,* who had moved with his widowed mother to Detroit shortly before the United States declared war on Germany. Mrs. Richards had left Detroit by the time I arrived there to pass the summer with friends in Rochester, and Will and I "bached" it in the Richards' attractive apartment on a street off Woodward Avenue. Our working hours were at variance. Richards, who had become the star man on the *Free Press,* reported to the city room in early afternoon and was through at mid-evening; I began my chores on the rewrite desk at 6:00 P.M. and finished well after midnight.

Since my afternoons were free I often visited the ball park where the prime attraction for me was Tyrus Raymond Cobb, the "Georgia Peach," then halfway through his twenty-four year career in the big leagues. He was an old story to Detroit fans; to me, who had never seen him before, his dazzling speed and daring on the base paths, his skill in the outfield, his power at the plate—the panache of the man—were a constant source of wonder and delight and, as I later wrote for *Life* magazine, I'd rather watch him spit on his glove than see the orthodox performances of almost any other player on the field.

A fiery and combative figure on the ball diamond, Cobb was often in rows with rival players and on more than one occasion invaded the stands to assault a heckling spectator. He stole thirty-eight bases the summer I watched him, far short of his single season record of ninety-eight; but whenever he essayed one of his extemporized dashes from base to base, the spectators were on their feet and the opposing athletes were as jittery as jumping beans on a hot griddle.

I recall an afternoon when he got a scratch hit in a game against the Cleveland Indians and started at once to taunt the Cleveland catcher, a stocky fellow with a German name. "Hey, krauthead, I'm going on you," Cobb cried, and his voice rang all over the ball park. "I'll beat your throw. I'm going to steal. S-t-e-a-l!" And sure enough, on the next pitch, which the batter ignored, he was off; the catcher, over-eager, made a poor throw, and Cobb hooked around second base in his famous fadeaway slide.

"Ah-aa-ah, I told you, krauthead," he chortled, brushing dirt from his flannels. "I'm going again. I'm going to steal. S-t-e-a-l!" It was showboat stuff. No one else but Cobb would have dared such insolent gasconading. He danced dangerously away from the bag, gesticulating wildly. The pitcher threw to second and brought him back in a head foremost dive. Then he threw a strike on the batter, but Cobb reneged on his threat to run. He touched the base, then pranced away from it. "I'm going, going, going!" he called, his challenge again resounding throughout the stadium. The tension was high. The spectators, out of their seats, were quivering on tiptoe.

The infielders were grim, worried and tight. The pitcher glanced nervously over his shoulder, then turned toward the plate. His windup was hurried, and with its first contortion, Cobb was running. The batter swung and missed, and this time the catcher, steadier than before, rifled the ball to third to beat Cobb's desperate bellywhopper by a split second, and the impertinent jackanapes was out.

He was always a show, the center ring attraction. Babe Ruth came into Detroit that summer with the Boston Red Sox; the stylish George Sisler, who the next year would hit better than .400, and three years later an astonishing .420, appeared with the St. Louis Browns. But Cobb was still the cynosure.

I met him for the first time through a young woman in Detroit, who, for the purpose of this narrative, I'll identify as Myra, which was not the name written on her baptismal certificate. Myra was a distant relative of my mother's and the only child of a well-known sporting man and restaurateur whom I knew as Cousin Fred, who had died some time before I started on the *Free Press*.

One day, returning from a sojourn on the East Coast, Myra stopped off in Rochester and passed the night under our roof. I liked her; she was a pleasant and personable young woman, but I had no romantic feeling about her, and besides, she had recently announced her engagement to a young man in Detroit. But at midnight the night she was our house guest, I was aroused in my chaste bed by a poke in the shoulder, and looking up I saw, in the fragile light cast into my room by a remote street lamp, Myra, stark naked. "I'm lonesome," she said, with a half sob, and cuddled into my bed. It was an unsettling experience. Myra had been assigned a room directly across the hall from the one occupied by my parents, and her tiptoed unclad progress along the hall to my chamber struck me as a very daring enterprise indeed. I warned her against talk, but she would talk; and when she presently left, her last remark did nothing to quiet my considerable alarms. "If I have a baby. If I do. . . ."

In the morning, when we met at the family breakfast table, there was nothing in Myra's manner that hinted at the episode of the night before, which now seemed as unreal as fantasy; and this impression was strengthened when she left that day for her home in Detroit without so much as a whispered word of endearment. The seething passion I might have prided myself I had aroused in an attractive young woman apparently was nothing of the sort; to Myra our midnight coupling had been merely a whim, a passing divertissement.

I had known that Myra knew Ty Cobb. If Cobb lacked the chiseled handsomeness of the orthodox matinee idol, his fame, his flamboyance, and his virility excited the adoration of many women, and he must have had a time of it fending them off. Perhaps Myra had once been enamored of the ball player, and perhaps Cobb had once shown her unseemly attentions, for Cousin Fred, before he died, zealously protective of his beloved daughter, had threatened to shoot him dead if he didn't "lay off."

In Detroit, when I settled there, I soon made contact with Myra. She was then married, unhappily, it turned out. We met occasionally, but our relations were purely platonic; no mention was ever made of our brief intimacy in Rochester. Whenever I did see her, Myra was kind and companionable and eager to help me become better acquainted with her native city. I told her of my admiration for Cobb as a ball player and one day when the Detroit club had no game scheduled, she proposed to show me the house where he lived, secretly hoping, I suspect, that we might also see the householder. It was mid-afternoon when we came to the house and Cobb was mowing the front lawn. I was surprised; it seemed a curious occupation for a figure of anthem status; infra dig. The great ball player greeted Myra warmly, bestowing upon her a wide and gracious smile. "Ty," she said, "you've got a new cap." He snatched it from his head. "Yeah," he said. "And d'you know what, Myra? I used to get these for seventy-five cents. Now, by God, they're a dollar!"

Cobb reputedly wound up with a couple of million dollars in an era before the propagation of sporting events by television induced the extravagant emoluments professional athletes receive today. He may have had high financial talents as well as athletic genius and he did have friends in the upper echelon of the Coca Cola Company in the early days of that booming industry. Or perhaps he appropriated the maxim of the ancient Greeks, that if you put a little on a little and do it often, the little will soon become big.

Like many other celebrated athletes I have met, whom their galleries idolize, Cobb seemed to me, when removed from the realm of his specialty, a person of no particular distinction; in a ball park I thought his performances Promethean, scarcely equalled, possibly never excelled.

* * * * * * * * * *

I never wanted to work steadily on the sports side of a newspaper, but occasionally I was assigned to do a sports story, and during an unconscionable long career in the newspaper business I chanced to see a great many sporting events and now and then told in my column "Seen and Heard" about some well-known athlete I had seen compete or with whom I had had personal relations.

Walter Hagen, the golfer, had moved from his native Rochester to Detroit a couple of years before I arrived there. Sometime after he won the National Open in 1914, Hagen was induced to quit the Country Club of Rochester, where he had learned his game and risen from caddy to club pro, to represent the Oakland Hills Country Club in Detroit.

I know almost nothing about golf (I never played a round in my life), but Hagen and his wife, Margaret, were friends of mine, and I occasionally visited them in a small house on the grounds of the Country Club of Rochester that had been put at their disposal at the time of their marriage. We called it Honeymoon Cottage, and it was sometimes the scene of revels, always arranged by Mrs Hagen, never by her husband.

Margaret Johnson Hagen was a lively, witty, stylishly dressed young woman, the daughter of the proprietor of a hotel in Rochester that had sheds out back in which farmers, coming into town with produce, who were the hotel's chief patrons, stabled their horses. Brought up in a hotel, where her meals had been prepared by the hotel's chef, Margaret had cultivated no culinary talents, and to make matters worse, Walter complained, she was a damn poor can opener.

She aspired to high life; she wanted to swing; to join what today would be known as the jet set. The time would come when Hagen's flamboyance, his imperiousness, and his command presence on a golf course would cause admiring sports writers to knight him—to dub him *Sir* Walter. In Rochester he was an abstemious and ingenuous young man, rather provincial in his attitude and tastes, who, leaving school in his early teens, had failed successively as a taxidermist and as an auto mechanic and hadn't done very well as a finisher in a piano factory. These were wintertime experiments. In the summer, although he dreamed of a career as a big league ball player, he was always on the Country Club links, and in the end decided that golf was his true metier.

Hagen was not married when he first won the National Open, which was played that year at Midlothian, outside of Chicago. In 1914 golfers were not rated on their money winnings. Walter received three hundred dollars for his victory, and returned to Rochester with little more panache than a factory hand punching a time clock in the morning. His vacation was over; he went back promptly to instructing club members in the niceties of a game in which he had won supreme honors. There was no dancing in the streets and streamers were not festooned between lamp-posts with huge stenciled letters Welcome Home Champ. The Country Club members were conservative souls; they liked their pro, they were pleased with his victory, but golf was a game with them, not a passion. Hagen had grown up around their course, he had been a caddy, a kid to fetch and carry ("Here, boy, take this brassie over to the pro shop") and overnight they couldn't canonize him merely because he had played a winning round in 292.

Walter seemed content to continue in Rochester as a teaching pro with leave now and then to play in a tournament. He accepted a role, which, in the early days of golf, was tantamount to that of a glorified servant, with equanimity. He had been born in farm country adjacent to Rochester, and it was Margaret Hagen's scornful dictum that while you could take the boy out of the country you couldn't take the country out of the boy. She taunted him; he had been champion of the nation. Why didn't he act the part? Live it up? She got him to wear fancy pants and fancy shirts and jackets. He himself got a gaudy automobile with a hood that seemed half the length of a city block and a motor the size of a shoe box. Margaret was a talented dancer (she and her brother had finished third in a dance contest sponsored by Irene and Vernon Castle when the Castles stopped in Rochester on a trans-continental tour), and she instructed Hagen in the art.

Often on Saturday night the Hagens and a party of friends danced to the strains of a lively orchestra in the Pompeian Room of Rochester's Hotel Seneca, and on one of these nights Walter telephoned the newspaper office where I was at work and asked me to join his party. He had something important to tell me. I hurried to the hotel, envisioning a news story. When I reached his table in the Pompeian Room, he said, "What d'you think? They want me to go to a new millionaires' club in Detroit."

I said, "Well you're going, aren't you?" "That's what I been asking him," Margaret interposed sharply. "The dope, he won't make up his mind."

Although Hagen and his wife were living rent free in a pleasant little house on the club grounds, Margaret had discovered that she was excluded from the social activities of the club. She was irked by this disbarment and taxed Walter for not doing something about it.

Responding to my question, Hagen said, "Gee, I don't know. I've always been around here. When I walk down Main Street, everyone knows me."

It was a naive answer. Detroit was a much larger city than Rochester. The new club, the Oakland Hills, wanted Hagen more as a playing representative than as an instructor. He would have a chance at all of the major tournaments. The financial rewards would be much greater than his salary and instruction fees in Rochester, where he was expected to teach not only golf, but, during the winter months, ice skating, at which he was no great shakes.

"You're a national figure now," I suggested. "You've won the American championship. You'll win it again. You're known to a lot of people beyond our Main Street."

"Well, I want to think it over," he said. "No hurry."

"We're going," Margaret said determinedly. But so far as I knew the matter was in abeyance for a week. Then, the next Saturday night, almost at the same hour he had telephoned me the week before, Walter phoned to urge me to come again to the Pompeian Room, where, when I arrived, he exultantly announced that he had accepted the Detroit offer, and I had a story for the newspaper.

In Detroit, Hagen experienced a metamorphosis. Any hay that had been in his hair in Rochester was brushed away; any aspect of the yokel that may have been in evidence disappeared. Almost at once he was invested in an aura of glamor, and the clothes he wore, as colorful as the spectrum; his unshatterable aplomb, on and off a golf course; his supreme confidence; the grace and power of his swing, and his seeming insouciance, even at moments of critical competition, created a dramatic excitement on golf courses similar to Babe Ruth's performances on a ball diamond.

Hagen emancipated the golf professional, even in England, where rigid class distinctions still prevailed. There the pro had little social status. Questing the British Open, a title no American had yet won, Walter entered that prestigious event in 1920, the year after he had won his second American Open. The championship was played at Deal. Denied clubhouse privileges, which amateur entrants were granted, Hagan glanced disdainfully into the tent where the professionals were expected to lunch, and repaired to a nearby fashionable inn for chicken livers en brochette and strawberries with Kentish cream. He returned to the tournament, finished fifty-fifth, and swaggered off the course as he had swaggered on it, and the British press had a field day. They piled derision on ridicule; wondered scornfully at the impertinence of an American champion, even *trying* for their sacred title. Hagen was as impervious to their invective as a cigar store Indian. "I'll be back," he promised; and two years later he achieved his first of four wins of the British Open.

I saw little of Hagen during the summer of 1919 that I lived in Detroit. After he won the American Open that year he resigned his lucrative post at Oakland Hills and was continually on the road playing tournaments and exhibition matches.

Mrs. Hagen did not accompany him on these travels. I met her occasionally in shopping marts and we'd lunch together. She had achieved at Oakland Hills a status that had been denied her at the Country Club of Rochester, but she was losing her hold on her husband. Walter had become the darling of golf courses, gushed over by fashionable women, a bon vivant who had far transcended the compass of Margaret's own high-life imaginings. "Walter goes away," she lamented, "and writes me pages and pages of golf. I want romance."

One afternoon I met her on Woodward Avenue and she invited me home to dinner.

"Walter's in town for a couple of days," she said. "He said he'd be home at six-thirty for dinner."

He didn't arrive until more than an hour later and brought with him a youth who had been caddying for him during the afternoon. His tardiness, which I thought Mrs. Hagen might have expected since he was notoriously unpunctual, and the introduction of an unexpected guest, aroused her wifely ire. She brought from the kitchen a couple of side dishes, and, as an entree, a ham that I must say looked a little the worse for wear.

"We got that old hacked ham again?" Walter remarked querulously.

"Shut up, you," Margaret answered testily. "I can remember, you had ham on the table, you thought it was your birthday."

Matters obviously were not well in the household. Some time later the marriage ties were severed and in time Walter essayed a second marital venture, this time with a divorcee. But marriage was definitely not his forte; he was as ill-suited for the restraints and ordinances of the conjugal state as a pirate. The second marriage was less durable than the first, and the story is that its dissolution began one night in a Florida hotel, when Walter, returning at a very unseemly hour, was discovered by the new Mrs. Hagen, as he hastily prepared for bed, to be without underwear.

"My God," Walter cried, when the deficiency was remarked by his outraged lady, clapping a hand sharply against his naked thigh, "I've been robbed!"

Walter Hagen was the gay caballero of the ancient and honorable Scottish pastime; a legend in his own time. His cavalier attitude toward a game he played with surpassing skill, but never seemed to take seriously; his extravagances, and the conjecture of fact and apocrypha regarding his dissipations; his impressive record of eleven national championships; the incident of his keeping the Prince of Wales waiting half an hour on the first tee, and his bravura performances on golf courses around the world fixed wide public attention on the game and helped to make golf the universally popular sport it has become.

* * * * * * * * * * *

The routine of the rewrite desk of the *Free Press* was not very exciting. I preferred to be outside, meeting people, doing general assignments as I had done at the *Democrat and Chronicle* before the war. The summer passed pleasantly enough, however. Richards and I contrived now and then to have the same day off and on these occasions we had fine times together. In the autumn Will's mother returned from her Rochester visit, and since the apartment was hardly suitable for three occupants, I engaged a dingy little cell in a rooming house.

I then began to long for my home city, and when the urge became insistent I wrote to Louis M. Antisdale, editor and publisher of the Rochester *Morning Herald,* who offered me a job by return mail. My only regret in leaving Detroit was the severance of my companionship with Richards. I would miss Will's chuckling good humor, his salty observations, his wit. I saw him only rarely after I returned to Rochester, but once, on his way to Europe, he stopped overnight at my family's house on Linden Street. I recall, on the occasion of that visit, his meeting with my father, whom he had never seen before. My father was a slim man of medium height, whose clothes, draped by the finest tailor in town, were ultra-conservative, as, indeed, was his punctilious deportment and much else about him. He diverted from this general pattern in one particular: he had a curious predilection for gaudy motor cars, and as Richards and I stood before dinner in the side yard of our home, my father tooled up the drive in a Cord, a big white underslung vehicle with pipes curling out from the side of the hood—super-chargers, I suspect—the raciest thing on the road. He stopped at my hail and got out.

"Jeez," Richards asked, wonderingly, "where's the blonde?"

CHAPTER TWELVE

Re-settled in my native city after an absence of more than a year and a half, I discerned, when I joined the city staff of the *Morning Herald,* a change in the attitudes and mores of my fellow townsmen.

Rochester prided itself on its orderliness: the "best governed city" was its boast. It was small enough to be manageable, and it had been managed for years with considerable expertness by a Republican boss who looked upon the community as his feudal fief. It was clannish, inbred, and self-complacent. The natives said Rochester was a conservative city. Some newcomers who attempted too quickly to penetrate its inner core and were repulsed by a carapace that seemed as stiff and bony as that of an eight-banded armadillo said "conservative" was a euphemism: the place was just damn smug.

A change came to Rochester with the close of World War I. With the tensions and edginess the war had created relaxed, the city experienced, as did other communities across the country, a new feeling of freedom. One result of this was a loosening of old restraints and reticences. Rochester did not throw off all of its traditional inhibitions; it did not go hog-wild. But it went a little wild. Many of the city's returning soldiers whose lives had been on the line, home safe, shot with luck rather than with German bullets, retained something of the eat-drink-and-be-merry-for-tomorrow-we-die spirit with which they had entered the service. They knew how cheap and brief life could be, so what the hell? The thing to do was live it up. And they did, in many instances. And veterans' get-togethers in the early post-war years often had an orgiastic character, with naked dancing girls and Corybantic revelry.

A craziness was in the air. The Era of Wonderful Nonsense, as it has been called, was in its inception. Ten years hence it would end with the crash of the stock market, which *Variety* hailed with the classic banner line:

WALL STREET LAYS AN EGG

The Eighteenth Amendment, which was supposed to prohibit the sale and consumption of intoxicating liquors, had not succeeded, and in Rochester as in other cities in the land, speakeasies were plying a flourishing illicit trade. Women, no longer restricted to the Ladies Sitting Room of the old-fashioned saloon, fronted the oaken strip, one foot on the brass rail, in peership with male patrons.

The younger generation had become a sort of cult with F. Scott Fitzgerald as its guru. The girls rolled their stockings at the knee, bobbed their hair, smoked cigarettes, and left their corsets in dance hall cloakrooms since the feel of whalebone stays had become repugnant to their male escorts. On joy rides they swigged from their boy friends' hip flasks. Fitzgerald had reported "petting" and "necking" in his earlier novels. There were indications that sex among youth had now transcended these trifles.

The *Morning Herald* was the liveliest newspaper in Rochester at this period, and it quite accurately reflected the spirit of the times. Its youthful staff were eager beavers who felt that they were "in" people, cognizant of what was going on, and it was true that the nature of our craft did provide us with a close view of the revolt that was taking place in manners and morals.

We knew the police and we knew the agents who were supposed to enforce the prohibition law, and did in some instances and didn't in others, depending often on the size of the bribe. We had easy access to speakeasies, which were being patronized by some of Rochester's most prominent and supposedly law-abiding citizens. Well known to us were the operations of a small, bold band of bootleggers who were spiriting whiskey in swift motor craft from the Canadian shore of Lake Ontario to obscure coves on the lake's southern perimeter.

Illicit gambling had become the concomitant of the illegal liquor traffic, and some of us patronized the resorts of such Runyonesque characters as Stack-Em-Up Joe, Black Barney, The Ox, Bearcat Beecher, Poker Lou, Danny New Yorker, and Potato Sacks. Reformers wailed to us that Rochester had become as wanton and wicked as Sodom and Gomorrah, but the mob had not moved in and there was no crime syndicate. And sixty years ago, contrary to the situation today, a man might walk alone in the dead of night in almost any section of Rochester without fear of being robbed, mugged, or murdered.

In the four years that I continued on the *Herald,* the assignments I worked on were often given to me by Mr. Antisdale. In 1920, for example, he sent me off with Governor James M. Cox, who was running for the presidency at a discreet distance behind Warren Gamaliel Harding, the Republican candidate.

Keen political observer that he was, I am sure Antisdale had no illusions about the governor's chances, but he was loyal to the Democratic party and he had me attached to the campaign entourage merely to attest to the *Herald*'s support of the aspirant. Cox was hardly a public idol, and on more than one occasion his managers needed to organize a claque to applaud and cheer and hip-hip-hurrah in order to gain attention when he detrained at some railway station.

Arriving in Rochester, Governor Cox thought it politic and politically astute, since the Nineteenth Amendment had recently been enacted, to visit the grave of the great suffragist, Susan B. Anthony.

The press delegation, which included a gamin-like little man with a Thoid Avee-noo accent who wore a disreputable fedora, shabby clothes, and carried a motion picture camera, followed the candidate to Mt. Hope Cemetery. There the governor, in doleful pantomime, removed his hat, bowed his head, and with a compassionate gesture laid a floral wreath on the Anthony headstone. He then turned with a sad shaking of his head and pronounced a low-voiced tribute, "A wonderful woman. A wonderfully courageous crusader."

He had started back to his limousine, when the gamin-like little man called sharply, "Hey, Guf'ner. My goddamn invention here got screwed up. Mind doing that again?".

The governor frowned with annoyance, but obeyed. He reclaimed the wreath, stepped back from the grave, paused a moment to resume the mournful countenance he had worn before, removed his hat, bowed his head, and with the same compassionate gesture replaced the wreath on the headstone; then repeated his previous tribute to the departed Miss Anthony.

"Thanks, Guf'ner," said the cameraman, and we all returned to the cars that had brought us to the cemetery.

* * * * * * * * * * *

Before George Brooks came to the *Herald* and he and I formed a friendship that continued until Brooks' death, my closest associate on the newspaper was a young man named Glenny Harris.

Harris had an engaging personality that won him friends and inspired confidences, and this I suppose is an attribute for a newspaperman; beyond that he had no talents to recommend him as a reporter. How he remained for two years on the *Herald*'s payroll was a mystery to me. I suspect though that he had ingratiated himself into the city editor's favor at a time when the staff was undermanned. The city editor, liking Glenny and beguiled by his charm and his Rabelaisian escapades, hadn't the heart to fire him.

The son of a prosperous small-town business man, Glenny had been educated in a fashionable preparatory school where he had been indoctrinated in the theory that "manners maketh the man," and drunk or sober I never heard him utter an improper word or display anything except the most punctilious deportment. He was tall, well-built, beautifully groomed and carefully dressed, with a red, fleshy, well-constructed face, and large brown, incongruously innocent eyes that protruded so far from their sockets that they might have been knocked off with a stick.

Glenny had a wife but he lived apart from her in an apartment in the heart of Rochester's downtown. I am sure he considered his connubial covenant a great error. He had an insatiable curiosity about women, and in affairs of the heart he was as loose-gaited as a jackrabbit. His apartment was only a short distance from the Hotel Seneca, the largest and most popular hostelry in town, and Glenny spent a good deal of his free time and time that he wangled from the *Herald,* around the hotel, which he seemed to consider a playhouse, or rumpus room. He was on familiar terms with room clerks, waiters, telephone operators, bellmen, and, particularly, with Bill Moffitt, the house detective.

Moffitt wanted a rigorous standard of morality maintained by the Seneca's guests and he was alert to discover and stamp out promiscuity among them. With Glenny Harris he was oddly placable and yielding.

The Lyceum, the city's grand old legitimate theater, stood next door to the Seneca Hotel, and the mimes and minstrels who performed in the theater usually put up at the Seneca. Harris was fascinated by theatrical people, and some of them seemed bemused by his charm. Now and then, when a musical comedy played the Lyceum, he would be seen dining with and beauing about one of the chorus girls, and on these occasions his blandishments were often sufficient to win him joint occupancy of the lady's room, for which, of course, the lady paid the rent during the three-day or week-long stand of the show. Moffitt always knew about these nocturnal divertissements, which he seemed to accept, in Glenny's case, as nothing more than amiable human weakness; he required only that they be confined to the nighttime hours the hotel employed him to sleuth about its corridors and recesses.

At the break of dawn, Moffitt would rap gently on the door of the room in which Harris was the joint occupant. "It's Bill," he'd whisper at the keyhole. "I'm going off now. Better get up and get out, Glenny."

In a much less conciliatory mood, he rapped loudly one early morning on the door of John Charles Thomas, the handsome, adored musical comedy and concert tenor, who was in Rochester for a concert engagement.

"We know you got a dame in there," Bill snarled. "We heard you call her up at the Hayward across the street and ask her over. I want her out of there. I want the both of you out of there. Open the door."

The door did open wide enough to allow Thomas to crack a whiskey bottle over the head of the importunate snooper, then close with a bang. It was not opened again until the police came to charge the singer with battery and assault. I was in police court later in the morning when he was arraigned. The incident made headlines but my recollection is that the charge was dropped, and Thomas hurried out of town after leaving a substantial recompense for the sore-headed house dick.

CHAPTER THIRTEEN

The theater and its people have always interested me, and while working for the *Herald* it was frequently my reportorial duty to interview some entertainer who was performing in Rochester. Occasionally a pleasant personal relationship evolved from these professional meetings. This was not, however, the case when I was sent to interview Ethel Barrymore, who was starring in *Déclassé* at the Lyceum.

At the great age I have now attained I am pretty much devoid of awe; sixty years ago, Miss Barrymore struck me as a creature of extra-dimensional quality; a goddess from the empyreal blue. I had seen her in several of her important roles, and it seemed to me that if she did no more than walk across a stage or read from the telephone directory, to observe the imperious elegance of her movements or to be charmed by her throaty, insinuating voice, would be worth the price of admission to any theater in which she appeared.

My talk with her was hampered by the sense of an overwhelming presence. I was more like a votary at a shrine than a newspaper interviewer. I finished, stuttering a "Thank you." I was about to leave the No.I dressing room, neither commodious nor luxurious, but one that Will Corris, the old showman who managed the Lyceum, had tidied up and ornamented for his adored leading lady, when Miss Barrymore spoke: "Young man, is there any *safe* whiskey to be had around here?"

Ward Vaughan had a place no more than a five-minute

walk from the Lyceum and I knew Ward's whiskey would be authentic. He had the best speakeasy in downtown Rochester and served, besides honest bottle goods, excellent food. And for all the mugs he ran with running whiskey across the lake from Canada, he was a man of gallantry and manners, noted among his raffish confreres for the mildness of his most violent expletive, "Jimminy Whittikers!" I envisaged myself arming this great personage up the darkened stairs of the back street building to Vaughan's second-floor hideaway and being admitted after the usual peek-a-boo through a sliding panel of the door. "Ladies and gentlemen—*Miss Ethel Barrymore!*"

What a triumph! What status I would attain!

My timorous proposal was rejected with a gesture of her eloquent hands and a protest in her *Alice-Sit-by-the-Fire* voice.

"Oh, no, no. I must have it here. I am not leaving."

I bowed, said I'd try and went next door to the Hotel Seneca. Crossing the lobby I encountered Glenny Harris.

Glenny was excited to learn that I had been with Miss Barrymore. I told him of the request she had made wanting whiskey. *Safe* whiskey!

"Ah, she's royalty," said Glenny. "The greatest lady of the theater. She's given a royal command." Glenny had read Shelley and Byron and Sir Walter Scott. " 'O, young Lochinvar is come out of the West,' " he recited with a little flourish. "We'll fulfill the mission. We'll go see Eddie McDermott."

Eddie McDermott was a Hotel Seneca bellman. He was a friend of Harris's and a source of liquid supply. We found him in a poolroom across the street. He would need fifteen minutes, he said, to procure four bottles of imported whiskey, and he was as good as his word. The bottles were handed to us in a battered satchel. I could have carried the satchel alone, but Glenny insisted that we deliver the token together.

Miss Barrymore was grateful. Glenny made a little speech. He told her that all his life he had worshipped her art and her person. He named several of her plays that he said he had seen. She listened with some attention and appeared to have forgotten my presence. When we left, it was Glenny's hand into which she pressed bills for payment for the liquor, which he protested, not too vigorously, that he did not want.

In the alley onto which the stage door opened, he said solemnly, "You know, meeting that wonderful woman has changed my life. I feel as if I have undergone an ablution; been purged." Glenny was often an apologist. I had heard him on other occasions lament his transgressions and resolve to renounce his wanton ways. "When I meet a woman of such nobility, I am ashamed. Ashamed of my sleazy little . . . liasons. My promiscuous ruttings." He shuddered and ran a hand over his eyes. "Believe me, I'm doing differently from now on."

He straightened his shoulders, marched out of the alley with a resolute tread, and went across the street to the poolroom to pay off Eddie McDermott.

Déclassé played three nights and a matinee at the Lyceum. I learned from Will Corris that Miss Barrymore spent most of her time in Rochester in the theater, a recluse in the No.I dressing room. She seemed morose and would see no one after my interview and the whiskey delivery Harris and I made.

Several years later, I had breakfast one morning in the Hotel Seneca with Lionel Barrymore, who had recently completed the motion picture, *Rasputin and the Empress,* in which Ethel and John Barrymore also appeared. I told him that I had interviewed his sister during the Rochester engagement of *Déclassé,* and without mentioning the whiskey Harris and I had taken her, remarked her strange behavior: how she had cloistered herself for hours in the shabby little dressing room of the theater, shut off from everyone.

"Yes, I understand," he said. "Her marriage to Russell Colt was breaking up at the time and she was very despondent. Was she drinking?"

"Oh, I don't know," I said. "I was only with her briefly."

* * * * * * * * * * *

I was a reasonably temperate young man, and I had none of Glenny Harris's sybaritic tendencies, but during the two years that he remained on the *Herald* we were often together during our off hours. Harris's extravagances not infrequently put him "out of trump," his own idiom for insolvency, and on these occasions I sometimes helped him entertain friends (usually lady friends) at dinner or late supper in the Hotel Seneca. He knew a number of theatrical people, one of whom was Frank (Fay) Darling, a native of the village of Lyons, thirty-odd miles northeast of Rochester.

I had met Darling through Harris. He had been for a long time musical director for Florenz Ziegfeld, the noted glorifier of American beauty. When I knew him he was back in his native village, let out because, as Ziegfeld once explained to me, "Darling began to think he was bigger than Ziegfeld."

Dismissed from the *Follies,* Darling resumed conjugal relations with a wife from whom he had been estranged for some time and the pair settled in a house in Lyons, in the cellar of which Mrs. Darling conducted a cursory traffic in illicit beverages.

I occasionally visited the Darlings and once took with me a graduate student from Oxford University who was curious about rural life in New York. I suggested that he might be interested in the transition of a Broadway character to the rustic life of a western New York village, and he agreed.

My companion was a small, frail, intellectual young man with a quiet manner and a soft voice. Introduced to the Darlings, he said very little, but I could see that he was keenly interested in Fay Darling. He was a picturesque figure with a bag full of anecdotes that concerned his Broadway career. If approached subtly, he could sometimes be persuaded to play the upright piano in the parlor, and he did so this day. It seemed to me that never before had I heard popular music rendered with such spirit, such bravura. Darling wore on his left wrist a heavy silver bracelet inscribed to him by Anna Held, Flo Ziegfeld's former wife and one-time star; and as he lunged at the piano with his body and his hands made great sweeps and parabolas, the heavy bracelet struck the keys and gave off grace notes that seemed extremely fitting.

In time we descended to the cellar bistro, where Mrs. Darling set out glasses and poured each a potion of what was represented as whiskey. I had been favored with this hospitality before and I was extremely chary. The stuff smelled (I tasted it tentatively, and surreptitiously poured it into a cuspidor) like radiator fluid. My companion, whose name was Struthers, to my concern, drank off three glasses of the amber liquid before he could be persuaded to mount the cellar stairs, a performance that required some assistance. In this ascent, his mild and gentle ways suffered an alteration. He became bristling and belligerent. A large police dog lay near the path as we left the house. Struthers, without provocation, kicked the animal hard in the snoot. "Sonofabitch!" he snarled.

I got him into the car, but we had scarcely left the limits of Lyons before he needed to get out. I waited several minutes while he writhed torturously in the grass at the side of the road and orally discharged the vicious liquid he had swallowed in the Darling cellar. He was better after his vomiting, his normal nature quite completely restored. We continued without incident into Rochester, and he thanked me warmly for what he said had been the most interesting day of his tour.

* * * * * * * * * * *

There was a good deal of theater in Rochester in the 1920's, with six and sometimes seven houses playing flesh shows. Across the street from the Lyceum was the Temple Theater, the home of big time vaudeville. The Temple had opened under the management of Mickey Finn, a small, slow-moving, low-voiced showman, who continued as manager for a number of years. Finn was a former newspaperman out of Detroit, but he had no sentimental feeling about his former craft and he had nothing to do with local journalists except those assigned to review his opening bill on Monday afternoon. His friends were downtown businessmen with whom he played cards at the Rochester Club. He ran what was called a "tight ship" and was notoriously stingy with passes.

Finn saw no glamor in show business; his only interest was the box office gross. The performers on stage seemed anathema to him, and his relations with them were confined to mere managerial requirements. He despised headline acts, necessary though they were. They cost more money than he liked to pay and the feature players often gave him a hard time with their absurd complaints and outrageous demands.

Women in the number one spot on his bill were usually more difficult than men; and when a woman performer began to display temperament (Mickey called it "temper") he kept away from backstage. The business of attempting to meet the headliner's demands and conciliate her grievances devolved then on Bert Caley, the theater's experienced stage manager.

The Temple had an arrangement with J. H. Moore, who had a vaudeville theater in Detroit, to accept each Monday the acts that had played the Detroit house the previous week, and one week the glamorous Fritzie Scheff came from Detroit to headline the Temple bill.

For a wage that Finn thought horrendous she had condescended to do a brief stint in variety theaters whose audiences she enchanted with "Kiss Me Again" and other numbers that had made her the most scintillating star in light opera. She was the pet of the carriage trade, queenly in aspect and imperious in manner. During her stand at the Temple, Bert Caley was ill with flu, and Mickey Finn had to suffer a week-long litany of the lady's discontents and importunities. She wanted this and she wanted that; she complained of disorders in the backstage alley and reminded Finn that Lillie Langtry had sometimes insisted that tanbark be laid on the pavement in front of the theater to soften street noises during her performances. She disparaged the hotel accommodations, the food in the restaurants, and protested the badness of the pit orchestra. It was a week of torment for Finn. And on Saturday night, after all the trouble she had given him, he had to give her a whopping big check. She studied the figures and saw that they were correct.

"You may now kiss my hand," she condescended.

Mickey, never quick on the uptake, waited a moment before he took the tips of the beautifully manicured fingers.

"Well," he said, "might's well kiss you hand. I been kissing your ass all week," and he bent and touched his lips in homage.

* * * * * * * * * * *

One Saturday night, following the last Rochester performance of the musical comedy, *The Midnight Whirl,* Glenny

Harris and I and a couple of bit players from the company were having supper in the Hotel Seneca when Richard Carle, the comedian who was co-starred with Blanche Ring, poked his head through the portieres of the Pompeian Room and beckoned to me.

I knew Carle from other Rochester appearances and thought him the funniest man on the stage. I left the table and joined him in the lobby.

He seemed distraught. "My wife's got a horrible cold," he said, and he wrung his hands dramatically. "God knows, it may be pneumonia. She needs a Whiskey Sling. Know where I can get some whiskey?"

It was not quite midnight. I looked around the lobby. Eddie McDermott, the bellman whose extra-curricular activity was selling bottled goods to hotel guests, was still on duty. I told Carle that McDermott might be helpful and I introduced him to the bellman and returned to my table.

The show moved the next day to Buffalo for a week's stand in the Erlanger, and that week I suffered an injury to my right hand that required a cast. I was unable to use a typewriter, and though I probably could have been of some use in the *Herald* office, I chose to malinger a few days and join my friends of *The Midnight Whirl* in Buffalo, and at the close of that engagement I went on with the company to Detroit.

Neither the Richard Carles nor Miss Ring traveled in the troupe car, but the company manager was aboard and he came to me with an angry inquiry.

"You know where Dick Carle got that whiskey in Rochester?"

"Wh-why, from a bellboy in the hotel, I think," I hedged, not wanting to admit my complicity. "He said his wife was very sick with a cold and needed a Whiskey Sling."

"Whiskey Sling, hell," the manager scoffed bitterly. "Goddamnit, don't you know? That pair are the greatest four-handed drinkers on the North American continent. Carle must have got a barrel of the stuff. He's been stiff as a board ever since we left Rochester."

And Monday night he almost recanted the showman's legend that "the show must go on." With a good house for the opening of *The Midnight Whirl,* he was late getting to the theater, the curtain was held almost half an hour, and Miss Ring angrily announced that contract or no, if Carle repeated his dereliction she'd leave the company and quit the tour.

Arriving in Detroit, I telephoned my old friend, Will Richards of the *Free Press.* We saw the show together and later went up to Carle's room on the eleventh floor of the Hotel Statler.

Carle was nurturing a better than week-long jag, but his old pro skills and his trouper's instincts had made it possible for him to give a creditable performance once the curtain rose and the music struck. I doubt if anyone in the audience was aware of his condition. Richards thought there might be a story in the comedian, but when we were admitted to his room it was difficult to get him to talk sense. He was good natured, laughing continually, but what he uttered was mostly gibberish. He had sent for a friend of his, Eddie Le Wroth, a comic who was playing in a local burlesque house. A sober little fellow, Le Wroth was remonstrating with Carle about his drinking, but Carle laughed and waved off his strictures.

A glass in hand, he sat in a chair near a partly-open window, for the night was mild. He was stripped down to his BVD's. He was painfully thin, and his long legs and arms had the narrowness and clay-like texture of the stem of a churchwarden. His thin, high-bridged nose was pinched at the tip by a pair of gold-rimmed pince-nez from which, ludicrously, depended a long black ribbon. He was a caricature. He spoke in a high nasal twang that always sounded as if he had a head cold. He was comic in every aspect.

"Why Eddie," he said, replying to Le Wroth's admonitions, "isha short life. Lesh make it a merry one. Eat drink—" he reached for a White Rock bottle on the floor next to his chair, poured the remaining contents of the bottle into his glass, which was half-filled with whiskey, and with a dismissing gesture tossed the empty bottle out the window.

"My God, Dick," Le Wroth cried, "you want to kill somebody?"

"Never has yet." Carle grinned fatuously. "Some's I'd like to, though."

Le Wroth flung the window full up and peered down to the street. There were passersby on the sidewalk, but apparently no one had been struck by the bottle.

Richards and I were shocked speechless. Le Wroth paced the room, excoriating his drunken friend. Carle remained in the chair, grinning and drinking from the glass.

Very quickly came a sharp rapping on the door. "Open up!" an angry voice in the corridor demanded.

As Richards, who was nearest the door, reached for the doorknob in reluctant obedience, Carle put down his glass. His fatuous grin replaced by a countenance of fear, he rose suddenly, staggered in bare feet across the room, climbed into bed and pulled the covers completely over his head, like a child in a thunder storm.

The bulky man who entered was a hotel detective. He glowered at Richards, at Le Wroth, and at me. "Who threw that bottle?" he demanded belligerently.

We shifted our feet and glanced furtively at one another.

"Who done it, I ask you?" the bulky man demanded again.

There was a stirring in the bed. Carle threw off the covers. He stood on his bare, pipestem legs, poised as if to orient himself; then, his skinny body bent low in homage, the pince-nez, with its flowing black ribbon still dangling from the tip of his nose, he weaved across the room, peered up from his bent position at the angry intruder, and extended a hand.

"Does you mind," he petitioned in his high-pitched nasal voice, "meeting me?"

I had seen Carle in *The Spring Chicken, Mary's Lamb, The Midnight Whirl,* and perhaps a couple of other shows, but I had never seen him in a comedy bit as funny as this one.

The detective took his hand and burst into a side-splitting roar, and the rest of us were similarly convulsed.

The tension was relaxed.

Le Wroth offered the detective a drink, an act that Carle observed with a look of stern disapproval. "No, no," he cried, hands raised in protest, "donja try to tempt me, Eddie. The pledge!"

Richards and I left shortly afterwards, and I went home the next day to boast that I had been on tour with a road show.

CHAPTER FOURTEEN

John Itta was an intimate of mine during the years that he served as maitre d' at the Hotel Seneca and also during the short period that he operated an elaborate but ill-fated restaurant which he called the Club Itta in a building formerly occupied by Rochester's leading social club, the Genesee Valley.

He was a dark, spare little man with a quiet manner and a soft voice, whose flat waiter's feet, invariably shod in sharp-pointed, highly-polished black shoes made an exact clock pattern of ten-minutes-to-two. The Seneca in his time was *the* hotel of the town, the place, in today's idiom, where the action was; and John was often part of the action. He was better known than anyone associated with the hostelry, including the manager. He was the personage of the Seneca. "Where's Johnny?" traveling men asked the minute they signed the register. He knew many prominent theatrical people. He was the pet of local patrons, who lunched or dined in the beautiful oak-paneled restaurant in the front of the hotel or danced at night in the adjoining Pompeian Room. If there was a large party, its sponsors wanted Itta to give it his personal attention. He was deputized to supervise the preparation and serving of comestibles at weddings, anniversaries, bar mitzvahs, and other celebrations. He was a party giver himself; he delighted on occasions to entertain a small group of friends, after hours, with exotic foods that were not on the hotel menu and spirits that he boasted came direct from foreign distilleries.

Itta was something of a tufthunter. As he said himself, he liked when name people were in the hotel "to be among those present." He was an ardent baseball fan. Early in Babe Ruth's career with the New York Yankees, Ruth and a small contingent of big league players visited Rochester on a post-season exhibition tour. The barnstormers displayed their skills in the International League park in the afternoon and put up that night in the Seneca. Ruth's first wife, a tiny woman whose head scarcely reached to her husband's chest, was on the tour, but very little in evidence; she was cached away in a suite in the upper reaches of the hotel.

With Ruth's arrival, John Itta was at once bustling in preparation for a party to honor the great power hitter, who was beginning to display the mischievous humors that later caused the Yankee management to drop his name for a time from the line-up. The party was held in the main dining room, and besides such athletes as Carl Mays, a Yankee teammate of Ruth's, Jeff Tesreau, formerly of the New York Giants, and a couple of lesser known big leaguers, Itta had invited three or four local friends, of whom I was one. It was a lively affair from the start, with prodigal offerings of food and liquid refreshment. It went on and on. Ruth was a robust dinner guest. He bubbled and roared in good-natured frolic, and now and then landed a playful blow that had the jarring effect of a wrecking ball on the shoulders of one of the other guests. His table deportment was less than Chesterfieldian. Sometime after midnight, in the general hubbub, we missed him. John was alarmed. "Where's Ruth? Where's the Babe?" he asked concernedly.

One of the local guests suggested that perhaps he'd joined his wife in their suite, which brought a laugh from one of the ball players.

"You don't know the Babe," he said. "He ain't that domestic."

A search was instituted, but the huge torsoed figure, with the debutante ankles was not to be found in any of the hotel's public rooms, nor in a couple of neighboring resorts that were investigated. We hesitated to signal a public alarm, but worry had supplanted our gay and festive spirits and the fun had gone out of our gathering. At two o'clock I started home, leaving the others in morose apprehension, and had scarcely reached the street when I saw Ruth hulking along the sidewalk toward the hotel entrance. He was a touseled figure. He had lost the tan cap that he usually wore canted at one side of his head, and I could see in the gleam of the street lamps, his polo coat was torn and mud-stained.

"Where in the world have you been?" I cried. "The rest of 'em are crazy worrying. They're still at the table. I'll go back with you."

Ruth shook his head determinedly. "Jesus, no. I gotta get upstairs. The old lady's going to bust the shit out of me."

It seemed an incongruous threat since I had seen the "old lady" and remarked her miniscule stature. But he went straight across the hotel lobby without pause and ascended in the elevator to his upper floor suite.

We learned later what had happened.

Someone had told Ruth about a resort called Cleo's, long indulged by the ruling burghers of the small city of Geneva on the theory that it provided a safety valve for the young of heart as well as for middle-aged romantics, and the Babe had sneaked away from our party, hired a cab and set out to investigate.

It was a run to the southeast of little better than forty miles, but the Babe never reached his goal. Somewhere along the way he persuaded the taximan to permit him to take the wheel; his piloting was erratic, the cab went off the pavement, and the home run champion landed in a roadside ditch.

Fortunately he suffered no more than the loss of his cap, a torn polo coat, and a charley horse. Had he mysteriously disappeared or been involved in some dire mishap, the news of either of these contingencies would have been heralded as a national calamity, for although Ruth had not yet reached the summit of his mighty powers, he was baseball's most glittering showpiece and one of the most conspicuous figures on the American scene.

* * * * * * * * * * *

Until we lost the honored guest, John Itta's party for Babe Ruth had been a lively and interesting occasion, but it had, for me, a worrying aftermath.

During the day the visiting ballplayers were in town, I spent some time prior to the party in the hotel with Jeff Tesreau, whom I had met in New York when he was pitching for the New York Giants. Our meeting in New York had been brief, and I doubt if he remembered it, but he made the polite gesture of saying that he did. In Rochester he and I hit it off very well. I liked Tesreau. He was a large rugged countryman from the back hills of Missouri, whose big city experience had veneered only lightly his native ingenuousness. His seven-year career with the New York Giants was distinguished the first year by a no-hitter; the following season he pitched twenty-six winning games; he figured in three World Series and retired with an over-all Earned Run Average of 3.26.

Recently finished as a big league player, Tesreau wanted very much to participate in the managerial side of baseball, and he told me that a wealthy New York sporting man had once promised to buy the Rochester baseball club, a member of the International League, and give him part ownership and the post of general manager.

"What happened?" I asked.

He shook his head sorrowfully.

"It was A.R. was going to buy the club."

"A.R.?"

"Arnold Rothstein."

"Oh, the gambler? Who fixed the World Series?"

"They *say* he fixed the World Series. I don't know. But now they wouldn't let him touch a ball club with the tip of his umbrella."

Of course everyone in America knew how a number of great but cheaply paid players of the Chicago White Sox (later denigrated the Black Sox) had been bribed to lose to Cincinnati in the 1919 Series. It was vastly more than a sports-event scandal; it was an obscene desecration of an institution guilelessly considered by the public so virginal and immaculate that it was apotheosized only a few cuts below reverence for motherhood and veneration of God. And the demonic catalysis of all this was generally believed to be "A.R.," as Arnold Rothstein was known to his associates in the vicious underworld practices upon which he battened. How in the world, I wondered, had this decent, rather naive countryman become intimate with a man who had been publicly denounced as "the most viperous person ever to infest New York?"

"How'd you know Rothstein?" I asked.

"Why, he's a pal of the boss. Charlie Stoneham, who owns the Giants."

Rothstein had been associated with Stoneham in the operation of bucketshops, and the two men had had cooperative interests in a gambling casino in Havana, Cuba. They were, as Tesreau said, pals; the owner of the baseball club and a man who had trafficked in stolen bonds, illegal whiskey, hard drugs; who played, when he could, with marked cards and loaded dice, a welcher; an abysmally low man, the king of the underworld.

It seemed as if baseball had a double standard. The meanly paid ballplayers (world beaters whose yearly income in some instances was less than four thousand dollars), who had sold out for what amounted to little more than a bag of peanuts, were banned from the game for life. But a club owner who had had as a partner in a gambling house the man who was supposed to have paid the Chicago players to lose could continue in the sport and profit handsomely from it.

Owning a ball club had become with Tesreau an idée fixe. He had lost the backing of Rothstein, but he professed to know other moneyed men in New York who would contribute to the purchase of the Rochester franchise, which, following a disastrous season, was up for sale. He needed, however, more money than he felt the New York people would come up with. He wanted me to promote some Rochester capital, and imprudently I allowed that I might manage to do so.

Big Jeff left town, and I made an earnest try to enlist the financial aid of three or four Rochester men I thought might be interested in sharing ownership of the club, but found in the end that all were indifferent to the project. I persisted. I went to less likely prospects with similar lack of success. I became rather desperate in my efforts, for every few days Tesreau would either write or call me on the telephone imploring me to tell him what progress I was making, and I had no progress to report. Presently he returned to Rochester. His prospective backers in New York had failed him, and he was relying on me to raise money for the purchase of the Rochester ball club, and I had to confess that as a promoter I was a dud. I hadn't been able to raise a penny, despite the sanguine hopes I had earlier expressed for success. Our rapport ended. My conscience troubled me to think I had unmeaningly deceived a man whom I liked very much. We parted, and the next I heard of Jeff Tesreau, he had moved to Hanover, New Hampshire, to operate a gas station and coach the Darmouth baseball team. He died in Hanover in 1946.

* * * * * * * * * *

Tesreau's telling me about Rothstein excited my interest in the gambler, whose nefarious activities following the exposé of the baseball scandal were often reported in the press. My interest was further quickened when I went one night to Reuben's restaurant in New York with a Broadway ticket broker who guardedly indicated a carefully dressed man with a white-on-white shirt and a black bow tie two tables away.

"A.R.," he said in an awed undertone. "Arnold Rothstein. The biggest man in New York."

"You mean the biggest crook?"

"Sh-sh," he cautioned in a frightened whisper. "Don't say that out loud. For all you know, there're two or three of his body guards in the place."

Of course Rothstein was not the "biggest man in New York," but he was a massive figure in the underworld; his influence was widespread; his poisonous talons reached deep into departments of the city's administration. And when he died in 1929, after being shot two days earlier in a room in the Park Central Hotel in New York, the murder became one of the most sensational homicides the city had known in years.

Rothstein died without revealing his assailant to the police officer assigned to question him at his hospital bedside, and the investigation that followed his death often seemed flaccid and energyless. The press badgered the police for their failure to solve the crime, but the police seemed to fear that if they very vigorously stirred the mephetic mess of the Rothstein case fumes of their own corruption would rise from the same stinkpot.

One suspect was named, however: George McManus, himself a notorious gambler. He had a brother on the New York police force and another, a priest. McManus' overcoat had been found in the hotel room in which the shooting had occurred, and it was also known that he had operated a poker game in which Rothstein had lost wagers amounting to six figures, and that instead of cash the loser had given markers—IOUs; and the IOUs had not been indemnified. Rothstein had implied that he was going to take his own sweet time about honoring them and let his creditors "sweat a little." It was a grievous default and the defaulter died, it was believed, because of it.

The police announced that they were conducting a nationwide search for McManus, but the quarry they sought had not run far from the scene of the crime. On the advice of a Tammany leader whom the police judiciously never questioned, McManus had allowed himself to be driven to a hideout in the Bronx by a hood named Bo Weinberg, an associate of the infamous hoodlum, Dutch Schultz, and later a victim of Schultz's displeasure. Weinberg's body, encased in cement, was dropped into the Hudson River.

McManus remained in hiding twenty-four days. The police were then informed that he might be found one morning in a barbershop in the Bronx, and there he greeted the detectives sent for him and willingly accompanied them to headquarters. He was indicted for murder but released on $50,000 bail, and in time—more than a year after Rothstein's death—was brought to trial. The trial had the overtones of travesty. When the prosecution finished its case, McManus was pronounced innocent and set free.

That was in 1930.

Four or five years later, George McManus, with a gesture of gallantry, performed a kindly service for my wife.

She met him in Florida, where she had taken our son, Bill, who was nine or ten years old and who, in January of that year, had suffered a critical case of pneumonia. For days it was touch and go. The crisis passed, but the boy's convalescence was dreadfully slow. It seemed imperative to his mother and me that he be removed to a softer climate; and one February morning, my wife, with Bill bundled to the teeth, set out from our Scottsville, New York, home in a luggage-laden little Essex for the deep south.

I had had an invitation from a Rochester friend who wintered in Palm Beach.

"If you're coming to Florida, come and stay with us. We've lost the butler, and we're pigging it," he wrote, "but you're welcome."

I had no intention of going to Florida, but I accepted the invitation on behalf of my wife and son. I told my wife to stop at the Palm Beach home of Russell Yates and his latest wife, and they might help her locate a place where she and Bill might live for the remainder of the winter.

Russell Yates was the youngest of three sons of Arthur G. Yates, an extraordinary entrepreneur, who had been president of the Buffalo, Rochester & Pittsburgh Railroad, who had a coal business and an ice company in Rochester and extensive interests in bituminous coal mines in western Pennsylvania. He had been a part owner of a large Rochester department store and had once profited from a local distillery that produced what was widely advertised as "medicinal whiskey." He had failed once, but failure had in no way depressed the grandiose motif of his way of life; and when, presently, he bounced back, he did so impressively—to the tune of three million dollars! Arthur Yates predeceased his wife, and at the widow's death the substantial estate was divided among her issue. When I knew him, Russell Yates was as busy as busy could be dispensing his patrimony.

Occasionally, before I was married, I had been a guest at parties given by Russell Yates in Rochester, and I recall starting out for one with Peggy Cussock, a pretty, aspiring young actress (formerly the favorite model of Penrhyn Stanlaus, the girly artist), who was a member of a summer stock company that was headed by Florence Eldridge, later the wife of Frederic March.

I was about to pull away from the curb in my small car when I was hailed by Solly Hershberg, a handsome, popular, fashionably dressed little man who owned a downtown jewelry store.

"Where you going?" Solly called. "The two of you—you're decked out as though it's a coronation."

"We're going to a party at Russell Yates'."

Solly wagged his handsome head sagely. "And a very good place to go, if you're enduring. I went to their anniversary party a week ago Friday night. I got home the following Tuesday."

Russell Yates was an expansive host, and when my wife and son reached Palm Beach in the little Essex, he and Mrs. Yates were bounteous in their reception. Russell, who had hypochondriac tendencies, was confined to the house with a good looking nurse and a real or imagined disorder. His condition was certainly not critical, and since he needed no nursing care from his wife, a lively and handsome young woman, on the night of the Clunes' arrival she took my wife to a wrestling match, leaving young Bill, an avid radio fan, in a room that was unequipped with a radio.

Next morning the boy said to his mother, "That Mr. Yates is an awful nice man, Mom. I was sitting alone in the room, and he called, 'Hey kid, come on in here if you want to hear the radio,' and I went in his room. I sat in a chair and he was in bed. And y'know, he's so nice, he let the nurse get right on the bed with him."

Mrs. Yates helped my wife locate an apartment just south of Palm Beach, and each day, after she and Bill were settled, my wife, a former Olympic swimmer, swam in the pool of the Breakers Hotel with Martha Norelius, a two-time Olympic winner, whose father was swimming instructor at the hotel.

Before she went south I had given my wife a wrist watch which she lost in the vicinity of the Breakers Hotel a week or so after she arrived in Florida. Although it was not a bauble of great worth, it was the most expensive present my economy of the time allowed. It had for Charlotte a sentimental as well as a material value, and in an ad she inserted in the Lost and Found column of a Palm Beach paper she offered a reward for its return.

When she returned to the Breakers to swim with Martha Norelius a couple of days after the ad appeared, a clerk in the hotel called, "Oh, Mrs. Clune. Your watch has been found."

"Who found it?" she asked.

"Mr. McManus."

My wife had read in the newspapers that the celebrated cartoonist of that name, whose comic strip, "Bringing up Father," was virtually a national institution, was a guest in Palm Beach, and she said, "Mr. McManus, the cartoonist?"

"Oh, no, no," said the clerk. "The *big* Mr. McManus. George McManus. He's in the pool now," and he left the lobby to identify a large man who was cumbersomely paddling about in the pool. He said to my wife when he left the water, "My chauffeur found your watch, Mrs. Clune. He's an honest man, and I want him to give it to you. There's no need of a reward. He's very well taken care of and his wife's my cook."

When he was dressed, he took my wife to his chauffeur, who presented her with the watch and to whom, over his protest, she gave the promised reward. She thanked the chauffeur and McManus. The latter was gravely courteous. "So glad to have been of assistance, Mrs. Clune," he said with a bow.

My wife's inquiries quickly established the identity of the *big* Mr. McManus. He was the big gambler who had arranged the poker game in which Arnold Rothstein lost more than $100,000, which he failed to pay, and McManus was the only person brought to trial for Rothstein's murder.

When my wife reported these discoveries in a telephone call from Palm Beach, I told her that I also knew something about George McManus. When he was in New York he was in daily telephone communication with Luke Smith, who operated the largest book-making establishment in Rochester, negotiating wagers on horses running on tracks all over America. The two men were old acquaintances. I told Luke Smith of my wife's experience with McManus, and asked, "Do you think George McManus really killed Rothstein?"

Luke threw out his hands in a gesture of horrified protest. "Oh, no. God no! Why, George wouldn't kill a fly. Of course," he added, after a moment's reflection, "he was in the room when Rothstein was shot."

The Chesterfieldian deportment McManus displayed to my wife was not consistently evidenced in his relations with women. In her popular book, *A House Is Not A Home,* the celebrated New York Madam, Polly Adler, told how, drunk, McManus once brought a small company of rollicking hoods to her establishment, who shot a bullet through a partition, abused her and her girls, whipped one who resisted their advances, with a buckled belt, and wrecked the interior of the place. Of course, the police were not summoned to quell the rioters. Later, Madam Adler wrote, a contrite McManus offered to pay for the damages and was told indignantly (and inelegantly) what he could do with his money.

CHAPTER FIFTEEN

Beth Sloan, I was told later, had, as a teen-ager, been a very lively number around the Busy B Drugstore in downtown Utica, New York.

I saw her for the first time, then well-grown, when I stopped one midnight at the Hotel Seneca to say "Hello" to John Itta and perhaps be favored with some gossipy bit that might be wrought into a news story, for the maitre d' was encyclopedic on matters that pertained to the hotel and the hotel's immediate downtown neighborhood.

John stood just inside the Pompeian Room, where a five-piece orchestra was banging out a popular dance tune. It was Friday night, the floor was fairly well filled, and my glance, flitting among the moving figures on the floor, noted several persons I knew—week-end regulars—remarked an aspersion of couples unknown to me, and suddenly, galvanically, fixed on an auburn-haired vision whose every aspect and movement excited urges that are necessary for the perpetuity of the human race.

"Wh—where did *that* come from?" I asked, for John's gaze on the auburn-haired charmer was as intense as my own.

He didn't divert his eyes. "God only knows. She dropped down like a ripe peach. She's been here before this week. Once with the Russell Yates' party. A dish, eh? A sexpot. Looks like Gloria Swanson."

"She does," I agreed. "Know her name?"

"Not yet. I'm casing her. I'll have the scoop soon."

I waited until the number was over, smitten, fascinated. I had never before seen the man with whom she was dancing, nor the couple they joined at a corner table for four. Rochester natives have no peculiar homogeneity. They are not distinguished by a peculiarity of dress, countenance, or manners; nonetheless, I was certain that no one at the corner table was indigenous to our fair city, and I left the Pompeian Room with the sorrowful notion that probably I would never see the auburn-haired enchantress again.

I was back in the Seneca the next midnight; and John Itta, as on the previous midnight, was again standing just beyond the threshold of the Pompeian Room, which, this being Saturday (night life in Rochester was conspicuously confined to the week-end) was crowded. Itta and I had a tacit reciprocal arrangement. He often provided me with news bits, and I often got his name into the newspaper. He was eager to please both because of our friendship and because I was a representative of the press. I spoke to him; he smiled benignly.

"She's here," he said, as if he apprehended my purpose in returning to the hotel. "I told you I'd get the write-up on her. The scoop." He made a discreet directional gesture toward the dance floor, but I had already discovered, in the maze of dancers, the siren who had beguiled me the night before. She was more elaborately gotten up than when I had first seen her; more flaunting in her carnal appeal. She was, as John Itta had denoted, a "sexpot."

"I know her now," Itta said. "Mrs. Beth Sloan. I'll make you acquainted."

And when the number was over and she passed with her partner not far from where we stood, John called, "Oh, Mrs. Sloan. This is Mr. Clune, from the newspaper."

She paused, smiled. "Oh," she said, "do you own the newspaper?"

"No," I confessed, "just work there. A reporter."

The smile blew off her face as though caught in a wind. She pressed her partner's arm and moved across the floor to a table arranged for eight or ten persons, with two of whom, I saw, I had a speaking acquaintance. I was piqued by her chilled attitude. Brushing me because I was only a reporter, not the owner of a newspaper! I decided that there was something of the bitch in Mrs. Beth Sloan, but the conclusion, rather than lessening my interest, sharpened it. I speculated vainly as to which of the men in the party was Mr. Sloan. It was crazy, I told myself, to indulge an emotional rapture over a married woman, but on a rash impulse I left John Itta and approached the table at which she sat.

There was a setup at every place and it was evident that more than a little had been drunk from flasks the men half-surreptitiously drew from hip pockets. I was greeted with boozy cordiality by one of the two persons I knew and given a round-robin introduction. A setup was ordered for me and a drink poured into it. There was no Mr. Sloan at the table, and before I left I learned that Mrs. Sloan had been divorced. A gay divorcee, obviously! I knew that much and now I resolved to know more about her, and that design was quickly realized. On Tuesday of that week I had lunch with her in the Hotel Seneca; on Friday I was briefly in her bed in a suite in the second most fashionable apartment in town.

Friday night was my single night off from the newspaper and I persuaded her—it was really not difficult—to dine with me at a place I thought precisely suited for the occasion, the White Horse Tavern, a few miles south of Rochester. It was managed by Jake and Emma, who were supposed to be living in sin, and it was a rendezvous for sinners. There were several small rooms if a couple desired complete privacy; the help was black and did not talk.

Our dinner was pleasant, the food good, and Jake, who, like John Itta was eager to pamper the press, sent in a bottle of supposedly imported wine. Beth Sloan tasted it, grimaced, complained about the vintage, but in the end drank more than her share. She professed to know about wine, though I doubt if she was a connoisseur. She talked knowingly about a number of expensive things: furs, jewels, show horses, and the more luxurious motor cars. She seemed to know the price of everything, and by the same token, the value of nothing. I enjoyed her. She was exceedingly ornamental. She was fairly amusing, ribald, far from profound, but—in today's vernacular—"street smart." Her ego was high. Her good humor, her charm—if it could so be called—cracked now and then, and the bitchiness I had discerned at our first meeting showed through the chipped veneer.

In our drive back to town a car in front of us sideswiped another car and the car that was hit veered into a ditch. It looked like a serious accident. I braked down and started to leap to the road. She grasped my arm and her voice was a gritty adjuration, "Don't be a goddamn fool!"

"Someone might be killed."

"If they're killed, what the hell can you do? Let's get out of here."

While we paused, another car stopped and two men left it and ran toward the ditched vehicle. I wondered angrily what sort of a companion I had? A woman with the humanity of a hooded cobra? I went on, as she commanded, my conscience troubling me. In the rear view mirror, I saw other cars stopping at the scene of the accident.

"You get mixed up in a thing like that, and you can never tell what'll come of it," she said, more conciliatory, as we continued along the road. "Subpoenas. Court actions. Your name in the papers. I got a rule. Never get involved."

"A good little samaritan," I said cynically. "A dear good little Christian, adhering to the golden rule."

"Horse shit," she said. "If you don't look out for *you*—for Number One—who's going to? I learned that with my fir—with my husband."

"Divorced?"

"Yes, the son-of-a-bitch."

She told me, and she seemed to become ugly in the recital, how she had married an older man "with money—a whole bank full of it" and found him closer, she said, than a dead heat at the races. "I didn't like him to begin with," she said. "He had a fat belly and all he talked about was his ancestors coming over on the Mayflower. I said, if they came over on the Mayflower, they must have rowed the boat. In the end, when he didn't loosen up, I went out and charged things—I got to say, his name was good for it. I charged a lot of things"—she laughed bitterly. "And that was the end of the romance."

I questioned her, but she mentioned no names. I had

discovered during the evening that while she appeared to tell a good deal about her past she was actually quite circumspect and it was difficult to pin her down to specifics. We hit a depression in the road, and she lurched against the side of the car. "Ouch!" she cried.

"Sorry," I said. "I didn't see that hole."

"It's my goddamn shoulder," she said. "I slipped off a stool while I was trying to hang a curtain rod, and hit my shoulder against the wall. It's been sore ever since."

"What have you done for it?"

"I need a massage. Like I used to have in New York. A masseur. I used to go to a fellow who was a real expert."

"A fellow?" I asked.

She laughed, and patted the back of my hand. "Shock you, darlin'? Of course he was a flit, but he was good. He had wonderful hands. He had movie stars for clients, Hedy Lamarr, and like that."

What she had told me, she knew very well, had inflamed my fancy. Was it Bernard Shaw who siad that love is three-quarters curiosity? I was imagining her now as a masseur had seen her and worked on her. I was putting myself in his place. It was a heady presumption. We had reached the city and were proceeding across town to her apartment on the East Side and I was speeding.

"I'm a good masseur," I said.

At Andover I had rubbed the kinks out of the arm of a boy who pitched a winning game against Exeter. I later coached a high school relay team and massaged the pulled muscle of my best sprinter. We stopped in front of the apartment house. Beth Sloan got out of the car. I waited, trembling violently.

"Well," she said, "are you going to fix my shoulder?"

It was a small but attractive apartment. Even in my eagerness, I noticed a Trinity College banner on a wall and a photograph of a man in an easel frame—not an old man with a "fat belly"—but a young, slim, handsome man. I saw a Psi U emblem. I asked no questions. We were quickly in bed and quickly out of it. I had heard that women who displayed great sexual allure were often sexually disinclined; this was definitely the case with Beth Sloan. She wanted only a massage.

"You've got wonderful hands, darlin'. Better than the flit's," she said flatteringly.

We agreed to lunch together in the Seneca the following Tuesday. After lunch she took me window shopping. She had seen a wrist watch in a Main Street jeweler's that she wanted very much, and she pointed it out to me in the show window. We went inside and priced it. I was shocked. Three hundred dollars! There was another in the window for one hundred dollars less. I took a deep breath and whispered in her ear, "Wouldn't that do?"

"Well, maybe," she said disappointedly. "The other's the one I had in mind."

When we parted she vaguely implied that we would meet again on Friday, but she went instead to Niagara-on-the-Lake for a week-end houseparty. And the following week end she said she was going to New York.

Over the telephone she was evasive, and I was sure she was putting me off. I began to suspect that the Niagara-on-the-Lake and the New York week ends were feigned. I inquired about her shoulder and she answered indifferently that it was okay. I finally won her consent to dine with me at the White Horse Tavern the Friday night after her supposed trip to New York, and by then, frantic in the fear that I was losing her, I took desperate measures to win her back.

After we had ordered dinner in one of the secret cubicles, I laid before her on the table a plush-lined jeweler's box. I had never before given a girl a gift of much value. This had taken a leg.

"Oh, darlin' " she cried ecstatically, when she opened the box. "It's the one I *really* wanted, not the other cheap one." She cosseted it lovingly then looked up with sudden apprehension. "But darlin', you didn't steal the other hundred, did you?"

The question implied no moral concern. Her only concern was that if I had stolen the money the theft might be discovered and the watch taken from her. I assured her that the purchase had been made with honest money but didn't explain that it had virtually exhausted my financial resources.

"You are a darlin'," she said. "Let's get through dinner

quick, and we'll go right home, and I'll have a hot bath and a wonderful rub."

I think it was Phoan Howard who ran a little racing paper for gamblers called the *Fireside Companion,* who pronounced the thesis, "Suckers can't wait." That was precisely my urgency; I couldn't wait to serve Beth Sloan in the menial capacity of masseur (although the work did have its attractions), and the Friday following my presentation of the three-hundred-dollar watch I was back again in her attractive suite rubbing her with perfumed lotions.

The famous Rochester Horse Show was soon to open its six-day stand, and Beth wanted to cut a figure around the arena boxes which were socially central at the show. She wanted, for the occasion, a bird of paradise for her hat and we found one after lunch one day, a real bargain, she said—for ninety-five dollars! I sprang. A couple of nights later, stopping at the Seneca, I saw her dancing with a handsome young man whose features seemed vaguely familiar. She saw me, waved, and brought him over. "I guess you never met Charlie," she said.

I laughed pleasantly as I shook hands with the young man. "Charlie who?" I asked.

"My husband, Charlie Sloan."

I felt as if a wrecking ball had dropped on my head, and I half wished it had, and driven me through the floor of the Pompeian Room. I was sure that the agitation that seemed to be wracking me to pieces must show in every line of my countenance and be as plain to Beth's husband as a pikestaff. He was, I saw, the man whose photograph I had seen in the easel frame in what I knew now was the apartment of Mr. and Mrs. Charles Sloan.

They were with a large party and they asked me to join them at the table. I contrived an excuse. I was acutely distressed. Charlie Sloan was a man I thought I could like. He was friendly, well-mannered, obviously intelligent, quite Ivy League—"Brooksie" in his tailoring, as it was known in that era. I wondered at the compatibility of the Sloans. I conjectured that they were in wide variance in such matters as taste, values, and ethics. I speculated as to how Charlie Sloan, as I had sized him up in this brief meeting, could have chosen a girl like Beth for a wife, and then thought ironically—wretchedly—of my own infatuation.

He told me he had been on a business deal on the West Coast most of the summer and that in two days he was leaving for New York. I asked how long he'd be in New York and he said a couple of weeks. I left then in a state of acute ambivalence, determined never to see Beth Sloan again and mad to know how I could contrive to be with her.

I cautiously telephoned her the next week. Charlie had left, she said; he was in New York. The Russell Yates' were having a party Saturday night, the Saturday before the opening of the Horse Show, to which both Beth and I had been invited, and we agreed to go together. She vaguely suggested, and I was enraptured by the hint, that we would break away early and go our own way. I had learned the Decalogue in Sunday School; I knew the Seventh Commandment. I also knew of the hortatory cry of the great and good St. Augustine, "Lord, make me chaste, but not yet!"

She was dressed to the nines when I met her, the bird of paradise in her hat, the watch I had given her on her wrist.

How, I asked, had she explained the watch to her husband.

She laughed. "Hah. That was easy. I told him I found it."

"Did he believe that?"

"Sure. Charlie's one of those people think if you get a little luck, you've got to crowd it. He made me go—he took me—to your goddamn newspaper office and made me put an ad in the paper describing the watch and telling where I found it." She laughed again and touched my hand. "Don't worry, honey. I didn't tell *really* where."

I suppose all deceits have to be contrived, but this seemed a peculiarly distasteful contrivance. I was still under Beth Sloan's thrall, but I was beginning to believe that perhaps there was a limit to her charms and I wondered how great the disenchantment would be if they were exhausted.

The Yates' party was a large and sumptuous one. In normal circulation among the numerous company, Beth and I were separated. Occasionally, passing from one room to another, I saw her, seemingly very cozy with a young man whose name I learned was Thompson, who had come on from Chicago to exhibit a string of hackneys at the Horse Show.

In mid-evening, growing eager about the tryst she had hinted at, I looked for Beth, found her in none of the rooms; looked for Thompson, and discovered that he too was missing. A friend told me they had left together half an hour before.

I waited until the festivities had almost run their bibulous course, hoping against hope. Neither Beth Sloan nor Thompson reappeared, and I left, bitterly disillusioned. The following mid-week she recited, in a telephone call to the office, an Alice-in-Wonderland fiction of what had happened at the Yates' party and suggested, since this was the last week her husband would be away, that we meet Friday night. I was tempted mightily; then a strength that I hardly believed I possessed asserted itself. I was through, definitely, intransigently, with Mrs. Sloan, and from that resolution I never departed. I saw her occasionally in the few months that she and her husband remained in Rochester, but our meetings were transitory. I learned that she and Sloan were ultimately divorced, and I saw her once after these proceedings. She returned to the Horse Show one year with a rakish looking fellow who apparently, from her glittering trappings, had provided her with more than a three-hundred-dollar wrist watch and a ninety-five-dollar bird of paradise. That was my last view of her.

Charlie Sloan married again, this time to a wife with whom he traveled the world, part of the way in the new Mrs. Sloan's private yacht. I think he deserved the break.

CHAPTER SIXTEEN

In 1921 I was having a fine time working for the Rochester *Herald*. My zest for newspaper work was pristine and untrammeled; and while the local side of our newspaper reported nothing of world-shaking consequence, there was an interesting variety to what we in the city room did and our reportorial tasks occasionally proved exciting. I continued to enjoy the favor of Mr Antisdale and I often had the top assignment of the day. Bylines were not common in those days but my news stories frequently appeared under my name and my vanity was piqued by the distinction. I was acquiring local prestige. But so far I had failed to do what I very much wanted to do, produce saleable fiction, and time was passing. I was thirty-one. In moments of retrospection, glancing back over my term of years, it seemed to me that there had been no highlights in my life, no notable fulfillment, and on these occasions I wondered if anything momentous would ever happen to me. This speculation persisted into the summer of that year; in the autumn I experienced an event of moment. I was married.

On Saturday afternoon, 2 July 1921, Hiram Marks and I were present at the world's heavyweight championship fight between Jack Dempsey and Georges Carpentier, the French challenger, in a huge wooden bowl in Jersey City, New Jersey. Marks at different times was the court, political, and business reporter for the *Democrat and Chronicle,* and we had been friends since before the war, when I also worked for that newspaper. He was a stoutish young man of medium height, quick, witty, acquisitive, and enormously energetic; he was both a skilled reporter and a very sharp entrepreneur. He always had money, for his outside interests paid more than his newspaper job, which, however, was necessary to the success of his extra-curricular activities. It gave him prestige and provided leverage for his promotional ventures. It helped him get his foot in the door.

He was a sort of unofficial exchequer in the city room of the *Democrat.* Newspaper salaries were low in those days, and newspapermen were often broke before pay day. "Hi," someone would whisper, "couldn't let me have a fin until the ghost walks, could you?" "The rent's due, and the wife's got me clean out of trump," someone else would complain. "If you could lend me a tenner until Friday. . . ." These were common petitions. And the petitioners were rarely refused. I, like most of the other workers in the city room, had been indulged by Marks's kindness. More than once he had "carried" me to payday. He had never seen a championship boxing match. When he learned that I was going to Jersey City he proposed that we go together, and I was pleased to have his company.

We arrived in New York the day before the match and found that the midtown hotels, anticipating a swarm of fight fans from all over the land, had outlandishly jacked-up their prices. Hi tried to beat the room clerks down to reason, but failed, smart trader that he was. He was annoyed by his failure. "I'll be damned if I'll be taken," he said; so we settled for a two-dollar-a-night-place in a shabby west side neighborhood, and suffered for our parsimony. The beds had other occupants besides ourselves, and the next day we itched and scratched on our way to Jersey City and through the four rounds that Dempsey needed to defeat Carpentier.

At breakfast the morning of the fight, Marks and I turned through three or four newspapers, the sports sections of which were so choked with stories of the impending championship that even baseball scores had a hard time squeezing in. Surprisingly, however, one of the journals I perused displayed on one of its sport pages a two-column photograph of two handsome, smiling, sun-tanned young women in swim suits. I identified them, before I even read the cut-lines, as the Misses Ethelda Bleibtrey and Charlotte Boyle, champions from the New York Women's Swimming Association. I admired their looks and what I had previously read of their achievements, and sometime since I had cut a picture of Miss Boyle from a magazine and pasted it in a scrapbook.

A short news item accompanied the photograph. It told that Miss Bleibtrey, a three-time gold medal winner at the Antwerp Olympics who had recently returned from an Australian tour, would be honored at a homecoming celebration the next day (Sunday) at the Brighton Beach Baths. There would be diving contests and other aquatic events, and, as the feature attraction, an exhibition of the Olympic champion and Miss Boyle, who had also represented the United States Olympic Team.

I showed the picture and story to Hi Marks and said, "I'm going to Brighton Beach tomorrow to see those girls."

"We got reservations on the sleeper for home tonight."

"We can cancel the space and make reservations for tomorrow night."

"But swimming," Marks said dourly. "What do I care about swimming? I can't swim. Or much, anyway."

"We're just going to see the swimming," I protested. "Not go in ourselves."

He was grumpy at first but finally consented. We changed both our hotel and sleeper reservations. And the next afternoon we were at Brighton Beach, both of us fully dressed in contrast to the light and airy costumes of the beachcombers and the scant attire of the bathers. Marks' corpulent torso was embraced by a waistcoat. He wore a derby hat. I suffered for him, although I, too, sweat profusely, and my exudation, like his, was aggravated by the itchy welts inflicted by bedbugs on our first night in New York. The temperature must have been close to one hundred in the shade and there was very little shade.

We idled about, waiting for the opening of the aquatic show. Marks unbuttoned his vest and opened his shirt to the dead, still air and made feeble sweeps with his derby to fan himself. He was a steaming figure of tragedy, a martyr to my obsession. When he pantingly announced that if he didn't escape the murderous rays of the sun he'd fall prostrate on the sands, we sought the shelter of a nearby merry-go-round shed, where Hi collapsed on one of the wooden benches that stood at intervals against the wall of the circular structure. I ministered to him briefly; then raised my eyes and saw, sitting together a couple of benches away, the two Nereids who were to star in the afternoon's entertainment.

"Hi! Hi!" I whispered excitedly. "They're here—in this shed. The two girls who are going to swim."

Marks rubbed a sweaty hand over a perspiring forehead. "You have 'em," he moaned. "I'll take a salt pill."

They seemed more impressive in the flesh than in their attractive newspaper photograph that had been the catalyst of this sweltering excursion. I left Marks and walked by their bench three or four times, ogling them surreptitiously. In my role of newspaper reporter I had often barged in aggressively where I was not wanted; I had intrepidly questioned persons who were hostile to an interview; I had cultivated the brassiness of my craft.

Now, however, not on official duty, I had strange misgivings, a woeful lack of confidence, and an enormous desire to meet, at least, Miss Boyle. I goaded my flagging spirit. I was on the point of accosting the two young women when they were summoned from the merry-go-round shed. I shook Marks out of his heat-induced torpor. "They've gone. Come on. The show's going to start," and I ran across the hot sands toward the swimming pool, Hi staggering after me.

Our seats were high up in the stands, a long way from the water's edge. No matter. Perhaps never before had I been so entranced by a performance in which women were the performers. The two stars demonstrated various swimming strokes. They moved through the water in their silk swim suits with the ease and grace of seals. At one point they did what was announced as the "double-oar." In this the two girls were attached to one another tandem-fashion, Miss Bleibtrey who alone used her legs in propulsion, in the rear, Miss Boyle in front, and the arms of both catching the water as rhythmically as the sweeps of a racing shell. It was a stunt, I later learned, they had performed by royal command for the Belgian queen following the 1920 Antwerp Olympics. Even Marks came to life enough to applaud.

I was reflective in the ride back to New York and in the sleeper jump to Rochester that night. I nurtured a vague sense of destiny. I was going to meet those girls, particularly Miss Boyle. I told Marks of my intent.

"Ha," he said. "She looks all right. They both look all right—from a distance. You meet her, and you'll get wised up. Be disillusioned. I'll bet she's a hard-boiled Annie from Brooklyn."

"I'm going to manage it someway," I said resolutely.

And I did. About six weeks later!

The Syracuse *Post-Standard* advertised a water show on Onondaga Lake that would be headlined by the "world's champion women swimmers," and I drove over for the exhibition with a friend of mine (not Hi Marks). On this occasion, exercising my newspaper prerogative, I sat during the exhibition with the officials, was introduced to the Misses Bleibtrey and Boyle, talked briefly with them during intervals when they were not performing in the lake, and invited them to dinner. They declined; they already had a dinner date.

My fragmentary conversation with Miss Boyle in Syracuse probably didn't total half an hour, but I was determined to expand my acquaintance, and with this design, I appealed to the resourceful Marks when I returned to Rochester.

"Hi, how can we get those girls to Rochester?"

"Oh, you met em, eh? How were they?"

"Charlotte Boyle is from Brooklyn," I conceded. "But not a hard-boiled Brooklyn Annie."

He grinned. "You're crazy about the girl, eh?"

"I didn't say that."

"I'll see what I can do."

Among other outside interests, Marks operated refreshment stands in two city parks. He had obtained these concessions through the good relations he enjoyed with members of the Park Commission, and he now exploited these relations in my behalf. He proposed to the Commissioners that a water show similar to the one in Syracuse, with the same principals, would be a fitting way to close the summer activities in the largest of the city's parks. The Commissioners accepted the proposal, and the exhibition was scheduled for the first Saturday afternoon in September at a point on the upper Genesee River where the stream bisects the wide acreage of Genesee Valley Park.

The two girls from the Swimming Association and a chaperon, Miss Charlotte Epstein, a redoubtable lady whose devotion to the association and its prominent performers was not unlike religious zealotry, arrived in Rochester the day before the exhibition, and were entertained that afternoon and evening at the home of Mr. and Mrs. Jim Sam Wadsworth in Geneseo, thirty miles south of Rochester.

Jim Sam was a member of the most distinguished family in the Genesee Valley. His forebears had settled in what was known as the Western Wilderness in 1790, and much of the vast acreage they acquired in the very early days of the nation's founding was still owned by the Wadsworth family.

Jim Sam's parcel, however, was negligible. He lived in a small, green-shingled house on a few acres a couple of miles outside of the village of Geneseo with his second wife, Bess. He had had an ample patrimony. It had come early and it had gone quickly. He raced horses, he rode to hounds, he played polo, he fought a war, he made extravagant wagers, and he backed a musical comedy. "We, Jim," his second cousin, United States Senator James W. Wadsworth, was once heard to remark, "have all the money. You've had all the fun."

Jim and Bess Wadsworth, the only members of the Wadsworth family I knew, had been friends of mine for some time, and it was their proposal that I bring the swimming girls, the chaperon, and any other guests I might select, to Geneseo for a party.

I asked a friend of mine, a handsome and gifted Dartmouth alumnus, who, in turn, gathered three or four of his Dartmouth friends, and the party, which began in mid-afternoon, extended well into the evening.

Impecunious though he was in a relative sense, Jim Sam was a celebrated host. He was a prominent member of the

Genesee Valley Hunt, the third oldest hunt club in the nation, which he later served as master. He kept out back a pair of excellent hunters, which Miss Bleibtrey and one of the Dartmouth men took out for a canter while I tried to talk seriously with Miss Boyle. It was a vain effort; there was too much activity and too many interruptions.

At dinner I was not seated where I wanted to be, next to Miss Boyle, but on the other side of the table, and I was disappointed to observe that she seemed more interested in what the man next to her was saying than she appeared interested in what I had said to her during our intermittent conversation of the afternoon. This dour speculation, however, did not lessen the enjoyment of a gay and festive occasion. Jim Sam's first wife had been "society." Bess (the first marriage ended in divorce) was a small-town girl of modest beginnings, well-learned in housewifely practices, and an excellent cook. Our host, a hulking figure at the head of the table, a man of graceful manners and notable wit, was in rare form. We sat at table in chairs that were carved with the insignia of his Harvard club, the exclusive Porcellian.

I was the unofficial escort of the New York visitors and I had breakfast with them Saturday morning at Powers Hotel, where they were lodged. Because of her amphibious habits Miss Boyle usually carried a bathing suit about with her, and at breakfast I learned that she had taken one to Geneseo the day before and carelessly left it in the Wadsworth house.

This, it seemed to me, was a providential ploy; the resounding knock of opportunity. I leapt at it. We would drive up to Geneseo right away and reclaim the bathing suit. Miss Boyle pooh-poohed the notion. She had other bathing suits and this one was not needed for the afternoon's exhibition. It wasn't worth all the bother. I protested that there was plenty of time between then and lunch to make the trip. It would be a pleasant ride on a bright, late-summer morning.

"Well," she said finally, not enthusiastically. "Okay."

The sixty-mile run to Geneseo and back was not a speed test in any sense. This was the first time that I had had Miss Boyle alone without interruption, and I made the most of it. But our talk was commonplace until the final stage of the journey. Before that I had rendered a few tourist-guide reflections on the beauties of the Genesee Valley countryside and pronounced several earnest recommendations of Rochester as a desirable place in which to live. It was only when we were within a couple of hundred yards of the hotel on our return trip, our progress blocked by a stationary horse-drawn van in the middle of the pavement, that I turned to my companion with a question that pulsed with romantic fervency.

"Miss Boyle, do you think you could ever live up here—I mean, where you would have to swim in fresh water?"

"You mean in Rochester?"

"Yes."

She laughed. "You know, I never before knew of *this* Rochester. I knew of the one where the Mayo Clinic is. A friend of mine is a nurse out there."

The wagon moved, and I maneuvered around it and pulled up at the curb at the side of the hotel.

"Think it over," I said, as she opened the car door to get out. "I wish you'd come back here, and live. I mean, and marry me!"

She made no answer but hurried into the lobby of the hotel, where she joined Miss Bleibtrey and the chaperon, who were waiting impatiently for lunch.

The aquatic show that afternoon was a great success. Several thousand persons gathered on the river bank to applaud the performance of the stars. That night I entertained the swimmers, the chaperon, and two of the young men who had been at the Wadsworth party, at dinner at the Club Itta, a gilded restaurant recently opened (and, soon, unhappily, to close) under the management of my friend John Itta, former maitre d' at the Hotel Seneca. We had a box party later at the Lyceum Theater. At midnight I put the three visitors on a sleeper that would take them back to New York. There had been no chance all evening to resume my petition to Miss Boyle or to put my proposal into appropriate language. She went off with the wave of a hand and left me with the desolate sense that I had failed to make my point.

The next day at Brighton Beach she set a world record for women at 220 yards, free style, and I took heart. She must have been advantaged in some way by her Rochester experience.

I did not see Miss Boyle again until the sixteenth of the following month. In the interim I persistently pelted her with pleading missives, and presently she agreed that if I would come to New York we might talk things over. We did, the day of my arrival, at lunch. That night Chris Dalton, noted as a crack timer of footraces, gave us, and a few of Miss Boyle's friends, a dinner at the New York Athletic Club. The next day my mother, whom I had importunately urged by telephone, arrived in New York, pinned a spray of orchids in the lapel of Miss Boyle's tailored jacket, and that noon we were married in the Little Church Around the Corner.

We went to Atlantic City for a honeymoon, and there I began to enjoy a reflected fame. If nothing noteworthy had happened to me before, I was now pictured in the New York press standing outside of the church with the world-record holder I had married. At Atlantic City we were photographed by news service cameramen as we were pushed in a wheel chair over the Boardwalk, and these "shots" were used in newspapers all over the country, and, to my delight (and the disgust of the new Mrs. Clune), in the *Police Gazette,* that old roué of journalism which I had been reading in barber shops since my youth.

As our acquaintance expanded, as our relations became more familiar, we ceased to address one another as "Miss Boyle" and "Mr. Clune"; but I knew almost nothing about my bride's background and she knew almost nothing about mine. We left Atlantic City, after a few days, for Rochester, where my wife met my father and my three sisters. Our family was small, closely-knit. We were bourgeois, conservative, unexciting squares. Marriage with us was a stay-put sort of an institution. It had its vicissitudes, but its vows had certitude. The Boyles, I discovered, when I gradually began to learn about them, were our exact antitheses.

CHAPTER SEVENTEEN

I met my wife's mother at the wedding in the church, but if the bride had a living father or sisters or brothers, I was not told of it at the time, and no relative other than her mother was present at the ceremony.

Mrs. Boyle was a pert, lively little woman, whose style of dress might loosely be described as "genteel gaudy." She was part French, part Belgian, and very much New York. She spoke the argot of the town; she was very *au courant.* I liked her instinctively. But I learned little about her or her family in our brief encounter; and it was not until the former Charlotte Boyle and I were settled in Rochester that I began to discover facts about my wife's family that aroused my newsman's curiosity, and the more I learned the more I was taken by the fancy that the Boyles were "story" people, perhaps worthy of a book. And, indeed, in time books were written about the paterfamilias, Joseph Whiteside Boyle. He was a man of romantic and adventurous cast, a legend in his own time, and I gloated when I read news dispatches from abroad that identified my father-in-law by such exciting epithets as "Modern d'Artagnan," "King of the Klondike," "the Morgan of the Balkans," "The uncrowned King of Rumania." And now and then I'd discover a sneaked-in line, "The paramour of a Queen."

My wife and I, I had thought, had a sort of record romance: two brief meetings, more than a month apart, and then marriage. Joe Boyle, my wife's father, was quicker than that.

He was a Canadian by birth, the youngest of three sons

of Charles Boyle, who operated a stud farm in Woodstock, Ontario, and raced a string of thoroughbreds on both Canadian and American tracks. Horses either owned or trained by Charles Boyle on two occasions won the Queen's Plate in Canada; and in New York, where he settled for a time, his racers won a number of important stakes on courses in the Metropolitan area.

Joe Boyle and his brothers, David and Charles, had been brought up around horses; they were expert in their management and training, and David, the second oldest son, initiated into racing as a youth, continued in the sport throughout his life. Young Joe, who had delighted in the freedom and outdoor activities of his father's stud farm in Woodstock, appeared to chafe under the restraints of New York life and one day, at the age of seventeen, without so much as a by-your-leave or a filial adieu, he ran away to sea. He was gone more than three years, roughing it before the mast, and during that period he never wrote a line to his family. "Home Sweet Home" for Joe Boyle was hardly a crewelwork legend to frame and hang on a wall.

He had articled himself to a sailing master at the Port of New York; and to that port he in time returned, a seasoned sailor, a large and handsome young man with a confident swagger. He had quit ship, tired of the forecastle of a merchantman. His brother David, he quickly discovered, was living in a Broadway hotel and doing well making book at the races. The brothers met and resumed fraternal relations. They were very much alike in physical structure, tall, powerfully-shouldered men, but there the similarity ended. Dave was shy, almost withdrawn; young Joe, arrogant and plunging. The former was in love with a gay and pretty divorcee, Emily Raynor, who lived in the same hotel, but it was some time before the infatuated bookmaker let his brother into his secret or presented him to the lady of his heart. The introduction was a grievous imprudence. Three days after Emily and Joe met they were married, and from then on the desolate and disenchanted Dave abandoned all hope of marital bliss and died a bachelor.

Joe's young and lively bride had an irrepressible urge

for high life. She had been married to the wealthy proprietor of a New Jersey silk mill, who was also billiard champion of the New York Athletic Club. She had a two-year old son, Bill, by Raynor, who was in her custody. Not long out of his nonage, Joe Boyle needed to do things quickly to provide his wife with the style of life to which she had been accustomed. Emily gravitated to costly fripperies. Her particular delight was to wrap her small, graceful Anna Held figure from ears to ankles in mink. It was a costly practice which her husband seemed to indulge; and during the early, endearing period of their marriage, "Mink" was his pet name for Emily, and friends also employed the nickname.

How, in a short period of time, Joe accomplished the transition from a rough-and-ready forecastle hand to the proprietorship of a successful feed and hauling business in New York is a mystery that none of his several biographers has successfully explained. He turned the trick somehow. His daugher, Flora Alexander, who has extensively researched her father's career, has attested in print that during her girlhood Joe Boyle's business succeeded so well that the family maintained homes in both New York and Red Bank, New Jersey, that both houses were staffed with servants, and that the Boyle carriage with the family coachman, was available when Emily desired to take the air or needed conveyance to some social function or the theater.

Boyle fathered three children by Emily, and another was on the way when he appeared to feel that the double yoke of domesticity and business was straitening his life into an irksome routine and damping his native free spirit. All his life his paramount interest had been sporting activities: racing, games, and pugilism; now, casting business and family aside, he went off on a barnstorming tour with Frank Slavin, the Australian heavyweight boxer who had come to America hoping to fight John L. Sullivan for the championship.

Joseph Whiteside Boyle, Jr., the first issue of the Emily Raynor-Joe Boyle union, was followed by Flora Alexander, Susan was next, and my wife, Charlotte, "who", according to one of Boyle's book-length biographers, "most nearly (of the four progeny) approached her father in superb physical capacity," was born shortly after Boyle quitted the familial hearth.

Flora Alexander has suggested that the temperament and propensities of her father probably unfitted him for the restraints and obligations of married life, and it would have been better if he had never married. I am happy, however, that he committed the error, if that is what it was, of matrimony; otherwise I should inevitably have married the wrong woman, rather than the one with whom I have lived for sixty-odd years, at times, to be sure "in antagonistic cooperation," as a distinguished Yale professor defined the marital condition; at other times, benign, with grace and cheer.

With the dissolution of his marriage, Joe Boyle consigned his two oldest children to the care of his parents in Woodstock and left Susan with the enceinte Emily, who was soon to deliver her last child, Charlotte. Once out of sight of his family, Joe seemed to put them out of mind.

His most profound biographer, Professor William Rodney of the Royal Roads Military College, British Columbia, suggests that the marriage failed in part because of a "certain shallowness of (Emily's) character that contrasts strongly with Joe Boyle's force and complexity."

In his long and carefully documented book, *Joe Boyle, King of the Klondike,* Professor Rodney virtually apotheosizes his hero, as did Kim Beattie in an earlier biography, *Brother, Here's a Man.* Boyle, in the consideration of both authors, could do little that was wrong, and no mention is made by either of his sins of omission.

Beattie, whose highly colored narrative postures Boyle in center stage of a fascinating cloak-and-dagger romance, says at one point, "All his (Boyle's) life his impulse has been to turn to the weak and buffeted—from whining husky puppy to overwhelmed nation . . ."

But there was an instance, not mentioned by any Boyle biographer, when the virtually destitute Emily made her catch-as-catch-can way to the Klondike in an attempt to gain unpaid alimony while her youngest child, back in Brooklyn, experienced a Christmas without a word of holiday cheer or receipt of a single token of the day.

Another time, when Emily and her daughter Charlotte, were hard-scrabbling in Brooklyn, Boyle, who at that time was referred to as the "Uncrowned King of Rumania," made a Sunday present of a five-thousand-dollar fur coat to his love bird, the Queen, who, under close scrutiny, might display something of the "shallowness of character" Professor Rodney attributes to Boyle's estranged wife.

* * * * * * * * * *

Boyle's tour with Frank Slavin, who was billed as the "Sydney Cornstalk," was hardly a howling success. The Australian's original purpose in coming to America, to fight Sullivan for the world's heavyweight championship, had been aborted before he and Boyle formed their manager-fighter partnership. The title match had gone to Gentleman Jim Corbett, who danced about and jabbed the Boston Strong Boy—whose big booze-filled belly swished and gurgled like a half-filled hot-water bag for twenty rounds—and knocked him out in the twenty-first. Slavin may have challenged the new champion, but if he did, the match was never made and it is likely that when Boyle took him on, the "Sydney Cornstalk" was beyond his pugilistic peak. Under Boyle's management he fought a few pirate battles in Canada for meager purses; the pair then moved across the border and briefly settled in Rochester, New York.

The time was to come when Joe Boyle would pass in and out of Buckingham Palace as though the place had a revolving door, confer with King George V and dine at the royal table. There was no premonition of this while he and Slavin were in Rochester. Here they managed a bowling alley for the Bartholomew Brewing Company and worked out in the shabby, loft building gym of the Rochester Athletic Club, the organization that my father later served as president.

They moved west in time. With no profitable match in prospect, they put on exhibitions of the manly art in lodge halls and other places of masculine assemblage, Boyle opposing his protegé in the ring; and there were aficionados in those days who believed that the manager was the better pug of the two.

Haltingly, they traversed the continent. They reached

San Francisco during the first fever of the Klondike gold rush, took ship to Skagway, pressed over torturous trails to Dawson City and the gold fields on the Yukon River. And there, with even greater alacrity than he had displayed in making a business success in New York, Joe Boyle came boomingly into his own.

His career was a brilliant, outsized extravaganza, and those who have attempted to put it into historical perspective have often been hard put to distinguish fact from fantasy. For a man of his flamboyant temperament whose career was a succession of dramatic exploits, Boyle seemed singularly indifferent to publicity during his life, and after his death those who desired to write about his activities at sea, in New York, in Alaska, in Russia, and in Rumania, needed, because of the scantiness of Boyle's own records, to depend mostly on outside sources for their biographical material.

He was an innovator and his operations were always on the grand scale.

Shortly after his arrival in the northern gold fields Boyle decided that placer mining with a pick and shovel was no way to get rich quick, a trick that he aptly performed, and he introduced the largest dredges the territory had ever seen.

John Hamill in his book, *The Strange Career of Mr. Hoover,* which went through more than a dozen printings, tells that the man who was to become the thirty-first president of the United States, once gave Boyle $1,350,000 in a deal that involved Boyle's Canadian Mining Company and a Klondike syndicate controlled by Herbert Hoover.

In *Brother, Here's a Man,* Kim Beattie estimates that in 1914 Boyle's huge holdings, known as the Boyle Concession, contained $50,000,000 of gold. "And the current belief was," Beattie writes, "that he (Boyle) had already personally amassed a fortune of $13,000,000, that he was only started and was potentially one of the richest men in the world."

In the rough and tumble, two-fisted, two-gunned milieu of the Klondike gold rush, where, as some wag remarked, "Men were men, and women ate their young," Boyle was as neat a fit as a die in a matrix. His years at sea, his propensity for strenuous activities, and his pugilistic tour with Slavin all helped to prepare him for the leading role he was quickly to assume in a frontier country of desperate and often lawless men who were scouring the frozen earth for riches. He was powerful of stature, he had enormous energy, unstinting courage, and a commanding presence.

The term, "King of the Klondike," was not misapplied.

Tex Rickard, western gambler and fight promoter, who later moved into the urban east to share the management of Madison Square Garden with the Ringling Circus people, had known Joe Boyle in the Klondike; he also knew Boyle's youngest daughter, who had swum exhibitions in the Garden's water-filled elephant pit.

I, too, knew Rickard, and one night during the Milrose Games in Madison Square Garden, I met him in the press box. My wife had recently given birth to the first of our four sons, and the newspapers had mentioned the fact that a former champion swimmer had become a mother.

"How's Sher-lit?" Rickard asked, in his nasal drawl. "How's the little boy?" He paused, reflectively. "Y'know, Sher-lit's father and I were pals in the Klondike. I had the saloon. Joe grabbed the rest of the place."

Joe's grip on what he had "grabbed" was still firm, and he was reaching for new acquisitions when, in 1914, the "Guns of August" heralded their dreadful devastation and Europe was inflamed in war.

Boyle had, besides vast material interests in the Klondike, a sentimental devotion to the region and to the "strong and restless (men), unthrottled by fear or defeat," whom the poet Robert W. Service represented as its inhabitants. His pride in the Klondike had caused him twice to send a hockey team to eastern Canada to compete for the Stanley Cup. Now he wanted a unit of Yukoners, identified by their territorial insignia, on the Western Front, and to this end he outfitted what was known as the Yukon Machine Gun Battery which, in time, he followed to England, where the detachment was in the final stages of training.

His intent was to lead the Yukoners in battle. The military authorities heard his petition for a command and granted him only the perfunctory title of Honorary Colonel. He was forty-nine years old. He had had no formal military training, although possessed of qualities that should have made him an excellent soldier in the field. He saw the unit he had organized and equipped go off to war with a husky puppy as a mascot, and he remained with the stay-at-homes in London.

Boyle's mining operations had been consigned to other hands for the "duration" but the "duration," in this instance, was infinity. He was never again to set foot in the Klondike. In London he wore an Honorary Colonel's uniform. It was elaborately cut, it had epaulets of gold leaf from the Yukon, and it gave him little more military status than a trigged-out light opera cavaliero on the stage. He chafed and fretted, outraged at the military ordinance that denied him participation in the most stupendous conflict the world had ever known.

Then, suddenly, with the collapse of Russia and the Bolshevik take-over, Joe Boyle was launched on a mad and romantic odyssey that took him first into the heart of havoc-ridden Russia, where he arranged the rescue of the Grand Duchess, and thence to the throne of her cousin, the Queen of Rumania. Boyle's biographers say that he was in love with the queen; Queen Marie spoke lovingly of Boyle.

"When Joe Boyle first entered my room, a stranger . . . , it was as though a rock had miraculously appeared before me, a rock upon which I could lean," the queen wrote in a foreword for Kim Beattie's book. ". . . All around were dark waves, storm, voices full of anguish against a background of flames; and all at once Joe Boyle was there, a stranger, and yet, somehow, not a stranger, because I seemed to have been waiting for him . . .

". . . My heart becomes soft when I think of him, soft with a great wistfulness and an aching longing . . ."

He was the strong man of a nation demoralized by war, by invasion, by disaffection, by a shattered economy, and by hunger, whose queen, with little support from the feckless and indecisive Ferdinand, was in desperate plight until the Canadian Colonel came by chance to her aid.

For a period of nearly three years, Boyle's administration of Rumania gave validity to the title which was continually affixed to him of "uncrowned king." He dictated policy, commanded what was left of the military, managed relief, directed agricultural operations, and served the queen as plenipotentiary extraordinary in Rumania's relations with other countries. His office extended to the domestic regime of the court. He went off to England with the youthful Prince Nicholas to enroll him in Eton, prior to which the pair were guests at Buckingham Palace. He brought about the annulment of the morganatic marriage of the irresponsible and profligate Crown Prince Carol; he was the loving guardian of the Princess Ileana.

He left Rumania after suffering a serious illness that brought Queen Marie to his bedside as nurse, and left a history of dramatic escapades and bravura exploits that have intrigued a dozen authors, whose accounts of Boyle's goings-on often have the melodramatic character of a suspense novel.

* * * * * * * * * * *

Boyle's next field of operations was Russia, where he attempted to implement a fantastic scheme to recover for Royal Dutch Shell the rich oil fields the Bolsheviks had confiscated. The scheme failed, to be sure; but it had been conceived on such a grandiose scale, and Boyle had displayed such daring and elan in its prosecution, that the failure had a kind of dramatic magnificence. And Boyle's derring-do in Russia added to his fame as the greatest soldier of fortune of the age.

"Col. Joseph W. Boyle . . . , who is popularly believed to hold the key to oil wells in Europe and Asia has returned to London," read an Associated Press dispatch from that city, 5 August 1922. "His activities at the Hague and Genoa conferences attracted more attention to petroleum negotiations than to most of the European statesmen.

". . . All Europe knows Col. Boyle as a friend of kings and queens, an adviser of prime ministers and a peace emissary between hostile states. He is believed to be closer to Lenin, Trotsky, Litvinoff and other Bolshevist luminaries than any other living man."

When Boyle died in April, 1923 in England, the New York *Morning World* devoted three columns to his obituary, which was illustrated with a picture of himself and Queen Marie. He was, the *World* declared, "the last of the D'Artagnans."

The *New York Times,* 17 April 1923, in its lead editorial which extended nearly a column, after a brief recital of Boyle's career in the Klondike and after telling of his activities during his first visit to Russia, (his main purpose had been to attempt to restore rail transportation and organize a White-Russian army for the eastern front; the rescue of the Grand Duchess had been an incidental achievement) went on . . .

"Then he (Boyle) went to Rumania, where his exploits have already passed into legend—too much legend, perhaps. He was soldier, statesman, rescuer of imperiled politicians, friend of royalty, and eventually pillar of the throne. He has left a big name in the Near East, where most visitors from the Atlantic world are gentlemen adventurers, at least outside of office hours, in these troubled and transitory times. Finally, he appeared in the most hazardous field of all, the great rivalry between international oil groups. At Genoa and the Hague he represented the Royal Dutch Shell organization. He held court and received accredited ambassadors; he almost attained the status and recognition of another Great Power. He warred against Standard Oil as Lloyd George warred against Krassin, and got almost as much space in the dispatches. He was credited with the erection of a magnificent political scheme, almost, but not quite executed, by which the Shell group would get all the oil in Russia, and in return for its promises Russia would finally concede Bessarabia to Rumania. It may have been fiction; certainly it didn't come true. But it illustrates the repute of Colonel Boyle that such stories should naturally attach themselves to him."

CHAPTER EIGHTEEN

Joe Boyle died quietly in bed in the home of a friend in Middlesex, England, a strange demise for a man whose fifty-five years of life had been a succession of madcap adventures and violent exploits. He was buried in England on the grounds of St. James Church, Hampton Hill. On the day of interment, the Dowager Empress of Russia sent a wreath to supplement the floral display the Rumanian queen had caused to be laid on the grave, and Queen Marie herself designed the elaborate headstone that marks the place of burial.

Boyle died intestate, and what became of the great wealth his biographers maintain he amassed in the Klondike gold fields, the better than a million and a quarter Herbert Hoover purportedly gave him, and another million, according to the *New York World* obituary, he won in a lawsuit brought against the Guggenheims, is a question that none of the investigators of Boyle's career has answered satisfactorily.

His fortune, if indeed it was as great as his biographers have represented it, seems to have slipped away as quietly as sand falling through the narrow tube of an hour glass. His three daughters, Flora Alexander, Susan, and Charlotte never saw a penny of the money. His divorced wife, Emily Raynor Boyle, received no bequest.

Emily Boyle died suddenly in our home in Scottsville. She suffered no lingering illness, and she was a lively and lucid little woman until shortly before her death. I often questioned her about her life with Joe Boyle, and I was fascinated with what she told me.

Queen Marie once mentioned Emily in her diary. She wrote, following a cozy after-dinner téte-a-téte with Boyle in a remote country seat in Rumania, ". . . I took Boyle into my room and we talked business, and curiously enough he for the first time spoke to me about his wife—she left him early in life declaring that he was going to be a failure and now he is King of the Klondike."

Mrs. Boyle told me nothing of the kind, and I am inclined to give credence to what she did tell me. While it lasted, her connubial career with Joe seemed a happy union. They lived together during most of the 1890's, two zestful and attractive young people whose resources permitted them to indulge their mutual taste for café life and the theater, and to patronize the metropolitan race courses, the favorite spots of Joe Boyle, who inherited his father's love of the thoroughbred.

"I can't recall a single serious quarrel we had before Joe left," his widow said. "He was wonderful during the years of our marriage. He loved to go, and we went everywhere: Rector's, Shanley's, Bustanoby's. Joe knew all sorts of people along Broadway: Phil Dwyer, the big race track man; Terry McGovern, the little fighter; Sam Harris, the Broadway producer; Kid McCoy; Diamond Jim Brady. I saw Bet-a-Million-Gates lose a lot of money—a wad, playing faro in Canfield's, in Saratoga. We were together at Monmouth Park the day Salvator, the famous race horse, set a record for a mile. I remember the chant they used to have, *They can bring 'em from the east, they can bring 'em from the west, but they c-a-n-t B-E-A-T Sal-vator*. Those were great days. Then, suddenly, Joe was gone"—she snapped her fingers—" just like that!"

"But why, if you were getting along so well?" I asked.

She shook her head wistfully. "Joe was a gambler, a sporting man. It was his life. Business—and he was very good at it when he wanted to be—bored him stiff. He hated to be tied down. He went off with Slavin, and once gone"—she waved her small hands—"with Joe, out of sight was out of mind."

And with two small daughters and a son to care for, there were times when Emily Boyle was hard pressed to make ends meet, particularly if the alimony wasn't forthcoming.

Then, without a word of warning, Boyle would pop back into New York. "And you'd never think," Mrs. Boyle said, "that he'd been away longer than overnight. We'd pick up where we had left off: the fancy lobster palaces, the theater, the race track. And presents! He'd shower me with 'em. And as suddenly as he returned, he'd be gone again. But we never fought or snarled at one another."

My wife had a somewhat similar report on Boyle.

He would come from the Klondike wearing a large western hat but never an overcoat, even in the coldest weather, and briefly play the role of a loving and indulgent father. "He was so big and handsome and the hat he wore caused people to turn and look at him," Charlotte said. "I was awfully proud to walk with him down Fifth Avenue and over to the Belmont Hotel, where he always stayed. What lunches he gave me, far more than I could ever eat. And he'd buy me things we'd see in shop windows. On one of his trips to New York he brought me a small nugget of Klondike gold which I wore on a charm bracelet."

Boyle's youngest daughter and I had been married a year and a half when Charlotte learned of her father's death. She was shocked since she had known nothing of his illness, but she was less grievously affected by the news than she would have been had Boyle been a devoted parent which, except on rare occasions, he was not.

Nearly three years had passed since she had heard from her father. He had written to her from London during the 1920 Olympic Games in Antwerp proposing a meeting in that city at the close of the games. The letter was delivered to the headquarters of the United States Olympic Team at a time when Charlotte and Ethelda Bleibtrey were in Paris for a series of swimming exhibitions, and her delayed receipt of it destroyed the chance of the meeting.

Irreverently, when I read in the obituary notices of the wealth Boyle was supposed to have had, I asked my wife what she was going to do with her patrimony: Buy a Rolls for herself? And perhaps a race horse for me?

"Don't start building a hope chest," she said cynically. "If there's anything there, young Joe'll have it."

Joseph Whiteside Boyle, Jr. had been for a time with

his father in the Klondike, and he probably knew more about his father's resources than any other member of the family, but the rapport between the two had ended some time before the elder Boyle's death, and my wife's surmise that her brother had sliced into their father's estate is unsupported by any known fact.

"A Broadway and London playboy, a flamboyant, much-married though minor figure," by Colonel Rodney's estimation in *King of the Klondike,* young Joe was not without capability. He was a counsel for Royal Dutch Shell and, on one occasion, was spokesman for a small delegation of Shell officials who came from London to solicit a staggering loan of $125,000,000 from Harry Haggerty, a former Rochesterian who served as fiscal officer for the Metropolitan Life Insurance Company. When young Joe died in 1955, he left his last wife with whom he had been living in Nassau, the Bahamas, in very comfortable circumstances, but hardly an heiress of millions.

The Boyles were a dispersive crowd with very tenuous sentimental ties. But I found that there were compensations marrying into a dismembered family. As a bridegroom, I was spared the ordeal of being ushered into the front parlor and exposed to the scrutiny of an entire company of in-laws. My meeting at the church with Mrs. Boyle was brief. And although I learned at that time that my wife had two sisters, I knew almost nothing about Joe Boyle, Jr. until, shortly after Charlotte and I had settled as newlyweds in the conservative city of Rochester, a long story with pictures telling of young Joe's liaison with the celebrated *Ziegfeld Follies* beauty, Kay Laurell, was circulated in newspapers all over the land. It was one of those lurid tales that the Hearst newspapers featured in their Sunday supplements, and it reported that Miss Laurell, posing as *September Morn,* had achieved a notable first: the first nude ever to be displayed in a Ziegfeld production. There was much more, including the announcement that Kay had had a child by Boyle.

I was not shocked but secretly rather pleased by this apocalyptic treatise. My profile was low. I had never been much in the spotlight until I married a Boyle; I enjoyed the reflected fame, and the notion I had early formed that the Boyles were "story" people was supported by this half-page exposé on my brother-in-law. My wife, however, found it less than edifying. She resented the scandal of familial association. And since the *Herald,* by which I was then employed, subscribed to the syndicate that issued the article, I was constrained to approach Mr. Antisdale, not to suggest that the story (which, after all, was news of a sort) be omitted, but played down.

He put a fatherly hand on my shoulder. "I've seen it," he said. "The *Herald* is a family journal. It won't be run here."

In a history of the famous girly shows, *The Ziegfeld Follies,* Marjorie Farnsworth devotes more than a page to Miss Laurell, and remarks at one point, "Her name became a synonym for undraped feminine loveliness and Kay was more than willing to have it remain as such. She knew she had a beautiful figure, slender like a boy's but softly rounded, and that it was her greatest asset on the road to fame. Ned Wayburn, who staged so many of the *Follies,* called Kay 'the original American Venus.' "

Miss Laurell became in time our sister-in-law. Joe took her to wife, briefly. What serial number she had in his succession of wives I cannot recall. An ambitious young woman, she left the *Follies* in which she had appeared with such notable players as Will Rogers, Ann Pennington, W. C. Fields, Mae Murray, Eddie Cantor and Ina Claire, to try Hollywood and the legitimate theater, but her success in neither venture was conspicuous. She was typed as a Follies beauty, and it was her destiny to remain as such, sempiternally.

* * * * * * * * * * *

During his youth and early manhood, Joe Boyle, Jr. was often around New York, and he and his youngest sister were good friends and frequent companions. He was an attractive and worldly youth and his sister was impressed by his knowing ways and flattered by his attentions. With Joe's first marriage these amicable relations ended, and in time the affection Charlotte felt for her brother was cooled both by long separations and by her feeling that he was grossly neglectful of their mother.

I never met young Joe and I never knew his father. I did meet Joseph Whiteside Boyle, Sr.'s older brother, David, who spent a Sunday at our home and excited in me the hope that we might meet again and again; that our relations might evolve into an intimate friendship. I was fascinated by the man. But he left and I never saw him again, for he died not too long after his Scottsville visit.

From Dave Boyle I derived a reflected impression of his brother, Joe. Both were men of large and rugged stature; their features were similar, and perhaps their style. But Dave was the quiet one. He was a man of charming manners, of sly humor, and of broad understanding that came not from book learning but from association with his fellow men.

He had been in racing all his life, he knew all its angles and he was wryly philosophical about what it could do to the compulsive gambler, particularly since the introduction of parimutuel betting on American tracks. In the days of the bookmaker, Boyle pointed out, the horse player could shop around for bargain prices; with the mutuels the odds were mechanically and irrevocably fixed. "The average horse player has a blind spot," he said. "He never figures the percentage the mutuels take from every dollar he bets. It can be disastrous."

His attitude toward racing was faintly snobbish. He seemed to feel that it was not a game for the hoi polloi, for people with welfare checks and the family grocery money, but rather for the likes of Ascot toffs in morning coats and silk toppers, who arrive at the course in road coaches.

Dave Boyle gave added support to my assumption that the Boyles were "story" people.

He once uncovered a "sleeper," a colt named Destruction, which did its time trials by the dark of the moon, and Dave promised his mother he would buy her an estate known as The Firs in Woodstock, Ontario, with the money the horse would win for him. He brought his brother Joe, and his father, Charlie, into the act. The trio laid quite a lot of money on Destruction, but the wagers were distributed among a number of bookmakers and the odds were not affected, as they would have been had the money been shoved through the mutuel windows. Run on a New York track, the race had the thrill of a 10, 20, 30, melodrama. Destruction, last away from the barrier, won by the proverbial nose, and Dave (and Joe and Charlie) had among them $56,000, more than enough for the purchase of The Firs.

Kim Beattie tells that story in *Brother, Here's a Man!* He fails, however, since the whoppers that escape the fisherman's hook and long shot horses that lose are hardly the stuff of romance, to mention the time Dave Boyle nurtured another "sleeper," which he thought an even tighter cinch than Destruction. He backed the horse prodigally and, disdainful of the other entrants, he ignored the progress of the race and was reading the comic strip "Barney Google" at a clubhouse table when his favored animal ran wide at the last turn and clean out of the money, cleaning Dave in the process. He had gone for broke; he lost everything, a thumping $27,000!

"After that," Dave Boyle told me during his Scottsville visit, "I was cured of an affliction I had suffered many years. I was through betting horses. It's a cliche, 'you can't beat the races,' but of course it's true. You can't. But there'll always be horse players. Allured by the hope of gain, hope springs eternal." He paused reflectively, and smiled. "It's an odd philosophy, the average horse player's. 'What d'you know?' is his frantic inquiry. He's always looking for the sure thing, the fixed race. But if he loses and he thinks the race has been rigged, he'll holler bloody murder."

Broke and in need of a livelihood, Boyle remained in the realm he knew. He became a racing official, first a placing judge, later a steward. He was a popular figure on Canadian race tracks. When he died a race was run in his honor: the Boyle Memorial. The president of the Fort Erie Racing Association invited my wife to be his guest and present the Memorial trophy. I went with her to Fort Erie. It was a ceremonial occasion. We were entertained at a sumptuous lunch and sat in the president's box. Charlotte saw the Memorial run from the judges' stand. They put down a red carpet when she descended to the winner's circle, where she was instructed to hold the bridle of the winning horse and hand up the plate to the jockey. There was applause. The band played, news camera clicked, and the horse, made fractious by this fanfare, reared up and tried to break Charlotte's hold on the bridle. She hung on resolutely, delivered the plate to the jockey, and started across the racing strip to rejoin the president in his box. As the gate opened for her, a tight-lipped horse player standing close paid her a terse tribute.

"Nice ride, sister," he said.

CHAPTER NINETEEN

The prominence that had come to me at the time of my marriage to a swimming champion did not end with the pictures and stories of our nuptials that appeared in newspapers the day after the ceremony, or with the circulation of news-camera shots of Charlotte and me being pushed over the Boardwalk in a wheelchair during our brief Atlantic City honeymoon. Back in Rochester, the modest local fame I enjoyed as a by-line newspaper writer was enlarged by the national celebrity of my bride. People wanted to meet the swimming star. Invitations to social events came from persons I had never known before. I was surprised to find that fellow diners in restaurants were eager for the new Mrs. Clune's autograph. We hadn't been settled in our apartment more than two or three weeks when I received through the mail a note addressed, "*Mister* Charlotte Boyle Clune, Rochester, N. Y."

Swimming as a competitive sport for women was in its early stages in this country when Charlotte was setting records and winning championships, and her pioneering achievements resulted in an exorbitant amount of publicity. I enjoyed displaying to guests at our apartment a fat scrapbook that contained cuttings from magazines and newspapers from all over the North American continent and from such far-away journals as the Sydney, Australia *Referee,* the Berlin *Sport-Spiegel,* and the *Hong Kong Telegraph,* telling of her exploits. James P. Sinnott had glorified her in verse in his column in the New York *Evening Mail* and Ripley ("Believe it or Not") had drawn her picture.

Charlotte was often spoken of as the "Sea Gate Flash," since she had lived for a time in the Brooklyn oceanside community of Sea Gate. The year before our marriage she and Ethelda Bleibtrey competed in a series of swimming races at the Hawaiian centennial celebration. The Prince of Wales, later King Edward VIII, making a tour of the world, stopped at the Islands for the celebration. A handsome, charming, zestful young man, the Prince was eager for new experiences. He wanted at once to try surfboarding off Waikiki, and Duke Kahanamoku, the famous Hawaiian sprint swimmer, and Charlotte and Miss Bleibtrey went with him, the Prince on the bow of the Duke's board.

They caught a wave and started in to shore and the Duke, with courtly solicitude, attempted to instruct the Prince in the subtleties of the sport. It was "Your Highness" this, and "Your Highness" that, and "If Your Royal Highness pleases." Naturally the Prince was not apt, this being his first try; he began to wobble on the front of the board and the Duke, striving at the opposite end to preserve its equilibrium, suddenly, as the situation became critical, lost all deference and deportment. "Eddie! Eddie!" he cried, "Eddie, for God's sake, step back!" It was too late. The board foundered, both riders were spilled into the sea and the long plank, after a plunge below the surface, rose in parabolic flight and came down smartly on the royal noggin. At which conjuncture the king-to-be loosed a string of obscenities that would have done credit to an East-End fishwife, but properly spoken, each with the cultured inflection of the Court of St. James.

The incident was reported in wire stories from Hawaii and later included in an Odyssean account of Charlotte's and Ethelda's Pacific tour, which was written by Paul E. Lockwood, then a *Brooklyn Eagle* sports writer, later chief aide to Thomas E. Dewey during Dewey's terms as New York governor and his candidacy for president. The saga consumed three-quarters of a newspaper page and was pasted into Charlotte's scrapbook.

Early in our marriage I myself began to put together a scrapbook that was devoted exclusively to post-nuptial news items, and I was surprised, now that Charlotte was nominally a Rochester housewife, at the continued mention of her name in newspapers and magazines. She returned once to New York to compete in a Metropolitan Championship, then announced her retirement from competitive swimming. She was still in demand. Promoters of aquatic events wanted her for exhibitions, and her appearance in Rochester, Buffalo, Toronto, and other places was heralded in sport page banner lines.

And that wasn't all. The month after we were married, the *New York World* magazine printed a story entitled "The Shower that shattered a Mermaid Friendship." The bank below, read:

"Charlotte Boyle's Wedding Indirectly Causes Break in Ranks of Women's Swimming Association and Loss of Its Long Held Monopoly in World's Records—All Because Ethelda Bleibtrey Wasn't Invited to a Pre-Nuptial Party."

It was one of those trumped-up, overwrought yarns intended to titillate stay-at-homes who, three score years ago, had no television to relieve the tedium of their Sunday confinement. It ran a full newspaper page, with pictures, and it was distributed to newspapers that subscribed to the *World* syndicate. I have before me a page from one of these subscribers, the *Sunday Oregonian,* of Portland.

There is a cut of Ethelda standing alone, another of Charlotte and Ethelda together, a pose of Charlotte sitting on a springboard, and a picture of Mr. and Mrs. Clune outside of the Little Church around the Corner. My wife is shorter than I. In this shot, I discovered, by use of a rule, that I had seven inches of vertical space on the page, she only five.

And the next month (the second following our marriage), the *World* published another piece, which also went out to its syndicate subscribers, "The Courtship of Charlotte Boyle," which purported to relate the intimate details of our romance, and which now and then did introduce into a preponderantly fictitious narrative a note of fact. My father was spoken of as Charlotte's "wealthy father-in-law," which he cynically remarked made no sense whatever; I was described as an "athletic looking young man . . . a graduate of Dartmouth College." In this instance I was confused with a friend of mine, a guest at the Geneseo party given for the swimming girls by Jim Sam Wadsworth, who was, indeed, a

Dartmouth graduate, and who did look like an athlete, which he was: a half-back good enough to be mentioned by Walter Camp, if not quite All-American caliber.

These paragraphs are being written half a year before the 1980 Olympic Games, and I asked my wife if she could recall the name of a single competitor in women's aquatic events in the last half-dozen Olympics. One name came to mind, Debbie Meyer, who won three individual titles in Mexico City in 1968. We were in Mexico City for the track and field program, but did not go near the swimming stadium. In a restaurant one day we met the parents of Miss Meyer, who told us distractedly of the difficulty they were having getting tickets to see their daughter win a championship. The name Debbie Meyer stuck. Beyond that, Charlotte could name no champions more recent than Helena Madison and Eleanor Holm, who won golds at Los Angeles in 1932.

The crack girl swimminers today, wherever and whoever they are, may be as photogenic as the girls of sixty years ago, but they are old hat—the novelty of a young woman competing in a swimming race in a sheer, one-piece silk swim suit has long since passed. And while the present day records are light years ahead of those of the early part of the century, the record holders are rarely shown in the national press and are obscure except to patrons and close observers of their sport.

Both Charlotte and Ethelda Bleibtrey, and pretty little Aileen Riggin, who won the fancy dive as an early teen-ager at the Antwerp Games—precursory figures in women's swimming—generated reams of newspaper copy. Women on bathing beaches were being enfranchised. They were throwing aside the ponderous habiliments of Victorian restraint—bathing costumes with sleeves to the elbows, skirts below the calf of the leg, stockings, and bathing shoes—for sensible swim suits. The pioneer swimming girls were the catalysts of this transition. They competeed in scant silks that accentuated the "female form divine" even more than Annette Kellerman's black tights; and though the Amateur Athletic Union, which certified their competitions, never promoted the thesis, it was the appeal of sex that attracted crowds to women's swimming and diving events.

Charlotte Boyle, before our marriage, won numerous national and metropolitan championships and got into the record books. As a youth and young man the notion of a world record had been a fetish with me. Now I was married to a young woman who had two or three. They were girls' records, to be sure, and for swimming, not for going the fastest mile on foot, the Promethean achievement of which I had dreamed. Nonetheless, I framed the plaques from the International Athletic Federation which attested to Charlotte's world supremacy and hung them on the walls of our apartment. They were the prize memorabilia of her career as a swimmer until, a few years after our marriage, the new edition of the *Encyclopedia Britannica,* in a way (it seemed to me) immortalized her and a former teammate in a paragraph that appeared under the encyclopedia's essay, "Swimming."

After explaining that swimming coaches were unanimous in the belief that the swift thrash of the six-beat crawl was too tiring a stroke for distances longer than one hundred yards, the essay continued:

> Late in 1917, however, two young champions of the Women's Swimming Association of New York, Miss Charlotte Boyle and Miss Claire Galligan, determined to give the six-beat crawl a trial and by the summer of 1918 they broke records with it over the regulation courses, 880 yd. and one mile. So convincing was this demonstration that it caused a sudden change of mind among coaches and competitors. The six-beat crawl immediately won favor in the United States, presently in other countries and within a few years it had become the recognized stroke the world over, not only for racing but for all around purposes.

CHAPTER TWENTY

In retrospect, it seems to me that the first dozen or fifteen years of my married life were the most exciting years I have ever known, and surely the most transitional. The 1920s, as someone defined the decade, was the Era of Wonderful Nonsense, and I suppose I participated in the common craziness, as did most of my contemporaries. I even got into the stock market, a daring exploit for one of my unadventurous spirit, through a man I knew whose daughter was married to young Thomas Lamont, who had recently been made a J. P. Morgan partner—an induction, the press said, worth a million dollars to the inductee. I was in only modestly, however, and out quickly. I had a profit of $1,000, the easiest money that had ever come to me. I was sorely tempted to try again. Resisting the impulse, I stood by, drooling, as Montgomery Ward spiraled into the stratosphere (439 and a fraction), with Radio Corporation, Harvester, Johns-Manville, and other offerings in pursuing ascendency. But my feet were cold; I couldn't quite believe the fantasy; and when the roof fell in that bitter October Thursday, 1929, I hugged myself for luck and congratulated my timorousness.

But the stock market wasn't the greatest excitement for me during that era. Two years after we were married we had a child—a boy—and I envisaged, as my father had at the time of my birth, the rapport I would have with my son and the manner in which I would direct his career; and of course the kid ultimately went off on his own tangent, and his designs and desires were entirely different from those I might have had for him. Two years later my wife, as the proprieties of the day would have it, was again in a "delicate condition;" and when the time came for her confinement I joined a small company of expectant fathers who were sweating it out, suffering mental labor pains, in a hospital anteroom. At one point during our ordeal, the obstetrician I had engaged showed a grinning countenance at the door and sprang the age-old gag, "Cheerio. I've never lost a father yet."

Presently a nurse came to the anteroom and beamed upon me. "Congratulations," she said, "you have a fine little boy."

The only boy in a family of three girls, in my own youth I had longed for a brother who might share my interests and activities. Now, the nurse had advised, my older son was to have a younger brother. It seemed to me a splendid arrangement, and the age difference was ideal. I thanked the nurse and rose exultantly. I was quite early in the morning. Mama would be unreceptive to my loving expressions until the fumes of the ether had passed. My tensions relaxed; I was in need of a hearty breakfast and I left the anteroom, descended to the main floor of the hospital, and was passing the reception desk when another nurse called, "Oh, Mr. Clune. Congratulations. You've just had another little boy."

"I know," I answered gaily. "Two now."

"No," she said, "three."

"Three?"

"You've had twins this morning—so far."

Twins—*so far!* I bolted through the door and into the street. Perhaps I was a chauvinistic pig, but I hadn't wanted a daughter, particularly. A son was fine; a second son. But not, good God, an eight-oar crew, or a baseball nine, right in the family!

I was tardy getting back to the hospital, fearful that some genetic prodigy had occurred during my absence. All was well, however; there were only two. Embarrassed by her fecundity, my wife avowed that there had been no twins in her family and that this sort of thing must have derived from mine. She was mistaken. A little genealogical dredging turned up the fact that there had been Boyle twins a few generations back, and my heredity showed nothing of the kind.

Bill Raynor, Charlotte's half-brother, in show business all his life, sent a characteristic telegram.

"What," the wire queried, "are you doing for an encore?"

Soon Charlotte was up and about and back again in the news. Press services sent out pictures of her holding the twins in her arms. We had moved from our small "honeymoon" apartment across from the University of Rochester campus to half of a double house not far from my native Linden Street. The summer following the birth of the twins, Charlotte inaugurated a career as a swimming instructor, first, briefly, at a huge salt water pool at a lakeside summer resort known as Sea Breeze Park, and later at Rochester's leading social club, the Genesee Valley, which continued nearly half a century.

We had room in the double house to entertain, and now and then girls from Charlotte's old club, the Women's Swimming Association of New York, would stop on their way to some aquatic event west of Rochester. Helen Meaney, Aileen Riggin, and Ethelda Bleibtrey, all Olympic winners, at one time or another were our guests. The callers were invariably accompanied by Miss Charlotte Epstein, the redoubtable manager and chaperon of the WSA, who one day appeared with a teen-ager, Gertrude Ederle, who was entered in the 50-yard Junior Championship to be contested that night at the Buffalo Athletic Club.

The kid was of German extraction, the daughter of an Amsterdam Avenue butcher in New York. Her coach, L. de B. Handley, thought she was a comer, a prospect for the Paris Olympics a year and a half hence. She was a stolid, undemonstrative girl with the shoulders of a lineman on a high school football team, as solidly built as a brick wall. I agreed to drive the swimmer, Miss Epstein, and my wife to Buffalo, a journey of less than three hours in our Ford, and that night the girl won the championship easily.

After that we heard little of her until 1924, and then not too much. Shd made the United States women's swimming team but was hardly a sensation in Paris. She finished third in the 100-meter championship and Olympic athletes behind second place are usually destined for obscurity.

Then, the following summer, we read in news dispatches from Europe that Gertrude Ederle, the third place finisher at the Paris Olympic Games, was back in France, at Cape Gris Nez, planning to attempt what no woman (and only five men) had accomplished, a swim across the English Channel. The proposed exploit excited some hoopla at first, but few persons believed the teen-aged challenger of the stormy waters between the French seaside village and the chalk cliffs of Dover would succeed; and this feeling was confirmed when, after an arduous several-hour try, Gertrude failed to stay the course and was hauled into a boat and returned to shore.

But the skeptics had not reckoned on the fortitude and resolution of the stocky girl from the pavements of New York who, defeated in her first attempt, was convinced she could succeed on a second.

Miss Ederle had developed her swimming techniques under the expert guidance of L. de B. Handley, the WSA coach, but there was a vast difference between paddling up and down a fifty-yard pool and churning the twenty-odd mile stretch of cranky waters between the French and English coasts. For this test she had as a mentor William Burgess, an Englishman, who himself had swum the Channel several years before.

After a series of coastwide training trials off Cape Gris Nez, always under the watchful eye of Burgess, Gertrude was ready for her big effort. Early in the morning of 6 August 1926, she stroked into the Channel waters and pointed toward the English coast, which she achieved fourteen hours and thirty-one minutes later.

Not only was she the first of her sex to swim the Channel, but the time of her crossing was considerably lower than that of any one of the five men who had performed the feat before her; and she returned to New York in Paris clothes, a gangling French doll in her arms, for the moment the most celebrated woman in the Western world.

When she was transferred from the liner that had brought her west across the Atlantic to the city tug *Macom* upon which awaited a welcoming delegation of municipal dignitaries in frockcoats and top-hats, every steamship within range tied down its whistlecord and the ear-splitting din from the harbor was heightened by the blare of on-shore sirens. Airplanes buzzed and dipped in homage and pelted her with floral offerings.

A motorcade had been formed to display the heroine to the city of New York, and from the dizzy aeries of cliff workers in the great canyon of lower Broadway, ticker tape and the torn pages of telephone directories fluttered down on the youthful idol until the streets were ankle deep in drifting paper. A great rolling roar followed the procession northward, bands played, and the leading citizens of New York rode with pride in cars that trailed out beyond the lustrous machine that carried Gertrude Ederle to the quintessence of fame. The president of the United States turned momentarily from his official duties to remark Miss Ederle's achievement and to wire her a personal message of congratulation.

The next day, the page one story in the *New York Times* opened with this paragraph:

> New York City yesterday welcomed Gertrude Ederle home from her victory over the English Channel with a demonstration that for numbers, noise, spontaneity and variety surpassed any previous reception to a distinguished person. No president, or king, soldier or statesman has ever enjoyed such an enthusiastic and affectionate outburst of acclaim by the metropolis as that offered to the butcher's daughter from Amsterdam Avenue, hailed as the 'Queen of Swimmers.'

In the days immediately following her triumphal return, the girl was virtually mobbed by hero worshippers whenever she appeared in public. For weeks her most trivial acts were considered news. During this feverish adulation, she received offers for personal appearances, endorsements, and other services which, the press reported, exceeded $1,000,000.

My wife and I had cabled her one of these offers. We did so at the instigation of Harry Mitchell, an old-time showman who had come to Rochester to succeed Mickey Finn as manager of the Temple Theater. The Temple was part of the

Keith-Albee vaudeville circuit, and Mitchell had been authorized to attempt to book Miss Ederle as a headline act. He knew Charlotte's relations with the girl, and we were instructed to offer her a flat weekly salary of $2,500.

Our offer was ignored. I presume it looked like peanuts to a girl who had been promised everything except the moon. Gertrude, who was under the partial sponsorship of Dudley Field Malone, the well-known New York and Washington lawyer, had signed a contract for a tour of vaudeville theaters that were not part of the Keith circuit for $6,500 a week. The tank act included two subordinate performers, Aileen Riggin and Helen Wainwright, a fine swimmer in her own right. In time the act was booked into the National Theater in Rochester, and during her week's stand, Gertrude spent a night in the house into which we had recently moved in the village of Scottsville.

We had brought her home from the theater through a late winter snowstorm in our sometimes erratic-performing little car, and while Charlotte was preparing sandwiches and hot chocolate, our guest, sitting with me before a blazing fire in the living room, asked,

"Henry, can anyone put more than $1,000 in any one bank?"

I was startled by the ingenuousness of the question. It seemed to indicate that despite the lavish weekly sum she was being paid, Gertrude was not getting rich, and this in the end was more or less true.

The contract she signed may have paid her $6,500, but apparently there was a joker in the fine print. Out of the money she received, she was required to pay the salaries and traveling expenses of the Misses Riggin and Wainwright, the salary and traveling expenses of a stage carpenter who was part of the entourage, and the cost of shipping the tank and other stage properties from one city to another, and in this instance (an atrocious miscalculation of scheduling) the act had jumped from St. Louis to Rochester, a distance of more than six hundred miles.

When Charlotte joined us before the living room fire with sandwiches and hot chocolate, Gertrude, continuing her discussion of the management (mismanagement, it seemed to me) of her tour, further surprised me with a remark that she had borrowed three hundred dollars from her father which she had not yet been able to repay.

We sat up until well after midnight and rose late in the morning. The Ederle act played a matinee as well as an evening performance, and Gertrude wanted to be in the theater at least an hour before curtain time. I went out to the garage to crank up our cranky little car for the fourteen mile run from Scottsville to the National Theater, and found the pesky thing had its dander up. When I threw the switch it sputtered, coughed, seemed to spit at me, and stalled. I ran back to the house and phoned the local garage. The mechanic was out for lunch. I returned to our garage, flung up the hood of the car, and frantically snatched at wires and tubes, then tried again to get a spark from the motor. The battery was dead—dead as a smelt in a brine barrel.

In desperation, Charlotte and Gertrude left the house and hustled on foot 300 yards over a wooded snow-covered drive that led to the main road. A motorist approached but gave only a cold, fish-eyed glance at the wildly wigwagging women at the roadside, and continued without a hint of hestitation on his way to Rochester. Two more similarly insensible drivers passed, unaware, of course, that they were brushing off a girl to whom millions had paid homage and who was still a pre-eminent figure of her sex. It looked as if the afternoon show would be canceled for lack of its star when Will Keyes, a kindly, sloppy old fellow who wore the same stand-up linen collar for a week at a time and had a sort of grocery store and coal office in a musty crypt in the heart of Scottsville, ambled up in his ancient, rump-sprung Chalmers touring car.

"What you doing, you two girls out here in the road, waving at people?" Will asked.

"This is Gertrude Ederle," Charlotte explained impressively. "The girl who swam the English Channel."

"Oh, the English Channel," Will said brightly. "I was there, onct. I crossed it." He peered down at Gertrude as he opened the car door. "You swam it? Why, what was the matter with the boat? It wasn't too costly when I made the trip."

The two girls got in, and the old blunderbuss of a vehicle ambled into town and delivered Gertrude in the nick of time at the theater, where a clamoring crowd of idolators waited at the stage door.

I got into town later in the day and arranged for Gertrude to meet a man I know who was supposed to be an expert on financial matters. I thought he might give her some advice that would help her get more than she appeared to be getting from her contract, which, if it were drawn by Dudley Field Malone, ought to be cached in the archives of the American Bar Association as an example of legal ineptitude.

I never learned if anything of benefit resulted from the meeting. At the end of the week, Miss Ederle and her tank act moved on to another city, and after that we saw Gertrude only at rare intervals.

The year after New York City tendered her the greatest reception ever accorded a "distinguished person," as the *New York Times* put it, Charles Lindbergh returned from his trans-Atlantic solo flight to a more tumultuous and extravagant welcome, and Gertrude's star was dimmed by the coruscations of this new Nova. Her fame simmered off, in time expired. The years passed. Persons I knew who vaguely knew that Charlotte had once been a notable swimmer irritated me with the query, "Let's see. Your wife swam the English Channel, didn't she?"

"No. That was Gertrude Ederle."

"O—oh, Gertrude Ederle . . ."

The name was unknown, the possessor of it an aging spinster long out of the public eye, who lived with a couple of other unattached women in a modest house in Flushing, New York. For several years during her residence in this house she was an immobile invalid as the result of injuries suffered in a fall down a flight of stairs. Now and then a newspaper writer will dredge up her name and do a nostalgic piece on a heroic performance that briefly topped all other athletic achievements during what has often been called the Golden Age of Sports of the 1920s, when Babe Ruth was on his way to his 714th home run, when Bill Tilden dominated world tennis, when Bobby Jones made golf's Grand Slam, and the Dempsey-Tunney boxing match did a million dollars at the gate. But who knows or cares today?

Sic transit gloria mundi.

CHAPTER TWENTY-ONE

I am a provincial by instinct, by design, and by practice, and although I have lived an unconscionable number of years, my life, I suppose, has been limited by my provincialism. I have never seen a purple sunset at Zanzibar, shot an elephant, ridden the Blue Train to the Cote d'Azur, tried sky diving, played a round of golf, or achieved a college (or high school) diploma. I was never active in battle or won a medal for anything.

But during the transitional years that immediately followed my marriage, besides experiencing the phenomenon of fathering twins, I was hugged and kissed by the prime sex symbol of the land, rode the engine cab of the famous 20th Century Limited, swallowed a red hose under the compulsion of an Amazonian nurse on the diagnostic assembly line of the Mayo Clinic, saw men die during the most violent uprising the state prison at Auburn had ever known, and sat one morning in a hotel room with the great Winston Churchill. There were other memorable occasions.

In the late 1920s, the Eastman Kodak Company perfected a process known as Kodacolor for the reproduction of natural colors in motion pictures, and I was sent one day to George Eastman's home, where a party was being held to celebrate the new invention.

Although Mr. Eastman was not at all given to flamboyance or personal display, he had a keen sense of advertising values, and in the promotion of Kodacolor he had the aid of a skillful promoter, General Oscar N. Solbert. An imposing and handsome West Pointer who knew all the blows and feints of social deportment, General Solbert, before he retired from the Army to serve Eastman and his company in a capacity that was never very clearly defined, had functioned as a sort of chargé d'affaires during the American tour of the Prince of Wales and had held other posts that required style and social aptitude.

He knew numerous persons of prominence, and it was his scheme to give cachet to the new invention by having it shown first before a select group of men of national and international renown. Included in the couple of dozen guests who were entertained in the great gray Eastman mansion with its multitudinous staff, were such scientists and inventors as Thomas A. Edison, Hiran Percy Maxim, inventor of the Maxim silencer for fire arms, and Sir James Irvine, noted British chemist and educator. Industry was represented in part by Owen D. Young and James G. Harbord, chairmen respectively of General Electric and Radio Corporation of America. There were newspapermen in the gathering: Adolph Ochs, publisher of the *New York Times;* Roy Howard, of Scripps-Howard Newspapers; and Frank Gannett, founder of the journalistic colossus that bears his name. But the prize catch of all, because of his triumphs as commander-in-chief of the American Expeditionary Force were so recent and so green in memory, was General John J. Pershing, the most celebrated American soldier of his time.

The party continued two days, and the showing of the new color film took place in the afternoon of the first day in Mr. Eastman's large living room. I interviewed several of the guests, as I had been instructed to do by the city editor of the *Democrat and Chronicle,* asking their opinion of the new process. All spoke glowingly of it. I got around in time to Mr. Edison. His hearing was impaired, and I wrote my questions on a slip of paper and he replied in kind, using a stub of a pencil he took from a pocket. I attempted to draw him out on matters that did not pertain to the demonstration, wanting to know, since I had heard that he was skeptical of much in Christian doctrine, what he thought of the immortality of the soul. He was an octogenarian with several years more to live. He smiled, winked, and put the pencil back in his pocket without writing another word.

I sat in the rear of the room during the running of the film. When it was over, I looked for General Pershing, but apparently he had slipped out of the room the instant the projector had stopped, and I found that he had left the house. He was standing on a flagstone terrace that offered a pleasant prospect of green, velvety walks partitioned by trim hedges, and a wide pattern of gardens, now in midsummer bloom. Adolph Ochs of the *Times* was at his side, and several other guests were grouped around him. I had an odd feeling that the stature of the others had suffered diminution in the presence of this erect, powerful-appearing man, whose jaw squared off like a granite cornerstone. The General was in mufti. He wore a correct double-breasted blue suit with a thin stripe of gray, and a gray fedora. He was meticulously groomed.

I approached the small company, of which the General was not only the cynosure, but the oracle. He was being questioned about political and international issues, and his auditors hung on his words as if they were unimpeachably prophetic. One of his interrogators, who perhaps was more to the left than Mr. Eastman would desire in a house guest, with some diffidence but also with some persistence, was wondering if General Pershing approved of sending the United States Marines into China to protect the properties of exploiting American industries. Was it right that fine young American lives should be imperiled for such a materialistic—such a purely commercial purpose?

I perked up my ears. The General's answer might be worthy of a headline. But it seemed to me that he was being a tiny bit circumspect, and I moved in closer and propounded what I thought was a pertinent query of my own. The oracle started to answer, still, it seemed to me, with something less than clarion directness, and had continued several seconds, when he stopped abruptly.

"Young man," he demanded, in a field marshal's tone, and his eyes bent upon me like a laser beam, "are you a reporter?"

The impulse was to click my heels, ramrod my back, and bring up a smart salute. I suppressed it.

"Y—yes sir," I admitted, and I thought of court-martial.

"Not a word—not a word of this is to be printed," he commanded, wagging a forefinger before my eyes. "Not a word, understand?"

"Yes sir."

I backed away from the assemblage, trying not to seem fugitive in my withdrawal, and soon left the Eastman estate. I have never been sharp in riposte: I have what someone has described as "staircase wit." All of the bright things I should have said on the instant come to me belatedly, usually as I am mounting the staircase on my way to bed. I was halfway to the newspaper office when my mind formed the trenchant retort I should have made to the General. I should have reminded him that I was no damn dog robber in his command but a member of the noble Fourth Estate: that neither he nor any other brass hat was going to tell me what I could or could not print. I was still in a ferment when I sat down at the typewriter.

Then I realized that the General had said nothing of significance during the time that I was within range of his voice, aborting the response to my question and being less than specific in answering the interrogator who had spoken before me. There was nothing here to write about, and suddenly I thought back to what had seemed at the time an epochal moment, my first sight of General Pershing (the second was on Mr. Eastman's terrace); the incident escalated in my fancy, and before I did the main story on the Kodacolor demonstration and the personages who had witnessed it, I indulged in a small vignette of recollection.

It was nearly ten years before, in the autumn of 1918. A lowly private in the army, I was walking alone along a road not far outside of Chaumont, general headquarters for the American Expeditionary Force. It was a pleasant afternoon and I was enjoying the graceful panorama of the French countryside when, suddenly, I saw a convoluting cloud of dust rise on the horizon, and, in front of it what I was sure was Jehovah's chariot coming on with the speed of light.

I leapt to the side of the road as a great shining vehicle, adorned with stars and occupied by a single star-decorated passenger, flew by. I threw the quickest and fanciest salute I could command and got a snap at the hat from the Olympian figure in the rear seat.

"My God," I exclaimed awesomely, as I was left besmirched in swirling dust, "It's him—HE—the General! Pershing!"

In the short piece I wrote for the newspaper about General Pershing I described the incident on the Chaumont road and remarked that being saluted by the commander-in-chief excited a heady sense of being in touch with divinity. I continued with a report of my actual meeting with the "divinity" on Mr. Eastman's terrace, explained my submission at that time to the General's order as a natural reflex of a former private under his command, and gently suggested that perhaps "our greatest captain and the outstanding American of his day" had been the least presumptuous in attempting to abrogate the noble ordinance that allowed a free press in this land of the free and the home of the brave.

The city desk seemed to like my small offering and gave it an arresting head and a place of prominence in the next morning's edition of the *Democrat and Chronicle.* I returned that afternoon to the Eastman house for the wind-up of the Kodacolor party. Several prominent Rochesterians had been invited to meet the visiting dignitaries, the large Eastman living room was crowded when I crossed its threshold, and, as I did so, I was startled by a stentorian pronouncement of my name.

"Clune! Clune!" the shout went up; and a large man, with a jaw like a granite cornerstone, handsomely tailored in a blue double-breasted suit with a thin gray stripe, was hurrying toward me from the far side of the room. "Clune," the name resounded, and a comradely arm fell across my shoulders and pressed tight, "that was a bully yarn this morning. Bully!" He was laughing. Laughing heartily! "Black Jack Pershing," who I had thought as solid and implacable as the pyramid at Giza!

The embrace ended; we shook hands, and quickly

parted. I was exultant as I circulated among the other guests in the room. I had known the touch of an accolade.

* * * * * * * * * * *

Nine years before Edward VIII, England's first bachelor king in 176 years, renounced his throne for an American lady, (who reportedly had cabled a Baltimore friend, "They say I'm a plumber's daughter. Send me something about the family." and got an answer, "Stop acting like a plumber's daughter.") I saw the then Prince of Wales cut a ribbon that officially opened the imposing structure that spans the Niagara River between Fort Erie, Ontario, and Buffalo, New York.

Performed in the middle of the Peace Bridge, the ribbon cutting was the climactic event of a day (Sunday, 27 August 1927) of posh ceremony. Leading statesmen from Canada, the United States, and England were present in the avowed interest of peace and international amity. President Coolidge had half promised to make a speech, but reneged. He deicded he needed a vacation and went off to the Black Hills of Dakota, where he was photographed wearing a feathered war bonnet, the gift of a friendly tribe of American aborigines. The war bonnet endowed him with all the dash and bravura of an Indian warrior—one of wood, in front of a cigar store!

His decision not to speak at the Peace Bridge celebration was briefly considered a violation of international etiquette and a breach of protocol. It was not at first thought fitting that England's future king should grace an occasion of such consequence unless his attendancce was complemented by the presence of the president of the United States. The difficulty was resolved when Vice-President Dawes and several cabinet members were delegated as stand-ins for the chief executive, and the affair went off brilliantly. It is possible that Mr. Coolidge was scarcely missed. If not a party-pooper, he was hardly a festive fellow; perhaps somewhat in the character implied in the remark of the irreverent wit, Wilson Mizner, at he sad moment of the ex-president's demise.

"Coolidge is dead," someone called to Mr. Mizner.

"How do they know?" was the dour and suspicious inquiry.

The Prince of Wales and his younger brother, Prince George, were first displayed on a speakers' stand in a compound on the Buffalo side of the bridge,; and it seemed to the select and formally attired audience who had seats directly in front of the stand and to thousands of groundlings farther back, that it would be difficult to team up two young men as appealing as these sons of the British royal family. They were beautifully turned out in cutaway coats and gray striped trousers; they wore high silk hats, and their clothes fell so gracefully on their slim frames that they might have constituted a natural integument. It was a warm day. There was some eye-lifting among the sartorial formalists when it was noted that the brothers had left off their waistcoats.

In the glittering array of notables at the Buffalo ceremony, which included such ranking figures as Stanley Baldwin, prime minister of Great Britain, and W. L. Mackenzie King, prime minister of the Dominion of Canada, the personage, next to the Prince of Wales, who most attracted me, was Alred E. Smith, governor of the state of New York.

I knew Al Smith slightly. I had met him on several occasions, one of which was a huge semi-public affair when his daughter Emily was married to John Adams Warner, son of J. Foster Warner, Rochester's leading architect, and Mrs. Warner. The wedding vows were exchanged in the Roman Catholic Cathedral in Albany, which was filled to capacity. The Tammany crowd came. It was a morning wedding, but some of them, indifferent to the precepts of Emily Post, were resplendent in evening dress—both black and white tie. Them that had 'em, wore 'em!

The wedding ceremony was very high church, and the party that followed, lavish—very high cake; and newspaper people were graciously received, since the governor already was being talked up as a presidential candidate.

Unfamiliar with the Roman Catholic ritual in such a high mass as this, I was determined to attempt to comply. In the pew directly in front of me was a man who seemed practiced in every form of the service, and I precisely imitated his movements. He was up, he was down, he was on his knees, over and over again, and I went with him, feeling almost as if I were engaged in some new routine of Swedish calisthenics. Presently, with a sharp movement, he raised his hand. I was only a flit behind him, but this was an extracurricular gesture. He struck at a fly that rested on the crown of his head.

And I recall a young man from the *New York Sun* who had come to the church in a flaming red shirt with a bow tie to match. He was assiduous and detailed in his observations. He did not stay put in a pew, but raced up and down the aisle, not wanting to miss a trick. Once, during a complicated bit of ritual, he stopped at my aisle seat.

"Jesus Christ," he questioned, in a sharp sibilant whisper, "what they doing now?"

At the Peace Bridge celebration in Buffalo, I first saw Governor Smith as he and Mrs. Smith were being driven in a Victoria toward the compound where the governor would join a notable company of statesmen, diplomats, and His Royal Highness, the Prince of Wales. He was properly attired for the occasion, frock coat, waistcoat, and plug hat. But the hat was canted on the side of his head, a cigar that seemed as long as a bowsprit jutted cockily from a corner of his mouth, and he had the careless posture of a Brother Elk on his way to a lodge clambake. Despite the correctness of his habiliments, the impression the governor gave at the moment caused me to agree in part with a snarling slanderer who stood with me at the street curb, "East side Tammany mug!" I wondered, with some concern, since the governor would represent my native state, how he would deport himself at a ceremony where the elegant formalities of international etiquette would prevail.

Mine were idle apprehensions. No sooner had Al Smith come within viewing distance of the assemblage, which he in his turn would address, than he underwent a metamorphosis. The cigar was discarded, the plug hat set aright, his careless posture straightened. He had assumed in a twinkling the grace of a courtier. I had seen him with the "boys" in a smoke-filled back room where he was completely in his element. Now, on a rostrum with a future king and a supporting cast of world leaders, he was equally at ease and in harmony with his environment. And when he was called upon, as governor of New York, to welcome the two royal visitors to the state's second greatest city, his speech was brief, self-effacing, and couched in language as polished as any heard that day from the speakers' dais.

His protean faculties gave me the feeling that here was a public servant who could adjust to almost any situation, and the confidence inspired by his bearing and performance at the Peace Bridge caused me, the next presidential year, to divert from a hereditary and habitual (but not passionate) devotion to the Republican party to cast a vote for Alfred E. Smith.

But it was not Al Smith nor any of the other commoners on the stand but the "golden boy," the Prince of Wales, who stole the show that commemorative Sunday in Buffalo. In the middle of the Peace Bridge, at the invisible line that separates the Dominion of Canada from the United States of America, he was beleaguered by a covey of newscameramen who had him going through a rigmarole of straight and fancy posing. He endured the ordeal with smiling good nature, a lively and compliant young man of enormous charm. The cameramen persisted, crowding him, wanting other shots,"What now, boys?" he asked. "Want me to stand on my head?"

All of us who were in fair juxtaposition to him were enchanted. I thought then that if the British Empire wanted a supersalesman, they had it in the Prince; and when, nearly a decade later, he renounced the British throne in favor of the lady from Baltimore whose mother had run a rooming house, I gave support to his decision in print. Oh, I was very oracular, very wise; and unsparing in my censure of those buckram relics of a decaying hierarchy, the Prime Minister, the Lord Chancellor, and the Archbishop of Canterbury, who had thrown up ground rules and called the king "out." It was some time later that I discovered that their opposition was valid; that had Edward VIII been allowed to enthrone Mrs. Simpson and place the queenly diadem upon her carefully coifed head, royal authority would have become an independent power in the state, in defiance of the British constitution.

Henry Clune and Monty in 1969, at home

Charlotte Boyle, swimming star, during her first Rochester visit in September, 1921

Ethelda Bleibtrey and Charlotte Boyle (right) in September, 1921, at the Rochester Athletic Club

A handicap race in 1920. Charlotte Boyle, entering the Brighton Beach pool in the far lane at the corner, eventually won the race, beating Gertrude Ederle, the English Channel swimmer (with arm out of water)

Henry Clune and Charlotte Boyle on their wedding day, 17 October 1921, in front of the Little Church Around the Corner in New York

The Lyceum Theatre on South Clinton Avenue in Rochester, razed in 1934, replaced by a parking lot

Billy Rose and Eleanor Holm

Joe W. Boyle, "King of the Klondike" (right) with an aide

Walter Hagen at the British Open, 1922, Sandwich, England

The Corinthian Theater on Corinthian Street in Rochester, where burlesque reigned in the 1920s, replaced by a parking lot at the end of the decade

Frank Gannett and Henry Clune in 1947

Charlotte and Henry Clune at Silver Stadium, Rochester, in 1971

CHAPTER TWENTY-TWO

George Eastman was a man of medium stature, sedentary in appearance and habit, with a paunch that protruded slightly under the white waistcoat he often wore. He had a cold eye behind steel-rimmed spectacles, a tight mouth, and a personality that encouraged human intercourse with something less than the quick response of iron filings to the attraction of a magnet. He was a bachelor, who perhaps needed a cutie in his life and probably never had one. He once said that he had never laughed until he was forty. In the last twelve or fifteen years of his life, I was occasionally sent by my newspaper to interview him in his office, in his theater, in his home, and on a couple of occasions, in New York, at the moment of his return from some European pilgrimage. He was courteous enough, and he may have smiled. I do not remember. But there was no fun in him, and a belly-laugh would have been beyond his capacity.

Eastman had devoted most of his adult years to the accumulation of a great many millions and to the perhaps equally dedicated objective of controlling the photographic business of the world. With these goals fairly well achieved and the years crowding up on him, in time he designated the management of the Eastman Kodak Company to other hands, and, knowing that he couldn't take it with him, he devised a scheme of divesting himself of his vast fortune; and the city in which he had built his industry and its university became the greatest benefactors of his largess.

A proud, lightly endowed little institution of excellent academic standards, the University of Rochester was, of course, elated to find itself suddenly star-crossed and possessed of a windfall of better than $50,000,000. It was a conservative place which very much reflected the decorum of the dignified theologian, Dr. Rush Rhees, who had long served it as president. It was determined, with all this new wealth, not to succumb to the vulgarisms of the parvenu, and it was only after grave counsels on the part of its administrators that it quit its tiny in-city campus, a ten-minute ride from downtown Rochester, for a spacious and attractive property overlooking the Genesee River that had formerly been the golf links of the Oak Hill Country Club.

The University of Rochester today is a vastly altered institution from the college that was seated on the small municipal campus. As its coffers swelled with gifts from other wealthy individuals besides Eastman, with monies obtained in fund-raising campaigns, and with contributions from foundations and other philanthropic agencies, the riverside property to which it moved became too tight a fit, and adjacent lands, including part of a city park, have been acquired for the continually expanding "greater university." It has a notable school of medicine which operates in conjunction with a huge hospital; a law school is in prospect; and remote from the River campus, in downtown Rochester, a music department, the Eastman School of Music, represents George Eastman's beginning interest in the university.

Although it was commonly supposed that the Kodak tycoon couldn't tell the difference between high C and the shriek of a stuck hog in a stockyard, music had a curious fascination for him. When, shortly after the turn of the century, he built a mansion on Rochester's most fashionable avenue, he caused a large organ to be installed in a main floor conservatory and hired an organist to come each morning for a private recital.

The organist took his place at the console the instant Mr. Eastman left his bed, and the recital continued while he bathed, shaved, and breakfasted, ceasing only when the master departed for the Kodak office. The morning routine was exact: Eastman's habits were as precisely regulated as the back and forth swing of a metronomic pendulum. He liked, in the early days, Wagnerian boomings, perhaps his notion being that the pomp and fury of *Kaisermarsch* would alert the numerous members of his household staff and overwhelm the sound of flushing toilets. His tastes softened later on, and the music became quieter and more meditative.

The organ was his first manifestation of a musical bent. Later, he introduced a series of Sunday musicales in his home which some of his guests doubtless enjoyed, and others, rigid for an hour and a half on not very comfortable chairs and less appreciative of the artistic fulfillment of a Brahms string quartet, suffered submissively, since to decline an Eastman invitation would be very much like snubbing royalty. Still later, in the flat, unequivocal voice in which he issued all of his directives, he announced that he would build a "concert hall and school of music surpassed by no other in the world," and the Eastman Theater, as the concert hall is known, pretty well certified the first purpose of his boast.

A nobly designed and handsomely appointed building, the Eastman Theater, which is owned by the University of Rochester, has suffered surprisingly little deterioration in its nearly sixty years of public use. It has a stage commodious enough for any reasonable theatrical or musical presentation, 3,400 comfortable seats, corridors and aisles ample enough to eliminate congestion, and an attractive decor that includes several Ezra Winter murals. It has, besides the main auditorium, a small hall for chamber music and other intimate entertainment which the founder dedicated to his mother, whose maiden name was Kilbourn. Kilbourn Hall is occasionally used to exhibit the accomplishments of members of the school of music, who pursue their studies in a building connected with the theater by a covered bridge, which, when the school introduced ballet classes and shapely young women in leotards romped across the elevated structure to rehearse on the theater's stage, became known as the Bridge of Thighs.

The theater in its early days offered motion pictures on its large screen and complemented the visible entertainment with an on-stage orchestra of sixty pieces, and for a time Eastman's handsome concert hall was a howling popular success, with eager patrons queued up each night half a block from the entrance. One night a week during the winter months the management suspended the motion picture entertainment and offered, at greatly advanced prices, a recital by a noted singer or instrumentalist, a symphony concert, a ballet or, at rare intervals, an opera. These were gala occasions.

The theater has a wide passageway adjacent to the main floor auditorium and the promenade (the Peacock Walk) through this at intermission on concert or opera nights, with the ladies of Rochester's *haut monde* aglitter with jewels and dressed to the nines, was an event almost equal in importance to the performance on the stage, were it the Boston symphony under the baton of Serge Koussevitsky or a Metropolitan Opera production of *Rigoletto.*

During the early days of the Eastman School of Music and the Eastman Theater, the founder daily visited each institution and imposed upon both a sort of unofficial superintendence. He was interested in the curriculum of the music school and concerned about the competence of the instructors. He was keenly attentive to the business operations of the theater, the quality of the pictures shown, audience reaction, maintenance—he wanted the place scrupulously clean. He overlooked few details. I was sent to the theater one morning to see him. He was attending a rehearsal of the newly formed Rochester Philharmonic under the direction of the handsome Englishman who had been appointed to conduct it and who later was to become *Sir* Eugene Goosens. Reaching under his seat, Eastman's hand came in contact with a wad of chewing gum. He stopped the rehearsal, had the house lights thrown up, and, half kneeling in the aisle, he struggled to dislodge the sticky gob with a handkerchief, his mouth grim. "Damn! Damn! Damn!" he muttered angrily. "These ingrates! These yokels!" He summoned an attendant, told him to dispose of the gum but return his handkerchief. And the rehearsal continued.

The Eastman Theater opened its doors to the public in the autumn of 1922, and that year George Eastman, entering the last decade of a life that would end with a self-inflicted bullet wound, began to display a broadening interest in his fellow human beings and to engage in activities for which he had had little time during the long years he was implacably devoted to the development and management of his company.

He became a fairly regular concert goer, and he seemed to enjoy the small flurry of ceremony his arrival at the theater on nights of these entertainments excited. A uniformed doorman would dart across the sidewalk to fling open the door of his shiny limousine, and Eastman, first to descend to the curb, would make little courtier gestures as he handed out two or perhaps three handsomely attired middle-aged (or better) matrons, members of an exclusive sisterhood known as the "gray-haired dynasty," who were attempting to direct the social career of their aging charm boy.

As the party crossed the crowded foyer, a way would be made for it; there would be much head-turning, discreet staring, and behind-the-hand whisperings. In the foyer Eastman would remove the hat he had worn to the theater and replace it with a black skull cap, which, were he lacking any other insignia of distinction, would make him the most conspicuous man in the audience. His march down the aisle would be rigid, with no turning to the right or left, though the ladies with him would bow and smile and wave triumphantly. "It was as if," a perceptive and amusing ex-actor who worked briefly as a critic for the *Democrat and Chronicle,* put it, "those old gals were flouting it over all the other aspirants for George's favor. 'Tonight,' they seemed to say, 'you sons-of-bitches, *we've* got him!' "

Besides the formal full-figged concerts in the theater, Eastman was occasionally present at musical and dance recitals given by the music school students. And as time went on he cultivated the acquaintance of some of the performers in the theater; and now and then, perhaps motivated by the appeal of novelty, he made personal contact with some of the embryo Paderewskies, the exiled Russian composers, the aspiring conductors, the long-haired male violinists and the short-haired female harpists, the ballet masters—members of a swelling company of instructors and students who had come from many places to the Eastman School of Music and the feast of artistic plenty they expected its Midas-like founder to provide.

George Eastman's relations with those "queer people," as conservative Rochesterians deprecatorily referred to the sometimes antic and madcap artistes who were forming around the Eastman Theater and the music school the first recognizable Bohemian colony the city had ever known, were not uninhibited, but tentative, cautious. At this stage of the game he was not going to get messy with opera girls or attempt any hanky-panky with a diva.

But he did seem beguiled by the statuesque operatic soprano, Mary Garden, who sang in the Eastman Theater and who, with her mother, was a house guest at Eastman's great gray mansion on the Avenue.

Arthur P. Kelly, press agent for the theater, had an inspired notion of posing Mr. Eastman at a piano with Miss Garden standing at his side, as though singing to the pianist's accompaniment, an aria from *Thais* or one of her other Metropolitan Opera hits.

"It'll be a honey," Kelly predicted. "We'll give the picture to the press services. It'll go all over the country."

Eastman was not at first opposed to the proposal. But he needed time to think it over, and his veto followed a night's reflection.

"No, Kelly," he said. "Everyone knows I can't play a note on the piano. It would be buncombe, fakery, to pretend that I can."

During her stay in Eastman's house, the sensational star of *Salome* brilliantly ornamented her host's table at a lavish dinner given in her honor. Some who were there thought Eastman fondled her with his eyes, and rumors of romance were quickly in circulation. They were as flimsy as feathers. George Eastman's congenital reserves were too deeply entrenched to be uprooted by a momentary infatuation, if, indeed, his interest in the diva was that intense. In any event, the relations between the pair ended abruptly and Frank Smith may have had an inkling of the reason.

Smith, better known as Whiskey Smith than by his given name, was an immensely popular, free-swinging soul, a sort of bon vivant, who had come to manage the Eastman Theater's box office (and, in time, to become house treasurer) from a most unlikely provenance. He had functioned in a similar capacity at the Corinthian Theater on the other side of town, which played burlesque shows of a deep purple hue.

Whiskey fitted in very well at the Eastman and he knew what ticket sales were all about. He outlasted manager after manager and other functionaries, who passed in and out of the theater as if they were in a revolving door, and remained until he achieved a legitimate age of retirement. He seemed to have more rapport with Eastman than any other person connected with the place. He knew, of course, of the Eastman-Miss Garden relationship.

"She put the bite on him," Smith said. "It chilled him. Y'know the boss. Zillions for good works and noble causes. Not a farthing for a personal touch. You try that, he's tight'ern a pipe wrench."

Arthur Kelly, like Smith, enjoyed good relations with Eastman. He lasted six years at the theater and left under his own volition. During this period he was reprimanded by his employer only once, and, as at the time he had attempted to pose Eastman as Miss Garden's accompanist, the issue concerned the Kodak head's intolerance of fakery and deception.

The newly formed Rochester Philharmonic Orchestra played its first out-of-town concert in Carnegie Hall, and two or three of the New York reviews were somewhat less than raves. It was one of Kelly's tasks to put together a pamphlet about the orchestra that would be distributed to potential subscribers. A fishmonger never cried "Rotten fish!" And what kind of a press agent would he be if he tried to promote his offering by admitting that it was less than great? His copy for the pamphlet quoted only favorable reviews. Eastman, suspicious of this felicity, summoned Kelly.

"Was everything written in New York favorable to the orchestra?" he demanded.

Kelly was forced to admit that a few sour notes had crept into some of the reviews.

Eastman was angry. He was not given to towering rages, but his cold flat words of scorn could be withering to one to whom they were addressed.

"Are you trying to deceive, Kelly? Are you cheating? I

won't have it. Put those poor reviews in with the others. If some critics think we haven't a fine orchestra, I want our supporters to know."

"Yes sir," Kelly said, and left, thankful that he wasn't fired on the spot.

George Eastman could be difficult on occasions, and the occasions were not infrequent. He was without flamboyance or swagger, but he had a very real sense of his position and his importance. He had set notions about what was fitting and proper, and he was intransigent in his adherence to these principles. I, perhaps, saw him more frequently during the closing period of his life than any other newspaper reporter. He would receive me with cold courtesy, bored, I am sure, by the need of the interview; and only in a couple of instances toward the end did our meetings warm into anything resembling social intercourse. An aging, unwell bachelor, alone and lonesome in his huge house with its multitude of servants, on these occasions he seemed pathetically eager for human companionship.

Eastman's stubbornness, his refusal to compromise when some principle or rule of conduct was involved, was amusingly manifested on one of the occasions when I met him in New York on his return from Europe. I have forgotten what my employer, Frank Gannett, wanted me to learn from Mr. Eastman, but he must have thought the interview important since he made detailed arrangements for it.

My instructions were to go to the foot of 90th Street and the North River and there board a yacht owned by a man who, Mr. Gannett said, was vice-president of the Lehigh Valley Railroad and a good friend of his. I would remain overnight on the yacht and be delivered next day to the ship upon which Mr. Eastman was returning from Europe.

Unfamiliar with yachts, I was very much impressed by this one. It was a seagoing craft, and it seemed to me as huge as a trans-Atlantic liner. I though of the reply J. P. Morgan is supposed to have made to someone who inquired about the cost of maintaining a yacht such as Morgan's *Corsair*.

"Anyone," Morgan told his interrogator, "who has to be concerned about the cost, shouldn't own a yacht."

The yacht owner may not have been a modern Croesus, but he was a prodigal host. When we descended from the deck to what I thought an elaborate dining salon, he pulled back a sliding panel in the wall with the remark, "Your boss wouldn't like this."

Mr. Gannett was a fanatical prohibitionist. What the wall cabinet displayed was a formidable array of illegal bottled goods. My host said, "We'll have a touch of cheer." He pressed a buzzer with his foot and instantly a small, uniformed Japanese, a veritable prototype of smiling, bowing obsequiousness appeared to do our bidding.

I spoke for gin, and the boy brought down a bottle of Boodles, expensive and high speed, which I had never heard of before. I should have been warned about its potency. We toasted Mr. Gannett, Mr. Eastman, Cornell University, my host's Alma Mater, the United States of America and, I think, the Statue of Liberty. We each sat at the end of a long table, like a couple of clubmen. In time the Japanese boy brought food in several courses.

I suppose the yacht drifted about New York Harbor (I never ventured on deck to get our bearings), and presently my host and I, both a little wobbly, retired for what was left of the night. The stateroom to which I was assigned, like everything else I had observed in this floating caravanserai, was first cabin.

The Japanese boy gently aroused me in the morning, drew a "bawth," and provided my host and myself with an excellent breakfast. In late morning we saw the liner that was bringing Eastman home come through the channel, and when she paused to take on dock officials, the yacht sidled up to her and I was raised to the deck, where I quickly found the object of my interview. He had come from Europe in the company of Harold Gleason, his breakfast-hour organist, and Mrs. Gleason, a lively, intelligent, and attractive woman of whom Eastman was particularly fond. General Oscar N. Solbert, who had become a sort of *fidus Archates* to the industrialist, running errands and performing a variety of services that had more to do with Eastman's private than his business life, was also there.

Solbert, who had come out from shore in a launch,

triumphantly announced that he had arranged to have Eastman leave the ship with him and avoid the irksome business of customs inspection. His luggage had already been examined and was mounded up waiting to be transferred to the launch. Eastman asked, "Are the Gleasons going, too?"

"No, I'm afraid—"

"Afraid of what?"

"I'm afraid we can't take them off with you. They can join you at the hotel."

"Well," the old man said, and his foot seemed to be banging on the deck in emphasis, "if they can't go, I don't go."

"But—"

"Only if they go," Eastman said again. It was an irrevocable decision.

Solbert bounded over the rail and sped into shore in the launch. The ship had not moved when he returned. Eastman was waiting in his deck chair. Long-faced, the general admitted his failure.

Eastman nodded coldly. The liner was soon warped into her slip and the great industrialist, along with the hoi polloi and his friends, the Gleasons, was harried through customs.

CHAPTER TWENTY-THREE

If the middling city of Rochester provided few news events of national or international importance, there was, nonetheless, much that was interesting to write about, and I pretty well ran the gamut of reportorial experience. I covered murders, (and sixty years ago a murder in Rochester was a very rare crime) prominent court cases, and political insurrections. I met visiting dignitaries, interviewed stage and screen stars, did an occasional sports story. Now and then I had an out-of-town assignment.

I was sent first to New York and then to Buffalo to tell about Billy Sunday who had lived a fairly rackety life as a big league ball player until religion sneaked up and gave a fillip to his conscience. He had displayed a lot of speed in the outfield for the Chicago National League team, he had stolen an impressive number of bases, and conversion had neither slowed him down nor abated his athletic energies.

He was an enormously popular preacher. He drew huge crowds into large auditoriums and into tents as capacious as the Big Top of the Ringling Brothers Circus. He moved about the land with an elaborate entourage, one of whose functions was to keep the tambourines in brimming plenty. I thought him an entertaining platform performer. I admired the vigorous and colorful language of his homiletic rants, though much that he said seemed nonsense; his spiritual message left me unconvinced. The recreants in his audience were not, however, numerous; at his call for redemption the sawdust trail was congested with fervent penitents and cries of "Hallelujah! Praise God!" resounded far beyond the canvas walls of his evangelical tent or the more substantial ones of his auditorium.

I was back-stage in Buffalo as he was revving up for his public appearnce. He was a study in concentration. He paced up and down a narrow corridor with angry strides, fists clenched, grimacing fiercely. He was like a method actor fitting into the mood. "God, oh, help me God," he'd mutter. "Help me punch these wicked sinners into some sense of your divinity. Ah! Ah!" he'd strike out like a boxer trying for a knockout blow. "These mealy-mouthed, these fourflushing Christians! Help me make 'em come to taw!" He'd shake his head and complain wearily, "Oh, I'm tired! So tired! But buck up, Billy. You gotta get these lazy backsliders up off their . . . their . . .." (I felt he wanted to say, 'big fat asses', but thought the adjuration too extreme) . . ." you gotta get 'em up to the penitential bench and know what it is to give themselves to Christ!"

He was probably sincere. He was a clean cut, scrupulously neat fellow until his mad antics on the rostrum caused his clothing to become rumpled, put his necktie askew, and brought sweat bubbling from his pores. He had been a good enough ball-player to last eight years in the big leagues, but his histrionic talents may have exceeded his athletic skills. He knew publicity like a Madison Avenue flack. He kept an alert eye on the evangelical exchequer, and he insisted on airtight contracts for personal appearances. From the platform he directed abuses to his hearers similar to the muttered defamations of his backstage warm-up, which his congregation submissively accepted, perhaps as a condition of absolution.

Over the years, I wrote about numerous revivalists from small timers in tiny gas-lit tents to Billy Graham, whose audience not only filled Madison Square Garden, but debauched into contiguous streets; and I saw young men, soldier boys and sailors, kneeling on the pavement mumbling prayers as Graham's pleas and demands were transmitted to their ears by amplifiers attached to the outside of the building.

Billy Graham may be a more rarefied spirit and a more

literate speaker than the late Chicago outfielder, but it strikes me that his play on words and his hortative techniques are very similar to those of the evangelical Billy who preceded him. From my observation the great difference between them is that Graham is able, by the use of electronic devices, to reach millions of listeners while Sunday's propagation of the Word was limited to those within range of his natural voice.

Sunday came into Rochester at the earnest solicitation of a group of local churchmen, but his stay was brief. He spoke one Sunday night from the stage of a theater. His appearance was without the trappings of a full-blown revival and his talk lacked the fire of his tent-show harangues. Graham also visited Rochester but he, too, was pretty well watered down. He addressed in orderly language a group of ecclesiastics and vestrymen in the academic quiet of the Colgate Rochester Divinity School.

Prior to either of these visitations, Aimee Semple McPherson, a Canadian farm girl who parlayed a Liberace-like talent for showmanship, a magnetic personality, and a remarkable gift of gab into a million dollar religious industry, staged a three-week revival in Rochester that was a howling success from the opening prayer to the final cries of "Hallelujah!" that sped Mrs. McPherson on her way to another profitable engagement.

Sister Aimee at the time was in the process of organizing what was to be known as Angelus Temple in Los Angeles, a huge gilded amphitheater in which for years she held center stage and played to untold thousands of frantic adherents.

In Rochester she took over a large barracks-like building that had formerly been the National Guard Armory and filled it to the Plimsoll mark at every session. She, I thought, had a more sovereign command over her audience than either Sunday or Graham or Gypsy Smith, another prominent evangelist I had heard. Men, women, and children were beguiled by her husky, far-reaching voice and her dramatic style. She reached out as if to embrace them, and seemed, by a miracle of levitation, to raise them to spiritual heights.

She was a stocky woman with a luxurious growth of chestnut hair which she piled high on her head, large dark expressive eyes, and strong but rather coarse features. She had the prominent nose of a conqueror, which, indeed, she was. In the pulpit she usually wore a white silk gown and a purple cape which billowed out seductively as she moved about the rostrum, and she often had a bouquet in her hands or a nosegay pinned to the bodice of her gown, which she would fling out to the enraptured throng in front of her. She delighted in feminine refinements. Off-stage she was slick and chic in clothes designed by expensive couturiers and she favored hats by the well-known Eugenie. Someone dubbed her the "religious glamor girl" and the term was apt.

In Rochester she not only preached what she defined as the Four Square Gospel, but professed a faith cure, and her congregation usually included several persons suffering from infirmities which they ardently believed the white-robed exhorter on the dais had the faculty to cure. The business seemed to me flagrant quackery. And one might have a twinge of compassion for the Sister's hopeful sufferers who, with her departure, would realize that their sight had not been restored, that their arthritic pains had not quieted, and that it would be injudicious to throw away their crutches and try to walk without them.

I was sent as a reporter only once to Mrs. McPherson's revivals, the night of her opening; but I returned several times on my own, fascinated by the phenomenon of her charisma and curious to know what it was that caused her hearers actually to prostrate themselves before her. And her appeal transcended the spiritual. At collection time she made it known that underwear buttons were not acceptable, and when the tambourines were fetched back to the altar they fluttered high, like celestial wings, with folding money of the realm. I know one sober, middle-aged burgher, who had acquired a modest fortune during the war manufacturing refuse cans for the army, who fell so fully under Aimee's spell that he was on the point of giving her (and God) his all, when his family interceded and saved his solvency.

Sister left Rochester, leaving converts all over the place and taking with her a substantial honorarium. She returned once more for a brief three-day stand in the same hall in which she had first appeared, but by that time she was fully established as the enchantress of Angelus Temple and a woman known to millionas, not only because of her evangelical endeavors, but because of a major episode in a career that had become an episodic continuum.

Leaving Angelus Temple one afternoon for a swim off of a Los Angeles beach, Sister Aimee disappeared and the belief was that she had suffered a heart attack or some other crippling disability and been drowned in the surf. With this report, a passionate keening arose from her stricken adherents, who wondered how God could have taken off a disciple who was winning converts to His name in astonishing numbers. Divers were employed to explore the floor of the sea in the area where Aimee was last seen, but no trace of the body was found. The evangelist's mother, Mother Kennedy, as she was known, a redoubtable and forceful woman who had served as adjunct at the Temple, sadly conceded her daugher's death and announced that she was prepared to take over Temple affairs and continue the propagation of the Four Square Gospel. Eloquent memorials were recited. Then, four or five weeks after she presumably had sunk to a watery grave, Mrs. McPherson was discovered wandering on the Arizona desert.

It seemed to her followers, mad with joy at her reappearance, that she had experienced the miracle of resurrection; Aimee, however, had a more temporal explanation for her recovery. She had been kidnapped, she said, and held rope-bound in a desert shack from which she had escaped by cutting the ropes with the jagged edge of a tin can.

Her story was heralded across the land in newspaper banner-lines and Sister Aimee was a very hot news item. She cooperated with the police in the desert search for the shack in which she allegedly had been held captive, but the shack was never located. She offered detailed descriptions of the persons she avowed had abducted her, but no one was ever apprehended and charged with the crime. She was haled into court and accused of fabricating the kidnapping story, and an attempt was made to prove that during her mysterious absence she was cohabitating with a man she had formerly employed as a radio operator at the Temple. Civil as well as criminal court actions evolved out of the escapade; there was a ferment of crimination and recrimination. Skeptics on the outside denigrated the priestess of Angelus Temple as a whited sepulchre and a religious charlatan. She suffered the slings and arrows of her detractors with admirable courage and continued her strenuous program of preaching and proselytizing. She kept her cool and her impregnable hold on her followers. Bonzes kneeling before the Dalai Lama were no more unflagging in their faith. Aimee Semple McPherson could do no wrong.

When the furor excited by the kidnapping affair presently abated, Aimee set off on a sort of tour of vindication that took her across the continent, and it was then that she made her second visit to Rochester. She eschewed in her short stay the tricky business of faith-healing; her bag was straightaway evangelism. I visited her twice. At the second meeting I asked the stereotyped question as to how she had escaped from the persons she said had abducted her. She favored me with her most charming smile, moved her hands expressively, and quoted from Proverbs.

"In my distress, I cried unto the Lord, and he heard me."

* * * * * * * * * *

Between the first and second Rochester visit of Aimee Semple McPherson, the city entertained (and was entertained by) a personage who, in a popularity contest would have won by millions of votes over even so beguiling a charmer as the oracle of Angelus Temple.

In the early spring of 1923, Rudolph Valentino appeared in the large, barracks-like hall in which Mrs. McPherson had held her revivalist meetings and filled it from wall to wall. His audience was predominately female, and the women in the seats seemed actually to want to leave them and swoon at the feet of the lean Latin with the come-hither eyes, the patent leather hair, side burns that were cultivated in the curving form of a scimitar, and a style of dress that was glitteringly point-device.

"I am not afraid with your arms around me, Ahmed, my dearest love, my Sheik."

It was as the sheik in one of his early pictures of that name that he established himself as the Great Lover and countless women all over the land fancied him as the paragon of his sex. Yet his first wife barred him from her bedroom, and the second, a glacial beauty who seemed impervious to his sexual allure, may also have refused to permit the consummation of the marital compact.

I was sent by the newspaper to report on this prodigy, whose appeal to women was so compelling that they actually attempted to get handholds on him and rend his impeccable tailoring from his back. There had been instances when riot squads were needed to save him from his frantic worshippers.

My wife of less than two years accompanied me to the hall and we had aisle seats a short distance back from the platform upon which Valentino and his second wife, christened Winnifred Shaughnessy but now known as Natacha Rambova, were to exhibit modern dance steps as the main part of the show.

To fill out the bill there would be an amateur dance contest and a competition for the title of "Miss Valentino," but neither Valentino nor his wife was to judge these events. The Valentinos were making their tour in a private railroad car, their schedule was tight, and they were slightly delayed getting to the hall. My wife and I were settled in our sets waiting for the show to begin when a young man named Ruddy, whom my wife had known at the New York Athletic Club and who was part of the star's entourage, espied her in the audience and hurtled down the aisle to petition her to serve as one of the "Miss Valentino" judges.

Some time before I had been pressed into service as a beauty queen judge and the experience had not been a happy one. I was abused not only by the contestants for whom I had not voted, but by the members of their families and their friends.

"Don't do it," I protested, "you can get stoned doing a thing like that."

"Don't worry, I'm not," she said.

"But you can meet Rudolph if you'll come up and judge," Ruddy urged.

"I can take a miss on that," Charlotte said. "Get on with your show. You're ten minutes late already."

I am sure her refusal made her unique among the feminine contingent of the audience. All around her women were drooling in anticipation of the appearance of the Great Lover, and when he did come on the stage he excited a mass ecstacy. There were moans and groans and a low-throated caterwaul of yearning. One heard "Oh-o-o's" and "Ah-a-a's," and "Oh, but he's wonderful!" "Fantastic!" "Grand!" Little shopgirls pulled out their gum and snapped it back against their teeth, and perhaps imagined themselves being borne across the desert, recumbent over the sheik's saddle.

Valentino was a striking figure, and I could understand the romantic appeal he had for women. He had begun his career as an entertainer dancing the tango, the maxixe, and other new steps, first as a thé-dansant gigolo, and later in stage exhibitions, and Natacha Rambova had also been a professional dancer.

The Valentinos were a stunning couple, and as Rudolph maneuvered his wife through various movements of the dance, as he whirled her about in mad gyrations or bent her far over and dipped sinuously above her or held her tightly in his arms, the hungry-eyed women in the audience were convinced that Natacha Rambova was the most privileged woman on the face of the earth.

Valentino's exposure to his worshippers was not prolonged. At the end of the dance routine he made a short speech telling of his disenchantment with Hollywood and how he desired to make pictures of higher artistic standards than those that had typed him as a sheik, which (although he didn't say this) had accounted for his vast popularity. He and Mrs. Valentino then took a bow and disappeared.

I left my wife and rushed back stage hoping for a word with the star, but Mrs. Valentino, a lady of elegant style and the precise, metallic lines of a steel engraving, very obviously the dominant figure of the duo, insisted that he leave the hall at once. He obeyed, giving me only a dismissing word and a wave of the hand. As he left the building, he was swarmed over by a clamoring crowd of women at the stage door who fought to touch him, to snatch at any available part of his clothing, and who, failing in these designs, would, I am sure, have prostrated themselves on the pavement and gloried in the stomp of the Valentino foot.

CHAPTER TWENTY-FOUR

Radio was beginning in the 1920s to whittle away the monopoly newspapers had long held on the dispensing of tidings. But the tidings impressed on newsprint had still a greater impact than those orally propagated by electromagnetic waves, and we in the newspaper business were rather disdainful of the town criers of the microphone.

We couldn't conceive of their seriously challenging our hereditary prerogative. We were still the people who kept the public informed of all of importance that was happening in the world. We were molders of public opinion. We gave impetus to civic movements, helped elect public officials, lighted torches for reform, and, on occasions, promoted obscure individuals into celebrity.

I was impressed by what I considered the power of the press. I nurtured small vanities and I began to fill a hat box with fan letters. The column called "Seen and Heard" that I wrote three, and later, four times a week, was not a column of advocacy. I dealt only occasionally with "big issues," but I had a fine time writing about all sorts of people and telling about interesting and unusual, if often trivial, events in town. When I now and then did express an opinion on a controversial subject, I excluded from the hat box notes from persons on the other side of the fence who might address me with the withering salutation, "Dear sir: You cur . . ."

I began to brevet myself for my achievements in the field of journalism. I took pride, for example, in what I managed to accomplish for a neat and courteous little Hollander who called at the office one day, explained that he was employed by several families in the fashionable east side section of Rochester, and asked if I ever wrote for a magazine in Holland. When I asked in turn how in the world I could do that when I couldn't write a word in Dutch, he took from a grocery bag a magazine published in Amsterdam whose format resembled that of the *Saturday Evening Post,* and opened it to a page that displayed my name, bold as brass, over a piece of fiction I had sold a couple of years before to an American monthly.

I was astonished. I had never been consulted about the sale of the foreign rights, and of course had never been paid for the use of the story in Holland. The Dutch translation of the title was similar enough to the English version to be readily deciphered, and in pilfering my text the thieves in Amsterdam had also appropriated three large woodcuts that had illustrated my piece in the American publication.

Angered to think I had been gulled, I was also a little set up, since this was the first time anything of mine had been translated into a foreign tongue.

The gardener said that each month relatives in Holland sent him their used copy of the magazine, and he offered me the copy that contained my story, which I was pleased to accept. I liked the gardener. He lingered on, wanting, I could see, to talk. He told me something about his early days in America, reported that his wife had died more than a year before and left him with five growing children. He was having a time of it, he said, trying to give parental supervision to his youthful brood while engaged all day providing their sustenance. He paused, then asked suddenly,

"Mr. Clune, could you get me a wife?"

Intrigued by the craziness of the proposal and flattered by the gardener's faith in my omnipotence, I allowed I'd try.

A few days later I told in "Seen and Heard" of my surprise when the gardener presented me with a copy of the Dutch magazine that contained my translated story; and I related the unusual request he had made and suggested, on scant evidence to be sure, that he would make some worthy woman a good husband.

I hadn't taken the matter very seriously; it was a whimsy that I thought might mildly amuse my readers. In time the incident passed from mind, and I had more or less forgotten the gardener when, a couple of months after his visit to the office, he telephoned.

"I've got a lady's going to marry me," he announced exultantly, and added an American vernacularism, "She's a honey!"

The lady had applied as a marital candidate shortly after I had published the gardener's request for a wife, and the pair had hit it off very well from the start. They had been "keeping company" ever since they first met, and the gardener told me that they were to be married in a quiet ceremony the following week. And the marriage was no tentative, fly-by-night sort of a covenant, as I learned later from the gardener's oldest issue, a daughter who, grown to young womanhood and married, held a responsible position in a bank in which I had an account. Rather, the daughter implied, my good offices had helped to effect a conjugal triumph, for, she said, her father couldn't have had a finer wife nor she a better stepmother.

* * * * * * * * * * *

Buffalo, sixty miles west of Rochester, was once more liberal in raunchy diversions than our own staid community, and occasionally, driving over there, I stopped at the Palace Theater, a narrow, dingy, spit-box sort of a place, where the girls in the burlesque show were allowed to strip down to a narrow G-string.

Lured on one of these occasions by reports that a show-stopper was featured in the Palace, I joined a line that queued out half a block from the ticket kiosk, bought a seat, suffered through a jumble of salacious comedy, awkward dance routines, and crack-voiced soloists to be rewarded in time by a brief, fascinating intermezzo—a dance and strip by a girl whose name was high in the marquee lights: Hinda Wassau.

The stage was blacked-out and a voice amplified by a loudspeaker proclaimed the management's pride in its scintillating star. The expectant hush that followed was broken by a great bong from the pit drummer and a spotlight darted above the main floor audience and fixed on a young woman in an elaborate evening gown. Executing a sort of saraband step, she moved slowly in the nimbus of the light to the low beat of the orchestra, and slowly, gracefully, began the removal of her clothing, a procedure that excited wave after wave of applause but not a single crude exhortation, "Take 'em off! Take 'em off, Hinda!" from the jam-packed crowd in the theater.

One doesn't need to be a Duse to star in burlesque, and the eminence Miss Wassau had achieved in this raffish, wrong-side-of-the-tracks entertainment was not the result of dramatic gift or unusual talent as a dancer, and she made no attempt to sing. But there was a quality about her that set her apart from strippers I had seen in other burlesque shows. They were blatant and obvious; she was subtle and delicate. And oddly, it was this subtlety and delicacy which made what she was doing seem almost decorous, that appeared to appeal to the groundlings, some in hip-boots and turtleneck sweaters, others with their caps still on their heads, who were the predominant witnesses of her "art."

She was small and lithe, and when her figure was all but totally revealed it appeared to be quite expertly proportioned, with all of its visible components in *esprit de corps*. Her face was small and her features had an interesting angularity. She had high cheek bones and her cheeks were sunken and, except for the red slash of her mouth, her skin was dead white. There was a hint of the exotic, of the mysterious about her. The sense of this was given emphasis by her name, Hinda Wassau, and the impression was not destroyed by the obvious fact that her platinum hair had come from dye pot rinsings.

I was as fascinated with Miss Wassau's performance, which did not last more than seven or eight minutes, as the other members of the audience and I told about it in "Seen and Heard." What I wrote was not a critique but a paean which became at times a little overwrought. At one point I suggested that her appearance on the Palace stage following the tawdry entertainment that had preceded it was not unlike the appearance on a concert stage of Fritz Reiner and a philharmonic orchestra following the performance of a high-school jazz combo. There were other extravagances.

My piece was enthusiastically received by Miss Wassau's agent, who ordered fifty copies of the edition in which it appeared. Two or three of its most glowing paragraphs were reproduced in letters an inch high, and my flattering comments were plastered on the facades of Midwest burlesque theaters in which this aesthetic strip teaser, as I had attempted to represent her, was appearing.

Fanny Brice, the comedienne, read on the outside of a theater what I had written and went inside to see for herself. She was impressed and proposed to Billy Rose, the Broadway showman to whom she was then married, that Hinda Wassau might do for a New York night club Rose was preparing to open. Rose took his wife's tip, and it was no trick to persuade Hinda to quit the murky, ragtag ambience of burlesque to strip for the carriage trade.

I met her for the first time when she was sharing billing with Gertrude Nissen, the singer who had once shared billing with the celebrated Mrs. Patrick Campbell, in Rose's new night club, the Casino de Paree. Other prominent performers on the bill were Jimmy Savo, the comic, and Eleanor Powell, the great rhythm dancer.

Miss Wassau worked the late show. She went on once a day, at 2:15 A.M. She was the star of the after-midnight entertainment; the pet of the sybarites who came in at that hour. She was doing very much what she had done in burlesque, only now she stripped in front of a curtain that resembled an elaborate Persian tapestry, under carefully adjusted lights, and to the accompaniment of a full orchestra.

I visited the café with a young actor friend of mine who, when I explained how what I had written about Miss Wassau had helped upgrade her career, insisted that we must meet, and exercising the freemasonry of his profession, he sought her out backstage and brought her to our table.

In a brief biographical run-down she explained that she was of Lithuanian parentage. As a kid, she had run away from her father's small Connecticut dairy farm because she hated milking cows, and joined the chorus of a burlesque show. She rose quickly to stardom in that peculiar metier; and now, she said, because of my good offices, she was featured in the hottest night spot in New York.

She reveled in her new position and she was acquiring the appurtenances that she felt went with it. She had moved into a first-rate hotel. She had an expensive fur coat, a new wardrobe, and a brace of Scotties which she led about on a rhinestone-decorated leash attached to a rhinestone-decorated harness. She had engaged a maid. She had had an offer to appear in a plush Palm Beach resort, but Warner Brothers was interested in testing her for the screen and she did not want to leave New York. "Look," she said, "what happened to Anna Sten?" This was the life; a long, long way from the four-a-day grind of burlesque.

Sitting next to her, I discovered that the exotic aura that had seemed to envelope her on the stage was an illusion. She was not ingenuous; she had been around long enough to have lost any dairy farm naiveté. But there was nothing arcane or mysterious about her. She was a pretty girl with thin features, an uptilted nose, and a humorous mouth. The actor and I liked her at once. Her gratitude for what she insisted I had done for her was profound.

In time Rose opened another fancy night club, the Casa Manana, and he moved Hinda to the new operation and put her again in the after-midnight show. She had a boost in salary. Walter Winchell called her the "highest-priced undressed woman in America." Her vogue expanded; patrons who arrived at the Casa Manana in limousines driven by chauffeurs in livery wanted her at their tables. She was projecting a Cinderella legend when, suddenly, her euphoric bubble burst.

New York was experiencing one of its periodic reform spasms. A hue and cry rose against what was called the libertinism of Broadway entertainment. Nudity had to go. The police stopped Hinda Wassau's performance. There was no appeal. She was "out." Broken-hearted, the girl went back to the burlesque wheel, still, to be sure, a star; but now the acclamation that reached her ears came not from admirers who knew about fish forks, caviar, and pressed duck, but from Tony Lumpkins who ogled her from fifty-cent seats in scrubby little back street showplaces.

Her return to burlesque did not, however, seriously constrict her economy. In her night club interlude she had become a sort of celebrity and the managers of the theaters in which she appeared made the most of this. Her name was always high in the lights, she drew 'em in, and the managers paid her accordingly. I saw her occasionally in various cities in the east in which she appeared, and at almost every meeting she provided me with interesting material for my column. Her name always apperaed in connection with these items and she appreciated the publicity.

Hinda Wassau was married for a time to Rube Bernstein, who, among other show business occupations, managed a road tour for the actor, Walter Houston. They were divorced. During the interim between her divorce and her marriage to a large, handsome man said to be a big Washington, D.C. gambler, she telephoned me from Philadelphia.

"I'm in a jam," she said. "I've got to have three hundred."

I whistled.

"Three hundred. That's a lot of money. How about"—and I wondered if I could get even that much up— "one fifty?"

"I've got to have three hundred!" she said desperately.

I didn't ask her then, and I never heard, what the jam was.

I was married, with three kids, and working hard to preserve my own economy. I had no right to scour up $300 and wire it to a burlesque woman in a jam, but somehow I managed it.

"Damn fool!" I said of myself. But the money was gone and the best thing to do was charge it off to some moonstruck fantasy and forget it, a resolution which, in time, I more or less fulfilled.

I had wired the money in mid-November.

I never wrote to Hinda Wassau nor heard from her. Then, one day early in the following March as I was leaving the office for lunch, a Western Union messenger handed me a notice to report at the Western Union office, and when I got there, there was my $300. It had been sent from Baltimore, Maryland. No message, only the money. It was like finding it.

I never saw Hinda but once after she returned the money I supposed she had accepted as a gift. She more or less quit show business after her second marriage, but occasionally some house manager persuaded her to make a week's "farewell" appearance, and she played one of these intermittent engagements in a slatternly old theater called the Embassy in Rochester. Her popularity seemed not to have diminished, and she virtually filled the house at every performance. I saw the show one afternoon and went back stage to say hello. Her husband was with her. They had driven up from Washington in a brand new Cadillac. They appeared in good marital form and I was pleased to think that a woman I admired on a number of counts—her integrity and inherent decency, her sense of appreciation, her always scrupulously groomed and shining person—was doing well. Our visit was brief and the least formal.

After that, I occasionally came across a reference to Hinda Wassau in an article in a magazine or in a book that dealt with show business, but we had no communication. Years passed. One day a man who identified himself as a Rochester native and who said that he had read my newspaper pieces for years, stopped in the office and handed me a torn piece of wrapping paper on which this brief greeting was written in pencil:

"Hello, Mr. Clune. Hinda Wassau."

"Where in the world did this come from?" I asked.

The man said, "My wife and I were driving home from Florida. Passing through Bethesda, Maryland, we saw a bakery and stopped and bought half a dozen cookies. While the little old woman back of the counter was putting the cookies in a bag, I wondered aloud how the weather was in Rochester.

"The clerk looked up, and asked, 'You from Rochester, N.Y.?'

" 'Yes,' I said. 'Why?'

" 'Do you know Henry Clune?'

"I said I didn't but I had read his column for years. Then she handed me this slip of paper. Do you know her?"

"Yes," I said. "I did know her once. Thank you very much."

I pondered; what lean days Hinda Wassau had come upon!

And the next day, since my visitor had left me the address of the bakery, I wrote her, thanking her for the $300 she had returned to me and suggesting that perhaps she could use some of it now. If so, would she please send me her home address?

I never received an answer.

CHAPTER TWENTY-FIVE

Bill Cox was a lanky, leggy kid whom I had helped get into Mercersburg Academy, which he left after a triumphant year as track star, to matriculate at a Rochester technical high school and set a world schoolboy record for running one mile. That was in 1924. The Olympics were coming up in Paris and although the boy was very good, I felt that he wouldn't have a chance at 1,500 meters (the Olympic mile) in which Joie Ray, our crack miler, and two or three other competent mature athletes would compete, and I suggested that he try 5,000 meters, a distance at which Americans had never shone. Ill-prepared to run this longer race, Bill tried it at the Olympic trials in Harvard Stadium, hung on, and finished, run out and wobbly, in fourth place; and fourth place finishers in all events, the Olympic Committee had announced, would make the team.

I had gone to Harvard with Cox, whom I liked to think was my protégé, although he was really a self-made athlete with only one year of expert coaching—the year he spent at Mercersburg; and the night following the trials I waited in the lobby of a Boston hotel, where the Olympic Committee was meeting, for official word that the boy had made the Olympic Team.

I sat during the interim with Mike Sweeney, who, in an era when track and field records were far more enduring than the transitory marks of today, had held the world high jump record for sixteen years. A companionable and personable man, Sweeney had served for years as athletic director at the

Hill School, Pottstown, Pennsylvania. He was a repository of athletic lore, and I was interested in his accounts of athletes and athletic competitions of another century. We were still together when Chris Dalton, who had given the dinner for Charlotte and me at the New York Athletic Club the night before our marriage, came down with a long face to announce that the Olympic Committee had decided not to take Bill Cox to Paris.

"But why—why?" I demanded.

"They say he's too young. Too inexperienced."

I was at once the knight-errant of the great and noble institution, the American press, prepared to right wrongs and bring injustice to book. "You tell 'em Chris," I pronounced majestically, "that if Bill Cox isn't taken to Paris, I'll tell the world that the Olympic Committe has reneged on its commitment."

Dalton left. I never knew whether he repeated my threat in the committee room, and I am not at all sure that the committee would have been much impressed if he had. But the fact is, two hours later he returned to the lobby, where I still sat with Mike Sweeney, with the announcement that the committee had reconsidered and that the schoolboy Cox was a member of the team.

I was elated with what I believed I had accomplished, putting an athlete on the American Olympic Team, and I boasted about my achievement when Bill Cox got a third place medal in the 3,000 meter team race at Paris, the only native Rochesterian ever to win an Olympic award.

* * * * * * * * * *

I was never a regular sports writer and I had no desire to be confined to that specialty, but first on the *Herald* and later on the *Democrat and Chronicle,* I occasionally wrote about sporting events, sometimes because I was assigned to do so, and at other times because I discovered in some event I was watching as a spectator something that I thought suitable for my newspaper column, which ranged unrestrictedly in subject matter.

Three years before I went with Bill Cox to the Olympic

Trials, Mr. Antisdale sent me to the opening baseball game, which that year was a considerable occasion.

The team of the year before had been tagged a "stinkeroo" by Bill McCarthy, the town's most authoritative baseball writer, and the epithet was not undeserved. The inept athletes had lost a sinful total of 106 games, twelve, at the nadir of their degredation, without the interruption of a single win. This sorry showing had winnowed out fans in great batches and the die-hard loyalists who still pressed through the ball park turnstiles wore a funereal aspect.

But during the winter the ball club had been sold by its Rochester owner to Walter E. Hapgood, formerly a crack Boston sports writer, and George T. Stallings, who, seven years before his arrival in Rochester, bench-managed the Boston Braves, taking them from dead last on July 4 to the National League pennant and a four-straight win of the World Series.

What Stallings had done was more than a conjuring trick; it was a miracle. And Miracle Man was the title bestowed upon him by general acclaim and if, when he arrived in Rochester, the exultant fans did not quite believe he could raise a Lazarus from the grave, they were certain that he would effect a redemption from the sins of the year before.

He did not, to be sure, repeat the miracle of Boston. That sort of thing is once in a lifetime. But he put a colorful and aggressive ball club in the field which finished second in the International League to the power-packed Baltimore Orioles. He repopulated the stands and fetched back to the ball park the faint of heart—the apostates of the year before—whose cheers soon mingled with the general chorus of approbation.

It was not my function to analyze the game itself, to record hits, runs, and errors. I was assigned to do the crowd story, to attempt to represent the humanness and color of the spectacle. It may have been the first of a series of opening day stories I did during the remainder of my tenure with the *Herald* and for a number of years after I returned to the *Democrat and Chronicle*. I never lost my zest for the event, but I am sure in time my pieces became stereotyped and I used to feel that I could pull from the files an opening day story of three or four years before and put it to current use with a few minor alterations.

I was never able to affect the blasé, world-weary I've-been-everywhere-seen-everything attitude assumed by some reporters as an insignia of their craft and as a token of their experience. I was an eager beaver, perhaps the perennial cub. My enthusiasms now and then got out of hand and I allowed my own feelings and sentiments to prejudice what probably should have been an objective piece of straight reporting.

In the spring of 1921, with a renovated ball club, a Miracle Man as manager, and Fred Merkle, a big power hitter with fouteen years experience in the big leagues (and five World Series) playing first base and acting as team captain, I was more a fervid fan than a paid observer. I was extravagant with metaphors. I compared the devotion of the crowds traipsing out to the ball park to Moslem pilgrims on their way to the stone at Kaaba. I saw the opening day parade, long, with all the chowder and marching clubs in glittering array; loud, with numerous brass bands; colorful, with decorated floats, and boozy with bootleg hooch, as a Roman pageant.

I liked what I had done; I had an exaggerated notion that I had achieved an epic. When I reported for work the day the story appeared, Mr. Antisdale beckoned me into his office. All of us in the newsroom admired and were fond of our employer, whom we secretly referred to as Uncle Louie. We feared him, too. He was a cultured man and never profane. He was not a ranter. But he could be shatteringly caustic, and it was a very real ordeal to suffer his reproof. Under stress he had a habit of pulling at the tips of his moustache, and he was indulging in this mannerism when I entered his office.

"Henry," he said, looking up at me with what seemed a forbidding expression. I wondered what I could have done wrong when I thought what I had done was so right. "Henry," he said again, still tugging at his moustache, "Mr. Hapgood of the ball club just telephoned. Mr. Hapgood is an accomplished and experienced big city newspaperman. He said he thought your story this morning the finest opening day baseball story he had ever read."

Mr. Hapgood's success in Rochester would depend in part on the good will of the press and his encomium could have been expressed as policy. I, however, accepted it as an unqualified tribute. Praise from Sir Hubert! And my employer was not unimpressed.

Although Mr. Antisdale never wanted me to work steadily as a sports writer, what Hapgood had said about my opening day story apparently caused him to believe that I should now and then be taken from the local side of the newspaper and lent to the sports desk. He seemed to feel that my reportage would be less standardized than the stories of the men to whom sporting events were commonplace. "You see things with fresh eyes," he said.

In the fall of that year he sent me to the Syracuse-Colgate football game which was always played at Syracuse. This was the big game of central and western New York. There were times when better football was on display at Ithaca, Cornell versus Yale, Cornell versus Princeton, Cornell versus Dartmouth, but these were Ivy League matches, eagerly attended by partisans of the contesting teams but of less interest to the general public than the traditional Syracuse-Colgate meeting.

On the day of the annual fixture (in recent years Colgate has been scratched from the Syracuse schedule), the city of Syracuse assumed a holiday aspect. Crowds streamed into town by motor and rail. Hotel lobbies were jammed with noisy rooters, and queues formed outside downtown restaurants. I was assigned only once to cover the Syracuse-Colgate game, but on several other occaions I witnessed the contest from the stands. It was always a lively and colorful spectacle; a good show on and off the field. I preferred, however, the games at Ithaca, where the setting was more picturesque, where the humor of the crowd was more temperate than the sometimes riotous goings-on in Syracuse, and where the game itself had more the character of a campus pastime than a public carnival.

Football at Cornell was accepted with civilized rationality. I am sure it was played with passionate intensity by the young men on the field, but the spectators in the stands (always preponderantly Cornell supporters) were not inclined to believe that great convulsions would tremble the earth in the event of a Cornell loss or that the game itself had any meaning to the world's vast billions. It was merely a pleasant college event with many pretty girls in attractive outdoor costumes, and young men very Brooksie, in the twenties and thirties, in contrast to the scuffy bindle-stiff campus apparel of today.

During the years that I worked for the *Herald* and during my subsequent long term employment by the *Democrat and Chronicle* I was present occasionally at one of the more important games at Ithaca, not because of any great devotion to football per se—its stratagems and Draconian disciplines and fierce competitive urges—but because I delighted in the ambience and setting of these contests. If the day was fair, picnic parties would form along the route to the stadium, and the tailgates of station wagons would be laid with inviting collations. I had seen football on other college campuses, but it seemed to me more attractive at Cornell than any other place I knew. And occasionally there were offbeat incidents that were worth writing about.

At an intense moment in a Dartmouth game, with the visiting team in a position to score (a touchdown, as I recall, would have given them victory), with everyone taut and on the qui vive, we were suddenly amazed to discover five men in the Dartmouth backfield, the extra player, a large man in an ankle-length coon skin coat who wore gloves and a derby hat, from the band of which a huge green feather waved defiantly.

He had crossed the sidelines and fitted into the backfield formation almost the instant the play was in motion and we heard, above the quick roar from the stands, his stentorian adjuration, "Score! Score! Score, men!" Then everything was in confusion. The players in moleskin swirled around the imposter in the coon skin coat, then banged into him. Whistles shrieked, flags were flung to the ground, and the big man went down with them. It was illegal, of course: twelve men on the field. But this was an act of alumni ardency, not chicane on the part of the Dartmouth coaching staff, and the officials, lacking precedent for this breach of rule, picked up their flags and declared no penalty.

The big man lumbered painfully to his feet and looked

about for his derby. It had been knocked from his head and crushed irreparably. Hs stood a moment bemused, his hands fumbling in his pockets; then a benign grin formed on his turf-smeared countenance and he brought forth a hip flask, intact. Sideline attendants assisted the intruder to his seat in the stands. The incident was reported by the press wire services and I myself devoted a column to it, but no one troubled to learn the name of the protagonist of a comic bit that tickled thousands, and he was denied, by this neglect, the renown he very much deserved.

* * * * * * * * * *

I have a vivid recollection of another memorable happening at Ithaca, this of a more dramatic character, that highlighted the coaching career at Cornell of the talented Carl Snavely.

Snavely never sought the soft touch. He had no design to aggrandize his reputation by running up tallies on pushovers, and he persuaded the Cornell athletic authorities to book two games with Ohio State on a home-and-home basis. It was absurd, of course; a team from the effete East, an Ivy League eleven, against one of the bully boys of the Big Ten. Ohio State was condescending about the mismatch. It was looked upon as a sort of light practice session—a pleasant respite in the middle of an arduous season—and Francis Schmidt, the Ohio State coach, spent the day before the game duck hunting. The teams met in the stadium at Columbus before a huge crowd that had come out to be amused and left in consternation when the final score went up on the board, Cornell 23: Ohio State 14.

It was a crazy moon-struck thing, the westerners said. An aberration. A fluke. And the following autumn Ohio State swaggered into Ithaca intent on a sacrificial oblation with Cornell the sacrificial lamb. And again the wily Snavely put an eleven on the field which routed the invaders, this time to the tune of 21 to 7; the eastern press had a field day, and I left the game, an exultant Cornell fan, to write about it in lavish imitation of Plutarch's account of the heroic deeds of antiquity.

CHAPTER TWENTY-SIX

Mr. Antisdale died in late spring 1923 and his nephew, who more or less inherited the newspaper, and the nephew's associates in its management, knowing that the deceased editor-publisher now and then had had me cover sporting events, sent me to the Dempsey-Firpo heavyweight championship in New York, and subtly hinted that I take with me William P. Barrows, principal owner and manager of McFarlin's, the leading men's specialty store in Rochester.

Barrows was a substantial advertiser. He was a prickly fellow whose humors were as erratic as the movements of a weathervane. Recently he had developed a grievance against the *Herald's* advertising department, and threatened to reduce his linage, and the *Herald's* managers apparently believed that a gesture of hospitality might appease his discontent.

He was a crack fresh-water sailor and the owner of the finest racing yacht on the south shore of Lake Ontario. He played polo. He had ridden cow ponies on a Colorado ranch where he had been sent as a youth to convalesce from an incipient case of tuberculosis, and he liked to assume the swagger of a ranch hand. He was tall, lean, craggy-faced, "the most handsome homely man I have ever seen," in the opinion of one woman admirer. The clothes he wore came not from the racks of his store, which held some of the most expensive ready-to-wear garments made, but from the noted Boston custom tailor, F. L. Dunne, and they fell with such ease and grace over his lanky form that Barrows, although he seemed indifferent to the distinction, was probably the best dressed man in town.

I was fond of the youngest of Barrows' three stylish and handsome sisters (Marie, the middle sister, whose second husband, Seaton Porter, reputedly possessed the fourth largest income in America, was the most celebrated beauty ever to originate in Rochester), and Bill Barrows and I were friends. The *Herald* managers knew this, and I acceded to their wishes.

I told Barrows I had an extra ticket for the Dempsey-Firpo fight, and that the *Herald* had advised me that I would have a due bill on the Vanderbilt Hotel in New York, which would provide food and lodging for two.

"Fake! Fake!" Bill scoffed, grimacing with disgust. "All those big money fights are rigged. Wouldn't walk across the street to see the thing."

The fanfare induced a change of mind. The press was making a great clamor about the match. It was talked about in clubs, in speakeasies, and in male gatherings on street corners. The public wanted the champion, Dempsey, who was stigmatized as a slacker because he had evaded the war and who had knocked out the glamorous French war hero, Carpentier, dethroned; and many hoped that "the wild bull of the Argentine pampas" might effect this desired end. Bill Barrows got caught up in the general ferment, and we went to New York together.

The night of the match we dined early in the Vanderbilt with a friend of mine, little Joie Ray, the Chicago taxi driver and the greatest mile runner in America, and a social and handsome friend of Barrows', Seth Brady, a polo player and Wall Street broker.

Barrows was leaving for Rochester on on early train the morning following the fight. I was staying over and Brady said to me, "I don't get down to the Street (meaning Wall Street) too early. When you get up in the morning, come down. We'll have breakfast together." I agreed. Joie and Barrows and I then left in a taxicab. The avenues leading north resembled a speedway with hundreds of cars racing toward the Polo Ground. Somewhere in the vicinity of 125th Street another taxi brushed fenders with ours, the drivers stopped, left their cabs, and an angry dispute ensued.

Barrows had a hair-trigger temper and fancied himself a "tough guy." Impatient after a minute's delay, he leaped from the cab and bristlingly intruded into the pavement altercation. He seemed, indeed, to want to take command. I called through the open door, "Bill, we're going to see a fight. Let's not get into one."

"Yeah, who do you think you are?" the offending cabbie asked, "Mayor Hyland?"

We had read in a newspaper that morning that Mayor Hyland was in a hospital critically ill with double pneumonia, his recovery in doubt.

Barrows' clenched fists uncoiled. A grin relaxed his taut features.

"No," he said after a moment. "I don't think I'm Mayor Hyland. And I'm damn glad I'm not."

Sheepishly he returned to the cab, and we continued without further incident to the ball park.

* * * * * * * * * * *

Never a devoted boxing fan, I have nevertheless seen a good deal of boxing and numerous championships at various weights, but never in the realm of what has been called the "sweet science" have I experienced anything remotely comparable to the excitement engendered by the Dempsey-Firpo bout.

It was an affray of such extravagant drama that Hollywood itself, employing its most ingenious devices for the creation of violent action on the screen, would have been hard put to match the gladiatorial orgy that set 85,000 spectators into screaming frenzy.

It was a breathless, starkly brutal combat between a hugely muscled Neanderthal man with black hair thick as couch grass matted on his chest, with scrub oaks for legs, and boulder-like fists that all but split the six-ounce gloves into which they were fitted, and a much smaller, lightning-quick man, as vicious and uncompromisingly aggressive as a tiger at bay.

The whole thing was over in less than five minutes, but

while it lasted it was unbelievable fantasy. Seven times in the first round Firpo went to the floor, and seven times he arose in murderous fury. He seemed to gain, rather than lose strength and fortitude in these brief tumbles; and during one of his perpendicular periods he bludgeoned Dempsey to the canvas, and a few seconds later, with a bull-like charge, catapulted him out of the ring, and the champion, legs bicycling madly over his head, landed assbackwards in the front row of the press section, his title saved by a very short whisker and the defending, upraised hands of sports writers, who shoved him back into the ring.

And at that moment, Bill Barrows, who had earlier decried the championship fight a fake, was schizophrenic. He bit his hand and teeth marks were on it hours later. He leaped from his seat, his arms gesturing crazily, his lean body writhing as though in agony. He was not alone in his delirium. It was epidemic in the ball park, one of the wildest scenes I have ever witnessed. I talked later with an ex-United States Marine, who had gone through the terrible first day of Chateau Thierry when the French were running back, hands raised in the air, crying, "Finisde la guerre," and fresh Americans were rushing French "75s" up the Paris Road and embedding their feet in the pockmarked highway, and holding on against one of the most savage offensives of the summer of 1918.

"Nothing I experienced then," said the ex-Marine, "from the stand of sheer thrills, transcended the first round of the Dempsey-Firpo fight."

Besides the action in the ring, there was a sort of Donnybrook outside of it, although no one except the persons involved paid it the slightest heed. Rough wooden benches had been erected over the entire playing field of the ball park, and during the frenetic first round dozens of bench sitters, each of whom had paid $27.50 for a squeezed-in-space, trying to climb up one another's back for a better view, collapsed the benches; there was grappling, kicking and fisticuffs, and before the precipitant spectators could get free of broken timbers and untangle themselves from the arms and legs of their fallen fellows and gain an upright position, the second round was over after a minute of slugging, and all they saw was the pole-axed "bull of the pampas" being carried in a comatose state to his corner.

My companion, Barrows, was nearly as done in as Firpo. He was completely wrung out. He came to after much persuasion, and in time we made our way back to the Vanderbilt Hotel. Too feverish to sleep, we discussed the mad phantasmagoria of the Polo Grounds for most of what was left of the night. It was dawn before I fell off to sleep.

When I awoke, Bill was gone and it was nearly ten o'clock. I was sure Seth Brady had by this time departed for the "Street", but I rang his room and was surprised to have him tell me that he hadn't yet breakfasted. "Come down when you're dressed," he said; and when I pushed open the door, he was still abed, still in pajamas, but wearing also a flowery silk dressing gown.

"I'm just calling room service," he said. "What do you want for breakfast?"

I asked for bacon and eggs, toast, coffee, orange juice and prunes. In fifteen minutes a white-coated servitor wheeled a small table bearing two silver-covered breakfast trays to the bedside.

"Come on," Brady said: and I leaped into bed, shoes and all, and the man fitted one of the trays over my knees. It was an experience. Only once before, confined in a hospital with pneumonia, had I been served breakfast in bed. Brady said he indulged himself in this manner every morning. He thought it cozy and club-like.

* * * * * * * * * *

I saw Dempsey win the world's heavyweight championship; I was present when he triumphed over Carpentier, Brennan, and Firpo. I was part of the immense crowd that witnessed his defeat by Gene Tunney in the rain-sloshed arena at the Philadelphia Sesqui-Centennial Exposition.

Losing to Tunney, Dempsey curiously gained a public esteem he had not known when he was successfully defending his title against a succession of challengers. The new champion, a cold, calculating young man who seemed to have worked out his destiny with slide rule exactness, had nothing of the appeal of the colorful fighter he dethroned. He appeared to want to divorce himself from the game that had made him a millionaire. It was felt that he was snooting his compeers of the squared circle to take up with persons of wealth and station and members of the intelligentsia. He boasted that he had read all of Gibbon's *Decline and Fall.* He lectured at Yale on Shakespeare, went on a walking tour with George Bernard Shaw, and, ultimately, courted and won an heiress of social status.

Prize fight patrons like their ring idols rough-hewn and in character. Jack Dempsey remained in character and eschewed pretense. In retirement, he opened a Broadway restaurant, where he was in constant comradely circulation among its patrons. He was a picturesque figure and popular at public functions. His World War dereliction seemed to have been forgotten, his popularity grew with the years, and although a two-time loser to Tunney, there were many who still thought of him as "champ" and addressed him by that diminutive.

His prestige continued until the United States became involved in a second World War, and the navy, hoping to capitalize on Dempsey's celebrity, granted him a commission; at once there were howls of protest and cries of defamation from individuals and patriotic groups who recalled how the great ring fighter had shirked the big fight in World War I. The clamor grew and became increasingly bitter. I did not share this feeling. I knew Dempsey slightly (he had gained in maturity, poise, and urbanity), I thought I understood what had happened in World War I, and I wrote an explanatory column in his defense.

A lean, hungry, tough hombre, little more than a hobo, who stole rides on freight trains and picked up cheap purses in tank town boxing rings, Dempsey in time was discovered by Jack (Doc) Kearns, a well-known manager of fighters, who took him under his managerial aegis.

Kearns was a cutie. He knew all the ins and outs of the sinister and savage business of the prize ring. He had formed a connection with Dempsey shortly before the United States entered World War I; he had a valuable protégé in hand, and he was determined not to lose him. When conscription was enforced and millions of young Americans were being inducted into the armed forces, Kearns wangled Dempsey out of the draft. There was a "work or fight" mandate. Kearns and Dempsey chose to work, or so they said. Kearns represented them as shipyard workers, and they were photographed in a ship yard.

But the photograph which was reproduced in the newspapers, probably without their intention, was hardly an edifying portraiture. It showed Kearns and Dempsey wearing patent leather shoes, stand-up linen collars, fashionable fedoras, and expensive looking overcoats. They seemed more like a couple of Broadway actors than workers dedicated to the patriotic task of helping build a war ship. With the publication of the photograph, Dempsey, particularly, became an object of vehement opprobrium. Throughout the remaining period of the war and during his postwar career as champion, he was constantly reviled as a slacker, and it was only with his loss to Tunney that the taunts and defamations abated.

At the time he came under Kearns' sponsorship, Jack Dempsey was not a young man filled with noble purposes or steeped in idealistic traditions. Nonetheless, it is reasonable to believe that, left to his own devices, he would have followed the example of vast numbers of his contemporaries and submitted without protest to the draft. But he had become the property of a very smart manager, and the smart manager pointed out that all that had been planned for him—a chance to make a great deal of money in a comparatively short time—would be lost unless he listened to reason. Dempsey listened. He waited out the war.

I incorporated the above speculations in the piece I wrote in Dempsey's defense. It brought harsh criticism from some; other readers sympathized with my thesis. I believed thoroughly in what I had written, and I was pleased one day to receive the following note:

> My Dear Henry Clune:—
>
> My good friend, Ed "King" Mahoney, of Rochester, has forwarded me a copy of your column, "Seen and Heard," in your issue January 10.

May I express my thanks and appreciation for the kindly editorial contained therein concerning me? I would like you to know that in these times it is comforting to be understood.

My warmest personal regards and gratitude.

Sincerely,
Jack Dempsey.
January 16, 1942.

CHAPTER TWENTY-SEVEN

One near-zero, pre-Christmas December day in 1929, I moved in limited compass about the front corridors of the state prison at Auburn, New York, during the most violent insurrection that grim, gray bastille had ever known.

In an initial gesture of revolt, a clique of desperate inmates grabbed the warden, the principal keeper, and several guards, and announced that the lives of the hostages would be spared only if the main gate was flung open and automobiles, with motors running, were ranked at the street curb to facilitate the prisoners' escape.

The main gate was opened in time, and cars with exhaust fumes pluming into the frigid air were parked in front of the prison. It was a ruse. The convicts' rush for liberty was met with rifle fire. The leader of the revolt, a lifer who once before had instigated a prison break, fell dead, his confederates retreated to a handy cell block, and thereafter for several hours the ancient keep reverberated with an intermittent exchange of rifle and pistol fire.

I had been frantically summoned by telephone from the restaurant in the Sagamore Hotel in Rochester, where I customarily lunched with a group of young bloods, and commanded by the city editor of the *Democrat and Chronicle* to catch the next train to Auburn. I made it by the proverbial skin of my teeth, sustained in my flight by a ten dollar bill lent to me by a wealthy table companion. I reached the prison in early afternoon, not long after the thwarted gate crash.

There was radio in those days, and news of the uprising had spread swiftly through Cayuga County, of which Auburn is the county seat, and from all over the area men bringing an assortment of weapons—squirrel guns, ancient fowling pieces, Civil War muskets, pistols, rifles, everything, except perhaps a harquebus—had converged, rabble-like, on the prison. One back road dairy farmer arrived with an ax over his shoulder, grimly determined, as were his fellow minutemen, to suppress the revolt before the felons escaped to rape, murder, and pillage the city and the adjacent countryside.

This heterogeneous mob, commingling in the offices and front corridor of the prison with an already assembled company of sheriff's deputies, Auburn police, prison guards, and state troopers, heightened a clamor and confusion that had prevailed since the inception of the revolt until, at the time I was admitted to the prison, it had the aspect of panic.

There was no organization, no unity of purpose, no command. Men bearing arms clumped and shoved and shouted about the corridors and brandished their weapons in displays of bravado, in such a reckless manner that it seemed a miracle that a gun was not accidentally discharged into the seething concourse of would-be besiegers. Everything was hugger-mugger; at sixes and sevens. And this situation continued until the end of the short winter day when the state troopers, with details of police from Geneva, Syracuse, and Rochester standing in support, took charge of the prison, wrought some order out of the general chaos, and brought the active insurrection to a nervous close.

Seven more rioters were shot to death in this closing episode, to bring the count of convicts dead to eight. But before this, the mutineers had murdered the principal keeper and shot, stabbed, and bludgeoned several of the hostage guards.

After it was all over, the second guessers, the theorists, the bleeding hearts, who were at far remove from the prison during the violence and bloodletting, suggested that the rebellion might have been quelled by attrition and the rebellious felons taken alive. This would have had no appeal to the state troopers who were on the firing line. They were taking no chances. A contagion of revolt had spread throughout the prison. Furniture and windows were being broken, steam pipes were pierced in mindless vandalism, and with the heating system out of whack the difference between the inside and the outside temperature was negligible. There was a constant cacophony as prisoners in sympathy with the rioters whacked hard objects against the bars of their cells and howled obscenities at the troopers, and only the fact that most of the inmates were locked in their brick and steel cubicles prevented a general uprising.

Before I arrived in Auburn and before the thwarted gate crash, a parley had been attempted: A Roman Catholic priest whose secular attentions and spiritual ministrations had won him friends among the prisoners, was deputized to attempt to negotiate a truce. His petitions failed. Tear gas was then employed in the hope that it would rout out the rebellious group from the narrow salient they defended with hand guns taken from the hostages, but the hostages suffered more from the gas fumes than their captors, who continued to hold both the hostages and their fortified position. The next procedure, the stratagem of the open gate and the get-away cars succeeded to the extent that it effected the liquidation of the leader of the revolt, and allowed, as his followers retreated in wild disorder, the rescue of the warden and other hostages.

W. O. Dapping, managing editor of the small city daily, the *Auburn Citizen,* was given a special award by the Pulitzer Committee for his coverage of the riot, and I too was cited, not for the two-column running story I wired into the *Democrat and Chronicle,* but for comments in my column "Seen and Heard." But mine was perhaps a dubious distinction.

Some time after the mutinous convicts had retreated in disarray from what had seemed the threshold of liberty and the prison gate had been slammed shut, a siege of the cell block in which they had taken refuge was inaugurated, and for a couple of hours I observed with shuddering fascination the unnatural behavior of men who were intent on killing their fellow men.

Huddled together in their small retreat, the prisoners had no more chance of escape than fish in a water barrel. Their only weapons were hand guns and their ammunition was limited. They knew, since they had murdered the principal keeper, that a charge of murder would be lodged against them if taken alive, and they formed a pact (which some adhered to) to die rather than be captured, and to bring death in this last ditch stand to any assailant within range of their guns.

The cell block in which the convicts made their defense was in what was known as the South Wing of the prison, and troopers engaged in the siege entered the South Wing from the corridor in which I circulated, as part of a milling throng, and there they returned after each sortie.

The troopers were at times imperiled, but they suffered no casualties; and the advantage was preponderantly with the attacking forces. They had the maneuverability, the big guns, limitless ammunition, the option of retreat, and a formidable contingent of police from four cities in reserve. A trooper would shoulder through the corridor crowd and sidle along a wall of the South Wing, seeking a living target. Soon we would hear the fierce crash of rifle bullets against a cell wall, a retaliatory pistol shot, perhaps a cry of anguish, and the rifleman would dart back to the protection of the corridor, wildly gesticulating, spewing profanities, always, it seemed to me, in a state of frenzy.

If a hit was made or a convict was killed, the announcement of either of these events excited a kind of orgiastic revel among the troopers and the motley crowd that swarmed the corridor, and ghoulish shouts and imprecations would transcend the ordinary noises of the prevailing hubbub.

I particularly observed a young trooper who, under ordinary circumstances, would have been as handsome as a movie idol, who stumbled into the corridor from the South Wing, his vision distorted by tear gas fumes. His cap of muskrat skin was canted over one eye, and the visible eye was tear-drenched. He had suffered no physical hurt, but the fury of his emotions had convulsed his features, twisting and fragmenting them until his face had the look of a gaping wound or something that had been stomped upon. He slumped down in a wooden chair, his neck resting on the headrest, and brushed his tear-filled eyes with the back of his hand. He laughed hysterically.

"I saw one of 'em die, the mother-f—sonofabitch! God, it was good. God, it was wonderful! He crumpled up and grabbed his gut and kinda wiggled. And down he went! I pumped another into the——!"

Someone handed him a tumbler half-filled with an amber-colored liquid which was being liberally dispensed among the troopers. He downed it in two gulps. Wanted more; was given more.

A man in civilian clothes—a chunky, hard-looking man wearing a checkered cap—stood over the young trooper, fanning him with a towel like a boxer's second in a prize ring. The trooper rose, took the towel, swabbed his sweaty face and blotted his tear-filled eyes. "I'm going back," he shouted challengingly. "I'm going back and get another one of the——'s! We'll kill 'em all, before this day's done."

When the siege finally ended and the mutinous convicts who had decided against the death pact had surrendered, prison attendants were sent into the South Wing to fetch the bodies of the rioters who had held to the pact. The corpses were brought out in makeshift litters, and as one of the litters passed where I stood in the corridor, a lifeless body slipped from it and lay supine on the floor, free of a bloodstained blanket that had been carelessly thrown over it. The two bearers did not at once resume their burden. There was a water cooler near the scene of the accident, and as one of the attendants leaned over for a drink, a uniformed police officer, with a great oath, lunged through the crowd, yanked a hand gun from a holster, stooped over the corpse, and fired a shot through its chest.

Two or three days after I returned from Auburn, reflecting on some of the scenes and incidents of the prison riot, I remarked in my column "Seen and Heard" that the siege of the South Wing was different from anything I had observed in my brief experience in the combat zone during the war. I had never participated in or witnessed hand-to-hand fighting, and artillerymen loading and firing a cannon at an unseen enemy miles away was a mechanical and impersonal exercise in human slaughter compared to the shooting of convicts at a distance of less than fifty yards.

I attempted in what I wrote to give a more detailed and

intimate picture of the scene inside the prison than had been possible in my news story. I philosophized briefly on the unnatural behavior of men engaged in the unnatural business of killing their fellow men. I reported the incident of the bullet fired into the corpse, remarked the rather schizophrenic conduct of the handsome young trooper who had suffered gas fumes, and mentioned an amber-colored liquid apparently provided as a stimulant for the men on the firing line. I had no intention of censuring the forces joined in a life and death struggle with a company of desperate and vicious felons. I thought what I wrote was commendably honest. The State Police, an agency I admired, and one in which, many years later, one of my sons served more than a dozen years, found no merit in my efforts.

Two months after the riot, I was sent back to Auburn to report the trial of six of the rioters who had been indicted for murder. A number of state troopers had been called as witnesses for the prosecution, and I was surprised to discover that they thought I had libeled them. I was a pariah, outside of the pale; their hostility was bitter and vindictive. I was enlightened by a trooper with whom I had been on friendly terms before the prison uprising. He called me aside the second day of the trial.

"You drive down here?" he asked.

"Yes."

"For God's sake, Hank, be careful. They got your number."

"My number? What do you mean by that?"

"That stuff you wrote in your column. The guy shot a hole in a stiff. The way some of our fellows blew their top. The amber-colored liquid—the whiskey. I'm telling you, you're shit with our whole organization."

"I wasn't being critical," I protested. "I wasn't trying to blow the whistle on anyone. I only wrote what I saw. But my number . . .?"

"Your car's license number. It's plastered on the bulletin board in every barracks in the state. One wrong move—even if it's only illegal parking—and they'll grab you. And get some judge to throw the book at you. Believe me."

I was astonished, and, at first flush, indignant. Reflection put the matter in a different light. I was very eager, in those days, for recognition. What I had written in my column about the Auburn riot would not, as had W. O. Dapping's reportage, win the acclaim of the Pulitzer Committee; but I had transcended the bourne of the *Democrat and Chronicle*'s circulation area.

My words were being mouthed all over the state, in revilement, to be sure—but weren't the white knights of journalism, in their implacable pursuit of the truth, often the objects of vilification? I was determined, from then on, to watch my motoring manners; but I was not unpleased with the proclamation of my name and license number in the barracks of the State Police. I felt, indeed, that I had achieved an honorable distinction.

CHAPTER TWENTY-EIGHT

When I first met her, Claire Luce (not to be confused with Clare Boothe Luce, the eminent widow of the late Henry R. Luce, founder of *Time, Life* and *Fortune*) was serving buns in the Hof Brau House, in Rochester.

A slim, delicately-formed girl with straw-colored pigtails dangling down the back of her Dutch dairymaid's costume, she moved among the tables with a tripping and sinuous grace that delighted the well-larded burghers, the mainstream of the restaurant's patronage, and titillated visiting firemen and other transients, who had discovered that the Hof Brau was the choicest eating place in town.

The popularity of the Hof Brau House derived not only from the excellence of its cuisine, but from its draught beer and Rhine wines. Although it continued in business for several years after Prohibition, the proprietors found that without the revenue from wines, beer, and spirits, they could not maintain their high standard in food, and they closed the doors of one of the finest restaurants Rochester has ever known; but the blonde bun girl had left before the closing.

Claire Luce had not been content to subsist on tips dropped into a bun tray that hung on silken cords from her shoulders or to submit interminably to the pats and pinches of fat old futzes with ogling eyes and lascivious urges. She had aspirations. She was determined that one day her name would be spelled out in lights, and she left town. That was some time after World War I.

One night, some time after the close of World War II, I dined with her in the Oak Room of the Hotel Plaza in New York. We had cocktails before dinner. Mis Luce offered me a cigarette from a rectangular gold case she handed across the table. I read on the inside of the upper lid the inscription, "To Claire from Randolph."

Margaret Wollf, whose father had owned the old Lyceum Theater and who had moved to Rome at the time of her marriage to Count Lorris Riccio, home for a brief visit, had told me that Claire Luce's engagement to Randolph Churchill was the talk of the French Riviera.

I boasted to Claire, "I knew of your engagement even before I read it in the columns."

She shook her head. "It's off," she said. "We're still very good friends, but we're—unengaged."

"Oh," I said. I observed my companion reflectively.

She had changed, to be sure, since I had first known her. She was worldly, sophisticated, chic, and very sure of herself. But she was still as slim and gracefully formed as when she had been the pet of the Hof Brau, and I speculated, as I had in the past, about the hidden strengths in this seemingly fragile physical frame that had kept Claire Luce in stern and unwavering pursuit of her goals.

And she had achieved notably. Her name had been high in the lights in New York, London, and Paris. Once, at the personal behest of the monarch, she had danced for the king of Spain. She had been acclaimed in *Time* magazine as the only American-born actress to play a leading Shakespearian role at the Stratford-on-Avon festival. And for a time—and this perhaps put her at the remotest remove from her bun tray and the Rochester restaurant—she had been the promised daughter-in-law of the great wartime master of the British Commonwealth, Winston Churchill.

She told amusedly of a dinner party she had attended with Randolph at the time of their betrothal at Chequers, the Churchill country place.

During the dessert, a large cat leaped up on the table and almost into the prime minister's dessert dish.

"It didn't bother Winston a lick," Claire said. "He fondled it and cuddled it, and presently let it loose to stray around the table top. He apparently was very fond of cats. Some of the other guests, I am sure, from the way they looked, didn't share his affection."

Ingrid Bergman, the Swedish actress, once lived with her husband Peter Lindstrom, who was studying at the university's medical and dental school, and her daughter Pia, in a small house in a modest neighborhood a block and a half from my native Linden Street in Rochester. I once interviewed her husband, but I never met the actress or her child. My wife knew Pia. She gave her swimming lessons in the pool of the Genesee Valley Club. This was before Miss Bergman's triumphs in such screen plays as *For Whom the Bell Tolls* and *Casablanca.*

Miss Bergman did not like Rochester; she never related to it, and the city could hardly claim her as a famous ex-resident. Claire Luce was indigenous to the town, and next to the distinguished playwright, Philip Barry, she is, in my memory, Rochester's most celebrated theatrical personage. She used to say that I gave her her start, a statement that I liked to hear, but know in my heart is untrue. I did, however, very early in her career, write about her activities, and in time in numerous columns, recounted her experiences with a kind of Boswellian amplitude and fidelity.

In her off hours in her bun girl days at the Hof Brau, Claire studied with the doyenne of Rochester's dance mistresses, Mrs. Florence Colebrook Powers, who was convinced, as was the girl herself, that she was destined for stardom. She danced and danced and danced long hours every day under her mentor's expert tutelage; but presently, feeling that her progress was slow, she scooted from under the Powers's aegis and flounced off with a third-rate Russian opera troupe which bogged down at some way-station, where, after a frantic search, Mrs. Powers found her protégée, bedraggled, hungry, and unpaid.

Returned to Rochester with the runaway, Mrs. Powers decided that if she were to keep her prize pupil ready at hand, she had better adopt her, and she did, legally. It was merely a stopgap. The kid's irrepressible urges negated any sense she may have had of filial duty, and soon she was off again, this time beyond recall. Her objective, New York: *Broadway,* New York!

The late Texas Guinan, chatelaine of a succession of Tenderloin night spots during the mad and febrile days (and nights) of bootleg hootch and blind pigs, whose cry "Hello sucker" forewarned each patron of her place of the exactions he might expect, one night, as I sat with her in one of her plush saloons, boasted that she had launched Claire Luce on a Broadway career.

"She came in here looking for a job," Texas said. "I sent her out to get her hair done, to have her nails done, and I gave her money for clothes. A shapely, pretty blonde kid, she could dance like crazy. I put her in my chorus line. Next, she was in the musical, *Little Jesse James.* After that—" Miss Guinan moved her bejeweled hands expansively.

Miss Luce has denied that she ever performed in a Guinan night club or received any benefits from the proprietress. But Tex was right when she said the girl could "dance like crazy," and it is true that not too long after her arrival in New York she was cast in *Little Jesse James,* where her glittering terpsichorean talents, remarked by Ziegfeld scouts, led to a prominent role in the *Follies,* with her name, perhaps more quickly than Claire herself had anticipated, high in the Broadway lights. From then on, for a period of several years, her career seemed an untrammeled triumph.

Her co-star and dance partner in a piece called *The Gay Divorcée* was the great Fred Astaire, whose former partner, his sister Adele, had left the boards to marry Lord Charles Cavendish. Miss Luce and Astaire danced half a dozen routines together, including the latter's famous "Night and Day."

She went to London with *The Gay Divorcée,* and there repeated her New York success; she crossed the Channel and brilliantly replaced the celebrated Mistinguett, in the Folies-Bergères; went to Madrid, where her dancing at a court soiree enchanted the soon-to-be-exiled Alfonso XIII.

Relentlessly ambitious, desiring to become a sort of Renaissance Woman—dancer, actress, painter, writer—Claire, upon her return to New York, turned to the legitimate theater. She was cast in the only feminine role in John Steinbeck's

Of Mice and Men, which, after a prolonged stand in New York, moved to London. In London Miss Luce achieved, as a dramatic actress, a greater vogue than she had known as a dancing girl; she became the toast of the town. *Of Mice and Men* seemed destined to continue interminably; but the war came, and Dunkirk. The show closed, but Claire Luce remained in the British capital during the dreadful ordeal of the blitz, displaying a fortitude and courage incompatible in one of her ethereal-like lightness and grace, her seeming incorporeality.

I had a note from her on the stationery of the swank United Hunts Club of London's West End. "I was bombed out of the Ritz the other night," the note read, "but expect to be back soon. Write me there."

One winter night during the blitz Claire gave a one-woman show in an army hospital. A bomb hit across the street. The show continued. Miss Luce finished her last speech before the intermission and stepped into the wings. "I won't go back," she cried distressedly. "I won't. Those men don't like me."

"Like you," the man in charge of the stage said. "Why, they're wild about you."

"No, no, no," she protested. "I haven't had a single hand. There hasn't been a patter of applause."

Sadly, the manager explained.

"But don't you understand, Claire? Some of these men were burned terribly at Dunkirk. Others have lost their hands. None of them is able to applaud."

The performer went back and finished the show.

* * * * * * * * * *

New York once had a compelling attraction for me. I was there frequently during the '40s and '50s, and on these visits I often met Claire Luce. She was pictorial, and I delighted in the attention she attracted in the restaurants to which I took her. She knew many people who answered to the description someone once gave of a celebrity (a person famous for being well-known), and liking to interpose prominent names into my newspaper column, these diversions were both enjoyable and professionally rewarding. I was pleased in her company to have her waved at by Marlene Dietrich, Anita Loos, William Shirer (Shirer took her one night to what he said was the best restaurant in New York, a small, unpretentious place on Third Avenue, and Claire and I went there the next week), and other personages.

One time after we had arranged to meet, I was put off by a Western Union message, "Sorry can't meet you for dinner Randolph (Churchill) just arrived; he wants to go everywhere and see everything."

Bill Clune, one of our sons, was doing very well in those years in New York (and in Europe, Mexico, Hawaii, Bermuda, and other places) as one of the highest paid male models in a business into which he had fallen by chance rather than chosen by design. He, too, knew numerous persons categorized as celebrities, and one day he asked me to a large and fancy cocktail party on East 57th Street. I told him I had an engagement with Claire Luce. "Bring her along," Bill said, and I did.

As we crossed the threshold of the host's elaborate apartment, a cry rose above the bibulous babble of a multitude of guests, and a woman darted free of the assembly and flung her arms around my companion. "Oh, Claire! Claire, darling!" she exulted. "It's so wonderful to see you!"

I was introduced to the first wife of Britain's prime minister, Sir Anthony Eden.

* * * * * * * * * * *

Claire remained nearly two years in England after the start of the war, and I once asked her why she had subjected herself to the London bombings when she might have returned to her native land.

"The English people had been wonderful to me," she said, simply. "I felt I had an obligation to stay there and try to help."

A girl of limited formal education, she taught herself to speak, read, and write French. She wanted to devise an English version of Dumas's *Camille,* and I once devoted long hours to typing out scenes from the play she translated from French into English.

She was a devoted painter, and presently had a one-woman show in New York. She very much wanted to write, particularly an autobiography, but published only one book.

In the first flush of her success as a dancing girl, when she was living in an exclusive Park Avenue hotel and being showered with attentions, Claire married a wealthy young man who, from what little I knew of the romance, seemed never to fit very firmly into the rather complex pattern of her life. They were separated, and she never tried matrimony again; but there were betrothals: a British air commander who was killed in action; Randolph Churchill; perhaps others. And before she left England, she became the goddess of a handsome young Irish fighter pilot, somewhat her junior, who wrote her a series of letters, florid, elegant, and completely worshipful, which, after the young man died in an air fight, Miss Luce compiled into a volume entitled, *Letters from Patrick.*

Perhaps the book might better have died a-borning. Love letters are dull reading except for the person to whom they are addressed, and it seemed inept of Claire to apotheosize herself by publishing a series of extravagant tributes from a young man who had made the supreme sacrifice. I had a sense of embarrassment turning through the pages of *Letters from Patrick,* as Miss Luce may also have had when she found, returning to Rochester to autograph copies of the book, that scarcely anyone came into the bookstore for her signature.

A couple of years after the close of the war, Claire shared billing and the lights above the Booth Theater with two excellent mimes, Sidney Blackmere and Donald Cook, in a mystery, *Portrait in Black.*

I saw the show the first Saturday night of its run. Friends had invited the actress to spend the week-end at a country place in New Jersey, and I agreed, after the final curtain, to escort her to the Lackawanna Station in Hoboken.

Waiting backstage while she changed to street attire, I was diverted by a profusion of messages of good will and congratulations from persons not only prominent in the theater, but in other fields, that were tacked above her make-up table. When we left the theater, Claire proposed that we stop at Sardi's, the theatrical restaurant.

I had previously found that leading ladies often conceive that their position in the universe is central, that their ordinances are sovereign, and that of course railroad trains and other accommodations adjust to their convenience. My suggestion that since the Lackawanna train was to leave shortly after midnight it might be well to proceed directly to the station, was brushed aside. Claire had a steak sandwich and a salad in Sardi's. The train had left five minutes before we reached Hoboken.

The leading lady's host was waiting at a station more than twenty miles away. I finally dug up a driver who agreed to try the trip for twenty-five dollars. It was a tortuous expedition. He would lose his way and twice had to arouse the occupants of a farmhouse to recover it. It was well after two o'clock when we delivered Miss Luce to the considerably annoyed friend with whom she was to pass the week-end.

I sat with the driver on the return trip. He was a Hoboken native who avowed that he and Frank Sinatra used to wash the windows of the city's trolley cars for spending money.

"We was pals, me and Frankie," he boasted. "I know his folks. Grand people. I want you to meet 'em."

"At this hour?"

"Oh, they'll be up. They're always up Sat'dy night."

"This is well into Sunday morning."

"Don't make no difference. They'll be playing pinochle down at the fire hall. They're always there Sat'dy night."

I pleaded exhaustion. I wanted only to return to New York and get into bed. He insisted on taking me to the fire hall where a card game was being played on a table set up next to a hose cart. I refused to leave the car. The driver was genuinely disappointed.

* * * * * * * * * *

After the '50s, I pretty well lost track of Claire Luce. Once in that decade, she wired me frantically that she wanted to play the mistress of the hero in a novel of mine, *By His Own Hand,* but Hollywood never bought the book.

Some time after that, Paul Crabtree, who managed a summer stock company at the East Rochester Playhouse, asked if I thought I could get Claire to star in a piece that would close the season. I phoned her; she came a-running and brought with her Francis Sullivan, a fine English actor. The night the show closed, she gave a party for my wife and me at a near-by inn at which Mr. Sullivan, a notable raconteur, proved as entertaining off the stage as he was on it.

The last I heard of Claire Luce she was living in the Gramercy Park Hotel in New York. The last mention of her in the press that I read was a line in the now defunct *New York Journal-American* in 1965.

"Topic at Monte Carlo," Walter Winchell wrote, "was zillionaire Aristotle Onassis' eyes for actress Claire Luce of H'wood while Marie Callas is over here."

CHAPTER TWENTY-NINE

Over a considerable period of years, I at various times quite extensively recounted the activities of Claire Luce, and once devoted a full newspaper column to the more distinguished of the two prominent Luce women, Clare Boothe Luce.

The occasion was Mrs. Luce's appearance as visiting star at the Summer Playhouse in Stamford, Connecticut. She had been engaged to play the title role in George Bernard Shaw's pleasant, witty, but rather dated comedy, *Candide.* The opening attracted a glittering audience that included politicos of national renown, leaders of café society, theatrical producers, actors and actresses, professional first-nighters, and leading metropolitan drama critics. It was ceremonial. There was fanfare, floodlights, autograph seekers, all the appurtenances of a Hollywood premiere.

At that time, the summer of 1945, Mrs. Luce was serving as representative of a Connecticut congressional district, and she was, perhaps next to Mrs. Roosevelt, the most widely discussed woman in America. Her gifts, as they were later to be enumerated by her biographers, would seem to give Clare Luce true claim to the title "Renaissance Woman," to which Claire Luce vainly aspired.

The issue of a chorus girl mother and a runaway father, she early displayed an intensity and aggressiveness that left those who attempted to compete with her spent and far up the track, as they say of failing horses at the race track.

She had been trained in youth at the Clare Tree Major

School of Dramatic Art. She had married, quite young, an older man of millions. Her biographers have said that she was a potential Olympic swimmer, the best equestrienne her riding associates had ever seen, a crack bird shot, a scuba diver. There is no mention that she defeated the late Willie Hoppe at 18:2 balk line billiards, but this may have been a statistical oversight.

Mrs. Luce had served as editor of the sophisticated monthly, *Vanity Fair;* she had been a brilliant and prolific war correspondent for *Life;* she had twice been elected to Congress; she had written several plays, one of which, *The Women,* played more than 600 performances on Broadway and made its author $2,000,000; she had married, after divorcing her first husband, the wealthy and powerful publisher, Henry R. Luce. She was a notable beauty and was said to have "the most beautiful legs in the world." At the time of Mrs. Luce's conversion to the Roman Catholic Church, the eloquent Bishop Fulton J. Sheen remarked of his most famous proselyte, "I have never met or talked to one with a more brilliant mind."

On the night Clare Boothe Luce opened in *Candide,* the New York critics were so unanimously disparaging of her performance that I was struck with the notion, reading the reviews, that they had made the trek to Stamford (when ordinarily they wouldn't have glanced twice at a summer stock company) with a collusive design to level a lady whose fortunes and talents seemed perhaps too numerous and too extravagant to countenance. They, and a sedulous imitator from a Bridgeport newspaper, mauled her, ran her through with verbal poniards, avowed that she couldn't act for sour grapes, and proclaimed her histrionic effort a pitiful disaster.

"I have seen the plain and ordinary failure," wrote one of Mrs. Luce's critics. "I have seen the dull and soggy flop. I have witnessed many a stinkeroo . . . But on Monday night I sat in a front row pew . . . during the embarrassing and inglorious spectacle of our lady from Congress laying so many eggs all over the stage that when the final curtain humanely ended the proceedings, George Bernard Shaw had turned into a veritable omelet."

In the end this sort of thing became tiresome, it was so

utterly unoriginal. It seemed even a little childish. For surely the critics had endured, with much less vitriolic disapproval, numerous performances by paid-to-play mimes as inept as they found Mrs. Luce's portrayal of a role that the theatrical trade had long considered actor-proof.

As I continued my perusal of the reviews, I envisaged (and so wrote in my column) the boys from New York spitting on their hands, jerking at their sleeves, and grittily remarking through their teeth, "We'll go up there and stick her. We'll stick her good. This is our chance. We'll let everything fall on her but the proscenium arch, and if that can be loosed, she'll get that, too. Hi-ho, and a heave ho, let's give it to Lady Luce!"

But the interesting part about this corpus of invective was that all who reviewed Mrs. Luce's performance agreed that she was a beautiful figure on the stage, a fact apparently so obvious to the other members of the audience that the critics themselves could hardly have ignored it and retained credibility.

"It was the first time, dear reader," wrote one of this company, "that these tired old eyes have feasted upon the delectable spectacle of blonde loveliness of our current high priestess of disunity.

"It was the first time I have felt the impact of Clare's utterly sexogenic appeal."

And the cynical, sophisticated, devastatingly witty Wolcott Gibbs of *The New Yorker,* who boasted that he had walked out of the theater after the second act bored stiff with the star's histrionic incompetence, had a different feeling about the appeal of her person. "She looked very beautiful, even so small, so terribly far away," he wrote.

It was, to be sure, a presumption on my part to take exception to what the eminent New York writers had written about a performance they had witnessed and I had only read about, but I couldn't help wonder how a woman who had been trained as an actress and who must have learned, writing several Broadway hits, something about stagecraft, and who had the immensely useful attribute of beauty, could be as bad on the stage as the critics made her out to be.

I devoted a full column to this sort of speculation, suggesting at one point . . . "that it is only natural that most of us who possess only one small talent and have had only a fair amount of luck should carp, cavil, and be ready to stone any person who has large talents in several fields of endeavor and a great deal of luck to boot. The critics couldn't disfigure Mrs. Luce's beauty. Most of them probably knew that she could write rings around them either in straight prose or in the dialogue of the theater. They knew that nothing they could say would upset her seat in Congress, pauperize her immensely wealthy husband, or debilitate his power; but they could sit stolidly back in their orchestra chairs and scheme up hard and bad things to say about her acting."

The column was headed, "Beautiful, At Least," and a few days after it appeared in the *Democrat and Chronicle,* it was reprinted in a Bridgeport newspaper. Almost at once I was assailed by letter, by telegram, and, in a couple of instances, by persons who paid toll charges in order to abuse me orally. One of these long-distance assailants denounced me as a "fink," and prefixed the epithet with a qualifier that shouldn't have been repeated over the telephone.

It wasn't only my mild defense of Mrs. Luce's stage performance that my detractors objected to; they appeared to be outraged that anything good should be written about a lady who, they seemed to feel, perhaps sharing the conviction of the drama critics, had been favored with too many of the assets that are the sublimated desires of humankind—fame, wealth, talent, success, beauty.

The tempest of invective spent itself quickly, and the whole business passed from my mind in time. I was vaguely aware that Mrs. Luce left Congress at the completion of her second term. Much later I was to learn of her appointment as our ambassador to Italy. In the interim I was surprised, and naturally pleased, one day to receive the following note from Sandy Hook, Connecticut, dated 5 October 1946.

Dear Mr. Clune,

Now that I am out of politics and there can be no suspicion (as sometimes, unhappily, there is) that a "thank you" note from a politico may be just an invitation to extend further favors—may I belatedly, and for that reason even more sincerely, thank you for the more than kind column you wrote about me last year? I liked it but very *much*. And altho' I've had far more than my share of newsprint, not all of it has been kind, and a surprising lot of it has been full of bitterness and jibes. This is to thank you for one review that was wholly generous.

Cordially yours,
Clare Boothe Luce

* * * * * * * * * * *

The ballyhoo years of the 1920s ended with the stock market crash of 1929; the era of depression that followed ended with the outbreak of World War II. Doubling as a reporter and columnist during these rather historic periods, I took all sorts of assignments. I was as busy as the proverbial bee. I was made a sort of tufthunter by the city desk and sent to interview a succession of notable (and notorious) visitors that included such various figures as Peaches Browning, a big pouty blonde girl, the protagonist of the New York tabloids, who boasted that she was "the most talked about woman in the world"; Scott Nearing, the intellectual Socialist, lecturer and writer; Gilda Gray, who emerged from a murky back street workmen's saloon in Cudahy, Wisconsin, where she danced for coins thrown at her feet, to gird her graceful figure in elaborate raiment, to ride in elaborate motor cars behind a chauffeur in livery, and to become (briefly) the biggest moneymaker on Broadway; Sir Hugh Walpole, the eminent British novelist; Emma Goldman, the anarchist, who once offered herself as a street prostitute to obtain money for the purchase of a pistol for her paramour, who shot, but failed to kill, Henry Frick, the steelmaster; Winston Churchill; madcap Tallulah Bankhead, whose penchant was removing her clothing in public; the romantically handsome Admiral Richard E. Byrd, who flew over both the North and South Poles and the Atlantic Ocean; Jean Harlow, the current sex goddess. That's a fair sampling; there were numerous others. And Yehudi Menuhin!

The city editor of the *Democrat and Chronicle,* a shouter,

a forthright fellow, whose shouts were often mixed with profanities, shouted at me as I was about to descend from the city room in the elevator, "Go meet Yehudi Menuhin. He's coming in on the Empire."

"Who's Yehudi Menuhin?" I shouted back.

"The Boy Wonder, for God's sake. He'll be getting off a Pullman. You can't miss him."

The city editor was at once busy with other directives, and although I was not bound in reportorial vassalage, it seemed best not to quibble over the issue, and I repaired to the New York Central Station. The Empire State Express, the railroad's crack daytime train on its New York to Buffalo run, arrived early in the afternoon in Rochester.

I stood near the Pullman steps as the extra-fare passengers descended, curious about Yehudi Menuhin, the Boy Wonder. I had been a few days before with Willie Hoppe, who, years before, had been an authentic Boy Wonder. His father, an uncompromising martinet, had brought Willie up virtually from the cradle to play balk line and three cushion billards, standing him on a box at the table and smarting him with a little switch when he missed a shot. At fifteen the boy was a world beater. I thought Willie might be resentful of his father's Draconian discipline and gently hinted at this. He looked off reflectively and said, without reproach, "Papa shot a wonderful cue himself."

I read the sport pages quite thoroughly, and, standing on the train platform waiting for the youthful prodigy I had been sent to interview, I discarded the notion that he might be a new Wonder Boy of billiards. But what was Yehudi Menuhin's genius? The name had a mystic connotation. . . . Then I saw, coming down the Pullman steps accompanied by a man whose solicitude and hovering attentions indicated managerial function, a youth with long hair and fat, bulging legs which were amply displayed in knee-length velveteen breeches. I had it at once. A musical Wonder Boy! I went along with the pair in a cab to the Hotel Sagamore.

We had proceeded a block or more when I asked brightly, "How long, Master Yehudi, have you been playing the piano?"

The question was like touching off a petard. The cab seemed filled with fire, wreckage, and the smell of cordite. My companions bent toward me as if to pitch me into the street. "Piano player! Piano player!" screamed Master Yehudi. "I'm not a piano player! I'm a violinist!"

"Oh, my God!" the manager cried, reaching under his hat and pulling at his hair. "Oh, my God! Why do newspapers send out ignoramuses to talk to genius? Why, why, why?"

It was difficult; indeed, it proved impossible to reconstruct our relations or for me to achieve any rapport with the manager and his charge. I had become an unspeakable pariah. I was not accepted in the Menuhin suite.

Back in the office, I sheepishly consulted the files and discovered that Yehudi had appeared as a soloist with the San Francisco orchestra at the age of seven; a year later he had given a recital on the stage of the Metropolitan Opera House.

So far as questions and answers went, my story of meeting with the Boy Wonder was a failure, but I did attempt to glorify the youth and prove to the manager that I wasn't quite the uncultured oaf he thought me to be.

Two years later, then out of velveteen knee pants, Yehudi Menuhin was again back in town for a concert at the Eastman Theater and I was sent to the Sagamore to talk with him. I had hoped that my gaffe at the time of our first meeting had been forgotten, but the former Boy Wonder had elephantine recall. I no sooner crossed the threshold of the suite than he leaped up from a settee, pointed an accusing finger at me, and cried out fiercely, "Here's that awful man again who called me a piano player!"

Our talk was brief and not very amiable, and I was dismissed rather curtly from the suite. And although I strove to say nice things about Yehudi, and did, in fact, say several nice things, my effort won no encomium. One can't be cavalier about genius, and it is best, I discovered, to be well prepared before encountering it.

* * * * * * * * * *

If my best efforts failed to please, or even placate Yehudi Menuhin, a performer of superlative talent, an interview

I had with Peaches Browning, a performer of no talent whatever who headlined a vaudeville bill at Loew's large new Rochester theater (and pretty well filled it at every performance), similarly won me no kudos. Peaches did write, but her missive was not one to drop into the hat box in which I lovingly preserved the occasional fan letter that came to hand.

"You cheap stiff," she scrawled fumingly on a postcard. "You small time scum."

She was a creature of what Frederick Lewis Allen, in *Only Yesterday,* which chronicled the years of craziness immediately preceding the market crash, defined as a "carnival of degradation." It had sunk the American intelligence to a very low ebb and gave support to H. L. Mencken's conclusion that no one ever went broke underestimating it. "Surely a change must come," Mr. Allen wrote; and it did, suddenly, when a modest and unheralded young man soloed what appeared to many little more than a gadget-equipped orange crate from New York to Paris, and a high white flame of pride rose over the land: Charles Lindbergh became the idol of his countrymen.

My visit with Peaches was made before the American spirit was purged and exalted by the Lindbergh flight, and George S. Brooks, my close friend from the *Herald* days, went with me to Loew's Theater. Then a New York City resident, a highly successful writer of short stories with a play soon to open on Broadway, Brooks was back in town for a short visit. He knew a good deal about Peaches and her spouse, whose marital shenanigans had made a tabloid idyll for weeks, and he was curious to meet her.

A stoutish girl with a legitimate peaches and cream complexion, a large red slash of a mouth, come-hither eyes, and a seductive swagger, Frances Heenan, at the age of fifteen, had married Edward Browning, a rich man "old enough by a considerable margin, to be her father," as the *New York Times* explained in a column-long obituary at the time of Peaches' death, thirty-one years after her teen-age marriage.

Browning, known to tabloid readers as Daddy, had always had a feeling for young girls, and the "power of the devil," in Saint Jerome's phrase, seemed "in his loins." In the beginning, his romance with Frances Heenan had a Cinderella character. Nothing was too good for the child bride. She was granted *carte blanche* in the matter of charge accounts and driven about in a peacock blue limousine by a chauffeur. All was sweetness and light until Daddy began to devise stunts for his darling.

Peaches had something of the physical aspect of the young women who pose in the raw for the centerfold of the nudie magazines, and whose swells and shallows, whose bovine placidity, and langorous attitudes convey a vague sense of contented cows. And if Daddy did not want Peaches stark naked on a catamaran or chased unclad along a beach by a dog, as John Derek offered poses of his wife, Bo, for *Playboy* voyeurs, he urged her to strip and parade before him; and a composograph purporting to depict one of these performances was displayed on the cover of the *New York Evening Graphic*. The composograph was captioned with Daddy's exhortation to his bride when she appeared to renege, "Woof! Woof! Don't be a goof!" It was a catchy one-liner and soon in the idiom.

The Brownings' conjugal career, begun in April 1926 when they were married before a justice of the peace, ended in less than six months, but the end was merely the beginning of the tabloids' field day. In the separation proceedings that followed the domestic break up, the bedroom goings-on of the pair were so extravagantly exploited by the *Graphic,* an enterprise of Bernarr Macfadden, the physical culturist, that the *Daily News,* hardly a Mrs. Grundy-sort-of-journal, protested that if this sort of salaciousness did not cease the public would be "drenched in obscenity."

Long before Peaches was divorced from Browning (she was subsequently divorced from three other husbands), theatrical agents were chivying at her heels, wanting her as a feature attraction in vaudeville. When she presently signed at what was announced a whopping figure and opened in a Washington, D. C. theater, they had to dust off the Standing Room Only sign and erect it in the foyer.

In Rochester, a more conservative city, crowds did not stampede into Loew's, but the house did a sound business during the six days of Peaches' appearance. George Brooks and I, visiting the star on the day of her Rochester opening, were admitted through the stage door. The vaudeville show had begun, but Peaches would not appear until later in the bill, the honored spot. As we waited backstage, a shadow flitted over the ceiling and Brooks asked, "What in the world makes that shadow?"

A woman stood near. "That's the acrobat swinging on a trapeze in the second act," she explained.

A man of charm and gracious manners, Brooks could be at times a cantankerous cuss, and at such times incorrigibly outspoken. And he had very determined prejudices. He had a great love for the theater, and I often thought he looked upon it as a house of worship. He was insatiably curious about all sorts of phenomena. He had read avidly the tabloid accounts of Peaches and Browning, but at the same time he was outraged to think that a girl who had no more theatrical talent than a frog has hair should be paid a good deal more money and be billed high above the true professionals who composed the other acts of the vaudeville show.

Brooks turned to the woman who volunteered the information about the shadow and recognized her at once.

"Oh," he snarled, and he bared his teeth like a wolf, "so that's it, eh?"

"I'm only telling you what's a fact," Mrs. Catherine Heenan said loftily. "I'm only traveling with my daughter, the star of the show. I, myself—I'm *not* a member of the profession."

"That a fact?" Brooks said quizzically. "Why, I thought you belonged to the oldest profession there was."

The remark was hardly one to put my meeting with Mrs. Heenan's daughter on good footing, but fortunately the older woman did not enter the dressing room while Brooks and I were visiting Peaches. An amply constructed girl who was striving, not without some success, to live up to her tabloid build-up of sexuality, she was a flaming figure in a skin-tight red dress who babbled effusively about her "career."

"I love golf, and pictures, and sculpture—statues, I mean," she told me. "You know, all that class stuff. I want to do something real grand in the theater. Play a great part."

"Like Cleopatra, in *Antony and Cleopatra?*" Brooks interposed.

"Oh, no, not that. Wasn't Cleopatra a prostitute? I don't want to get that kind of a role."

She said she had taken up not only golf, but tennis, and handed me a photograph, for publication—she said—showing her rushing toward the net on pumps with heels as high as stilts, a racket, which she grasped half way up the shaft, raised for an overhead smash.

Brooks and I observed her "performance" from the wings, and I was constrained to write that "the girl couldn't sing, dance, act—and she made no attempt to whistle." It was probably that and some other gratuitously unkind things I said, together with Brooks' remark to Mrs. Heenan, that provoked Peaches' vituperative postcard.

Peaches Browning was not the only non-talent to be elevated to headline position in vaudeville during the "carnival of moral degradation." In their determination to give the public what they believed the public wanted, promoters filled the Academy Theater in New York by displaying on its stage Kiki Roberts, the red-headed moll of the slain "Legs" Diamond; a rival syndicate booked the mobster's widow for a vaudeville tour at $1,500 a week.

Neither of these attractions graced our fair city, but I did briefly encounter the "Shooting Stars," in the less prestigious medium of burlesque. The two girls were a week at the Corinthian Theater.

I have forgotten their names. One of the pair had been the inamorata of an elderly millionaire named Stokes, who lived in the Hotel Ansonia in New York. At the time his infatuation was at perihelion, Mr. Stokes wrote a number of impassioned letters to his youthful sweetheart, which, when his ardor cooled, he very much wanted to recover. He tried first to purchase the *billets-doux;* the price wasn't right. He then attempted to wrest them from their possessor by the use of force.

The struggle took place in the presence of a girl friend of Mr. Stokes' former candy-lamb, and the two young women, joined in Amazonian sisterhood, defended the cherished letters on the barricades. The siege ended when the recipient of the correspondence peppered the elderly gentleman around the feet and ankles with a small-calibered gun. There was an arrest but the girls were quickly free, and almost as quickly on the stage of Hammerstein's Roof, billed as "The Shooting Stars." Alan Dale, the Hearst drama critic, reviewed their premiere. He wrote the next day:

" 'The Shooting Stars,' who shot a millionaire, last night opened a week's engagement on Hammerstein's Roof. If they want to last another week, they better shoot another millionaire."

The talent of the pair was more scant even than Peaches', and neither had the latter's blonde full-bodied carnality; together they had had nothing remotely comparable to the reams of copy and the expansive gallery of photographs that Macfadden's Evening *Graphic* had bestowed upon Daddy's erstwhile pet. They had two or three songs and no voice to render them. I recall one, "Way up the River We will Row, Row, Row," which seemed to have no relevance whatever to their careers. They spoke of the little gun that had been fired at Mr. Stokes' nether extremities, remarked the infidelity of aging millionaires, did a quick skirt dance, and bowed off.

"The Shooting Stars" were accompanied to Rochester with a rumor that both had fallen in love with the "straight" man of the burlesque troupe and fallen out as a consequence. The story was that they had had a girl fight, pulling hair, scratching, calling names, perhaps kicking and biting. Word of this had reached a New York theatrical weekly, which wired a request that I question the ladies about the rhubarb, and I visited them backstage at the Corinthian. The actual gun wielder reluctantly admitted that there had been a row, but averred that the trouble was now over and their relations were again benign. When I attempted to press her for details, she became fiercely indignant. "Well," she asked, a hand pressed against a projecting hip, her eyes an angry glare, "do you think we're going to talk about a thing like that, for God's sake? We care something about our reputation."

I sent what little I learned to the theatrical weekly, which made a small squib about a sequel to an *affaire d'amour*. But by then "The Shooting Stars" had pretty well run out their string, and like so many similar phenomena of the epoch, soon disappeared from public view.

CHAPTER THIRTY

Al Moss and Henry James were both writing men, but in all other respects save one, they were vastly disparate—the difference between them as great as the distance between Al's spare, barracks-like walk-up flat in Rochester, New York, and a pagoda in Hong Kong. Their single other likeness was the friendship they enjoyed with Sir Hugh Walpole, the prolific and immensely successful English novelist, and the deep affection Walpole felt for both. He invariably addressed James as "My dearest Master;" he spoke of Al Moss as "My dearest friend in America."

Henry James, of course, needs no introduction. Al Moss was a newspaper reporter who had entered the profession in a time before newspapers started sending out scouts to recruit Nieman scholars.

A printer's devil in the composing room of the *Democrat and Chronicle,* Moss entertained the notion that romance and adventure spangled the career of a newspaper reporter. He itched to renounce his respectable union wage for the skimpy un-unionized pay of a reportorial worker, and he pleaded with the city editor for a chance. Given one, he in time proved his worth and was made a member of the city staff. That was before World War I when he served in the army. Upon his discharge, he did not reunite with the paper that had given him his start but went over to Rochester's leading afternoon journal, the *Times-Union,* as a police reporter.

The assignment fit him like a pinched-back coat on a

boulevard dandy. He knew police procedure as well as the police chief himself. The cops on the beat were both his professional associates and his personal friends. He had fathomless news sources. It was said that he could come away from the communion rail of a cathedral with a juicy police story.

Moss was an oddly visaged man. His physiognomy had all the facets of caricature. As pliable as modeling clay, his features responded readily and extravagantly to such emotions as disapproval, annoyance, impatience, and contempt. He seemed to have no neck, which gave him a frog-like appearance and defied any attempt at elegance in neckwear.

"Al assumed a gruff, even fierce demeanor to conceal a very soft-hearted, sympathetic nature, and he could change instantly to delight in appreciation of a good story or a sharp remark," said John W. Brown, one of his *Times-Union* colleagues.

"But his sense of humor sometimes took a morbid turn. On a dark, cold, rainy day he'd say, 'This is no day to go up in the attic. You might find an old piece of rope lying around.' He was not in militant opposition to a growing tendency to introduce women into newspaper city rooms, but he took a rather jaundiced view of the practice. To Al, all girl reporters were 'Little Bo-Peeps.' "

He was a very good reporter, if hardly an Addisonian prose stylist. But in the days before World War I and in the years that immediately followed the war, the main content of newspapers was news, not the magazine pieces that today, with television stealing the headlines, consume great sections of newsprint. And Moss put a lot of news on the copy desk, at times to the distraction of copy readers sensitive to proper English usage.

He, like the rest of us in the newspaper business in that era, was not opulently compensated for his efforts. Today the practice of moonlighting is rigidly forbidden by the rich Gannett newspapers in Rochester, but there was a time when a fellow who wanted to work for a newspaper and live decently needed something going for him on the side. There were numerous openings. A political writer would plug, for pay, an aspiring politician. A drama critic would act as press agent for a theater. Hotels and amusement parks wanting mention in the press would hire a reporter to make sure that they got it. Before the market crash when everything was boom-boom-booming, a shrewd and enterprising member of the *Democrat and Chronicle* city staff, who did what was known as the business and financial beat, did so well in the promotion of one of the city's banks that the bank granted him close to a six-figure loan.

Al Moss once attended an execution in the death chamber at Sing Sing, and he thought he might eke out his newspaper wage by lecturing on capital punishment, pro or con, as he anticipated public sentiment on the issue. He hesitated, vaguely mistrustful of his ability to speak in public. Glib talker though he was in ordinary conversation, he habitually talked through his teeth, since a cigar, which seemed an indigenous appendage to his malleable features, was invariably clamped in the corner of his mouth, and he wondered if he could talk in public without it. While he was still contemplating the matter, he discovered a teen-aged Indian boy who was curing illnesses by the laying on of hands and the administration of an herb medicine he had concocted on some Indian reservation.

The Indian boy was doing fairly well in the boondocks, but Al, a congenital city dweller, soon removed him from crossroad meetings and hamlet gatherings and boldly presented him in a Rochester hall, where he was an instant hit.

Probably the Indian boy's therapeutic boondoggling was as flagrant a quackery as Aimee Semple McPherson's faith healing, but some of us were more amused than outraged, and I know I wrote a long piece about the youthful healer, largely at Moss's persuasion. The manager and the youth made wide claims for the latter's talents. The herb medicine, both asserted, could cure rickets, liver complaint, relieve arthritic pains and the distress of stomach ulcers, grow hair on a bald-headed man, and straighten bowlegs; by laying on hands, the kid could dissipate melancholy and neurasthenic despair.

It was a bonanza while it lasted, but the howls of medical men and the anguished protests of their societies prodded the police, who reluctantly whispered to Moss that he would have to get a new racket; and the Indian boy descended from the rostrum and disappeared under the waters of Lethe.

His ambition baited by his first success as an entrepreneur, Moss looked about for another attraction; he found one in James J. Corbett, one-time heavyweight champion of the world. Possibly to relieve the stigma of Corbett being a professional bruiser, the promoter had him talk at a Sunday night service in a Universalist church the night before he was to lecture in a downtown hall. At that juncture, Al learned what farm boys know from the beginning: if you want to keep your cabbage, don't put it in front of a rabbit.

Sunday, the church pews were filled; Monday, the hall in which Corbett spoke for profit was virtually empty.

But Moss was learning the tricks of the trade of peddling platform performers. He made a contract with the Lee Keedick lecture bureau in New York and brought in, besides several lesser speakers, the controversial Margaret Sanger, well-known birth control advocate; Billy Mitchell, former air force commander, who was court-martialed and suspended from the service after he had revealed things about the service that in time proved eminently true; and Arthur Conan Doyle, whose audience, on the *qui vive* in anticipation of Sherlock Holmes thrillers, was disappointedly subjected to a long discourse on spiritualism.

Moss had booked these attractions only for their one-night stand in Rochester, and their promotion was subordinate to his regular job on the newspaper. Now he wondered why, with his experience, he shouldn't quit scouring the police beat for the *Times-Union* and make the lecture circuit a career. He spoke to the Keedick people about this; they agreed to make him a full-time representative and entrusted him, after he quit the newspaper, with the American tour of Hugh Walpole.

Walpole had lectured in this country before, and his popularity as a platform speaker was said to be greater than that of any other English novelist since Charles Dickens' American readings of the previous century. He and Al Moss, precisely opposite in every possible way, achieved, oddly, an almost perfect rapport at their first meeting.

A bachelor, an aesthete to his finger tips who felt that nothing "seemed to matter in comparison to 'Art,' " Walpole was an avid bibliophile and a notable collector of paintings.

He made a fortune through his novels, increased it with fees from his lectures and high pay as a Hollywood screen writer. He was a compulsive purchaser of paintings. He owned works of Renoir, Gaugin, Manet, Tintoretto, Cezanne, Constable, Boudin, Turner, and many others, which went, at his death, to the Tate Gallery in London.

Walpole's luggage on tour was rather unwieldy. He carried with him a collection of favorite books, pictures, etchings, statuettes and other bibelots, and the instant he arrived in a new hotel he and Moss were busy removing any decorations the room contained and replacing them with the writer-lecturer's array of ornaments. This was an unvaried procedure, even though the room was to be occupied a single night. Walpole protested that he could not relax or sleep in a chamber that was not made intimate and liveable with a display of his own books and virtu.

The Walpole-Moss tour extensively covered the Middle West, and Rochester was one of the last cities on the itinerary. Moss had asked me to interview his charge, and I called at the Sagamore Hotel, where both men were engaged in the business of interior decorating. As I entered the room, Moss attached to the wall a small Raoul Dufy engraving, and Walpole, before he responded to Moss' introduction, stood a moment in critical observation of a Max Beerbohm poster he had just hung.

"Hugh's staying here only one night," Al said proudly. "Tomorrow he's coming over to my place for a couple of days."

I had been in Al's "place" and I wondered if the novelist would consider it the prerogative of a house guest to attempt to relieve its grim austerity by the distribution of art objects that represented his own rather precious taste. Moss' independent notion of "Art" was a bathing girl on a calendar advertising a garage.

Walpole was an eager, bubbly man with an astonishing flow of talk. He had traveled extensively and had had wide experiences. He had been in and out of Russia several times during World War I, and his description of these visits was vivid. He knew many persons of front-page fame in politics, in the military, and in other fields. He was an intimate of such celebrated English men of letters as Shaw, Kipling, Arnold Bennett, Galsworthy, and H. G. Wells, and he had lively anecdotes about some of them. I was particularly curious about Wells, whose *Outline of History* was enjoying a vogue similar to the mah-jongg craze or the devotion to Émile Coué's therapeutic litany, "Day by day in every way I am getting better and better."

When I spoke about the popularity of Wells' book, Walpole said, "The Middle West is seething with Wells and his *History*. Thousands and thousands of copies are being sold. One is considered rather beyond the pale if one hasn't read it—or professed to have read it. There are, of course, quite a formidable number of pages. I sometimes wondered, when some starry-eyed young thing would rush at me with a gushing petition, 'Oh, do tell us about Mr. Wells and his divine *History*,' if the starry-eyed young thing had actually stayed the course or given up, in the discussion of Early Latium or the career of Alexander the Great."

He paused reflectively. "It's curious about you Americans' enthusiasms. They gush up volcanically, and as quickly sputter out. Like guttering candles. I am sure that many who are avidly devoted to Wells' *History* have never heard of Herodotus and have never read a line of Gibbon. In some instances, I don't believe they even know about such American historians as Fiske and Parkman. But H. G. is immensely in fashion today. His popularity rivals that of your frozen confection, Eskimo Pie."

Henry James had been dead several years before Walpole's visit to Rochester under Moss' sponsorship, but it was James about whom he mostly wanted to talk. He spoke worshipfully of the great novelist, whom he referred to as "Master." Moss, who remained in the room during the interview, was patently bored with the subject.

Moss' career as a full-time lecture agent was short-lived. It continued only during his tour with Walpole, and at the close of that pilgrimage he returned to his native métier, the police beat for the *Times-Union*. One night, several years after Walpole's death, I chanced to meet Al in a Rochester bar. He was in a reminiscent mood. He recalled interesting episodes of his association with the novelist and remarked, with some pride, that the time Walpole was dubbed knight, *Sir* Hugh had informed him of the honor by cable.

"Hugh was really a great fellow," Al said. "Y'know, one of his ancestors was a big shot years and years ago. Famous. The Earl of Oxford. But it wasn't that he boasted about. His big thing was being palsie-walsie with Henry James—not *Harry* James, for God's sake, who married Betty Grable. *Henry!*"

"I know," I said. "He talked to me a good deal about him."

Al nodded. "That's right, I remember. He'd go on and on about him. He was always trying to get me to read his books. I tried one, *The Golden Bowl.* Jesus, the sentences the man wrote. They were like a tunnel without a light in it, you could never find your way out. What the guy needed—what Henry James needed like crazy, was a damn good copy reader."

Walpole's Rochester visit, with Moss as his cicerone, was marked by one amusing incident. The novelist had been invited to one of George Eastman's Sunday musicales, and he had accepted the invitation since he was spending the weekend at Moss' walk-up flat. Occasionally at these affairs, which brought out a good slice of the city's *haut monde,* the Kodak head seemed to take a sort of dead-panned satisfaction in springing on the assembled company some person of national or international prominence, and this Sunday Walpole was to be the pet seal. Al drove him over to the imposing Eastman ménage on East Avenue in his shabby little Chevvy and let him off at the front door. Walpole started up the steps, turned, and saw Moss still behind the wheel of the car.

"Come on, Al" he called impatiently.

Moss shook his head. "Why, I'm not invited," he said. "They just want you."

"Well, to hell with that," Walpole exclaimed indignantly, "The man means nothing to me!" and he started to climb into the Chevvy.

Moss was at pains to persuade him that even if he didn't care a hang about the musicale or the host who was giving it, it was politic in Rochester not to snub an invitation from the city's leading citizen, and Walpole rather disgruntedly entered the house. In the course of the evening he was called upon to say a few words. "I am very glad to be in Rochester for a few days," he said at the beginning. "For this is the home of my dearest friend in America, Al Moss."

I wrote a glowing piece about Walpole and had a note from him saying that mine was the best interview printed since he had been in America. In those days, I had not yet come to realize that sniffing flattery could become as habit forming, if perhaps not as pernicious, as smoking hashish. I accepted all tributes whole hog, dropped the note tenderly into the hat box in which I preserved written encomiums, and only later realized that as Al Moss had persuaded Hugh Walpole that it was good policy not to run out on Mr. Eastman, he had also persuaded him that it was good policy to butter up the press.

CHAPTER THIRTY-ONE

Tallulah came to town in 1937; as did Winston Churchill, who knew and admired her. He came four or five years earlier. I spent an hour with Sir Winston in the Sagamore Hotel; a Sunday afternoon with Miss Bankhead in her suite in the same hostelry. The experiences were at variance.

I had seen Miss Bankhead in several plays and was particularly taken with her in *Reflected Glory,* the story of an actress torn between desire for a husband and family and the urges of a career. The critics found it tacky and pommeled it; but all had glowing things to say about the person and performance of the star. She was at that moment, it seemed to me, the most glamorous lady of the stage, and upon my return home (I had seen the piece in New York) I wrote a rave notice about Tallulah, which apparently, was picked up by the actress' clipping service.

Reflected Glory had only a brief run, and rumor was about after it closed that Miss Bankhead was intending to experiment with both matrimony and Shakespeare. The lucky man in the first venture turned out to be John Emery, a slim, handsome fellow, a sort of road company John Barrymore; in the second, Tallulah was cast as the snake-bitten empress of the Nile in the great bard's *Antony and Cleopatra*.

One day there came to the glorified broom closet that passed as my office in the *Democrat and Chronicle* building, a ponderous, slow-moving man with a curved handled cane hooked over his arm, an overcoat with an astrakhan collar, a wide expanse of cravat purpled in its center by a huge amethyst, a homburg, and a British accent thick as a London fog.

He bowed, removed his homburg, and laid his walking stick across the desk. He was a man of elaborate courtesy.

"I understand," said he, "that you are a warm admirer of that great lady, Miss Tallulah Bankhead."

I conceded my admiration.

"I am the agent," he explained, "in advance of *Antony and Cleopatra,* in which, of course, Miss Bankhead will play the second figure in the title. The drama will open a week from Monday. I have come, because of the gracious things you wrote about her, to invite you to spend Sunday afternoon with Miss Bankhead. The Sunday afternoon before the opening. You will find her charming, wonderfully zestful, fascinating, unpredictable"—he hesitated and gave me a small smile and a nod—"and, perhaps, slightly drunk."

I accepted the invitation. I was eager for the rendezvous. I had never seen Tallulah Bankhead except on the stage, but legend was that her antics away from it were often as entertaining as her footlight performances. My visitor gave support to the legend.

In gentle voice, his diction precise, he recounted some of her whimsies.

"She is a lady of great *joie de vivre,*" the agent explained, "and because she is congenitally uninhibited, if taken with the fancy, she might do a flip on your Main Street at high noon, join a firemen's parade, spit in the eye of an ogling and lecherous old gentleman in the first row, or—if you'll pardon the reference—pee in the jardiniere in the hotel lobby that holds the rubber plant."

Timidly I suggested, "And she takes off her clothes, readily, any time, any place."

"Yes, yes," he agreed soberly. "It is one of her predilections. A creature of impulse—but a lovely, lovely person. You'll adore her."

At that period of her career Miss Bankhead resided, when in New York, at the Élysée, 60 East 54th Street, the street floor location of the immensely popular Monkey Bar, presided over by a singing-pianist, Johnnie Payne, who flounced back and forth in a rocking chair as he made mad flourishes over the keys of the instrument. A glass of liquor always rested above the keyboard, from which, during brief musical lapses, he drank copiously. He was a Bankhead devotee. He improvised, and most of his improvisations made reference to the glamorous lady of the Élysée, who, returning to the hotel late at night, often stopped at the Monkey Bar to join Payne in song. The anticipation of these impromptus brought crowds thronging to the café, and I myself had gone there two or three times in the hope of witnessing one of these informal performances, but Miss Bankhead never appeared. Payne, however, was a show in himself. One of his songs closed with the line, "My canary has rings under his eyes—Tallulah's back in town!" He ended this, as he did every number, by swallowing the contents of the glass and flinging the glass over the piano, where it crashed among the shards of numerous other similarly discarded tumblers.

Following the English advance agent's instructions, I called at the Bankhead suite at three o'clock Sunday afternoon. The door was flung open by a vision in an elaborate costume of purple and gold, a couturier's oddity which displayed, below a skirt glittering with sequins, white pantalets with ruffles. There were other baroque embellishments. The vision had a playscript in hand.

"Come in, dahling," she welcomed in a throaty, sort of whiskey voice. She closed the door, reached for a tumbler on a nearby stand, touched it to her lips, and declaimed with a wide histrionic gesture:

"O happy horse, to bear the weight of Antony!
"Do bravely, horse! for wot'st though whom thou movest?
"The demi-Atlas of this earth, the arm
"And bourgnonet of men. . . ."

She broke off. "That's one hell of a line, don't you think? . . . Oh, dahling! Help yourself," and she indicated bottles and glasses on the stand.

I was surprised at her tininess. I was fairly nimble in those days, and I had the notion that if she stooped only slightly I could leap over her head. She seemed scarcely five feet, and although she had a little more girth than when I had seen her in *Reflected Glory,* her miniscule figure was still pridefully proportioned, and I half expected that at any moment it would be totally revealed. It wasn't.

She talked nineteen to the dozen, scarcely stopping to replenish a glass. It wasn't an interview, it was a monologue. I did inject a question now and then, but it was usually brushed aside, and she continued in the flow of her own rhetoric. She was an ardent fan of the New York Giants, and Mel Ott, the great outfielder, then well into his glittering 22-year career, was her particular idol. He had joined the Giants as a teenager fresh up from the canebrake country, identified then because of his youth, as "Master Melvin," and Miss Bankhead adoringly referred to him by that pseudonym. I had a feeling that it was he, rather than Antony, whom she considered *"The demi-Atlas of this earth, the arm/And bourgnonet of men."*

I remained more than two hours in the suite, and my hostess, tippling intermittently, became, as the press agent had reservedly predicted, slightly drunk.

She was ceaselessly in movement, intensely vivacious, and never at loss for a word. She launched off on a discussion of a recently thwarted design, which she said she had shared with every other prominent young—or not so young—actress in the land, to be "li'l ole honeychile," and play Scarlett O'Hara in *Gone With the Wind.*

"They told me I was too old," she shouted in vehement scoff. "Too old! Goddamnit, look at me, dahling. I'm still virtually an ingénue, virginal—almost!"

She wiggled violently in her baroque costume and I was half fearful, half hopeful that she would wiggle clean out of it, and for an instant I think that was her intent. She was taken by a new mood. She struck a pose and read another of Cleopatra's lines, *"Give me my robe,"* her throaty voice petitioned loud enough to penetrate the walls of the suite, *"put on my crown; I have/Immortal longings in me: now no more/The juice of Egypt's grape shall moist this lip. . ."* she stopped and moved to the stand and raised a glass, "Egypt's grape! Horseshit, dahling! Horseshit! It's nothing like Haig and Haig pinch bottle. But drink up, join me in another tumbler. Don't let me split a quart amongst one."

I am a modest drinker; two is usually my limit. Urged on by a lady who "deared and dahlinged" me, who never asked my name and hadn't the least interest in knowing it, I slightly over-matched myself; I knew then what Johnnie Payne meant when he attributed the rings under his canary's eyes to Tallulah's return to town.

Now and then she did other snatches from the role she was to play the next night before a capacity audience, and these bits, together with other extempore divertissements, were much more entertaining than the Cleopatra she played opposite the Antony of Conway Tearle, a rather long-toothed mime from Hollywood. I saw Tearle as Antony on the stage, but remembered him more vividly from discovering him one afternoon during the show's Rochester run sitting in a high-legged wall chair in the Hotel Seneca's billiard room, dramatically gotten-up in an Inverness cape, a flowing black silk cravat a foot wide, a poet's hat with a huge limp brim, and shoes with patent leather lasts and pearl-gray cloth uppers, secured, not by laces, but by large brown buttons. The shoes fascinated me. At that ingenuous stage of my life I aspired to fame, and I resolved, if it were ever achieved, that my arrival would be signaled by a pair of shoes similar to Tearle's. Octavius Caesar was played by John Emery, the new *Mister* Tallulah Bankhead, with an ineptitude that complemented the renderings of the other members of the cast. And although on opening night Tallulah won salvos of applause on her first and closing appearances, she was miles out of her element attempting Shakespeare. The whole thing was a woefully misbegotten enterprise, and perhaps made excusable the dredging up by a local critic of the ancient gag about the audience' enjoyment of the scenery being marred by the actors getting in front of it.

In her free association monologue, Miss Bankhead spoke of Philip Barry, who, a few years before, had written *Holiday* purposely for Miss Hope Williams, as, later, he wrote *The Philadelphia Story* for Katharine Hepburn. She admired Barry's style and scintillating drawing room wit and thought he might do a play for her. I attempted to impress her with the fact that Barry was a native Rochesterian, who had gone from a local high school to Yale; I boasted that he and I were friends, but the thematic tributary was engulfed and silenced in the swollen main stream of her talk.

She mentioned George Cukor, who had directed her in two Hollywood pictures and who had tested her for the Scarlett O'Hara role in *Gone With the Wind;* but she gave no heed to my interposition that I had known Cukor since the 1920s, when he managed a highly successful summer stock company in Rochester.

She talked about Herman Shulman, who, two years later, was to direct her in the Lillian Hellman drama, *The Little Foxes,* the greatest hit of her career. I knew Shulman slightly. He had been brought to dinner at our house in Scottsville by George Brooks, whom Shulman had engaged to do a rewrite. A man of brilliance and wit, the director was a bleeding heart for all minorities, the disadvantaged and the downtrodden, and was suspected of having Communistic leanings. After dinner Brooks, Shulman, my wife, and I went into Rochester to witness *Macbeth* with the enfeebled septuagenarian Robert Mantell in the title role. Shulman thought the drama farcical, which, because of the age and infirmity of the leading player it may have been; but it seemed to me that for one of his professed humanity, his ridicule of the ancient tragedian's performance and his bursts of laughter throughout were unkind almost to the point of cruelty. I didn't find Shulman much to my fancy.

With no prompting by me, Talullah diverted to sex. "I've tried it standing on my head," she avowed. "On a swinging trapeze. I've got lockjaw from it, and the bends. Dahling, you ever try it in a howdah on an elephant? It's sort of rippling. But good."

I blushed and looked at my watch. I had forgotten, beguiled, enchanted, completely under the spell of my hostess, that I had been instructed to send for a photographer. I telephoned the city desk. "Goddamnit, it's about time," the city editor snapped.

The photographer arrived in fifteen minutes. He was a small, shy young man. He had only recently been hired by the newspaper and he lacked entirely the aggressiveness and hubris of most newspaper cameramen. He was meek in the presence of this tornado of femininity. He adjusted his camera.

Miss Bankhead flung herself on a settee, kicked her heels over her head, and gave the cameraman a toothy grimace.

"Take it now, you little bastard," she urged. "I'm smiling!"

He did. We left together. In a long career as a newspaper reporter, I have interviewed innumerable ladies of the stage; but this, the afternoon with Tallulah Bankhead, was an experience beyond all others. It was unique.

* * * * * * * * * *

My remark at the beginning of this chapter that I had passed an hour in the Hotel Sagamore with Sir Winston (Churchill) was incorrect on one point. At the time of his Rochester visit, the former British secretary of war and air had not been knighted; that came twenty odd years later. Shorn, at the moment, of all official investiture, he was merely *Mister* Churchill, a private English citizen on a lecture tour. The subject of his talk was "Gold," which seemed hardly appropriate to the times; for this was the nadir of the Great Depression, with men selling apples on street corners, with soup kitchens established across the land, and gold, to vast millions of Americans, was no more than a mirage in the distant sky, the wistfully yearned-for grail at the tip of the rainbow.

Churchill's arrival excited no furor and his talk at the Eastman Theater the first night of his two-day visit was scantily attended. The morning following the lecture I was admitted to a suite in the Sagamore by a bulky-shouldered man with a huge unlighted cigar in his mouth, who was loosely encompassed by what looked like a moth-eaten dressing gown, and whose feet were fitted into scuffed carpet slippers.

His greeting was little more than a grunt, and he dropped into a chair, lighted the cigar, and lifted the top of a port bottle on a nearby table stand. He did not pour. He was about to do so when his instinctive courtesy restrained his hand. There was only one glass.

"Yes," he said, peering at me over spectacles that had slipped far down his nose and dangled precariously at its tip, "young man?"

I was not actually a young man, I had been a reporter for quite a number of years. I had met—in the touch-and-go encounters newspaper people have with celebrities—numerous men and women of national and international renown, and usually managed the interviews fairly well. Mr. Churchill was not cooperative. It was like pulling teeth to get a scrap of usable information.

He was not rude or discourteous, but he seemed to feel that there was no need of a reporter taking up his time with questions that were not very vital when he wanted to smoke his after-breakfast cigar in peace and when only one glass reposed next to the port bottle on the table stand. His answers to my inquiries were brief and, if the question was not to his fancy, monosyllabic or deliberately evasive. It was he, I quickly found, who controlled the colloquy, not I.

For several years in the middle of the nineteenth century, Leonard Jerome, the colorful, wealthy, sporting father of Churchill's glamorous mother, Jennie, lived in Rochester, and latter-day residents cherished the notion that Jennie was born in the fine Jerome house in what originally had been the city's most fashionable precinct. I mentioned this, hoping that it might incite a flow of talk. It didn't.

"My mother," Churchill said flatly, "was born in Brooklyn."

The halting dialogue came to a close and the story I got from it was hardly inspired. It was, indeed, rather dull. And since Churchill was not at the time a very hot news personality, my piece was not prominently displayed. I had been baffled in this vis-a-vis. But my frustration had not dulled my perceptions and I was deeply impressed by the quality of the man I had attempted to interview. And though I did not discover in the figure in the moth-eaten dressing gown and the scuffed carpet slippers the Promethean grandeur that the world in time would come to recognize, or see in the eyes that peered at me over the dangling spectacles the shine of prefigured destiny, Winston Churchill struck me as the most formidable person I had ever met.

He left town the night after his lecture. There were wealthy and socially prominent persons in Rochester who felt the depression, to be sure, but who were still solvent, who still pursued their habitual style of life. A group of these fortunate citizens arranged a dinner party for the former British cabinet member; it was gay, and Churchill, who seemed to feel that a depression was something that one would in time manage to muddle through, was a lively and very engaging guest. When the dinner was over, he was given to the charge of General (Colonel, at that time) Oscar N. Solbert and the socially prominent and wealthy Samuel E. Durand, who drove him several miles south of Rochester to a station on the main line of the Lehigh Valley Railroad, where he was to board an east-bound train.

It was a rollicking excursion, and as the party careered through rural reaches of western New York, the voice that would later enthrall and give hope to the entire free world rent the nocturnal stillness with a bit of doggerel Churchill had picked up in a recent visit to Jamaica, Durand and Solbert joining in the chorus.

"Mam-my don't want," he and his fellow choristers bellowed bibulously, "no rice, no peas, no coconut oil. All she wants is handy-brandy—all the time."

Less than a decade after Churchill's Rochester visit England was at war, and the reins of government, fallen from the unsure hands of Neville Chamberlain, were delivered into his. From then until the end of the greatest holocaust the world has ever known, the old-school-tie boy, the product of England's privileged and luxurious aristocracy, (who once arrived at the French Riviera villa of Maxine Elliott, the celebrated American beauty, with the boast, "Do you know, my dear, I managed all the way from London without my man,") when pressed into a sticky corner, with the odds dead against him, was as tough and doughty as a pug at a *Stag at Sharkey's.*

The old boy had it; he could take it and he could dish it out. England lived—raggedly, desperately, hand-to-mouth, in the days of her greatest anguish—but lived, by the faith he gave Her and by the example of his indomitable courage. At a moment when his native island was encompassed by disaster, with England's weakening ally, France, about to collapse, with the Nazi hordes raging through the Low Countries with the design of a cross-Channel invasion, he spoke unflinchingly to his people: "I have nothing to offer but blood, toil, tears and sweat."

And at the time of the debacle of Dunkirk when England stood alone against the might of the totalitarian states, "We shall defend our island, whatever the cost may be; we shall fight on the beaches, we shall fight on the landing grounds, we shall fight in the fields and in the streets, we shall fight in the hills; we shall never surrender. . . ."

And again, bidding his people to have hope, to hope and believe, to have strength, and again to hope, "Good night then, sleep to gather strength for the morning, for the morning will come. Brightly will it shine upon the brave and the true; kindly upon all who suffer for the cause; glorious upon the tombs of heroes—thus will shine the dawn."

As these and other image-fixing words came over the radio from Britain's Prime Minister during the most critical period of the war, I recalled my first impression of the chubby man in the shaggy dishabille who several years before had given me a difficult hour in the Sagamore Hotel. I had thought then that he was a man of very unusual quality. Now my first impression was fortified by the stirring testimony of his wartime leadership. Winston Churchill, it seemed to me, was a very great man, perhaps, at the moment, the greatest on our globe.

CHAPTER THIRTY-TWO

One afternoon late in the winter of 1932, Edmund Howard, assistant manager of Loew's Rochester Theater, took me backstage to meet the headline attraction. I had a brainstorm during the visit and wrote a piece for the paper in imitation of the language of *The Song of Songs.* My piece appeared under the title, "The Temptress and the Scribe (A Parable)." In the parable I denoted the theater as the Temple of Loew and told how Edmund Howard and I, penetrating the rear reaches of the Temple, ". . . after many windings . . . came at last to a small portal of the inner sanctum upon which Edmund rapped thrice, and from within came, like unto the ringing of a bell of pure gold, a voice saying, 'What message bringest thou me?' And Edmund made answer, 'No message, O Beautiful one, only a Scribe.'

"Thereupon the portal was thrown back, and lo, a vision of great comeliness, stood Jean, the daughter of Harlow. And Henry the Scribe, gazing upon her, quoth, "Tell me, O thou whom my soul loveth, where thou feedest, and if thou feedest upon the herbs and meats of The Sagamore, may I come and feed with thee?' And Jean, the daughter of Harlow, gazed upon Henry the Scribe, and made answer, 'Thy neck is like the tower of David, builded for an armoury, but thy raiment is slovenly; whence comest thou, and why?'

"And Henry the Scribe was sore distraught, a faintness and dizziness came to his temples, and he grasped at a small pillar for support, so surpassing was her comeliness. And he spake again, saying, 'Behold, thou art fair, my love; thou hast eyes like blue doves within thy locks; thy hair is like a flock of snow-white goats that appear from Mount Gilead; thy lips are like a thread of scarlet. Rise up, my love, my fair one, and come away, ere the thoughts of mine little children take hold of me and bring me back to reason and the path of righteousness.' "

I was in the presence of Jean Harlow no more than six or seven minutes, and I had scarcely any talk with her. She was a slim, pretty girl with a platinum hairdo so slick that it seemed as if the color of her hair had been applied by a brush. Fully bespangled, as ornamental as a wedding cake, she was all ready to go on stage when Howard and I were admitted to the dressing room. She was on a tour of the East, making personal appearances in various theaters to help promote *Red Headed Woman,* the picture which, with the previously produced *Hell's Angels,* had boosted her to stardom and established her as the new Hollywood sex symbol. She had not yet made *Dinner at Eight,* which would certify her talent as a comedienne. She was twenty-two years old, with one broken marriage behind her and two more to come, and she had only a handful of years left. Four, to be exact; she died at the age of twenty-six.

I made quite a thing of the "Parable." It occupied all of my column space. It was a novelty for the staid and sometimes stodgy *Democrat and Chronicle,* a rather daring innovation. It attracted considerable reader interest. On the day that it was printed a messenger brought me a large (about two foot square) portrait photograph of the subject of the column with the inscription, "To Henry Clune, with all my love. Jean Harlow." A note that accompanied the photograph was couched in similar heady language.

I saw Miss Harlow's stage appearance, which was little more than a walk-on, from the wings; I saw nothing more of her during her week's stay in Rochester. But a couple of weeks after she left town I had another note from her which exalted my "Parable" as the greatest thing that had ever been written about her, and I began to feel, my ego clean out of hand, that

I had achieved a classic. The note's opening salutation read, "My Dearest Henry." I answered warmly.

In time I had a response to my letter. I wrote again, another "My Dearest Henry" missive came back, and for the next couple of months Jean Harlow and I were in intermittent correspondence. I was beginning to think I must be a pretty hot number to have won the devotion of this scintillating new star when the illusion was suddenly shattered.

One night at a large party at which I was a guest, the assistant drama critic of the *Rochester Evening Journal* (a short-lived Hearst newspaper) in support of his bibulous boast that he and Jean Harlow were in loving correspondence, passed among his fellow guests a note from the actress, and I read, when the note was presently handed to me, a couple of endearing paragraphs under the salutation, "My Dearest David," David being the given name of the critic. I return the *billet-doux* without comment and left the party at once, chastened, deflated, feeling almost as if I had been cuckolded.

I was disgusted to think how naive I had been to allow myself to be taken in by this faithless and meretricious siren of the screen, but I was alert enough now to realize that I had been gulled by Miss Harlow with a deliberate design.

The country was still mired in the Depression, and the movie industry, like businesses of more essential character, was feeling the pinch. The amusement dollar was straitened. Movie theaters were often scantily populated. A rising young star needed all the help she could get from the press, and Miss Harlow apparently was determined to cultivate the newspapermen she met on tour and enlist them firmly in her cause by addressing each with a "My Dearest" letter similar to the one the Hearst critic had displayed at the party and the ones I cherished in secrecy.

I gave myself a period of grace so as not to write angrily, but I wrote Miss Harlow in time, and without mentioning the discovery I had made, suggested that our correspondence had been a lot of nonsense since I was sure she wouldn't know me from a bunch of beets, or, indeed, if she stumbled over me. Her response was instant and almost tearful in its protest. She sacredly avowed that she would know the author of the "Parable" in a crowd of thousands—how could she ever forget him? And if I ever got out to the Coast (and she hoped I might very soon) I was, please, please, to call her at once, and allow her to prove by her bounteous hospitality the sincerity of her endearments.

And it happened that that summer I did go to the Coast. The Olympic Games were being held in Los Angeles, and I was sent by the newspaper to cover the track and field events. I arrived in Los Angeles the Saturday before the games opened, and that night I took Ray Mandery, a former Rochesterian, and a young woman friend of his, to the Coconut Grove in the Ambassador Hotel.

Mandery was several years my junior. He had been a popular beau around Rochester, partly because he was a pleasant and attractive young man, and partly because he always had a Packard car at his disposal since his father had the Packard agency. It was believed that the elder Mandery had made a million dollars selling Packards, but he had died leaving a large family, the fortune somehow disappeared, and Ray, in Los Angeles, was employed as a sort of gentleman chauffeur for the movie actress, Clara Kimball Young.

In those days the Coconut Grove was very much the "in" place in Los Angeles, and this night, with the Olympic Games opening in two days, it was jam-packed, and prominent in an assemblage that included visitors from all over the world were numerous Hollywood personalities, who, as they danced by our table, were identified by my guests.

"There's Joan Crawford," one or the other might say, indicating some elaborately gotten-up young woman on the dance floor. Or Norma Shearer, or Myrna Loy, or Carole Lombard. I took their word for it. It seemed a veritable galaxy of stars. Once, when my companions rose to go out on the dance floor, I stood up in gentlemanly deference and pushed back my chair as I did so. It impinged upon a passerby "Oh, I am so sorry," I apologized, turning; and got an acrid rejoinder from a glamorous lady. "Well, I should think you would be."

"That's Constance Bennett," Mandery whispered back of his hand.

(A number of years later, Miss Bennett came to Rochester to play for a week with a summer stock company, and I told in my newspaper column of my encounter with her in the Coconut Grove. She invited me to call on her, and I did. "I just want you to know," she said, "that I'm not as nasty as you tried to make me sound.")

I had no talent as a dancer and that night in the Coconut Grove I encouraged my young friends to dance whenever they felt inclined to do so and not concern themselves about me. I was entirely content to sit alone. The music was by Phil Harris' great orchestra. I was fascinated by all that I saw, and my eyes constantly swiveled over what seemed to me a fantastic pageant. At one point when Ray and his girl were on the dance floor, I saw a vision all in white, white from her tiny slippers to the off-white of her platinum head, leave a table with a man in a dinner jacket, and start for the exit. "Well," I said to myself in triumph, "there's one *I* know." I leaped up and hurried into the hotel lobby. Jean Harlow and her companion, who seemed slightly less than her height, were stopped by an autograph seeker. I approached and fronted her.

"Hello Miss Harlow," I said.

Her smile was professionally cordial, she wanted to seem gracious to an admirer, but her eyes were a blank.

The lobby of this fashionable and sophisticated hotel was well peopled, and Miss Harlow was surrounded at once by a considerable covey of gawkers. Whether they were tourists or natives I had no way of knowing. But their wonder-stricken attitude at being in the near presence of this symbol of the supposedly glamorous world of Hollywood was similar to the bedazzlement the blonde charmer would affect if she appeared suddenly in the lobby of a hotel in such hinterland cities as Terre Haute, Indiana; Bradford, Pennsylvania; or Rochester, New York. Their mouths gaped open so wide in wonder that flies might have buzzed in and out without hitting a tooth.

"I told you," I pronounced bluntly, "that you wouldn't

know me from a bunch of beets—even if you stumbled over me."

Miss Harlow performed an elaborate exercise in histrionics. She made wide gestures with her hands, wrung them dramatically, ran one over her alabaster brow, her eyes closed as if in evocative supplication.

"I know! I know! I know!" she cried. "It's just slipped my mind."

But she didn't know from nothing.

"Tell me, please," she pleaded.

"Henry Clune," I said, and started to back away.

Then I had a bid at fame. The blonde sex symbol flung her arms around me and kissed me roundly, and I could almost hear the gawkers' gasps of marvel.

"Henry! Darling!" She broke from me and turned to her small companion. "Paul this is Henry Clune from Buffalo—I mean," catching herself, "Rochester, who wrote that fantastic Biblical story about me. The one I framed."

I shook hands with Paul Bern, Miss Harlow's second short-term husband who, rumor had it, beat her mercilessly on their wedding night in sadistic revenge for his impotence.

They were leaving the Coconut Grove for the Airport, an illegal gambling resort, and she pleaded that I go with them. I was tempted; it would have made a great story for the readers back home. But I didn't have much money, and I also had the obligation of my guests on the dance floor. I declined under what appeared to be Miss Harlow's frantic supplications.

"Well, you must come to lunch Monday," she insisted, and she scribbled an address and her unlisted telephone number on a slip of paper.

I explained that I had to be in the Olympic Stadium late Monday morning and lunch would be impossible.

"Breakfast then," she amended. "Phone me at nine o'clock, and I'll send my chauffeur for you. He's a Jap. After breakfast, he'll drive you to the stadium."

I had been naive about the letters. I wasn't going to fall again for these siren blandishments. "This is all unnecessary," I said. "You can't really mean it."

"Oh, darling, you know I do. Nine o'clock sharp, Monday morning."

I had another hug and we parted.

Ray Mandery protested that I had been crazy not to have gone to the Airport. He and his girl would have understood.

"It would have made a good story," I said. "But I'll see her Monday morning."

"I wonder," Ray said dubiously.

I called the number she had given me promptly at nine o'clock Monday morning. The voice that answered said, "I'm the butler."

"I was supposed to call Miss Harlow at nine o'clock," I explained.

"Miss Harlow's in bed."

I phoned again at 11 o'clock, just before I went to the stadium. The same voice answered, "Miss Harlow's down at the swimming pool."

"Tell her, please, that Henry Clune from Rochester, telephoned."

I gave him the name and the telephone number of the hotel in which I was registered. It was a hostelry in downtown Los Angeles where the rooms cost, as I recall, $2.50. It was not an impressive address.

I remained in Los Angeles until the Games were over. I never had a call from Miss Harlow.

At Christmas that year I had an elaborate card from her. "My dearest Henry," it read. "Why didn't you get hold of me when you were in Los Angeles last summer?"

The romance had petered out. I made no answer.

* * * * * * * * * * *

The Olympic Games in Los Angeles, the tenth revival of the ancient Greek festival, provided more agreeable entertainment than any of the Olympiads I have attended in later years. Tickets sold for a reasonable price and there seemed to be enough for all who desired them. Spectators were not subjected to the crowding and discomfort that was common when the Games became more universally popular; there was ample housing and no need for visitors to lodge forty or fifty miles from the stadium gates, a not unusual inconvenience in Mexico City, Munich, and Montreal.

Los Angeles in 1932 was a swiftly growing city, but it had not yet become the sprawling, unwieldly, smog-clouded metropolis of today. It was a friendly community which combined something of the character of an out-sized Midwestern town and a Riviera resort. Its people, many of them Midwestern transplants, were friendly and hospitable.

The Games were held under ideal conditions. The fabled California sun shone unstintedly, and the city and state had done themselves proud in providing the most modern accommodations for the various sports. The competition among the world class athletes was exciting, records fell with reckless abandon, and there was very little of the haggling and dissent that in other years had mocked the Olympic ideal of sportsmanship and international comity.

My prime interest was the center ring, the huge coliseum with capacity of more than 100,000, where the track and field events were held. My dispatches to the *Democrat and Chronicle* were devoted mostly to these contests. I had only a cursory interest in the swimming program, but I knew L. deB. Handley, coach of the women's team, and I visited him one morning in the swimming stadium.

Although the swimming competition would not begin for two or three days, the natatorium was an animated and colorful scene. Male swimmers were churning up and down the pool, and others, who had finished their workouts, were disposed in various attitudes around the pool, their muscular, scantily-clad bodies statue-like under the refulgent rays of the sun. There was horseplay and a multilingual exchange of lively banter among these eager, friendly, attractive Olympic aspirants. The stadium seemed pervaded with an admirable spirit of fellowship.

I had supposed that the Americans would dominate the swimming events and remarked this to Handley. He shook his head dubiously and pointed to a group of squat, bandy-legged young men of yellow complexion who were tossing beachballs about and bandying jocosities with flashing, white-toothed laughter. They seemed the personification of healthy, happy, high-spirited youth on holiday; but this impression was suddenly dispelled at the approach of a small, dark-visaged, authoritative man, who addressed them in the sharp, commanding tone of a Marine drill sergeant. The ball tossing ended, the laughter ceased. They were transformed on the instant into a disciplined company which formed around the small man, its members taut, soldierly, and rigidly attentive to his swift, harsh words.

"Those kids," Handley said, "will probably win every race on the program."

"The Japs?" I was astonished. "Why, when did they get so good?"

"They're very, very good," Handley attested soberly. "You watch when that little fellow, the head coach, puts them through their paces. I thought the shogunate, the military dynasty in Japan, ended in the last century. That coach and his charges may be a hold-over."

Handley had an appointment. He introduced me to Fred Cady, the Olympic diving coach, and left. The Japanese were entering the water, and Cady and I watched a grueling practice session under the direction of the small man, who, standing at one end of the pool, stopwatch in hand, shouted commands as each swimmer approached. We did not understand his words, but we inferred from their tone and his gestures that he was demanding greater speed. Faster! Faster! Faster! he seemed to shout. And if some mistake was made, some imperfection observed, the erring swimmer was called out of the water, roundly castigated, and sent back to correct his fault. Cady marveled at the thoroughness of the Japanese training.

"This isn't sport with these people," he said. "This is war. This dedication has a nationalistic purpose. The Japanese are determined to prove their superiority over the white race. Why, any one of these swimmers would willingly die to finish in first place, confident that in such a death he would gain immortal glory. They have exactly the same attitude as the Japanese soldiers. They're burning with racial pride. It's too bad what they'll do in the men's swimming. Just too damn bad!"

And Cady's and Handley's prognostications were stunningly validated once the swimming program was under way. There were six races on the card and the Japanese won five. I was in the press box the night a Japanese lost the 400 meter free style to Buster Crabbe, an American, by no more than a fingertip. Crabbe, the most surprised person in the stadium at what had happened, soared off on his fame, and in time became a movie Tarzan. The Jap dragged himself from the tank and spoke over the radio to Tokyo, not to apologize for his defeat, but to incriminate and self-accuse himself for the scandalous disgrace he had brought to his country. He was crushed; utterly abject. One wondered if on leaving the stadium he would hang himself or cut his throat with a scimitar. He seemed on the verge of hara-kiri.

That was in 1932, and few of us had any conception that a second World War was in the offing. But less than ten years later, by their strike at Pearl Harbor, "the confident and overlusting" Japanese appeared to have achieved the supremacy they so passionately desired in the swimming tank at Los Angeles. Exulting in the devastation they had wrought on that "date," as President Roosevelt defined it, "that will live in infamy," they had become masters of vast areas of sea and land. They were arrogant and flouting in their stunning successes, talking even of moving into the White House. Time went on, the tide of battle changed, and the Japanese began to lose the war. They were smashed on the atolls and islands they had ruthlessly expropriated; their ships were sunk, their aircraft shot out of the sky. They were losing, but there was no retreat; only greater savagery in resistance.

When we heard of the utter desperateness of their holding on, and how members of the Kamikaze Corps willingly offered themselves as human conveyances of high explosives and blew themselves to "glory" on the decks of Allied vessels, I thought back to the desperateness of the Jap boy who lost to Buster Crabbe, of the shogun commander who directed the swimmers' training, and of Fred Cady's remark, "This isn't sport with these people. This is war."

CHAPTER THIRTY-THREE

The girl swimmers and the other female athletes at Los Angeles were not quartered in the Olympic Village, but in the Chapman Park Hotel in a pleasant section of the city, and one night I dined there as the guest of Miss Charlotte Epstein, manager of the women's swimming team. Besides Miss Epstein, I knew Eleanor Holm, a backstroke swimmer from the New York Women's Swimming Association, who had been a guest at our house in Scottsville on a couple of occasions.

The backstroke is not a style of natation that ordinarily would beguile my fancy, but Eleanor Holm was no ordinary backstroke swimmer. She was a personage, the cynosure of the multi-national assemblage in Chapman Park whom the girl reporters wanted to interview and news cameramen pursued for cheesecake shots.

She was a small, dark-haired girl with slim graceful arms and legs, a broad laughing mouth, gleaming white teeth, sparkling eyes, pretty as a picture; and pert and cocky as she was pretty. There was no side to her; no mysteries or subtleties. She was as wide open as a Macy show window. The daughter of a Brooklyn fire captain, she was proud of her paternity. Married, in time, to a multi-millionaire showman, she might arrive by Rolls Royce at a Broadway opening, dripping sables, bedecked with diamonds brilliant as kleig lights, and shout across the crowded lobby, "Get a load of this, will you? The fireman's daughter!"

She was in her late teens at Los Angeles, and she was

as confident of winning the 100-meter backstroke as if she already stood on the victory podium, the gold medal dangling from her neck.

"I'll swim away and hide on the rest of 'em," she predicted, and on the day of the race she virtually did as she promised.

Once the games were under way, newsmen sought another figure at Chapman Park, Mildred (Babe) Didrikson, who had no pulchritudinous qualities but considerable talent at running the hurdles, throwing the javlin, high jumping, and putting the shot. The newspapers called her the "Texas Flash," and said that she was a whole track team in herself.

I met her the night of my visit to the hotel. She was a pinch-faced, thin-lipped kid with a gruff Texas drawl, lean and limber as a buggy whip. She was no person for feminine frills or fripperies. She wore shabby slacks and a sweater, no lip stick or rouge. Her hair was cut short. I think it was Paul Gallico, the sports writer, who dubbed her the "Muscle Moll," and remarked that he could imagine seeing the Babe in a chair next to his in a barbershop. She boasted that she had always played boys' games, never dolls or keeping house.

Women track athletes failed then as they fail now to excite my enthusiasm. Sixteen years after the Los Angeles games, I was asked by an English journalist in the press box at the London Olympics why it was that the United States produced so many male champions at track and field and so few good women performers. I gave him what I thought was a good answer and later repeated it in a piece I wrote for Arthur Daley, sports columnist for the *New York Times*.

In America, I said, our raciest women were found in such places as the Stork Club, not in shorts and spiked running pumps on a cinder track. I added a comment of Lawson Robertson, coach of several Olympic teams, that "The Olympic Games were devised as a world championship in athletics, not as a tournament in sex appeal."

There were other similar animadversions and what I wrote consumed all but half an inch of Mr. Daley's space. He himself explained that neither of us was a misogynist; that we both appreciated, respected, and delighted in women, but deplored their engagement in activities in which they were egregiously ill-suited.

As a former track and field writer, Daley wrote that he had often suffered "watching female footracers and hardware heavers burlesque a noble sport," and he wished they would abandon the practice.

He was more temperate than he had been in a previous column when he suggested that women track and field athletes be loaded into an open boat and pushed out to sea, a fate as harsh as H. L. Mencken's proposal that "all female athletes . . . be shipped to the white-slave carrels of the Argentine."

Arthur Daley won a Pulitzer Prize for sports reporting, a specialty he practiced for the *Times* for forty years. He died suddenly while still in the newspaper's service. I have often wondered how he would have reacted had he lived to see the *Times* name a woman sports editor. And I wonder how the lady editor would feel about Arthur's anti-feminism, at least as it concerned women in track and field.

Babe Didrikson won several medals at Los Angeles and after that began to capitalize on her fame. She was good at all games that were played with balls: golf, basketball, soccer, baseball. I once saw her doing fairly well in a Rochester pool hall against a local hustler. But golf, in the end, was her big thing. It became her, she was a good solid pro and she readily adapted to the country club mode. She went in for feminine refinements, wore handsomely cut sport clothes, a girdle, and slips with pink lacy shoulder straps that showed through her spotless white shirtwaists. She had her hair "done" and visited the manicurist.

The Babe, who had made an earlier visit to Rochester as a member of a woman's basketball team, came the last time to play an exhibition round over the course of the Oak Hill Country Club, later the scene of two National Opens and a PGA championship. She was accompanied by her husband, George Zaharias, a huge fat man, with two cauliflower ears, once known on the professional wrestling circuit as "The

Crying Greek from Cripple Creek." Chomping on cigars which he never lighted, Zaharias followed his wife around the course, proudly declaiming on her exploits.

Mrs. Zaharias was central in a foursome that included Charlie McKenna, long-time Oak Hill professional, and two young local pros. She was engaging, enormously good natured, and full of chatter.

"I'll hitch up my girdle and belt this one a country mile," she'd boast; and her tee shots often went 200 yards or more, straight as a rule. Her volubility continued even during the delicate play on the green where a cathedral hush is expected; but no one protested, and the crowd laughed at her quips.

She banteringly addressed McKenna, a granddaddy, as "Pops." Her lively talk threw the young players off their games. She bemused them and ruined their concentration. Old Charlie McKenna, paying no mind to her prattle, kept on sawing wood and his card, when the round was over, was the lowest of the four. A good-sized gallery followed the match, and all were pleased with Mrs. Zaharias' golf and her comic by-play.

The club planted a tree in her name in one of the numerous coppices that add variety and arboreal splendor to a course that is notable both for its playability and its beauty. Babe died at a too early age of cancer, but the tree still stands with her name on a plaque attached to its bole.

* * * * * * * * * *

Babe Didrikson's post-Olympic career was brief and only modestly successful; Eleanor Holm's, a sunburst of glamor, gold, and glory.

A year after her backstroke triumph in Los Angeles, Miss Holm married Arthur Jarrett, a handsome crooner and band leader, and went on tour with her husband. She sang with the band. I have known Eleanor for more than forty years and never heard her sing a note; but they paid her to sing, so she must have had talent, though I suspect that the appeal of her person was greater than the appeal of her voice.

Jarrett, his band, and Eleanor went to the West Coast, and there Mrs. Jarrett enjoyed a vogue. She was an Olympic champ, and a very pretty one to boot; a party girl, with a predilection for doing what came naturally. She was cultivated by the smart people of Hollywood and Beverly Hills. She swam in their pools, played with them, drank with them. Warner Brothers tested her for the screen, put her on the payroll at $500 a week, and sent her to Josephine Dillon, Clark Gable's first wife, for acting instructions. She had a new kind of appeal. Her healthy, outdoorish naturalness made the over-decorated run-of-the-mill Hollywood starlet look like a dime store bauble on a Christmas tree.

But Eleanor, in those days, loved to swim. It was her inherent talent. Winning an Olympic championship was a pragmatic accomplishment, not an endeavor that depended upon the whims of a movie director or the chancy favor of the public.

The Berlin Olympiad, which promised to be the greatest extravaganza of its kind yet staged, was coming up. Mrs. Jarrett itched to remount the victory stand and have the eyes of the world momentarily fixed upon her again. In time she returned East with her husband and his band, quit the night club circuit, and adopted a training regimen. She had no trouble making the women's Olympic swimming team, and in the summer of 1936, with scores of other United States athletes, she sailed on the S.S. *Manhattan* for Europe.

In mid-ocean she experienced the crisis of her life. They booted her off the Olympic team.

The athletes on the S.S. *Manhattan* were restricted to second-class. As a night club feature and a potential movie star, Eleanor had first-cabin instincts. One night she escaped the team chaperonage and ascended to the upper deck, where Charles MacArthur, the playboy playwright and husband of Helen Hayes, embraced her, toasted her, made her, as it were, the Sweetheart of Sigma Chi. Champagne was drunk and high-jinks indulged in. There was nothing monstrously scandalous about the episode, but news of it quickly reached the ears of Avery Brundage, the grand panjandrum of the Olympic Committee, and his fellow members, and Miss Holm's slight defection became a *cause celebre*.

Mr. Brundage had been an athlete of sorts in his youth. In maturity, he had become the Sir Galahad of amateur sport.

A multi-millionaire, he could more easily adhere to an Arthurian code of amateurism than, say, a black Olympic boxer from the ghetto. He was outraged at Eleanor's escapade. It seemed treason to him and the other members of the committee. The girl herself protested that she had done only what came naturally. She had been drinking champagne for years. She was a member in good standing of the Amateur Athletic Union, but she had no notion that there was a connection between that agency and the Women's Christian Temperance Union. She appealed to reason, but the high moguls held inexorably to their decision.

A petition that she be reinstated was signed by most of the members of the Olympic team. The petition was discarded as a scrap of paper. Eleanor was devastated, sunk, overwhelmed with remorse. She was sure that back home she would be branded as the traitor the Olympic Committee believed her to be and the disgrace would haunt her the rest of her life.

And back home Miss Holm had become the heroine of a first-cabin farce, the glamorous Champagne Girl. The newspapers gave her front page attention and mocked the bluenose Olympic officials who had thrown a pretty girl off the team merely because she had had a sportive evening with a celebrated playwright and his friends. The whole thing was treated as a lively jest by the newspapers, and a great deal was written about Eleanor's beauty, her talent, and her zest for life. She knew nothing of this at the time, and when the ship docked, she went on to Berlin, not as a competitor, but as an outcast—a pariah—to watch from the stands a Dutch girl win the backstroke championship she had hoped to retain for her country.

Eleanor Holm Jarrett returned to New York, not in disgrace as an ousted member of the United States Olympic Team, but to enjoy sympathetic front-page treatment by the press and to become known for her shipboard shenanigans to millions who would never have heard of her as a backstroke champion. The newspapers, still in the dog day doldrums, eagerly and voluminously revived the Holm-Brundage-MacArthur incident, and now their stories were enlivened by quotes from the Champagne Girl herself. There was Eleanor's remark that while Mr. Brundage was severe about an Olympic athlete enjoying a few glasses of champagne, he wasn't above "pinching the broads' behinds." No detail was overlooked. There was a story that Helen Hayes, incensed by MacArthur's bibulous attentions to the swimmer, was turned from her resolution to leave the ship at Cork only by the pleas of her contrite husband that she remain aboard until Cherbourg. The tenor of all that was written was favorable to Eleanor. "The girl who had rocked two continents," as one impassioned journalist described her, was envisaged by the public as an enchanting nymph who had been abused by a group of heavy-handed boors.

All of this was avidly read by the greatest publicity hound in New York, an inexorably ambitious little Broadway huckster who was spending thousands of dollars every year to keep his name in the newspapers; and along comes this Holm doll to grab more space for drinking champagne on the S.S. *Manhattan* than the ship itself would get if it hit an iceberg and sank.

Billy Rose got his start in life as a shorthand writer. He was a speed demon and won championships at the art. He made good contracts because of his skill, one in particular. He took dictation from Bernard Baruch, millionaire stockbroker, "park bench philosopher," confidant and counselor of Presidents, and a friendship developed between the two men that continued until Baruch's death. Rose had a broad threshold of tolerance when it came to persons who might help him in his eager Alpine ascent. His tastes were catholic. Arnold Rothstein, the man who was supposed to have "fixed" the World Series, card cheat, bucket shop operator, ultimately shot to death for a gambling debt, was one of Billy's pals and business associates; and for a time the notorious mob leader, Lucky Luciano, was vaguely connected with one of Rose's enterprises.

Rose had come to Broadway as a lyricist in Tin Pan Alley. He wrote numerous songs, some on his own, others with a collaborator. He had great facility. He was very apt with words and very adroit in employing the talents of others for his own advancement. Those who have attempted to investigate the career of the Fabulous Billy Rose, as he was denoted in one extensive biographical sketch, have found it difficult to determine which songs were his original creations and which were composed with a collaborator whose name may have been left off the sheet music. If Rose did not write the hit, "I Found a Million Dollar Baby in a Five and Ten Cent Store," the title is believed to be his. It is typical Rose.

Rose did well as a song writer, but the field was too restrictive for one of his inexhaustible energies and horizonless ambitions. He wanted fame, wealth, power—the world in a hand basket. He quit matching words to Tin Pan Alley tunes and became a Broadway entrepreneur. During part of the prohibition period he managed a resort known as the Back Stage Club. The place was small but enormously popular. There was food, and illegal liquor. "Don't drink it," Arnold Rothstein, abstemious himself, advised Rose, "sell it." And Rothstein, influential with the police, saved the place from raids.

The Back Stage Club had a band, a dance floor, and Miss Helen Morgan, a small dark-haired, provocative girl, whose sultry rendering of "The Man I Love" never failed to win a rapturous response. She stood at first next to the piano accompanist, but the dance floor was tiny, and Rose, always the utilitarian, saw that her slight figure was taking up space that could be used by paying patrons. "Sit up on the piano and sing," he told the girl. She did. And thenceforth, Helen Morgan never assumed another pose. She was celebrated as the girl on the piano box.

Rose was soon engaged with more ambitious projects than the Back Stage Club. He put a show on Broadway (it was his boast toward the end of his career that he had produced at least 100 shows and sold more than 100 million tickets to the public); with repeal, he opened a succession of night places that served food, drink, and offered excellent vaudeville entertainment at a reasonable price. His profits came from volume. The Casino de Paree served food to a thousand table sitters. He had what was known as the Billy Rose Music Hall. The Casa Mañana was said to be the largest cabaret in the world. His most durable venture of this sort, the Diamond Horseshoe, continued eleven years.

Insatiably questing for more gold and greater glory, the Mighty Mite or Bantam Barnum, as Rose had become known, persuaded John Hay Whitney to invest a large sum of money in a huge extravaganza, *Jumbo,* which Rose put on in the New York Hippodrome. Its success inspired him to attempt larger and more extravagant productions. He went to Texas to stage a multi-million-dollar spectacle for the Fort Worth Centennial Exposition, thence to Cleveland to introduce, at the Great Lakes Exposition, a colossal water show with Eleanor Holm as leading lady.

When Rose was in his late twenties, he married Fanny Brice, his senior by more than half a dozen years. She was not a beauty or a woman of great physical allure; she was a comic genius. Rose envied her name in the lights, her prestige, and the prominent persons who were her admiring intimates. Always the opportunist, "he sought," in the words of Earl Conrad, one of his biographers, "to aggrandize to himself her name, her fame, her public attraction."

Billy didn't like it, but he knew, in the early years of his marriage, that the Broadway wiseheimers referred to him as Mister Fanny Brice. The epithet was not apt for long. Rose quickly emerged from the nimbus of his wife's celebrity to achieve headline status of his own. His successes rolled on and the top press agent in the town, with a corps of assistants, kept his name continually before the public. Billy was eclectic. He saw Eleanor Holm as a sort of goddess of publicity, ready-made for his promotions and productions. He sought her out and signed her to a contract. In 1937, the year after her sensational expulsion from the Olympic team, he put her and Johnnie Weismuller in the water show in Cleveland. Two years later, Eleanor became the star of the New York World's Fair, the aquabelle of Rose's Aquacade, and Billy had his first million.

But before this, Mr. and Mrs. Arthur Jarrett had legally dissolved their marital compact, and Rose, who had been courting the latter ever since the Cleveland show, left the lamenting Fanny Brice with the excuse, "It's no fun being married to an electric light," and at the close of the first year of the New York Fair he and Eleanor Holm were married.

One day thirteen years later, Rose returned to New York from a diversionary expedition in Canada with a blonde named Joyce Matthews; the pair quarreled as they ascended to Rose's office in the Ziegfeld Theater building and the girl locked herself in the bathroom and slashed her wrist.

The police came, a tourniquet was applied to the wound, Joyce lived, and Billy Rose, for once in his life not relishing publicity, made a remark that should be listed in *Bartlett's*. "Now is the time," he said, "to have a wife. I'm going to call Eleanor."

This was not, however, the end of the affair. It was merely the prologue to a comedy of manners of Gothic design.

Eleanor Holm was not a mean or vindictive soul. She had broad tolerance. She suggested at first that Billy might have cheated a little; it was only what other men did without being caught. But no true reconciliation was effected, and Rose continued to see the blonde charmer who had made a theatrical gesture to take her life because of him.

Soon Eleanor and Billy were in court. Eleanor wanted a legal separation and $1,000,000. Rose countered with a divorce action. The litigation became perhaps the most sensational divorce case New York had known in the first half of the century. It was billed in newspaper headlines as the War of the Roses; it beguiled millions of readers, and at times crowded the Korean War and other capital news stories off the front page. Determined to hold tightly to his greedily acquired possessions, Rose resorted to guttersnipe practices. His vile innuendoes and the scurrilities he directed at his estranged spouse revolted even his case-hardened Broadway friends.

In the end the Roses were divorced, and Billy made an out-of-court settlement. Eleanor didn't get her million, but she was given what seemed at the moment a very substantial sum, and, in supplement, $700 a week to live on. She also had furs, jewels, and a lovely Renoir nude, a Sunday present from Rose at a time the pair lived in peace and good accord. Only the lovely Renoir turned out to be "not quite genuine," which is a little like being "slightly pregnant." Released from Miss Holm, Billy married Miss Matthews. They were divorced three years later; but hope, as Doctor Johnson remarked of a second marriage, triumphed over experience and they tried it again. The second union ended more quickly than the first in a Mexican divorce.

Rose died in 1966. A codicil to his will contained this clause, "To my former wife Eleanor Holm, $10,000." It was a niggardly bequest for a man who died leaving millions; but better, Eleanor may have remarked, than being hit in the head with a sharp stone. And it was I, she said, who got her the money.

The story might be of mild interest:

Shortly after midnight one winter morning early in World War II, I entered Lindy's well known Broadway (New York) restaurant for an after-the-theater snack. It was a place well-peopled at night with an assortment of Broadway characters, the fabled "Mindy's" of Damon Runyon's fiction. My eyes blinking in the garish lights, I had scarcely crossed the threshold when I heard a feminine cry, "Henry! Henry!"

Eleanor Holm Rose bounced up from a table that was occupied by several other persons and waved frantically. I went over.

The dominant figure in the group was the miniscule Billy Rose. He was holding court. Lou Holtz, the musical comedy comic was, this night, court jester. He was filled with quips and smart sayings, a veritable *Joe Miller Jest Book.* I didn't think him very funny. Others at table were Sylvia Sidney, a stage and screen leading lady, and her actor husband, Luther Adler; Clifford Odets, the playwright, whose drama *Clash by Night* Rose had produced, and his wife, Luise Rainer, winner of the Academy Award for the finest performance in pictures, and another woman whose name I have forgotten.

Rose and Eleanor had been married only a short time and were living in a large apartment on the top floor of the Hotel Warwick while an elaborate five story house they had taken on Beekman Place was being prepared for occupancy.

Rose was engaged with another theatrical enterprise. He had obtained the rights to Ernest Hemingway's Spanish War play, *The Fifth Column,* which was in rehearsal in New Haven.

"Billy's got to be in New Haven tomorrow," Eleanor said. "Let's you and I have dinner and see a show."

I was delighted at the proposal. Eleanor was in the fullest bloom of her career, a small, sparkling, elegant girl, better known because of her starring role at the World's Fair than any theatrical star in town, and as glamorous, surely, as any glamor girl on Broadway or on movie lots of Hollywood.

Rose, at the other end of the table said, "Yeah, take her, Henry. You'll be doing me a favor. I'll appreciate it. Bring her back here tomorrow night after the show."

Eleanor said she hadn't seen *The Man Who Came to Dinner,* the hit of the season.

"We'll see that," I said assuredly.

"Yeah, you'll like it," Rose said. "It's a great show."

I remained at the table for bacon and eggs. Before I left, it was arranged that I would pick up Mrs. Rose at the Warwick the next evening, we'd dine at "21," and go on from there to the show.

In the morning I set out blithely to obtain the best seats in the house for *The Man Who Came to Dinner,* and by midday I was worn out and discouraged. The theater and every agency I tried turned me down flatly. A ticket agent I had known for years who had never failed me before, shook his head disconsolately. "Not a chance," he said. "Not a living chance. The house is sold out weeks in advance."

My bright hopes of triumph shattered, I was glooming in my hotel room in the afternoon when a friend from the *New York Times* knocked on the door. I told him of my desperate plight. He said he knew a wealthy stockbroker who could conjure up tickets for any show in town. He told me to go ahead with my plans for the evening and he would telephone me at "21" and advise me if the tickets were available.

I called at the Warwick early in the evening and tried the Rose number on the house phone. There was no answer, no sound of ringing, but suddenly the bell captain blustered up to me, seeming on the point of snatching the muted headpiece from my ear.

"Who ya trying to get?" he demanded.

"Mrs. Billy Rose."

He was hostile and very suspicious. "Whatja want her for?"

"I'm to take her to dinner."

"To take her to dinner," he repeated angrily. He hesitated as he looked me over with detailed scrutiny. "Well, wait here."

He disappeared. The phone was still dead. In a minute he returned and grudgingly conceded, "Well, go on. Ring her."

The bell captain stood at my elbow as I told Eleanor I was in the lobby. She said to come up. As I started for the elevator, the bell captain grasped my arm. "Here, take this," he commanded, and he handed me a baggage check, larger than a silver dollar, with a number on it. "Give it to me when you come down."

The apartment was huge. I thought it must occupy the entire top floor of the hotel. Eleanor had instinctive taste, and the rooms were delightfully appointed. Rose had recently become a collector, and two or three important paintings hung on the walls. Mrs. Rose was dressed to the nines, and I gloated in anticipation of the reflected glory I would enjoy as her escort. We were about to descend to the lobby when the telephone rang, and Eleanor ran to answer it. The conversation was fairly long.

"That was Billy, calling from New Haven," she explained, when she returned.

"Everything all right?"

"He wanted to make sure you hadn't stood me up."

"Fat chance of that," I said.

We passed out of the hotel and had gone a hundred feet when I thought of the baggage check.

"I've got to go back," I said.

"What for?"

I showed her the check. "When I went up to get you the bell captain gave me this. He told me to return it when I left."

"Well, I'll be goddamned," Eleanor exclaimed, with an embarrassed laugh, "Oh, that Billy!"

I realized then that she was under very close surveillance.

The maitre d' at "21," beaming on Mrs. Rose, solicitous to know her pleasure, showed us to a table and put two waiters at our service. We were having cocktails when a third servitor, in an act of swank, came to attach a telephone to "Mr. Clune's table." My friend from the *Times* informed me that two tickets, "down front," were in my name in the box office.

At the theater Eleanor was the cynosure of scores of eyes which, since I clung to her like a lamprey to a rock, could not exclude me from their admiring gaze. What a night, I thought happily, for an apple knocker.

Since Rose, returning from New Haven, would not hold court at Lindy's until after midnight, Eleanor proposed that we stop at the Beachcombers, a recently opened night club that was in great vogue. The place was packed and a considerable crowd waited hopefully at the entrance. The velvet rope was up, guarded by attendants. I was sure we'd have no chance, but my companion pulled me up to the barrier. "Oh, *Mrs. Rose,*" one of the attendants said; the rope came down and we were in.

I delivered Eleanor to her husband at Lindy's some time after two o'clock in the morning. Rose was sitting at the same table he had occupied the night before, but a different group of courtiers surrounded him. I thanked him for the high privilege of having his wife for the evening, and he thanked me for the service he said I had performed in entertaining her during his absence. I returned home the next day, and a few days later Eleanor wrote that Billy had had several anonymous letters telling him that his wife had been out on the town with a strange man. "Nice people," Eleanor remarked. I suggested that the authors of the letters must have been myopic. For surely, I said, no one with normal vision would have mistaken me for a Broadway playboy or a cuckolding *flaneur*. On the contrary, mine was an avuncular image; a kindly, fiftyish old fellow in town to see the sights, perhaps the possessor of a dairy herd and a seckel pear orchard in some rural precinct—

Green Valley, Illinois; Tunbridge, Vermont; Scottsville, New York.

My wife and I saw very little of Eleanor during the years of her marriage to Rose. I did, however, spend an Easter Sunday afternoon at the house on Beekman Place, where I blunderingly shook hands with the butler, mistaking him for a house guest. There were half a dozen servants. Billy gave me a tour of the establishment and I was duly impressed, as, of course, he wanted me to be. He was at pains to show me his Rembrandt, his Frans Hals, and other notable paintings, and he boasted that kings and queens and the Florentine Medici had dined off of an elaborate gold service he displayed in a cabinet.

Not too long after her divorce from Rose and before she contracted a third marriage, Eleanor came to our house for the winter holidays. She insisted that Christmas dinner without champagne, a luxury in which we ourselves had never indulged, would be a pallid repast, and Christmas Eve we all piled into the car and went in search of a couple of bottles. Our quest took us three villages away. When we returned and I opened the front door and threw on the light, I suffered a paroxysm I might have experienced were a pistol pressed at my temple. I was speechless, unable to utter a command or kick at our new bull terrier puppy, who was asleep in the folds of a $6,000 matched mink coat our guest had carelessly dropped in a corner of the living room when we left.

A miracle had been wrought. The puppy (notorious, as are all bull terriers, for tearing to pieces anything they can get their teeth into) had fallen asleep without chewing a single mink. "God be praised!" I intoned tremblingly. It was not an expletive; it was an ardent hosanna.

The former Mrs. Rose came back one summer to perform, with the collaboration of my wife, her sensational aquacade act in the pool of Rochester's leading social club, the Genesee Valley. Later, she moved to Florida, married Thomas Whalen, and we often saw her during winter visits to that state. She lived sumptuously, high up in a high-rise in the northern reaches of Miami. She had been a *Time* cover-story girl, and the only decoration on the front cover of an issue of *Look*. She was still a very attractive woman and a wonderfully kind hostess.

She seemed to know everyone of prominence in Miami, and whenever we were with her I collected names that could be dropped resoundingly into my column "Seen and Heard." She took us to a party given by Ethel Merman, who had recently co-starred with Marilyn Monroe in the film, *There's No Business Like Show Business.* With Eleanor we were guests of Sonny Werblin at a clubhouse lunch party the day Mr. Werblin's horse, Silent Screen, highly favored to win the rich Flemingo stake at Hialeah, ran wide at the stretch turn, clean out of the money, to lay a funeral pall over a small company that had anticipated a very lively celebration.

One day, as we sat at lunch in the Palm Bay Club with the then Mrs. Whalen, Colonel and Mrs. Cloyce J. Tippett came to the table, and I was pleased to talk briefly with the former "Liz" Whitney, divorced wife of the immensely wealthy John Hay (Jock) Whitney, our former ambassador to the Court of St. James. The Tippetts left, and one of the chairs they vacated was taken by Harold J. Gibbons, once the aide and closest confidant of the president of the International Brotherhood of Teamsters, James B. Hoffa, whose mysterious disappearance has never been resolved. I was entranced by the variety and spice of Mrs. Whalen's friends and acquaintances.

Several months before Billy Rose's death, a query in a syndicated newspaper feature "What in the world has become of Eleanor Holm?" cued me to write a column about the time I had taken Eleanor to "21" to dinner and to see *The Man Who Came To Dinner* and needed a baggage check to get her out of the Hotel Warwick. I embellished the incident, trying to amuse my readers, and broadly hinted at the close watch Rose was keeping on his bride. Eleanor saw the piece and clipped it.

Not long after the column appeared, Rose returned to New York after surgery performed by a Houston specialist and Eleanor visited him during his convalescence. Their divorce litigation had been tumultuous and bitter, but that was of the past. The second Mrs. Rose was not a woman to nurture a grudge or indulge in vengeance to the point of obsession. In an attempt to amuse the patient, she read him my piece, and she said he laughed until his incision hurt at the part about the baggage check; and it was this, she avowed, that got her the line in the codicil of Billy's will, "To my former wife Eleanor Holm $10,000."

Perhaps she over-stated the case, but I like to think that I may in some way have recompensed a gracious lady for her many kindnesses to my wife and me.

CHAPTER THIRTY-FOUR

George Plimpton, the perennial novice (and editor of the *Paris Review*), wrote an interesting book about his experiences trying almost everything in the athletic line from quarterbacking a professional football team to stunting on a swinging trapeze with a troupe of circus aerialists. And Paul Gallico, while writing sports for the New York *Daily News,* once got knocked out by Jack Dempsey in order that he might describe the sensation for his readers. Such daring enterprises to obtain a story were well out of my range. But now and then I did divert from the ordinary routine to seek a novel piece for the paper, and I went off once on what I defined as the Great Adventure. My wife thought the term extravagant.

"Henry," she told friends, "went out to get the pulse of the country, and got nothing but a blister on his heel."

"But I did hitch to Chicago," I boasted, which was not quite true.

"Yes," she countered, "and came back in a lower berth on the North Shore Limited, with breakfast in the diner."

Franklin Roosevelt was in the White House, the country was gradually emerging from the Depression, I was brim full of energy and seething with a desire to do something innovative. So one day I left Scottsville on foot with an itinerary that would take me first to Chicago, on to Kansas City, Missouri; then a southeast swing to Hot Springs, Arkansas, and home by easy stages. I was sure I would have a hatfull of adventurous tales for my readers.

I left on a bright May morning. The dogwood was in bloom and birds were in chippering chorus as I passed through our grove to the main village street. I breathed deeply of the clear, invigorating air and whistled—I am not dead sure, but I think—Waldteufal's *Skaters' Waltz.* I moved blithely through the short business section of town, turned west at the Catholic Church, and heard the honk of a car behind me. Well, I thought, here's my first ride. It wasn't. It was my wife.

"You forgot your raincoat," she called, flaunting it through an open window.

"I don't want it," I announced emphatically. "Go back. Don't be chasing me all the way to the Mississippi River."

She turned the car without another word and retreated.

I went on again, whistling. I transcended the village limits and delighted in the prospect of the open country. The terrain was undulating and varied. Wooded lots were thickening with new foliage; broad stands of winter wheat, luxurious in their verdant softness, contrasted pleasantly with bare brown patches of earth, fitted, but not yet seeded, with the season's crop. Cattle grazed in rolling, tree-studded meadows. A farm kid jockeying a small tractor in a nearby field waved a greeting. "Hiya," he called; I waved and answered in kind.

I felt wonderful, uninhibited, loose as ashes; a 48-year-old Road Kid out on his own, without a care in the world.

I had sent by express to Chicago a suitcase with good clothes, in the event that I decided to remain in that city two or three days before returning to the road, and I carried no pack on my back. I wore a pair of old pants, a shabby jacket, heavy workman's shoes, and woolen socks. One of the socks had been darned at the heel. I should have known better. In my youth, I once walked all day with the famous pedestrian, Edward Payson Weston, who instructed me in the care of a pedestrian's feet.

I didn't mind walking. I had declared to myself that come what might I'd never resort to the technique of those lazy hitchhikers who stand at the side of the road and wag a thumb. I'd keep on walking, and if my industry failed of reward, I'd plod on resolutely, even unto the setting sun.

I was a fair piece outside of Scottsville and numerous

cars had passed me without a flicker of interest, when a fellow with a heart in his rib cage stopped a few yards in front of me. I ran with a glad cry to accept his hospitality.

"It's a warm day for walking," he said. "Where you trying to get to?"

I thought it best to seem modest in my purpose and answered, "Erie, Pennsylvania;" Erie being the first city on my planned route to Chicago.

"Well, get in," he said. "I'm going south, but I gotta cross Route 20. That's the road goes right through Erie."

He was a nice man and we talked about the weather, crops, the state of the nation, and my good Samaritan wondered vaguely from where I had come, and I answered vaguely. I think he thought my provenance Bridgeport, Connecticut.

He let me off when we reached Route 20. I thanked him and again turned my face to the west. The sun was well up now, and it's midday rays had a midsummer intensity. I trudged on, no longer whistling; and suddenly a painful fact impinged upon my consciousness. Like Achilles, I had a tender heel.

Route 20 is a federal highway that ends, I had been told, at Portland, Oregon. It looked like a long road. It looked like a very long road after I had walked perhaps eight miles, the darned heel of my sock an increasing irritant; I had seen, it seemed to me, 500 cars going west and never an encouraging glance from the occupants at the limping hiker on the gravel shoulder of the pavement. I clenched my teeth and refreshed the memory of my resolution. I wouldn't use the thumb. But I began to look around wistfully at the sound of an approaching motor and indicate by a gesture of the index finger that I too was anxious to go west. No one gave me a tumble. Not for another mile or two.

Then a small car shot by doing a neat sixty. I heard a shriek of brakes and the driver stopped a hundred yards down the road. I sprinted, fearful that he would go on, my foot crippled by a sore heel. He was a handsome young man with a small waxed mustache and modish clothes.

"Where you going?" His tone was angry, the inquiry almost a command.

I told him my immediate destination was Cleveland. He fixed me with full scrutiny. He hesitated. "Well, get in." The invitation was less than cordial.

"Thanks," I said, dropping wearily into the seat beside him.

He put the car into gear. "You know," he said, "I've made a rule for myself never to pick up anyone."

"Well, I'm glad you broke it this time," I said gratefully.

For a moment, his eyes fell again full upon me. "I wouldn't have broken it now," he assured me, "except that you remind me of a fellow I've seen in Rochester."

"I'm grateful for the resemblance."

"Fellow named Clune," the driver said. "Henry Clune."

I was startled. It seemed like clairvoyance. Then I laughed.

"I give up, that's me," I confessed. "Where'd you ever see me in Rochester."

He chuckled, displaying an amicability I hadn't supposed he possessed.

"Last New Year's Eve," he said. "At a formal dance at the Genesee Valley Club."

* * * * * * * * * * *

At Fredonia I suggested, since I had been caught out of character, that I buy the lunch. Our relations had become felicitous. The driver identified himself as Thomas H. Truslow of Geneva. He carried me to the Erie city line. Quitting the comfort of his front seat to struggle westward on foot, my heel now hurting like an ulcerated tooth, was almost traumatic. Why, why, I wondered, as I saw Truslow's sedan disappear in the opposite direction, had I attempted this absurd enterprise? At my age? I had tried to look like a hobo and I must have succeeded, for no one apparently wanted anything to do with a shabby wayfarer who might turn out to be a robber or worse. Cars fled by me in an unceasing parade. Chicago seemed as remote as the Pleiades.

I was less than an hour out of Erie when a ratty little old car, squeaking, rattling, its motor a discordant snort, slowed to my crawling pace and the fellow at the wheel called, "Where you going, pal?"

I told him, as I had told Truslow: Cleveland.

"Hell of a place to go if you're looking for work. Nothing doing over there. I been looking for a job myself for two months. C'mon, though, I'll take you a piece, you going that way."

I noticed the tires. They looked dangerous. But this was the first act of grace I had known since Tom Truslow had stopped for me and I wasn't being choosy. The rear of the car was cluttered with junk, the disarray surmounted by two small girls on the seat who leaned against one another in sisterly somnolence.

It was good—it was wonderful—to be riding again. The driver, to whom I at once took a fancy, told me his name, said that his wife had died the year before and left him with the two girls; that he used to operate a thirty-ton crane in Erie, but the bottom had dropped out of the job market, and he wondered wryly if it would ever be restored.

"Y'know," he said at one point, "if I didn't have these kids, I'd go along with you to Cleveland. We'd shack up. Together, maybe we'd find something. What do you do, pal? What kind of work? You a steel worker?"

"No," I said, not knowing what to say; then, as a random shot, "I work with horses."

"Jeez, I wish you could come with me," the driver suggested. "I'm going over to my father's farm, 'bout forty miles from here, to cut wood. One of his horses got the heaves bad. What makes that?"

Secretly I had no idea. I told him, though, that it might be diet—or old age. We had gone twelve or fifteen miles. We went another five, then, what I had feared happened. A tire popped.

I set the jack and the driver removed the flat tire and replaced it with a spare. The spare was worn to the canvas. If another blowout occurred, I couldn't in good conscience walk off and leave a father with two small girls and only three wheels. I had accepted his hospitality, and I was involved in his fortunes.

We went on slowly, cautiously; for my part, fearfully. Ten miles after we passed from Pennsylvania into Ohio the driver announced with genuine regret that he would have to leave the east-west highway and turn south. In my hobo get-up I looked more impoverished than he. When I got out, I dropped a five-dollar bill on the seat.

"Jesus," my benefactor exclaimed reverently, and his eyes popped out so far a derby hat could have been hung on them, "you got money!"

"I'm all alone," I said. "I got no kids. Good luck to you."

"Pal, *good* luck to you. I wish t'hell we could hook up, and try to make it together."

The shambling, rattling old car with its bum tires had been a luxury, and when I saw the unemployed crane operator disappear south on the intersecting road my early resolution lost its sinewy firmness. My inclination was to stand on the ballast of the highway and jerk a thumb, but the cold eye of a highway patrolman caused me to reconsider. I had painfully proceeded a short way when a sporty white car with an Illinois license shot out from a roadside tavern and the driver hailed me.

"If you're going to Cleveland, buddy."

"You're heaven's gift," I said, hobbling up to him.

He was a stout, flashily dressed man, with a red closely shaved face and sharp little bead-like eyes. He said he was a salesman for vending machines, pinball games, and such, and I suspect that all that he sold was not quite legitimate. He had had, very obviously, more than a Coca-Cola in the tavern.

"You're a lucky stiff," he said, wagging his head assertively. "Out on the road, nothing to worry about. Free as the air."

"I got a blister on my heel."

"Hell, a blister on your heel. I got a blister back home, where I live, just outside of Chicago. On my back. Twice a day she wants me to call in and give her the report when I'm out on the road making a living. She thinks I'm some goddamn Lothario. You know Lothario, buddy?"

"A kind of a lover," I suggested.

"Natch. She thinks I'm a Lothario." He laughed and seemed happy about her suspicions. "She thinks I'm jumping in and outta beds like street cars. Every day, she's trying to check me out, like some goddamn G-man."

He was a lively companion. He entertained me with accounts of Rabelaisian episodes that seemed to warrant the suspicions of the lady in Illinois. He drove swiftly. I rode with him to the Hotel Statler. He gave his car to the doorman. I bought a toothbrush, a pair of socks, a bottle of iodine, a bandage for my heel, and went over to the YMCA for a seventy-five cent flop.

In the morning I went west on a bus, left it at Norwalk, Ohio, and chanced it again on foot, my bandaged heel hurting only slightly. Almost at once I got a ride for twelve or fifteen miles; then a second—a dandy—clean into Toledo. But my vagabond view of this great land of ours gave it a Cyclopean dimension. I was suddenly appalled at the prospect of making it to Chicago, to Kansas City, to Hot Springs, Arkansas, and home, without a bus, a plane, or a train ticket, and I took a train into Chicago. I slept that night in another YMCA and in the morning, deciding that my age opposed further peregrinations afoot, I reclaimed my suitcase from the express office, changed my clothes, and registered in the Hotel Stevens.

And that night I dined at the Drake. The music was soft, the service faultless, there were well dressed men and pretty women at adjacent tables. I had squab with truffles. I returned home before the week was out, as my wife pointed out, on the North Shore Limited. My Great Adventure had lost its luster and sort of petered out. But you can't be a good Road Kid with a blister big as a silver dollar on your heel.

* * * * * * * * * * *

I have always been a doodler: on a paper napkin in a lunchroom, on the margin of the directory in a telephone booth, on the pocket notebook I always carry, waiting my turn in a barbershop or the dread summons of a dentist's office; doodling, but not drawing. Fritz Trautmann, a highly respected instructor, in whose class in freehand drawing in old Mechanic's Institute (now the Rochester Institute of Technology) I enrolled, disparaged me, not mincing words. "Heinie", Mr. Trautmann said, "as an art student you can't even draw your breath. You're lousy."

I withdrew, my yearning to imitate Max Beerbohm or those cartoonists in *The New Yorker* who seem to say, with a few trenchant strokes of a pencil, more than many an author can tell in half a dozen manuscript pages, suppressed by the master's mockery, but not vanquished. The next year, learning that Elmer Messner, a fine newspaper cartoonist would teach a class, I returned to try again. Elmer was a friend of mine. He encouraged me, at times even coddled me. But I seemed unable to do little more than make sweeping lines which gave no indication of design. I read Ruskin about the pre-Raphaelites, but that scarcely helped. And I was vaguely disappointed with the subjects on the model stand: a standing lamp, a place setting for a dinner party, a bowl of apples, a broken bicycle pump. No naked women, as I'd half expected.

My class met once a week, Monday night. Mechanics Institute was in downtown Rochester, in the area in which the city had been founded in the early 1830s. Next to one another on Spring Street, no more than a three minute walk from the class room, stood two of the oldest dwelling houses in town, each then given over to a commercial enterprise. In one, George Humphrey, a relative of Humphrey Bogart (the actor's mother had come from Rochester), managed a second-hand book store of such distinction that customers came to it from all over western and central New York. In the other house, a colorful downtown character operated a saloon on the main floor and opened on Sunday an upstairs assembly hall where the saxy moans and brassy stridencies of a jazz orchestra drew youth to the place like lepidoptera to the fluttering flame of a candle.

Jack Foran, who called the resort the House of Foran, had had a varied career. He was a sailor in the Navy in the first World War, a bootlegger during Prohibition, a pugilist in the light heavyweight category. He had a saloon and a partnership in a racing stable. He was a handsome fellow, talky and opinionated. He would bone up on various subjects and lecture on them authoritatively: chamber music, the best way to prepare sauerbraten, paleethnology, the breeding of fighting cocks, Freud's dream theories—his range was wide. He had a habit of poking a finger sharply into the chest of his captive audience and demanding angrily, "Am I right?"

Although Foran had not been a prizefighter of notable talents, he was a large and formidable figure, and generally the disposition of his auditor was to defer to his belligerent inquiry. "Yeah, you're right," the auditor would concede. "You're dead right, Jack."

When racing was suspended during World War II, a reporter asked Foran, a compulsive horse player, what he was going to do now that he was bereft of his absorbing avocation. His prompt answer was printed in the press: "Unable to indulge in the mental calculations I formerly practiced, I am now busy resolving Einstein's quantum theory of specific heat."

He was a great one for politics and religion, especially religion. He wanted a pulpit for his homilies and he had one behind the oaken strip of his café. He talked of Zen Buddhism, the New England transcendentalists, Taoism, the Roman Catholic and Greek Orthodox Churches, Calvinism, theosophy. He professed great admiration for Richelieu, whom he had discovered in his encyclopedic reading. He reveled in the Cardinal's machinations and extolled his imperial rule. He delighted to shock his listeners.

"You know what the Pope said about Richelieu?" he asked, leaning importunately over the bar and bending a hard gaze on a mild little patron who probably had never heard of his Red Eminence.

"No, Jack. What's the Pope say about Richelieu?"

"He said, 'If there's a God, the Cardinal will have much to answer for. If there isn't—well, he's had a very successful life.' "

"Aw naw, Jack. Now where'd you hear all that?"

"You haven't read Ranke?"

"Ranke? Who's Ranke?"

"My God, man! *von* Ranke's *History of the Popes,"* and with a dismissing gesture—a gesture indicating that it is absurd to attempt to carry on a discussion with the ignorant and the uninformed—Foran moved along the bar to serve another patron and astonish him with a new facet of his erudition.

Foran's martinis were celebrated. They were called "bombs". "One is good," the adage went, "two's too many, and three's not enough."

It was my custom Monday night to stop at the House of Foran for a martini. The martini served as an anodyne to the suffering caused by my classroom ineptitude. One Monday night I took two. The effect was apocalyptic. I realized on the instant that my talents as an artist were unexpandably narrow, I saw the futility of carrying on and decided to abandon the freehand drawing class then and henceforth. I spoke to the proprietor, knowing him to be well traveled. "Jack," I asked, "you've been in Youngstown, Ohio?"

"Indeed I have."

"What sort of a place is it?"

The Spring Street academician wagged his handsome head. "Earthy," he pronounced. "I should say, quite an earthy community."

Imprudently, I took a third martini, well over-matching myself. It was a catalyst. It sent me zooming into the night. At midnight I crossed from Pennsylvania into Ohio, and very early in the morning tooled into the city of Youngstown. Little Steel was on strike. I had been reading in the newspapers of this "protest of grievances." I had read that 60,000 of the city's population of 175,000 were out and I thought it would be interesting to tell my readers of this traumatic civic dislocation.

I parked my car and engaged a taxi driver who said he had formerly been a steelworker. He was a hulking, hard-faced fellow with a long Hungarian name. His first name was Al. I paid him five dollars and asked him to show me places where the strikers congregated. I liked Al. We were soon as clubby as a couple of Brother Elks; and presently, telling me I had paid enough, he invited me to share the front seat and ride for free.

Our tour continued from shortly after midnight until four o'clock in the morning. During it we visited various resorts which enjoyed, at this late hour, a lively patronage, where Al delivered or picked up "fares," and the three big steel mills, the Republic, the Sheet and Tool, and the Carnegie unit. I had expected to see fights, riots, all sorts of violence. There was no disorder; no police in evidence. At each plant gate a few pickets were clustered around a portable radio listening to music or an all-night disc jockey.

"I think if the men had full say about it, ninety percent of 'em would go back to work," Al said.

"But why would they go back to work? They must have voted to strike."

"There's only Little Steel in this town," Al explained. "Sixty thousand is only part of the hundreds of thousands of steel workers who'll go out in a few days—if the strike lasts. These fellas gotta go along with others 'cause they're loyal to the union. We'll go over to the Republic Café and you can talk to some of the guys. I'll leave you there and make a couple of calls and come back later."

The Republic Café, like much else I had observed in Youngstown, was, as Jack Foran had suggested, "earthy." It stood directly across the street from the Republic steel mill, the latter a great sprawling plant that extended along the copper colored waters of the Mahoning River. This night the mill was like a giant suddenly rendered impotent; a Goliath felled by David's sling. A faint flag of smoke rose dispiritedly from a chimney that was part of a battery of enormous stacks, but there was no vast glow of red from the hearths and boilers inside. A plant that had the capacity to turn out more steel in two or three months than many countries are able to produce in a year was silenced by a dispute of labor.

It was not difficult to engage in conversation with the men at the long, crowded bar, although there was a brief period when my dress, and particularly my haberdashery—I was the only man present with a linen shirt and a necktie—made me suspect. Soon, however, I was accepted in fellowship and found myself at a wall booth with five striking steelworkers, one a powerful black man.

The oldest man of the group, a Pole with a seamed face and great gnarled hands, said, "We ain't too sore at the company. They got their rights same as us. But this thing can't go on too long or we'll all be sore'n hell at each other. We want the pension. I'm fifty-seven—in three, four years, I won't be much good any more. And I got three kids and the old woman. You tell him, Hunk."

Hunk had wanted to talk all along, but the others had attempted to shush him down while they expressed their own opinions. He was diffcult to repress, and the oldest of the group decided to give him his tongue. He was Irish, a squat, bulky-shouldered young man with angry eyes and a granite slab for a chin. He wasn't like the others, comfortably mellow with beer. He had been double-dipping into the whiskey and he was truculant and blasphemous.

"Don't know why I should be talking to this guy," he declared, thumping a fist on the table top so violently that the glasses jiggled, his angry eyes holding me in a basilisk stare. "Looks like a goddamn scabbing spy."

I tried to tell him that I was merely a traveler passing through town. He profanely rejected the explanation, but a minute later grasped my hand across the table, said we were pals, told the others that I was okay.

His humors were mercurial. I lost favor as quickly as it was achieved. Hunk seemed to resent my necktie, said it made me look a "sonofabitch of a FBI."

When the others attempted to temporize, he turned on them, telling me that they were a "bunch of sonsofbitches of pickets . . . I wouldn't stand on one of them goddamn picket lines," he announced vehemently. "No, by God, not if they put a gun on me."

I timorously suggested that if there were a strike, pickets must be necessary, but Hunk shouted in reply that the picket line at the Republic opened every day to allow 150 men to pass through to man the boilers, a concession that outraged every principle of unionism. The black man, soft-voiced and temperate, interposed.

"You can't let them fires out, Hunk," he said. "You let them fires out, and them big boilers, cost maybe four or five million, ain't no good, and what we going to do if we go back to work and no fires?"

The oldest member of the group supported the black man's thesis. "He's right, Hunk. They gotta keep maintenance. I don't want to be off no longer than this strike, and God knows, a couple of weeks is long enough. You weren't here in 1937. We was shut down eighteen months then. I don't want that to happen again, me with three kids and the old woman."

Hunk was irreconcilable. He'd let the whole plant rot and go to hell before he'd let a man cross the picket line. He got up, fuming, and went over to the bar.

Another man said, "What we want most is the pension.

You get old in a steel mill fast. We got these raises, Murray (Philip Murray, president of the United Steel Workers Union) got 'em for us. Ten and fifteen cent raises. What we'd rather have is for that to go into a pension."

Al returned and I left the Republic Café on the front seat of his cab. We went out of town to a roadhouse and picked up two steelworkers. Al let one off after a couple of miles and the other left us a few minutes later.

"What's the price for Mike and me?" the last passenger, whose huge shoulders threatened to burst the red flannel shirt he wore, asked Al.

"Fifty cents 'll do it, Smitty."

"I ain't no free loader, strike or no strike," Smitty said. He pressed two dollars into Al's hand.

"No, look here, Smitty," Al said. "When you're working again, okay. Not now. Gimme half a buck and take this back."

Smitty ended the argument by getting out of the cab. "Smitty's a right guy," Al said, when we moved on. "Most of these guys are okay. He's been with the Republic seventeen years. He'll gamble on anything. You heard him want to bet me fifteen hundred against my cab the strike'll be over on the fifteenth of the month."

"I heard him. I thought it was just talk."

"Well, Smitty was half leveling. He'd bet it if he had the dough."

"You think the strike will be over then. I heard him say the government wouldn't let it go on, losing all this money from income taxes."

Al shrugged and lighted a cigarette. "I wouldn't know," he said. "Smitty might know something."

CHAPTER THIRTY-FIVE

With time out for military service during World War I and a couple of brief reportorial experiments in large cities, I served as a small city newspaper worker for nearly sixty years beginning in 1910 and ending in 1969. For the greater part of this term I wrote a column which was perhaps the most conspicuous printed matter in the newspaper. It was set in two-column measure on the left side of the first local page; its enduring appearance gave it, in time, a sort of institutional character, and it made me a prominent figure in the community.

I liked very much the prestige I enjoyed, the letters the column inspired, the invitations to various and sometimes novel functions that came to me, and the belief that seemed implicit in not a few of my readers that I had the wisdom of Solomon—that I was encyclopedic. There were times when I seemed to be a sort of father confessor or a Dear Abby, long before Dear Abby became the phenomenon she is now. I recall being awakened by the telephone long after the middle of the night—perhaps at three o'clock in the morning—and hearing a fervid feminine petition, "Is it true, Mr. Clune? Tell me. Is Betty Grable really going to have a baby?"

My first city editor, the late Morris Adams, whose memory I revere, had this precept:

"The first business of a newspaper is to inform the public, and on every conceivable subject. If the public thinks we are omniscient, that's fine. We'll prove it."

To catalogue the requests for information that came to me over a long period of years would require a chapter in itself. They were a mixed bag. I can think now of being asked to fix the date of Pickett's engagement at Five Forks; repeat, for an interrogator on the telephone, the second stanza of William Blake's "The Tiger"; name the place and give the date of the featherweight championship "Terrible" Terry McGovern lost to Young Corbett; the year and month of the Chicago Fire; and decide whether Michelangelo or Raphael painted the *Sitting Madonna.*

The answers rarely came off the top of my head. But the office had an adequate morgue, a tattered encyclopedia, and the sports editor had a collection of record books. But there were times, even with these aids, that I was stumped. Donald F. Southgate, a man of whom I had never heard until I opened his letter, sought my advice about sky diving. Mr. Southgate explained that he was shortly to leave his post as president of the Shur-On Optical Company, and he thought sky diving might be an engaging hobby.

The office repositories of knowledge had no information on the subject, and I was constrained to tell my correspondent that he had appealed to a very unlikely source; that I myself so lacked daredevil propensities that I was apprehensive even on roller skates. Ours, however, was a felicitous correspondence, and from it I gained the friendship of a fine and interesting man, once described by the press as a "Renaissance Man." The epithet was extravagant; but Don Southgate did have a variety of talents and wide interests. A widower, he lived on a handsome, beautifully maintained estate not far from Geneva, New York. He had a notable collection of jazz records, and several leading jazz artists were his friends. In midlife, he successively took up ballroom dancing and figure skating under professional instruction. He was spoken of as a gourmet cook. He was a collector of rare books, a skillful equestrian, a crack bird shot, and a fisherman. He was persistent and unsparing in his efforts to master any pursuit that engaged his fancy. Our friendship, which I cherished, continued until his death from natural causes, not as the result of a sky diving accident, since, prudently, he never adopted the sport as a retirement activity.

* * * * * * * * * * *

Letters are a boon to a fellow writing a newspaper column; they are the barometer of his readership, and even the ugly ones have meaning. Since, for the most part, my pitch was to entertain the readers rather than agitate them with heavy-duty "think" pieces, I was spared much of the recrimination and abuse that must come to columnists who grind political axes and beat drums for social and governmental reforms. I was, I suppose, a sort of male Pollyanna. I loved the letters, and they came from a wide assortment of persons and dealt with a variety of subjects.

By letter Jeff Davis, King of the Hoboes, entreated me to make the convention of the Knights of the Road, to be held in 1947 in Miami, Florida. "All the good boes'll be there," Jeff wrote, "and you're one of us." Indeed, a few years before, Davis himself had sponsored my initiation into the Knights at a convention in Buffalo. But I had had no experience riding blind baggage or hiding out in freight cars. Because of this and the remoteness of Miami, I declined the convention invitation.

H. L. Mencken, brilliant satirist and critic, thought by many to be a dreadful curmudgeon, curiously requested ("My apologies for bothering you") a piece I had written about President Roosevelt at a time when the privileged scion of the wealthy Roosevelt family, the boy from Groton and Harvard, decided to "soak (his own kind) the rich." Mencken had seen only part of the column and wanted a full transcript. I was complimented and eager to comply. He thanked me profusely and ran what I had written straight down the center of the editorial page of the Baltimore *Evening Sun.*

A letter from Who's Who, Inc. asked me to fill out an accompanying biographical questionnaire, which I did. The next year, the material I had provided appeared in a volume called *Who's Who in the East,* which seemed to me a sort of vainglorious come-on. Next, I supposed, there'd be a *Who's Who in*

Monroe County. In this instance, I did not return the questionnaire, and explained to the Who's Who people my failure to do so. Recently, I informed them, my name had been transferred from the tiny Scottsville section of the Rochester Telephone Directory to the main Rochester listing, which struck me as a greater distinction than a paragraph in *Who's Who in the East,* or in the West, or in the center of the nation. My relations with the Marquis Company ended on that note, and my name has never since appeared in their publications.

* * * * * * * * * * *

One day, a couple of years after the close of World War II I had a note from C. Lloyd Fisher, of Flemington, New Jersey, telling me that while sojourning at the sanatorium in Clifton Springs, a village thirty-odd miles east of Rochester, he had started reading "Seen and Heard" and liked my little *feuilletons* well enough to take out a subscription to the newspaper.

Subsequently, I now and then had a brief epistle from Mr. Fisher commending something I had written in the column, to which I always gratefully responded. He apparently was a sports fan and urged me to write more about sports. I was not inclined to act on the suggestion. Sports seemed fairly easy for me, but a great many of my readers were women upwards of middle life and I knew that every time I went off on a sporting topic I alienated, for the moment, the members of this devoted sisterhood. But Mr. Fisher liked also the vignettes I often did of family life, elaborations of incidents in our own menage, and these were very popular with the elderly ladies. I used to say that it was a tough way to make a living, exploiting in print our parental trials and marital disquietudes; but if this sort of thing lapsed very long I was sure to be asked, verbatim or in substance, "When you going to have a fight with your wife, or raise hell with your kids?" There was nothing I wrote in the newspaper that had such general appeal.

Several months after the first note had come from Mr. Fisher, he wrote from Clifton Springs where, he explained, he went twice a year to relax from the pressures of his legal practice, inviting my wife and me to dinner the following Saturday night at the Belhurst Club, an elaborate eating place in Geneva, New York, a few miles southeast of Clifton Springs. I was eager to accept. I wanted very much to meet this patron from New Jersey who had swelled out my ego fit to burst.

It is an hour's drive from Scottsville to Geneva, and from the moment we set out the name of our prospective host kept strumming through my head. "C. Lloyd Fisher! C. Lloyd Fisher!" I kept repeating in my mind, nagged by the notion that I had heard the name somewhere before the beginning of my correspondence with its possessor. And suddenly, as we were passing through Canandaigua, I was struck, as was Saul on the road to Damascus, with the light of revelation.

"I've got it," I cried. "I know about Fisher. *C. Lloyd Fisher.* It just came to me."

"What do you know about him?"

"He was the lawyer for the fellow convicted of kidnapping the Lindbergh baby."

"You mean the lawyer for Bruno Hauptmann?"

"Exactly."

My wife moved from me on the seat as though I were a leper. "Turn around," she ordered angrily, "we'll go home. I wouldn't think of accepting hospitality from anyone who defended that unspeakable beast."

Instead, I pressed heavily on the pedal, excited at the prospect of meeting the counsel for the defense in one of the most famous criminal trials in the history of the country.

Mr. Fisher greeted us cordially in the corridor of the Belhurst Club. He bore no resemblance to the monster my wife had conjured up in fancy, and she was reconciled by his graceful bearing, his wit, and his keen intelligence. Besides ourselves, he had assembled eight or ten other guests, all from New York or Clifton Springs. I have a lingering memory of the dinner itself, a sumptuous repast, for the proprietor of Belhurst, an old friend of mine, provided roulette in a locked room upstairs, and the profits from this gaming-house staple allowed him to serve *haute cuisine.* I have, however, no recollection of the other guests, to whom I must have seemed extremely rude, since, from the moment I met our host until we started home that night I persisted in questioning him (I sat next to him at table) about the Hauptmann trial. I was totally absorbed in what he told me.

Mr. Fisher was associated in Hauptmann's defense with Edward J. Reilly, a noted Brooklyn criminal lawyer, and it would be difficult to conceive of two men committed to a more unpopular cause. Before a single juror was selected, Hauptmann already had been adjudged by vast numbers of the public as the fiendish slayer of the infant issue of America's greatest hero. "We were pariahs," Fisher said. "Reilly and I were thought to be beyond the pale of civilized society. I was barred from the church I had previously attended and life-long friends passed me on the street without speaking."

During the trial, Fisher and Reilly received between 4,000 and 5,000 letters daily. Most of these were bitterly accusative, some contained threats to their persons; but there were instances also when the writers encouraged the lawyers' efforts to protect the constitutional rights of the defendant, and persons of this stamp, who desired justice to prevail over public clamor, contributed more than $100,000 to Hauptmann's defense.

The two lawyers quarreled openly over details of legal procedure before the end of the trial. Later, when arrangements were being made to appeal the guilty verdict, the breach was partly closed. But new disagreements soon completely severed their relations, Reilly withdrew from the case and all subsequent efforts to appeal the conviction—and the matter ultimately reached the United States Supreme Court—were directed by Fisher.

Fisher described Reilly as a flamboyant figure who strutted about the Flemington court room dressed like a matinee idol or a Broadway playboy, spats, striped trousers, a fancy coat with a boutonniere in the lapel, and whose patronizing and overweening attitude antagonized the panel of country jurors.

The Brooklyn lawyer had been engaged as defense counsel by a New York newspaper with the idea that if Hauptmann confessed to the crime, Reilly would provide the newspaper with an exclusive story of the confession.

There was no confession. Fisher, who was with the condemned man in the death house, was emphatic about this; and Hauptmann went to the electric chair professing an innocence that numerous legal analysts are not today inclined to discredit.

Reilly's performance as defense counsel won little favor with several of the historians of the Hauptmann trial, whose works I consulted after the dinner party at Belhurst. One of these authors wrote:

"His (Reilly's) reputation as a sharp-witted criminal lawyer was not fully proved at the Flemington Courthouse. . . . In the conduct of the case there were glaring examples which negated his perspicacity . . . Reilly tried the case as though he were playing a game, and he was so objective in his handling of Hauptmann that the defendant, as a person, seemed not to exist for him."

In *The Crime and the Criminal . . . Psychiatric Study of the Lindbergh Case,* Dr. Dudley D. Schoenfeld, in a portrayal of Fisher, wrote in part:

"C. Lloyd Fisher . . . was thoroughly familiar with all of the ramifications of the Lindbergh case. Before he undertook the defense of Hauptmann, he defended John Hughes Curtis (charged with obstructing justice in the Lindbergh investigation) in the Hunterdon County Court House. Well versed in law, he took a subordinate position during the conduct of the Hauptmann trial. It was only after the trial that he emerged as the defendant's sole champion. Throughout the trial his attitude toward Hauptmann bespoke personal conviction of his client's innocence. He was solicitous, courteous, friendly and ever ready to take exception, and on occasion differed openly with his colleague's opinion of the proper conduct of the case. When at one point Mr. Reilly conceded the body of the baby found on the outskirts of Hopewell to be the Lindbergh baby, Mr. Fisher, emotionally affected, was heard to say, 'You are conceding Hauptmann to the electric chair.' He was so disturbed he hurriedly left the court room.

". . . Until the day of Hauptmann's execution he fought tirelessly for his vindication and seemed to sustain a personal loss in the death of a man whose championship was to him of deep significance."

During the period of appeal, Fisher traveled thousands of miles to question persons, many of them prisoners in state and federal prisons, who professed that they knew the real kidnappers or asserted that they had information that would prove Hauptmann innocent.

"I chased down everything," Fisher related, "but my inquiries were all futile. Most of the prisoners I visited hoped to trade spurious information for a pardon."

After Hauptmann had been electrocuted, Fisher was taken to California by Arthur Brisbane, famous editorial writer, for an interview with William Randolph Hearst at the latter's great estate at San Simeon.

"Mr. Hearst was virtually slavering at the mouth, hoping that I would tell him that Hauptmann had confessed to me in the death house," Fisher said. "It would have been a great story for his newspapers and probably a very good fee for me. But he hadn't confessed and I wouldn't perjure myself to say that he had."

Before we left Belhurst my wife, who had heard a good deal of the story the lawyer told me, was not only fully won over to our host, but convinced, as I was also, that C. Lloyd Fisher believed to the marrow of his bones that Bruno Hauptmann had not killed the Lindbergh baby, and ever since that night I have had an uneasy feeling that the state of New Jersey, in this instance, may itself have been guilty of murder.

CHAPTER THIRTY-SIX

I was not by enrollment an America-Firster in the late 1930s and early 1940s, being an inveterate non-joiner with no club, union, American Legion, lodge, church, or any other like affiliation; but my sentiments were strongly with the America First Committee, which wanted to preserve the peace of the nation, as Europe at first inched toward another great war and then plunged into it.

I was opposed to European entanglements. In my newspaper column I frequently departed from the genre writing that was its hallmark (small local incidents, anecdotes that concerned local people, vignettes of family life) to become rhetorical, fancying myself a prophet.

"The newspaper headlines have quieted their screams that the world is on the brink of war, but sage commentators on world affairs write with fatalistic conviction that the greatest world catastrophe it is possible to conceive is imminent. It is a shuddering thing to hear the death march rumbling in the distance and to feel that these bright, clear mid-summer days are merely the lull before the ghastly fires of the *auto-da-fé* are lighted and the torture of tens of millions of people begun.

"Can it be? Is it possible that the forces of destruction are so out of hand that no check can be given them? Must one day soon a falling bomb burst upon an unprotected city or a high explosive shell gash a pretty countryside, flinging the quivering, red-wet fragments of men, women, and children into the air? Is this the beautiful necessity that gives meaning to life, inspiration to human hearts, purpose to human action?"

I went in quite extensively for this sort of thing, and my employer, Frank Gannett, whose name today is identified with the most numerous group of newspapers in America, approved of what I wrote.

Mr. Gannett mistrusted President Roosevelt, and I professedly did too. He also despised the president, and made a strenuous, misbegotten, and expensive effort to gain the Republican nomination and oppose the incumbent's run for a second term. He failed, of course. The convention pretty well ignored him, giving the nod to the Barefoot Boy from Wall Street, Wendell Willkie.

I continued my pleas for strict neutrality after Great Britain and France declared war on Germany, and I persisted in this vein when a shooting war succeeded months of what was called the "phoney war," and was castigated for my pains by ardent Anglophiles and Francophiles, who dubbed me Herr Clune and defined me a "Nazi at heart."

With Hitler's armies in seeming all-conquering momentum, there was a growing disposition for an American expeditionary force; and raising, as I said, my tiny voice in protest, I quoted the president's promise to American mothers and fathers in a campaign speech in Boston, ". . . I have said this before, but I shall say it again and again: your boys are not going to be sent into a foreign war." I don't know how President Roosevelt suffered, but my stand, supported by some readers, was fiercely attacked by others. I didn't mind. The boss, a sort of America-Firster himself, was with me; and I felt complimented when a couple of college history professors took pen in hand to roast me to a turn in column-long Phillippics in Letters to the Editor.

I held staunchly to my guns until one afternoon in early winter, my parents having driven out from Rochester for Sunday supper, I went down to Byron Losee's drugstore for a quart of ice cream for dessert. Scottsville was an independent rural community at the time, not a place to bed-down city workers, and Losee's drugstore was as indigenous to the village as the watertank, the feed mill, Will White's barbershop, and the coal office and general store of the brothers Keyes. It was also the only place in town that sold ice cream.

Byron Losee was a quiet, sedentary man, who appeared to pass half his life, or better than twelve house a day, in his store. He looked over the marble counter with a grave face, and his hand trembled as he reached for the ice cream scoop.

"We're at war," he said, seeming to sense my ignorance.

"At war?"

"They bombed Hawaii."

"Who?" I asked incredulously.

"The Japs."

"I can't believe it. What part of Hawaii?"

"Place called Pearl Harbor. Our navy's gone. Blown up, sunk in the sea."

I hurried home with the tragic news. None of us was a radio addict. My parents listened mostly to Amos and Andy; our favorite program was Rudy Vallee, singing "Vagabond Lover," or one of his current hits. Now we tuned in full blast, and every feverish word we heard added to the already Cyclopean dimension of the Hawaiian disaster.

I remembered a column I had written on Japan in 1931 when her army had overrun Manchuria and the leaders had set up a puppet state in that country.

"The militarists have believed for years that eventually America must, as they express it, 'have trouble with Japan.' I have been told by professional soldiers that the 'trouble' was imminent just prior to the World War (1914–1918), but first the spectacle of America mobilizing a vast expeditionary force with surprising speed, and later the Tokyo earthquake, temporarily removed from the Japanese mind thoughts of open hostility with the United States."

At another place in the column, telling of the indifference of the average American to what was happening in the Far East, where a raised petard might blow us all into another World War, I quoted the man in the street, "What do we care if all the Chinks and slant-eyed Japs and red Russians start a melee. Hell, maybe we can sell 'em some goods for their war."

Well, I knew Rochester junk dealers who had made a

good deal of money selling tons and tons and tons of scrap iron and other substances that might be wrought into military projectiles to Japan; and I thought of my teen-age sons, soon to be eligible for military service, who might become targets for Japanese missiles made from materials that made the junk dealers rich.

If the military and naval people considered Japan a potential enemy in the years that immediately preceded World War I, the circumstances that deteriorated the relations between that country and the United States in the months immediately preceding the Pearl Harbor attack, would seem to have displayed Japan as a greater menace than ever.

President Roosevelt's refusal to confer with the Japanese emperor and this country's insistence that Japan clear out of Indochina and China was too much for the pride and arrogance of a people who for centuries had believed in the infallibility of their military might.

Japan joined the Axis, quit the League of Nations; and in a stratagem that American military experts now consider brilliant—for all of President Roosevelt's declamation of its infamy—devastated, in a sneak air attack, a fleet of American warships idling about Pearl Harbor, its guard down, as fair game as sitting ducks on a mill pond.

The president very much wanted us in the war despite his rhetorical promise to American mothers and fathers about their stay-at-home sons, and he had his wish that fateful December Sunday.

"He lied the American people into a war because he could not lead them into it," cried Clare Boothe Luce; and there are critics today who believe the president deliberately ignored foreknowledge of the Pearl Harbor attack in order to hasten our inevitable participation in the European conflict.

Polio had rendered the commander in chief of our armed forces a wheel chair invalid. In one of my anti-war columns I applauded Ernest Hemingway's pronouncement: "No man or group of men incapable of fighting or exempt from fighting should in any way be given the power, no matter how gradually it is given to them, to put this country or any other country into war."

But now we were at war, soon to be in up to our armpits. I no longer could oppose our participation in "herd slaughter," and became, in my column, a flaming patriot. One of my sons, whose various physical disorders made him a draft reject, went into a war plant. My wife joined the Red Cross Motor Corps and became an airplane spotter on the roof of the Scottsville schoolhouse. She had a uniform, a card that certified her for service, and a key to the school. Two or three nights a week she let herself into the basement of the deserted building, ascended to the third story, made it through a trap door to a cupola on the roof to scan the night sky for enemy planes that might dump a bomb load on Keyes's store and coal office, Will White's barbershop, or the Greek's saloon, about the only strategic targets our small community had.

Our oldest son left Manlius School to join a parachute combat regiment which helped, with an air drop, to reclaim Corregidor; and one of his younger brothers, after two years at the Hill School, became a member of the Fourth Marines.

We learned presently that both sons were on the West Coast, waiting to be shipped to the Pacific, but the names of the embarkation stations were withheld from us. Then, late one morning, I had a call at the newspaper office from a San Diego, California operator, who asked me to call a certain San Diego number at precisely 12:30 P.M.

Our oldest son had been in service several months longer than the Marine, and I was sure that he now had his "orders," and it was he to whom I was to speak. If that were the case, I wanted his mother also to have a chance to say good-bye. I left the office, hurried home to Scottsville, and attempted at the prescribed hour to call the San Diego number. The channels were clogged to Chicago. There was a ten minute delay. Then the report, "The man who was waiting for your call has left. We can't locate him."

I appealed to the Home Service of the Red Cross, who reported, to my astonishment, that it was not the paratrooper who had awaited my call, but the Marine; and the Marine had gone; his new address, care "Fleet Postoffice, San Francisco."

I related the incident in the column, gave a brief biographical sketch of the youth and wrote, in closing:

"At this point I am not thinking of the Four Freedoms or the Atlantic Charter or the emancipation of the subjected peoples of Europe and Asia, nor of the more perfect world which the heavy duty thinkers, whose guess is no better than mine, predict will result from the war. What I am thinking, with a sick feeling deep in the pit of my stomach, is that a son of mine may now be well into the Pacific and that he went without a chance to say good-bye. I'm just one of the ordinary run-of-the-mill little guys in America with a kid gone to war, and the welfare and well-being of that kid is the most important thing in the world to me. It is because so many of us are in the same boat, beset by the same concerns, that I have dared to exploit so personal a matter as this to such length. And yet, what else could I have written today?"

If this seems bathos today, it wasn't during the war years. Lafayette R. Blanchard, managing editor of the newspaper, who had one issue—a son just turning draft age—came to me, his voice atremble. "Heinie," he said, dead sincere at the moment, "You've done it today. You don't need to do another column this year."

It was then late April. I kept on working.

My contribution to the war effort was negligible, but I did have a vicarious sense of participation because of a voluminous correspondence carried on with service men from the Rochester area who were stationed all over the globe. I was complimented by their confidences; I sympathized with their complaints; and I was eager to comply with their occasional requests.

In India, Rochester soldiers were engaged in heated debate with compatriots from New York City, insisting that a ring of sweetened dough fried in deep fat was a fried cake, a term discredited by the metropolitan polemists, who contended that the only definition was doughnut. Would I decide? A company in the Aleutians had no reading matter. One appeal in the column was enough; they received a boatload of magazines and books. An Air Force navigator in England bet his tentmate a month's pay that Joe DiMaggio had hit safely in fifty-four consecutive games, not fifty-six; I was sorrowfully constrained to tell him he had lost the bet. That sort of thing was common; but nothing I did was as important as my wife's driving for the Red Cross, no matter what her contribution to the war effort on the schoolhouse roof.

I worried, though. I worried unremittingly about our two sons. Besides my newspaper job, I had become the "Voice" for the Eastman Kodak Company's weekly radio program, a very pleasant and remunerative engagement but exacting, and I was writing a book. I was underweight, twitchy, and I had developed a gastric complaint. The village doctor, no great medical academican but a little fellow with sound good sense, who practiced without a receptionist, a medical secretary, or a nurse—who received patients in his shirt sleeves, his suspenders showing, and who could competently deliver a baby or help a farmer deliver a calf—sent me, when his own remedies failed, to a famous Midwest clinic. "You'll have some fun, anyway," he promised. "It'll be an experience."

It was.

I was a walking patient, not confined to a bed, and the procedure was solely investigatory. It was assembly line medicine. I was given a metal device with a number, a sort of king-size baggage check, and sent on my way. I was hustled from one dimly-lit crypt to another and subjected in each to some small or large indignity. I was poked and prodded mercilessly. In one station, I was asked to drink a tepid, gruely mixture which tasted like melted down tennis balls, while dispassionate scientists observed by x-ray the act of ingestion. I was laid out flat on cold slabs and stood against others. Someone would shout through the crepuscular gloom, "Take a deep breath . . . hold it . . . breathe." I tried, on a couple of occasions, to engage an operative in social chat. No chance. "Next!" he'd bellow, and shove me toward the door.

The last stop on the line was a chamber larger than the others, well lighted, with a cot along one wall. When I closed the door, I was confronted by a large lady in starched, spotless white, who had a determined jaw and very much of a no-nonsense air. She held a red hose in her hand. It wasn't a garden hose and it wasn't a fire hose. It was shorter and thinner than either, and it had at one end a metal gadget, like a sinker on a fish line.

"Good morning," I said pleasantly.

The salutation was unheeded.

"Here," she said, attempting to hand me the hose, "swallow that."

It was an incredulous suggestion.

"But really," I protested, "I couldn't. That's impossible. I've never swallowed a hose in my life."

"Well," she said grittily, "you're going to swallow this one."

And as I gaped in wonder, realizing that she actually meant it, she shoved the thing into my mouth and tried to force it past my epiglottis.

We grappled. She was an expert at judo. She tried various holds, and one finally put me on my back on the cot. But in these exertions I disgorged the hose and saw it writhing on the white sheet like a horrid red snake. I bit her, but she snatched her hand away before I drew blood. She put her knee on my chest, which forced open my mouth, and she got the hose into my gullet, this time for a sounding. The metal gadget at the end went clear to the pit of my stomach. She worked a pump at her end of the hose and brought up, I know not what. Perhaps the residue of a dry martini.

We were engaged in combat more than half an hour. I was told later that the ordinary hose-swallower managed the trick in four or five minutes. When I left I tried to make amends for my unseemly behavior. "Have a nice day," I called to the lady, whose immaculate starchiness had become considerably rumpled. There was no response.

The final diagnosis was that I had a duodenal lesion, an ulcer. I named it Llewellyn for no sound reason, and now and then discussed it in the column. Readers told me about theirs and we exchanged symptoms. When the stress caused by overwork and war worries relaxed, the thing subsided; presently it went clean away. Breakfast has always been my banner meal. Recovered in health, I returned to my pre-ulcer menu: orange juice, bacon and eggs, toast, cereal with cream, two doughnuts, coffee and a plate of prunes. A physician spoke to me warningly about cholesterol, but I was confused about the term. I thought he was talking about a fear of being confined in narrow places. Claustrophobia!

CHAPTER THIRTY-SEVEN

God grant that it be averted, but in the event of another World War, the civilian population of the United States will know nothing of the immunity from terror and attack it enjoyed in the interval between Pearl Harbor and VJ Day. With the arsenals of the world bursting with nuclear weapons of "improved" intensity, the universal devastation these devices of scientific savagery will wreak will make Hiroshima and Nagasaki seem like parochial disasters. All will be in the same fix; one may run, but there'll be no place to hide.

During the war, my wife was sometimes scared climbing through the nighttime Scottsville schoolhouse to her vigil on the roof, but she never once saw anything remotely resembling an enemy plane. She had a lively time with her fellow volunteers in the Red Cross Motor Corps, and the experience made an interesting topic for her bridge group. We knew few privations. I worried, once our sons joined the colors; but the feverish activities of the war years were an anodyne for my concern; my economy improved with a fine outside job, and there were occasions of notable interest.

I went frequently to New York and always returned with enough material for a couple of columns. I was assiduous in collecting names of persons of some prominence, which I eagerly dropped into "Seen and Heard." Subscribers seemed to delight in reading of the exploits of an apple knocker on the Main Stem, and I did my best to gratify their interest. I had a few friends in New York who were able to open doors that ordinarily would have been closed to me and bring me into contact with people remote from my ken.

One morning I went down to the headquarters of the Third Naval District at 90 Church Street, Manhattan, to visit an old friend, Captain John T. Tuthill.

Captain Tuthill had originated on Menlo Place, the second street south off of Mt. Hope Avenue from my native Linden Street. He had left Rochester many years before to publish a newspaper in Patchogue, Long Island and to plug—at every opportunity—the United States Navy, in which he had served on a ship during the first World War, served as a reservist during the interval between the wars, and was, at the time of my visit, publicity director for the Third Naval District.

He was a bright, urbane, cocky man, whose devotion to the Navy, begun in youth, continued with unflagging zeal throughout his life. He was not of great stature, but he had a very definite air of presence, of command. I was fond of him. I admired his poise and self-assurance.

Some time before I called upon him, Tuthill had directed a huge show in Madison Square Garden for a naval benefit. In this, as in other promotional enterprises, he had had the assistance of Hollywood stars, leading Broadway players, such celebrated journalists as Walter Winchell and Ed Sullivan, and numerous other well known men and women. His range was wide. He was a friend of Bernard Baruch, the so-called advisor to presidents; and Richard Aldrich, theatrical producer and husband of the glamorous English actress, Gertrude Lawrence, was one of his uniformed aides.

My stay in the captain's office was brief. The place was feverish with activity. Our conversation was continually interrupted by the intrusion of a secretary or an aide, and the telephone seemed to ring every three or four minutes. Once he spoke into the mouthpiece in a tone considerably less stern than the language of a battleship's bridge. He was saying, "Yes, yes, Minnie, dear . . . OK. . . . Yes, Minnie, darling. . . . At seven. I'm bringing a friend."

I knew, of course (since he was a solid family man) that these endearing terms were merely rhetorical; that they represented the floridity of Broadway and the theater to which, in recent months, Tuthill had been widely exposed. I listened, nonetheless, with curiosity. He finished, replaced the phone in its cradle, and gave me a sharp glance. And now it was the captain speaking.

"Put on your best suit," he ordered tersely, "and report at the St. Regis tomorrow night. At seven."

"But why?" I asked.

"Never mind. I'll meet you there."

I intended to persist in my inquiry, but the door opened and an aide entered with a sheaf of papers for a signature. "Yes sir," I said meekly, and departed.

I arrived at the St. Regis at the appointed hour the next evening, if not a glass of fashion, as close to it as I could manage. Captain Tuthill was prompt, as a navy man should be. We had barely settled in the lobby when who should appear but Mrs. Vincent Astor.

Known to her intimates as Minnie, Mrs. Astor was the eldest of the three married and marrying daughters of the noted Boston brain surgeon, Dr. Harvey Cushing. Her sister Betsy, divorced from James Roosevelt, the president's son, married the multi-multi-millionaire, John Hay (Jock) Whitney, and Barbara, a third sister, after separating from Stanley G. Mortimer, Jr., became the wife of William S. Paley, chairman of the two billion dollar Columbia Broadcasting System. The adage was, "the Cushing sisters done well."

A slim, lively, gracious young woman, the former Mary Cushing had assisted Captain Tuthill in various projects that were part of his tour of duty and the two were close friends. They had business to discuss, but this was quickly finished and we adjourned to one of the hotel restaurants for dinner. I was curious about Mrs. Astor's husband, who had inherited one of the great American fortunes. I learned that he was an ardent yachtsman and that he had lent his luxuriously appointed yacht, *Nourmahal,* which was almost as large as a trans-Atlantic liner, to the navy, in which he served as a non-combat officer. He was also, Mrs. Astor told me, a railroad buff. He had a miniature railroad in Bermuda, with small locomotives which he operated himself, and she displayed, as a token of this hobby, a gold oblong cigarette case with a train of cars delineated in diamonds on the outside of the upper lid.

When the check came, the captain and I made a pretense of struggling for it, but Mrs. Astor snatched it from our hands.

"Poof," she said. "Don't be silly, boys. After all, Vincent owns the joint."

It was true. He did own the St. Regis at the time; and I went home with the incident vividly in mind and wrote a piece for the paper, "The Check for Mrs. Astor."

A week or so later, trouble developed in our septic tank, and I went to the old fellow in the village who had installed the tank to ask him what to do about it. He suggested that what he called the leach bed was plugged and that if I got a grubhoe and opened a channel that led to the bed of the old Genesee Valley Canal, about two hundred yards below our property, everything would be fine and dandy. This was Sunday afternoon, and the old fellow didn't want to abandon his siesta.

I got a grubhoe and struggled through brambles and knee high grass to the canal bed. It was an early July Sunday of greenhouse heat and sultry to boot. I removed my shirt and worked in my undershirt. Gnats and other unpleasant things attacked me. I was hot and soiled. I plied the grubhoe fiercely. Then, suddenly, came revealment.

What, I angrily asked myself, was I doing around that mephitic channel, sweating like a coolie, when only a few days before I had dined with Mrs. Astor? It seemed an abysmal indignity; I flung the grubhoe aside and went up to the house to bathe, though the bath water backed up in the tub owing to the plugged leach bed. And I wrote about the experience in the paper.

A few days after the little squib appeared in "Seen and Heard," I had a note from New York on heavily monogrammed paper.

"Dear Mr. Clune: I'm so glad I helped you open your sewer pipe. Mary Astor."

Of course, I'll never make *Burke's Peerage*. But thanks to Jack Tuthill, I got awfully close to the *Social Register*.

* * * * * * * * * * *

J. R. Cominsky, an old friend of mine, who had left the city editorship of the *Democrat and Chronicle* for the *New York Times* and left the *Times* to become the publisher of *the Saturday Review,* arranged an interview for me, during one of my wartime visits to New York, with a man I very much wanted to meet.

Late one afternoon, following Cominsky's instructions, I rang Somerset Maugham, the English novelist and playwright, on the house phone of the old Ritz-Carlton Hotel, and a voice with a pronounced British accent said, "Will you come straight up to six eleven, please?"

Six hundred eleven was not a hotel room, but an elaborate suite, and the living room into which I was shown was as handsomely furnished as the living room of a gracious private home. There was a highboy, a large sofa, comfortable chairs, a commodious writing table. A graceful vase that held long-stemmed roses reposed on a coffee stand. There were interesting pictures on the walls, which I learned were the possessions of the occupant; and books, books, books, everywhere.

A young man with a broad, pale forehead and the aspect of an intellectual was leaving. "This is the bearer of a distinguished name, Henry James," Mr. Maugham said, but made no other comment.

Somerset Maugham was a figure in my Pantheon. I thought him one of the great story tellers, and story tellers are the writers I fancy most. He never won the Nobel Prize in literature, the double-dome critics sometimes chilled him off, but the reading public held him in a collective embrace. The reading public bought something like 30,000,000 copies of his books, a figure likely to provoke the sneering epithet, "rank commercialism," from some existentialist poet at Prairie View A and M or an avant-garde novelist with an untidy beard, a dirty T shirt, a pair of broken sneakers, and no readers in a Greenwich Village tea room.

I had heard that Maugham had a slight impediment in his speech, and this was at once apparent. He was courteous enough, but not enthusiastic about our meeting. He suggested a martini and tried to ring room service. There was a delay. "Th-th-this is a nice family hotel," he stutteringly complained after half a minute, "but the service is lousy;" and he disappeared into another room and reappeared with a concoction of his own.

I felt privileged being with a man I greatly admired, though I had no sense of the abject servility once displayed by the late Alexander Woollcott. Meeting Maugham by chance in a crowded elevator, fat Alex dropped to his knees, grasped the author's hand, called "Master! Master!" to the novelist's considerable embarrassment.

The martini my host prepared was excellent, but it failed to bring us into rapport and I was wondering what sort of a story I might obtain from this rather difficult man, when I touched a responsive chord.

I had been reading *The Razor's Edge,* the latest Maugham novel. It wasn't up to *Of Human Bondage,* which I considered the author's masterpiece; it hadn't interested me as much as *Cakes and Ale* or *The Moon and Sixpence.* It was still, it struck me, a very sound performance.

I told Mr. Maugham I had been going slowly with the novel, that I had been more than a week at it. And I added, "I like to sip it and enjoy everything about it. I am reading it as I suppose a connoisseur would sip a fine brandy. I'll be very sorry to finish it."

Slouched in a half-somnolent attitude on the sofa, my host came suddenly alive. He fixed me with an alert and interested eye.

"You know, Mr. Clune," he said, in his halting speech, "You have paid me a very real compliment."

I wondered why, and asked him. He tossed a hand disdainfully.

"I am always being exclaimed over by some woman at a dinner party," he said. "Oh, Mr. Maugham, I picked up your book last night and couldn't put it down until I finished it.' That probably means that she picked it up after dinner and read it until two o'clock in the morning. I read twenty books to obtain the material for one chapter of *The Razor's Edge*—the chapter on mysticism. I thought about the book for years and spent a year writing it. And some damn silly woman thinks she has complimented me, telling me she read it in one night."

At the top of his bent, some years before my meeting with him, Maugham had often been called the finest stylist writing English prose. And shortly before my visit I read an editorial in the New York *Daily News,* suggesting that those who wanted to learn to write correct and economical English, study the master, Somerset Maugham.

But Maugham, I learned from questioning him, learned from such masters of English prose as Joseph Addison, Jonathan Swift, Edmund Burke, and the essays of John Dryden.

"I worked my guts out," he said. "I studied the great exponents of English prose word for word. If I was going to spend my life learning to write, I could only believe the task worthwhile if I considered literature one of the most important of human pursuits. Early, I learned the value of rewriting and re-rewriting. Today, writing is no easier for me than it was when I started. I have to work just as hard."

Maugham was a successful playwright before he turned to the novel, which he thought more worthy of his serious efforts. He produced many splendid examples of the modern short story. One of the longest of these, *Rain,* when adapted for the stage, gave a sort of immortality to the dazzlingly gifted Jeanne Eagels. He practiced in the great tradition of the essay.

He made more money stringing one word after another than any other author (up until his time) with the possible exception of George Bernard Shaw, and delighting in the amenities of life, he was happy to be able to enjoy them. Posterity, which remembers only authors who have been read extensively, will pass final judgment on his talents. For my part, my hour in the Ritz with the master, as I, like the *Daily News* and Alexander Woollcott, thought of Maugham, was one of the most interesting interviews I ever had as a newspaper reporter. The resultant piece brought a gracious note from its subject, which I cherish to this day.

* * * * * * * * * * *

Our two sons returned from the war unharmed physically, if needing some psychological adjustment to fit them for the resumption of civilian life. We had beaten a very desperate game. We hugged ourselves for joy. Untempered at first, our exultations were soon quieted by the sad reflection that our neighbors and closest Scottsville friends had suffered the personal tragedy of war that we so fortunately had escaped.

Colonel Carey H. Brown and his wife Derryle, who occupied a handsomely decorated farmhouse three or four hundred yards south of our property, and the Eugene D. Browns, who lived in the family homestead a similar distance to the north, each lost a son in the war, and the Carey Browns knew a second bereavement when their younger son, a veteran of both the World and the Korean Wars, died in a post-war Air Force plane crash.

Nick Brown, the issue of the Eugene Brown's, a handsome, brilliant young man, assigned, because of his academic talents to a military language school, was snatched from his studies in time for the Battle of the Bulge, thrown into the breach to help stem the onset of the Nazi hordes, and died in the unpracticed role of an infantryman.

The two sons of Colonel and Mrs. Brown, like their father, were West Point graduates. Carey H., Jr., the older by a couple of years, commissioned in the Field Artillery when he left the Academy, transferred to the Air Force and served, as did his younger brother, Alston L. Brown, as a fighter pilot in Europe. Both were recipients of the Air Medal and the Distinguished Flying Cross. After numerous air encounters, Carey Brown was assigned to experiment with a new type of army plane and died when the plane crash-landed on an air strip in England. That was in the second last year of the war. In the last year, Alston Brown was shot down over the German lines and held prisoner until VE Day.

My wife and I never knew young Carey Brown. He and his brother were cadets at the Military Academy when, in 1941, his parents moved to Scottsville from Rochester, where the family had lived ever since Colonel Brown retired from the regular army. The Scottsville property included, besides the fine old farmhouse, 150 acres of Genesee Valley pasture land. It was the Colonel's intention to operate a dairy farm as a sideline to his position as manager of Engineering and Manufacturing Services for the Eastman Kodak Company. The project was delayed several years. After Pearl Harbor, the Browns ended a brief Scottsville residence and moved to Kingsport, Tennessee, where Colonel Brown served as an engineer for the Holston Ordinance Works.

Our friendship with the Browns began when they resettled in Scottsville after the war, and it was then that we came to know and admire Alston, who, with his attractive wife and small children, occasionally visited his parents' dairy farm. He had been a lively and extremely popular youth in his high school days in Rochester, and his wartime exploits—he had flown a fighter plane in the Korean War, and received a second Air Medal—his handsomeness, his style, and his spirit, enveloped him in a sort of Promethean aura. He served in the Air Attache's Office in Japan after the Korean War, later was assigned to duty in the United States, advanced to colonel, and given command of the 56th Fighter Squadron at Wright-Patterson Air Base, in Dayton, Ohio.

* * * * * * * * * * *

One night, a few days before Christmas 1956, Mrs. Brown and my wife drove in our car to a theater in Rochester. Later that evening, Colonel Brown stopped to pick up his wife. We had a few minutes together before the women returned. A serious, soft-spoken man, of quiet charm and precise deportment, the Colonel was in uncommonly high spirits. The next day he and Mrs. Brown were driving to Dayton for a holiday visit with Alston and his family. It would be his first opportunity, he said, to play Santa Claus for his grandchildren. They would be up early to pack the car with gifts and jams and preserved fruits and other products from the "farm," as they referred to their Scottsville property. When the women returned, Mrs. Brown, much more voluble than her husband, expansively previewed the expedition of the morrow.

We waved the Browns good-bye, adding the usual holiday salutations and remarked in the morning that they had a fine clear day for the Dayton journey.

At dinner that night we tuned in the radio news. The announcer reported in a swift, unvaried monotone various local happenings; told that Oswego, a small city northeast on Lake Ontario had suffered a crippling snow storm; went on in the same even, undemonstrative voice intended, I suppose, to certify his reportorial objectivity,

"Lieutenant Colonel Alston L. Brown, son of Colonel and Mrs. Carey H. Brown, of Scottsville, was killed today when his Air Force fighter plane exploded near Dayton, Ohio . . ."

There was more, of course, to the report than that. We were stunned. Horrified. "Turn it off," my wife cried. "Oh, what a terrible, terrible thing to happen!"

Alston and his wife, Jean, had visited our house late in the summer. They impressed us then, as they had at other meetings, as two of the most spirited and attractive young people we knew.

All that night we agonized over the Browns, whose gay expedition to celebrate Christmas with their son and his family would have such a tragic denouement.

The elder Browns did not return to Scottsville at once. There was the sad business of the obsequies. The remains of Carey, Jr., had been brought from England and interred in the West Point Cemetery, and now the body of his younger brother was laid in that hallowed acreage. Colonel and Mrs. Brown were back at their farm two days before Christmas. They had many friends in Rochester who attempted to relieve their sorrow, but under such circumstances flowers, notes, and oral expressions of sympathy and condolence seemed woefully inadequate. My wife said, "We'll have them for Christmas dinner."

It did not seem to me the proper thing to do, since the Browns' presence might damp the spirit of our own family's celebration. She insisted and she was eminently right. They came. There were no tears, no demonstration of any kind. Before dinner, the Colonel and I, leaving the others, went into a room that is more or less my own preserve. I mixed a drink. No mention was made at first of the subject that preoccupied the thoughts of us both. In the end, it could be avoided no longer.

I knew superficially what had happened. The young

colonel, flying a new type of aircraft, discovered a flaw in the intricate mechanism and radioed that he was coming down. He was sure he could make the airstrip. He was told to delay his descent and make one more circle of the field, but the plane was losing altitude, and before he could parachute the engine exploded.

I said to Colonel Brown, "Alston had a wonderful life. He did the sort of thing he loved and for which he was eminently fitted. He made a great success of life."

"Yes," the colonel said slowly, "they told me out there that his was one of the very top commands in the entire service. We are proud of that. He was only in his thirties."

"But he lived so fully," I persisted. "So many men carry on to a great age, but only putter through life. Your son lived every minute. Lived brilliantly. He savored the great experiences."

The grave, quiet-voiced man who sat with me waited a moment before he spoke again. "But it may have been that his death was unnecessary. That his life was wasted, in the end." And he told me that he had heard from sources that seemed exact that the reason his son was told to delay his descent was because another airplane was idling on the landing strip. This was in violation of a rigid order that an aircraft touching down be instantly removed from the runway. In the few seconds that elapsed before the field was cleared, Colonel Alston Brown was killed.

I had not known of this before, and burst out in angry denunciation.

"If that had happened to one of my sons," I cried, "I'd be bitter against the person guilty of that criminal neglect until I died. I'd never get over it. I'd shout the name of the culprit from the housetops."

The colonel shook his head.

"No Henry, that wouldn't be the thing to do," he said. "My son's gone. I can't bring him back. But why—why by publicizing a thing like that, ruin the life of another young man?"

This was Christmas Day. And this man sitting in my home, in the greatness of his spirit, personified what, to my perhaps limited understanding, is one of the great lessons Christ taught. Charity, and forgiveness, and love of one's fellow men.

For God sent not His Son into the world to condemn the world, but that the world through Him might be saved.

CHAPTER THIRTY-EIGHT

I was born in early February 1890. If my life had been lived in reverse my natal day would have come less than ten years after Cornwallis surrendered at Yorktown and the thirteen colonies became the United States of America. Less than thirty years before I was born human beings were being sold as chattel in this "land of the free and home of the brave." In my youth an ice cream soda cost five cents, you could send first class mail any place in the United States for a two cent stamp, buy a newspaper for a penny.

One day, a few years ago, Mrs. Harry Moss, dining at our house in Scottsville, told quite casually about her brother walking on the moon, and picking up stones, or whatever lies on the surface of the moon, as lunar samples. After dinner we went out in the yard and looked up at the moon. It seemed awfully far away, but Mrs. Moss wasn't fooling about her brother padding about on it. He is Charles Conrad, Jr., who commanded one of the Apollo outer space missions.

"There's nothing seems at first so wonderful, so great,
But that man's wonder will not presently abate . . ."

I saw the introduction of the safety bicycle, the automobile, and the airplane. As a boy in high school, when I wanted to do my homework at night, I struck a match, turned a switch on a wall bracket, and ignited a gas jet. I recall the first commercial motion picture, *The Great Train Robbery,* shown as an after-piece in a vaudeville theater; and the excitement in our home when a telephone was installed; radio and television were lesser miracles.

About the time I was born, horses stopped hauling street cars through my native city of Rochester and the transit system was gradually electrified. Later—years later, and at a time when I was well out of knee pants—they motorized the fire department and the thrilling spectacle of a brilliant red pumper, in mad career behind a galloping three-horse hitch, passed into limbo, along with the canvas-topped circus, the family farmer, the steam locomotive, and the hunchback whale.

Nothing, someone has said, is as immutable as change; and it may be that the changes that have taken place during the time I have endured on this earth have been more numerous and more radical than the changes that occurred in any similar period of recorded history.

I remember very well the turn of the century, and the hope and promise the transition encouraged. It was a new age, an epoch of enlightenment.

All, of course, was not well with the world; there were vast wrongs that no millenium would correct. We were told by missionaries that natives died from lack of food in the streets of Calcutta and Bombay, and we heard of fearful privations in other places remote from our ken. In our own land there were great abuses still to be corrected: gross exploitation of labor, sweat shops, unsafe mines, mills and factories in which workers were held in serfdom. There were areas in our great cities where men, women, and children were huddled in habitations of filth, squalor, and festering depravity. There were ravaging epidemics that medical science had not yet managed to control. The black man, enfranchised by constitutional amendment, was, in point of fact, a second class citizen. But new attitudes were forming on all of these matters and the public conscience appeared to have become more sensitive. Laws were being enacted to prohibit the employment in industry of children of tender years, lynchers were being prosecuted, there was a growing sentiment for prison reform and the abolishment of capital punishment. The notion that the brutal and casual infliction of pain and death was an evil requisite of society had been abandoned.

And there were new attitudes about armed conflict. Very early in the new century President Theodore Roosevelt mediated a treaty that ended the short-lived Russian-Japanese

War, and the feeling was that henceforth civilized nations would find means other than mass slaughter to resolve their political differences. It was a high hope. It persisted fourteen years into the epoch of enlightenment. Then an archduke of whom most of us had never heard, and his wife, were slain by assassin's bullets in a place called Sarajevo, obscure to me, and I am sure to my Linden Street neighbors, and soon Europe was enflamed in a war of such savagery that 100,000 men might die in a single battle.

Since then—since the "guns of August" (1914) boomed their dreadful devastation, man (or the so-called human race) has killed more than 100,000,000 of his own kind. He has managed this Cyclopean slaughter by the employment of every device for exquisite torture and death his genius for gadgetry has managed to contrive. Today, the epidemic of violence that rages through society, and is reflected in our addiction to the axe murders and gang shootings that compose so much of the entertainment in our movie houses and on TV, conduces to the notion that violence is our desired way of life—and death. And those dreaded piles, the London Tower and the French Bastille seem now, compared with Auschwitz and Buchenwald, almost suitable for human habitation.

Some time ago, a group of psychiatrists explored the subject of violence in a two-day seminar in Rochester, but how effective their conclusions were in lessening the incidence of violence I never learned. The psychiatrists were concerned with the parochial aspects of violence. To explore the subject fully, investigators would need to look beyond the mugger in the street or the rapist in the park or the murderer in an alley and penetrate the chanceries of great nations. For in these august halls decisions to make war are taken. And today, with arsenals bursting with nuclear weapons, war can be such a sovereign act of violence that both sides may be liquidated in a Pyrrhic victory and removed from the stage of history.

In the very early days of the Christian experiment, the Roman, Seneca, said, "We are mad, not only individually, but nationally. We check manslaughter and isolate murderers; but what of war and the much vaunted crime of slaughtering whole peoples?"

EPILOGUE

Our house rests on a rise, and I delight on a soft summer evening, before the glow of the sun dims out in the west, to sit on the terrace out front and gaze across the Genesee Valley. The prospect is broad and delightfully varied. There are verdant swales and wooded uplands and now and then a cultivated field, and not, in immediate view, a single standing man-made structure.

On such occasions, sitting alone in the dead silence that often prevails at that hour, all sorts of speculations pass through my mind. The other evening, my recollection went back a long way to the incident of a man I knew only slightly crossing the aisle of a New York Central parlor car and taking a vacant chair next to mine.

He said peremptorily, without a preliminary remark, "I often wonder about you."

"Wonder about me? About what?"

"I've been reading your column for years. You write about all sorts of famous and successful people. Don't you ever have a desire to emulate them? Are you content, meeting those kinds of people, just to stay here—a small city newspaper reporter? Don't they provoke your envy?"

Envy! I mentally mouthed the word a moment. Then said, "You know, it's a funny thing. For the life of me, I can't think of anyone I really envy."

"You're kidding."

I assured him that I wasn't, but I didn't expatiate on

my position. I didn't tell him that I hadn't always been exempt from that execrable passion; that as a youth I was once anguished by it.

On Gregory Street, three streets from ours, lived a friend of mine named Fred, whose father was a bartender but who seemed more devoted to the avocation of breeding fighting cocks than to the job that provided his livelihood. His family lived wretchedly. It was said that Fred's mother was hard pressed to put food on the table for Fred, her other issue, and herself, while her husband indulged his game chickens with *haute cuisine* that included cakes made with suet and liver and half a dozen eggs. He kept the birds in a shed out back that was equipped with crude apparatus to exercise them for strength and agility. Poor as the family fared, Fred had two dogs. They were mongrel, mangy, half-famished creatures, but they were Fred's pride and joy and I desperately envied his possession.

I had ice skates, a flexible flyer, and a small red bicycle with wooden handlebars, but more than anything in the world I wanted a dog. My mother, who was usually susceptible to my entreaties, on this issue was inflexible. She was a meticulous housekeeper. She disliked dogs or any other pet that might disrupt her domestic arrangements.

Then a miracle occurred. Christmas morning I was awakened by a faint yipping in the cellar and ran down to find in a cage contrived of chicken wire and an upturned laundry table a bull terrier my father had bought me in unusual defiance of my mother's domestic ordinance. He was all white except for a black patch over his left eye. He seemed a thing of surpassing wonder. I was enraptured. I have never since had a gift of any kind that excited such ecstacy.

I named him Rip. The tag symbolized his habits and temper. He was a lively and often intractable puppy. Although forbidden the front of the house, he managed now and then to invade it. He destroyed my mother's prize sofa pillow. He had the mischievous conceit, if he succeeded in one of his forays, of using the legs of the dining room table for a fire hydrant or the bole of a tree. He tore to pieces the new derby hat I was to wear to Sunday School with my first suit of long pants. He killed the cat of a cranky old maid who lived outside of our social clique at the far end of Linden Street, and shortly after suffered a strange malady that took him off.

For days and days after Rip's funeral I was inconsolable. When the paroxysm of my grief quieted, I pleaded for another dog. My mother's objection this time was sovereign. There'd be no more dogs in her household. Resigned this time to this dictum, I resolved that when I was old enough to be on my own, I'd have a bull terrier. The resolution was fulfilled. In the years that we have lived in Scottsville, I have had successively five bull terriers, each at times something of a trial, for the bull terrier is very definitely an individualist; all fine companions and loyal and intimate friends.

To the best of my recollection, Fred, my youthful friend from Gregory Street, was the last person to provoke my envy; and so far as desiring to emulate anyone, which my inquisitor in the parlor car seemed to think should be my natural inclination—pshaw! That, it strikes me, would be absurd.

I sometimes gloom about the world, but I do so under forced draft. They say it is in a horrible state, but I know of its horrors mostly from reading of them in the newspaper. I have been graced with providential felicity. Benjamin Franklin, a stand-out in my pantheon, once said, "Were it offered to my choice, I should have no objection to a repetition of the same life from the beginning, only asking the advantage authors have in a second edition of correcting some faults in the first."

I could pretty well subscribe to that thesis. I have known no great triumphs. Flowers have not been flung in my path; I have heard no cries of "Viva!" But I have done almost everything I wanted to do. In the vespertine quiet of a warm summer evening, on the terrace in front of our house, I have occasionally heard a whispered query, Where would you rather be than here? The answer is prompt and inevitable. Nowhere else in the world. Except for a couple of departures in early manhood in futile quest of greener pastures, I have lived all of my long life no more than fifteen miles from the place of my birth; thirty-seven years in the city of Rochester, fifty-five years in the same house with the same wife in the village of Scottsville. I always had a lurking wish to appear considerable in my native place, and in a career of nearly three-score years in the newspaper business in Rochester I achieved status and a desirable prestige. I always liked it here. I am pleased and proud to be *locally,* internationally famous.

Fairport High School.

AGE IS ALL A POINT OF VIEW . . . Memo to Lawyers Co-operative editor **David Oliveiri**, who turned 40 on Wednesday, and to anyone else celebrating one of those so-called trauma birthdays (you know, 16, 21, 30, 40, 50, 65, etc.): It's all a matter of perspective — and most of us are spring chickens, relatively speaking. Consider the case of Rochester's highly respected retired journalist **Henry W. Clune**. At 97, he's currently vacationing in Clearwater Beach, Fla., and spends every day taking a slow but persistent walk up the beach. At one point, we understand, he was stopped by two solicitous ladies, who asked, "Are you all right? Is there anything you need?" Clune's reply: "Oh, to be 96 again!"

Henry Clune

PAINTINGS